J. MIKUSIŃSKI · THE BOCHNER INTEGRAL

Pure and Applied Mathematics

A Series of Monographs and Textbooks

Editors **Samuel Eilenberg and Hyman Bass**
Columbia University, New York

RECENT TITLES

Samuel Eilenberg. Automata, Languages, and Machines: Volumes A and B
Morris Hirsch and Stephen Smale. Differential Equations, Dynamical Systems, and Linear Algebra
Wilhelm Magnus. Noneuclidean Tesselations and Their Groups
François Treves. Basic Linear Partial Differential Equations
William M. Boothby. An Introduction Differentiable Manifolds and Riemannian Geometry
Brayton Gray. Homotopy Theory: An Introduction to Algebraic Topology
Robert A. Adams. Sobolev Spaces
John J. Benedetto. Spectral Synthesis
D. V. Widder. The Heat Equation
Irving Ezra Segal. Mathematical Cosmology and Extragalactic Astronomy
J. Dieudonné. Treatise on Analysis: Volume II, enlarged and corrected printing; Volume IV; Volume V; Volume VI, in preparation
Werner Greub, Stephen Halperin, and Ray Vanstone. Connections, Curvature, and Cohomology: Volume III, Cohomology of Principal Bundles and Homogeneous Spaces
I. Martin Isaacs. Character Theory of Finite Groups
James R. Brown. Ergodic Theory and Topolological Dynamics
C. Truesdell. A First Course in Rational Continuum Mechanics: Volume 1, General Concepts
George Grätzer. General Lattice Theory
K. D. Stroyan and W. A. J. Luxemburg. Introduction to the Theory of Infinitesimals
B. M. Puttaswamaiah and John D. Dixon. Modular Representations of Finite Groups
Melvyn Berger. Nonlinearity and Functional Analysis: Lectures on Nonlinear Problems in Mathematical Analysis
Jan Mikusiński. The Bochner Integral

In preparation
Charalambos D. Aliprantis and Owen Burkinshaw. Locally Solid Riesz Spaces
Michiel Hazewinkel. Formal Groups and Applications
Thomas Jech. Set Theory
Sigurdur Helgason. Differential Geometry, Lie Groups, and Symmetric Spaces

THE BOCHNER INTEGRAL

by

JAN MIKUSIŃSKI

ACADEMIC PRESS   NEW YORK   SAN FRANCISCO   1978

A Subsidiary of Harcourt Brace Jovanovich, Publishers

CIP-Kurztitelaufnahme der Deutschen Bibliothek

Mikusiński, Jan
The Bochner integral. – 1.Aufl. – Basel, Stuttgart: Birkhäuser, 1978.
(Lehrbücher und Monographien aus dem Gebiete der exakten Wissenschaften: Math. Reihe; Bd. 55)
ISBN 3-7643-0865-6

Copyright © 1978 by Birkhäuser Verlag Basel.
(Lehrbücher und Monographien aus dem Gebiete der exakten Wissenschaften, Mathematische Reihe, Band 55)
ISBN 3-7643-0865-6 (Birkhäuser Verlag)
North and South America Edition published by
ACADEMIC PRESS, INC.
111 Fifth Avenue, New York, New York 10003
(Pure and Applied Mathematics, A Series of Monographs and Textbooks, Volume 77)
ISBN 0-12-495850-8 (Academic Press)

Library of Congress Catalog Card Number 77-84176

Printed in Switzerland

Preface

The theory of the Lebesgue integral is still considered as a difficult theory, no matter whether it is based the concept of measure or introduced by other methods. The primary aim of this book is to give an approach which would be as intelligible and lucid as possible. Our definition, produced in Chapter I, requires for its background only a little of the theory of absolutely convergent series so that it is understandable for students of the first undergraduate course. Nevertheless, it yields the Lebesgue integral in its full generality and, moreover, extends automatically to the Bochner integral (by replacing real coefficients of series by elements of a Banach space).

It seems that our approach is simple enough as to eliminate the less useful Riemann integration theory from regular mathematics courses.

Intuitively, the difference between various approaches to integration may be brought out by the following story on shoemakers.

A piece of leather, like in Figure 1, is given. The task consists in measuring its area. There are three shoemakers and each of them solves the task in his own way.

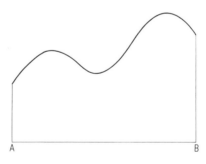

Fig. 1

The shoemaker R. divides the leather into a finite number of vertical strips and considers the strips approximately as rectangles. The sum of areas of all rectangles is taken for an approximate area of the leather (Figure 2). If he is not satisfied with the obtained exactitude, he repeats the whole procedure, by dividing the leather into thinner strips.

The shoemaker L. has another method. He first draws a finite number of horizontal lines. To each pair of adjacent lines he constructs a system of rectangles, as indicated in Figure 3. He finds the sum of areas of those rectangles, by multiplying their common height by the sum of lengths of their bases. He proceeds in the same way with each pair of adjacent lines

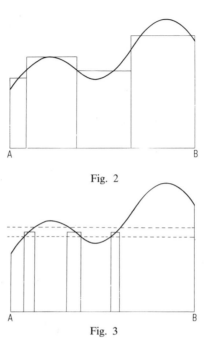

Fig. 2

Fig. 3

and sums up the obtained results. If he is not satisfied with the obtained exactitude, he repeats the whole procedure with a denser set of horizontal lines.

The third shoemaker applies the following method. He takes a rectangle a_1 and considers its area as the first approximation. If he wants a more precise result, he corrects it by drawing further rectangles, as in Figure 4 or similarly. It is plain that, in case of Figure 4, the areas of rectangles a_1, a_2,

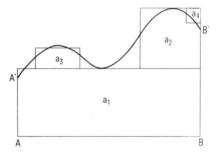

Fig. 4

a_3 are to be taken with positive signs, while the area of a_4 is to be taken with negative sign.

The reader acquainted with the theory of integration will easily recognize that the constructions shown in Figures 2 and 3 correspond to the Riemann and to the Lebesgue integrals, respectively. It is surprising that the construction in Figure 4, which is so simple and natural, never was exploited in integration theory, before. This construction illustrates the idea of our definition in Chapter I, where the details are presented rigorously in the analytical language.

The main features of the theory are displayed in Chapters I–VII. We first select 3 basic properties **H**, **E**, **M**, and further properties of the integral are derived from them. Consequently, the theory applies not only to the Lebesgue and to the Bochner integrals, but also to each integral satisfying **H**, **E**, **M**, e.g., to the Daniell integral (see Chapter VIII, section 5).

Chapters VIII–XV contain some more special topics, selected after the taste of the author. Each chapter is preceded by a short information about its contents. There are also two appendices.

The galley proofs of the book were read by my friends Czesław Kliś, Krystyna Skórnik and my son Piotr Mikusiński. They introduced a number of improvements and corrections. It is a pleasure to express my thanks to them.

Jan Mikusiński.

Contents

Chapter I

The Lebesgue Integral

We define Lebesgue integrable functions as limits of series of brick functions (i.e., of characteristic functions of intervals) with a special type of convergence (section 3). This definition is equivalent to the original Lebesgue definition, but avoids mentioning measure or null sets. The integral of an integrable function is obtained, by definition, on integrating the corresponding series term by term. Although this definition is very simple, it requires a proof of consistency, for the function can expand in various series. That proof is preceded by two auxiliary theorems (Theorem 3.1 and Theorem 3.2) and makes the core of this chapter.

1. Step functions of one real variable

By a *brick* we shall mean a bounded half-closed interval $a \leqslant x < b$, where a and b are finite real numbers. A function whose values are 1 at the points of a brick J, and 0 at the points which do not belong to that interval, will be called a *brick function* and the brick J, its *carrier*. In other words, a brick function is the characteristic function of a brick, its carrier. By the *integral* $\int f$ of a brick function f we understand the length of its carrier: thus, if the carrier is $a \leqslant x < b$, then $\int f = b - a$.

By a *step function* f we mean a function which can be represented in the form

$$f = \lambda_1 f_1 + \cdots + \lambda_n f_n, \tag{1.1}$$

where $f_1, \ldots, f_n$ are brick functions and $\lambda_1, \ldots, \lambda_n$ are real coefficients. It is easily seen that the sum of two step functions is again a step function. Also the product of a step function by a real number is a step function. In other words, the set of all the step functions is a linear space. We assume as known the fact that, if necessary, we always can choose the brick functions $f_1, \ldots, f_n$ in the representation (1.1) so that their carriers are disjoint, i.e., have no common points. This implies in particular that the modulus (absolute value) $|f|$ of a step function is also a step function. By the integral $\int f$ of the step function (1.1) we mean

$$\int f = \lambda_1 \int f_1 + \cdots + \lambda_n \int f_n.$$

We assume as known the following facts. The value of the integral is independent of the representation (1.1). This means that, if we have another representation for the same function

$$f = \kappa_1 g_1 + \cdots + \kappa_p g_p,$$

1

then

$$\lambda_1 \int f_1 + \cdots + \lambda_n \int f_n = \kappa_1 \int g_1 + \cdots + \kappa_p \int g_p.$$

The integral has the following properties:

$$\int (f + g) = \int f + \int g,$$

$$\int (\lambda f) = \lambda \int f \quad (\lambda \text{ real number}),$$

$$f \leqslant g \quad \text{implies} \quad \int f \leqslant \int g.$$

In other words, the integral is a positive linear functional on the space of the step functions. Moreover

$$\left| \int f \right| \leqslant \int |f|.$$

We shall still prove

Theorem 1. *Given any step function f and a number $\varepsilon > 0$, there is another step function g and a number $\eta > 0$ such that*

$$g(x) - f(y) \geqslant 0 \quad \text{for} \quad |x - y| < \eta,$$

$$\int g \leqslant \int f + \varepsilon.$$

Proof. Let $f = \lambda_1 f_1 + \cdots + \lambda_n f_n$ and let $[a_i, b_i)$ $(i = 1, \ldots, n)$ be the carrier of f_i. We assume that g_i is a brick function whose carrier is

$$\left[a_i - \frac{\varepsilon}{2 n \lambda_i}, \, b_i + \frac{\varepsilon}{2 n \lambda_i} \right).$$

This interval is greater than $[a_i, b_i)$, if $\lambda_i > 0$, and smaller than $[a_i, b_i)$, if $\lambda_i < 0$. If $a_i - \dfrac{\varepsilon}{2 n \lambda_i} \geqslant b_i + \dfrac{\varepsilon}{2 n \lambda_i}$ happens to hold for some i, then we put $g_i \equiv 0$. Letting $\eta = \min\limits_i \left| \dfrac{\varepsilon}{2 n \lambda_i} \right|$, we evidently have $\lambda_i g_i(x) - \lambda_i f_i(y) \geqslant 0$ for $|x - y| \leqslant \eta$ and $\lambda_i \int g_i \leqslant \lambda_i \int f_i + \dfrac{\varepsilon}{n}$. Hence the assertion follows for $g = \lambda_1 g_1 + \cdots + \lambda_n g_n$.

2. Step functions of several real variables

The functions of q real variables $\xi_1, \ldots, \xi_q$ can be considered as functions of a point $x = (\xi_1, \ldots, \xi_q)$ in the q-dimensional space $\mathbf{R}^q$. By a *brick* J in $\mathbf{R}^q$ we shall mean the set of the points x such that $\xi_i \in J_i$, where $J_1, \ldots, J_q$

are one-dimensional bricks, as in section 1. In other words, J is the Cartesian product $J = J_1 \times \cdots \times J_q$ of q one-dimensional bricks.

By *brick functions* we mean characteristic functions of bricks; the bricks are called the *carriers* of the corresponding functions. Thus, a brick function admits the value 1 on its carrier and vanishes outside it. By the *integral* $\int f$ of a function whose carrier is $J = J_1 \times \cdots \times J_q$ we understand the product of the lengths of $J_1, \ldots, J_q$. Thus, if $f_1, \ldots, f_q$ are characteristic functions of $J_1, \ldots, J_q$, we can write

$$\int f = \int f_1 \cdots \int f_q,$$

where the integrals on the right side have been defined in section 1.

Since our notation is the same in the case of several variables as in the case of one real variable, the definitions of a step function and of its integral can be repeated without any change. Also their properties are word for word the same, and Theorem 1 remains true (provided by $|x - y|$ we mean the distance between the points x and y). The proofs are essentially similar to those for a single real variable.

3. Lebesque integrable functions and their integrals

Given any real valued function f, defined in $\mathbf{R}^q$, we shall write

$$f \simeq \lambda_1 f_1 + \lambda_2 f_2 + \cdots, \tag{3.1}$$

where f_i are brick functions and λ_i are real numbers, if

1° $|\lambda_1| \int f_1 + |\lambda_2| \int f_2 + \cdots < \infty,$ *and*

2° $f(x) = \lambda_1 f_1(x) + \lambda_2 f_2(x) + \cdots$ *at those points x at which the series converges absolutely.*

The functions satisfying (3.1) will be called *Lebesque integrable*. By the integral $\int f$ we understand the sum

$$\int f = \lambda_1 \int f_1 + \lambda_2 \int f_2 + \cdots.$$

We do not know, at first, whether $\int f$ is determined uniquely. However this will follow from the following basic theorem:

Theorem 3.1. *If 1° holds and, for every x, the series $\lambda_1 f_1(x) + \lambda_2 f_2(x) + \cdots$ either converges to a non-negative limit or diverges to $+\infty$, then $\lambda_1 \int f_1 + \lambda_2 \int f_2 + \cdots \geq 0$.*

Proof. Let

$$M = |\lambda_1| \int f_1 + |\lambda_2| \int f_2 + \cdots$$

and let ε be any fixed number with $0 < \varepsilon < M$. Since M is finite, there is an index n_0 such that

$$\sum_{n_0+1}^{\infty} |\lambda_i| \int |f_i| < \varepsilon. \tag{3.2}$$

Let

$$g_n = \sum_{1}^{n_0} \lambda_i f_i + \sum_{n_0+1}^{n_0+n} |\lambda_i| \, f_i \qquad (n = 1, 2, \ldots). \tag{3.3}$$

By Theorem 1, given any positive number ε, there are step functions h_n and positive numbers η_n such that

(i) $h_n(x) \geqslant g_n(y)$ for $|x - y| < \eta_n$;

(ii) $\int h_n \leqslant \int g_n + \varepsilon \cdot 2^{-n}.$

We evidently may assume that the sequence η_n is decreasing.
Let $k_n = (h_1 - g_1) + \cdots + (h_n - g_n) + g_n$. Then $k_n(x) \geqslant h_n(x)$ and, by (i) and (ii), we have

(I) $k_n(x) \geqslant g_n(y)$ for $|x - y| < \eta_n$;

(II) $\int k_n \leqslant \int g_n + \varepsilon$;

(III) $k_{n+1} \geqslant k_n$;

the last inequality follows because $k_{n+1} = k_n + (g_{n+1} - g_n) + (h_{n+1} - g_{n+1})$ and from the fact that the differences in the parentheses are non-negative. We shall show that, given any number $\delta > 0$, we have

$$k_n \geqslant -\delta \quad \text{for sufficiently large } n. \tag{3.4}$$

In fact, suppose, conversely, that there is an increasing sequence of positive integers p_n and a sequence of points $x_{p_n} \in \mathbf{R}^q$ such that $k_{p_n}(x_{p_n}) < -\delta$. It follows from (3.3) that the functions g_n are non-negative outside a fixed bounded interval (brick) J. Thus all the x_{p_n} must belong to J. Consequently, there is a subsequence t_n of p_n such that x_{t_n} converges to a limit y. Of course

$$k_{t_n}(x_{t_n}) < -\delta \qquad (n = 1, 2, \ldots). \tag{3.5}$$

On the other hand, there is an index $n_1 > n_0$ such that $g_{n_1}(y) > -\delta$, for the sequence g_n converges, at every point x, to a positive limit or diverges to ∞. Hence by (I) we have $h_{n_1}(x) > -\delta$ for $|x - y| < \eta_{n_1}$. Since $x_{t_n} \to y$, there exists an index $r > n_1$ such that $|x_{t_r} - y| < \eta_{n_1}$. Consequently, we have by (III), $k_{t_r}(x_{t_r}) \geqslant k_{n_1}(x_{t_r}) > -\delta$, which contradicts (3.5). This proves that (3.4) is true.
Since all the k_n are non-negative outside J, we may write instead of (3.4), $k_n \geqslant -\delta k$ for sufficiently large n, where k is the characteristic function of J.

The function k does not depend on δ. Thus, we can choose δ as small as to get the inequality $\int k_n \geqslant -\varepsilon$ for sufficiently large n. Hence and from (II) we obtain $\int g_n \geqslant -2\varepsilon$ for large n, i.e.,

$$\sum_1^{n_0} \lambda_i \int f_i + \sum_{n_0+1}^{n_0+n} |\lambda_i| \int f_i \geqslant -2\varepsilon$$

for sufficiently large n. Letting $n \to \infty$, we hence get

$$\sum_1^{n_0} \lambda_i \int f_i + \sum_{n_0+1}^{\infty} |\lambda_i| \int f_i \geqslant -2\varepsilon.$$

But $|\lambda_i| \leqslant \lambda_i + 2|\lambda_i|$, thus

$$\sum_1^{\infty} \lambda_i \int f_i + 2 \sum_{n_0+1}^{\infty} |\lambda_i| \int f_i \geqslant -2\varepsilon,$$

and by (3.2)

$$\sum_1^{\infty} \lambda_i \int f_i \geqslant -4\varepsilon.$$

Since ε may be chosen arbitrary small, we have $\sum_1^{\infty} \lambda_i \int f_i \geqslant 0$, which is the required inequality.

From Theorem 3.1 we obtain, as a corollary,

Theorem 3.2. *If f is integrable and $f \geqslant 0$, then $\int f \geqslant 0$.*

Proof. Let ε be any positive number and let (3.1) hold. There is an index n_0 such that (3.2) holds. At all the points where series (3.1) converges absolutely, we have

$$\sum_1^{n_0} \lambda_i f_i + \sum_{n_0+1}^{\infty} |\lambda_i| f_i \geqslant 0. \tag{3.6}$$

At the remaining points series (3.6) diverges to ∞. Thus, by Theorem 3.1,

$$\sum_1^{n_0} \lambda_i \int f_i + \sum_{n_0+1}^{\infty} |\lambda_i| \int f_i \geqslant 0. \tag{3.7}$$

Since $|\lambda_i| \leqslant \lambda_i + 2|\lambda_i|$, this implies

$$\sum_1^{\infty} \lambda_i \int f_i + 2 \sum_{n_0+1}^{\infty} |\lambda_i| \int f_i \geqslant 0. \tag{3.8}$$

Hence, in view of (3.2), we obtain $\sum_1^{\infty} \lambda_i \int f_i \geqslant -2\varepsilon$ and, by the definition of the integral, $\int f \geqslant -2\varepsilon$. Since ε is arbitrary, the inequality $\int f \geqslant 0$ follows.

From Theorem 3.2 it is easy to deduce the uniqueness of the integral $\int f$. Suppose that we have, besides (3.1), another expansion of the same function

$$f \approx \kappa_1 g_1 + \kappa_2 g_2 + \cdots. \tag{3.9}$$

Suppose that the values of the integrals corresponding to (3.1) and (3.9) are F and G respectively, i.e.,

$$F = \lambda_1 \int f_1 + \lambda_2 \int f_2 + \cdots \quad \text{and} \quad G = \kappa_1 \int g_1 + \kappa_2 \int g_2 + \cdots .$$

We must prove that $F = G$. In fact, we have evidently

$$0 = f - f \approx \lambda_1 f_1 - \kappa_1 g_1 + \lambda_2 f_2 - \kappa_2 g_2 + \cdots ,$$

and this implies, by the definition of the integral,

$$\int 0 = \lambda_1 \int f_1 - \kappa_1 \int g_1 + \lambda_2 \int f_2 - \kappa_2 \int g_2 + \cdots = F - G.$$

Applying Theorem 3.2 to the function 0, we get $\int 0 \geqslant 0$, and hence $F - G \geqslant 0$. Since the role of expansions (3.1) and (3.9) is symmetric, we obtain similarly $G - F \geqslant 0$. Thus, there is the only possibility $F = G$. This means that *the value of the integral does not depend on the choice of its expansion* (3.1). In other words, the integral is determined uniquely.

In particular, given any step function $f = \lambda_1 f_1 + \cdots + \lambda_n f_n$, we can always write $f \approx \lambda_1 f_1 + \cdots + \lambda_n f_n + 0 \cdot f_{n+1} + 0 \cdot f_{n+2} + \cdots$, and this implies that $\int f = \lambda_1 \int f_1 + \cdots + \lambda_n \int f_n$. Thus, our general definition coincides, in this case, with the former definition in section 2.

The uniqueness of the integral being proved, it follows directly from the definition that

$$\int (\lambda f) = \lambda \int f \quad \text{and} \quad \int (f + g) = \int f + \int g.$$

That means, together with Theorem 3.1 that the integral is a linear positive functional on the space of integrable functions. Note the following immediate corollary of Theorem 3.1,

$$f \leqslant g \quad \text{implies} \quad \int f \leqslant \int g.$$

We are also in a position to prove that, *if $f \approx \lambda_1 f_1 + \lambda_2 f_2 + \cdots$, then in every brick there are points x at which the series converges absolutely*. In fact, assume, conversely, that there is a brick such that the series $\lambda_1 f_1(x) + \lambda_2 f_2(x) + \cdots$ does not converge at any point of it. Let f_0 be the characteristic function of that brick. Then evidently we also have $f \approx f_0 + \lambda_1 f_1 + \lambda_2 f_2 + \cdots$ and hence $\int f = \int f_0 + \lambda_1 \int f_1 + \lambda_2 \int f_2 + \cdots$, which contradicts the uniqueness of the integral.

This result can be strengthened. Let $f \approx \lambda_1 f_1 + \lambda_2 f_2 + \cdots$ and let f_0 be the characteristic function of a set Z on which the series $\lambda_1 f_1(x) + \lambda_2 f_2(x) + \cdots$ does not converge absolutely. We shall show that then $\int f_0 = 0$. In fact, we have evidently $f - f_0 = \lambda_1 f_1 + \lambda_2 f_2 + \cdots$, which implies that $\int (f - f_0) = \int f$. Hence $\int f_0 = \int f - \int (f - f_0) = 0$.

The property $\int f_0 = 0$ shows that the set Z is small in a certain sense. We say that Z is a *null set*. Generally we say that a set is a null set, iff the integral of its characteristic function vanishes. We have shown that, *if $f \simeq \lambda_1 f_1 + \lambda_2 f_2 + \cdots$, then the series $\lambda_1 f_1(x) + \lambda_2 f_2(x) + \cdots$ converges absolutely almost everywhere*, i.e., everywhere except for a null set. We may also say that property 1° implies that the series in 2° converges absolutely almost everywhere.

Theorem 3.3. *If f is integrable and $f_a(x) = f(x - a)$, then f_a is integrable and $\int f_a = \int f$. In other words, the integral is translation invariant.*

Proof. This is obvious, if f is a brick function. If $f \simeq \lambda_1 f_1 + \lambda_2 f_2 + \cdots$, where f_n are brick functions, then it is easy to see that $f_a \simeq \lambda_1 f_{1a} + \lambda_2 f_{2a} + \cdots$, where $f_{na}(x) = f_n(x - a)$. Hence $\int f_a = \lambda_1 \int f_{1a} + \lambda_2 \int f_{2a} + \cdots = \lambda_1 \int f_1 + \lambda_2 \int f_2 + \cdots = \int f$.

Chapter II

Banach Space

The definition of an integral given in the preceding chapter extends automatically to vector valued functions, provided the coefficients λ_i in the considered expansions are vectors of a given Banach space and the symbol $|\lambda_i|$ is meant as the norm of λ_i. Since the Banach space has become very familiar in mathematics, we need not to give many examples of it. However we recall its definition and state a few fundamental theorems on convergence in it. Vector valued functions and their integrals will be considered in Chapter III.

1. Vector space

The rules of addition of vectors are like for numbers, namely:

(1^+) $\quad a+b=b+a$;

(2^+) $\quad (a+b)+c=a+(b+c)$;

(3^+) $\quad$ The equation $a+x=b$ is solvable.

It follows from (1^+) to (3^+) that the solution x of the equation $a+x=b$ is unique for any fixed pair of elements a, b. That solution is called the *difference* of elements a, b and denoted by $b-a$. The difference $a-a$ is called *zero* and denoted by 0. Such an element is unique and does not depend on the choice of the element a in the difference $a-a$.

The fundamental properties (1^+) to (3^+) have been chosen so that all the other properties of addition and subtraction follow from them. Thus we can carry out the calculations involving addition and subtraction according to the usual rules, as for real numbers.

A vector can be also multiplied by any real number; the result of such a multiplication is another vector. Using Latin letters for vectors and Greek letters for numbers, the fundamental properties of the multiplication by a number can be formulated as follows:

$(1^{\cdot})$ $\quad (\lambda+\mu)a=\lambda a+\mu a$;

$(2^{\cdot})$ $\quad \lambda(a+b)=\lambda a+\lambda b$;

$(3^{\cdot})$ $\quad \lambda(\mu a)=(\lambda\mu)a$;

$(4^{\cdot})$ $\quad 1a=a$.

These properties have been chosen so as to imply, together with (1^+), (2^+), (3^+), all the remaining rules concerned with addition, subtraction of vectors and multiplication by a number. Evidently, rules $(1^{\cdot})$ to $(4^{\cdot})$ are also valid, when we assume that all the letters (Latin and Greek ones) are numbers. This remark implies that, practically, we can perform calculations (involving addition, subtraction and multiplication) as for real numbers, but the following restrictions should be preserved: the sum and the difference can be formed only when both elements are either vectors or numbers; in a product of several factors only one of the factors can be a vector.

We say that a set of any elements is a *vector space*, if the addition of elements and a multiplication by numbers are defined and properties (1^+) to (3^+), $(1^·)$ to $(4^·)$ are satisfied. The set of the geometrical vectors and the set of real functions (defined in a common domain) are examples of vector spaces. In this book we restrict ourselves to vector spaces with real coefficients, i.e., we shall not be concerned with vector spaces with complex coefficients.

In order to verify whether a subset X of a vector space is itself a vector space, we need not check all the properties (1^+) to (3^+) and $(1^·)$ to $(4^·)$, it suffices to verify only that:

1°   If $a \in X$ and $b \in X$, then $a + b \in X$;

2°   If λ is a number and $a \in X$, then $\lambda a \in X$.

The set of all the functions defined on a common set K is always a vector space, whenever the values of those functions are in a given vector space. Thus a set of functions (not necessarily of all functions) from K to a given vector space is itself a vector space, iff it satisfies 1° and 2°.

2. Normed space

The modulus $|a|$ of a complex number a has following properties:

(1^m) $|a + b| \leq |a| + |b|$;
(2^m) $|\lambda a| = |\lambda| \cdot |a|$ (λ real number);
(3^m) $|a| = 0$ implies $a = 0$.

Also in the space of geometrical vectors, if $|a|$ means the length of the vector a, the above properties are fulfilled. More generally, given any vector space, if to every element a there corresponds a real number $|a|$ so that (1^m) to (3^m) hold, then $|a|$ is called a *norm* of a and the space is said to be *normed*. The norm is always non-negative, for $0 = |a - a| \leq |a| + |a|$. It is a generalization of the notion of modulus and, as a matter of fact, does not need any separate name. For that reason, the norm will be called in the sequel just a *modulus*. Thanks to properties (1^m) to (3^m), the computations involving a modulus are to be carried out in the usual way, as for numbers.

3. Convergence and absolute convergence

We say that a sequence a_1, a_2, ... of elements of a normed space *converges* to an element a, and we write

$$a_n \to a \quad \text{or} \quad \lim_{n \to \infty} a_n = a,$$

if, given any number $\varepsilon > 0$, there is an index n_0 such that the inequality $n > n_0$ implies $|a_n - a| < \varepsilon$. Since that definition is identical with the routine definition of the limit of a numerical sequence, also its properties are similar, of course when restricted to the operations discussed above (addition, subtraction, multiplication by a number and modulus). Thus in particular, if $a_n \to a$ and $b_n \to b$, then $a_n + b_n \to a + b$ and $a_n - b_n \to a - b$. If $\lambda_n \to \lambda$ (λ_n numbers) and $a_n \to a$, then $\lambda_n a_n \to \lambda a$. Finally, if $a_n \to a$, then $|a_n| \to |a|$.

A series of elements of a normed space

$$b_1 + b_2 + \cdots \tag{3.1}$$

is said to converge to b, if the sequence of corresponding partial sums

$$a_n = b_1 + \cdots + b_n$$

converges to b. The limit b is called the sum of (3.1),

$$b_1 + b_2 + \cdots = b.$$

We say that series (3.1) *converges absolutely*, if the series $|b_1| + |b_2| + \cdots$ converges (to a number).

Theorem 3.1. *If a series* $a_1 + a_2 + \cdots$ *of elements of a normed space converges and, moreover, if it converges absolutely, then*

$$|a_1 + a_2 + \cdots| \leq |a_1| + |a_2| + \cdots.$$

Proof. Let $a_1 + a_2 + \cdots = a$. For any number $\varepsilon > 0$ there exists an index n_0 such that $|a - (a_1 + \cdots + a_n)| < \varepsilon$ for $n > n_0$. This implies

$$|a| < \varepsilon + |a_1 + \cdots + a_n| \leq \varepsilon + |a_1| + \cdots + |a_n|.$$

Hence we get, for $n \to \infty$, $|a| < \varepsilon + |a_1| + |a_2| + \cdots$. Since ε is arbitrary, the required inequality follows.

The notion of absolute convergence can be extended to sequences. We say that a sequence $a_1, a_2, \ldots$ converges absolutely, if the series $a_1 + (a_2 - a_1) + (a_3 - a_2) + \cdots$ converges absolutely, i.e., if $|a_1| + |a_2 - a_1| + |a_3 - a_2| + \cdots < \infty$.

Theorem 3.2. (Riesz). *From every convergent sequence in a normed space we can select an absolutely convergent subsequence.*

Proof. Denoting by a the limit of a_n, we can choose an increasing sequence of indices p_n such that $|a_{p_n} - a| < \varepsilon_n$, $\varepsilon_1 + \varepsilon_2 + \cdots < \infty$. Then

$$|a_{p_{n+1}} - a_{p_n}| \leq |a_{p_{n+1}} - a| + |a - a_{p_n}| < \varepsilon_{n+1} + \varepsilon_n,$$

and consequently

$$|a_{p_1}| + |a_{p_2} - a_{p_1}| + |a_{p_3} - a_{p_2}| + \cdots < \infty,$$

which means that the sequence $a_{p_1}, a_{p_2}, \ldots$ converges absolutely.

An infinite matrix of positive integers will be called a *rearrangement of positive integers*, if it exhausts all positive integers and each positive integer appears in it only once.

We say that a series $a_1 + a_2 + \cdots$ is *composed* of two series $b_1 + b_2 + \cdots$ and $c_1 + c_2 + \cdots$, if there is a rearrangement of positive integers

$$p_1, p_2, \ldots,$$

$$(3.2)$$

$$q_1, q_2, \ldots,$$

such that $b_n = a_{p_n}$, $c_n = a_{q_n}$.

Theorem 3.3. *If an absolutely convergent series $a_1 + a_2 + \cdots$ (consisting of elements of a normed space) is composed of two convergent series $b_1 + b_2 + \cdots$ and $c_1 + c_2 + \cdots$, then*

$$a_1 + a_2 + \cdots = (b_1 + b_2 + \cdots) + (c_1 + c_2 + \cdots).$$

Proof. Let $s_n = a_1 + \cdots + a_n$, $t_n = b_1 + \cdots + b_n$, $u_n = c_1 + \cdots + c_n$. Since t_n and u_n are convergent, it suffices to prove that

$$s_n - t_n - u_n \to 0.$$

$$(3.3)$$

Let (3.2) a rearrangement of positive integers corresponding to the considered series and let r_n be the least positive integer which does not appear among $p_1, \ldots, p_n, q_1, \ldots, q_n$. Then the difference $s_n - t_n - u_n$ can be represented, after cancelling equal elements, as a combination of elements a_i with $i > r_n$. Hence

$$|s_n - t_n - u_n| \leq |a_{r_{n+1}}| + |a_{r_{n+2}}| + \cdots.$$

Since $r_n \to \infty$ and the series $a_1 + a_2 + \cdots$ converges absolutely, formula (3.3) follows.

By induction, the foregoing result can be generalized to the case when a series is composed of any finite number of partial series. We are going to formulate and prove an analogous theorem also for the infinite case. We say that a series $a_1 + a_2 + \cdots$ is composed of infinitely many series $a_{i1} + a_{i2} + \cdots$ ($i = 1, 2, \cdots$), if there is a rearrangement of positive integers

$$p_{11}, p_{12}, \ldots,$$

$$(3.4)$$

$$p_{21}, p_{22}, \ldots,$$

$$\cdots$$

such that $a_{ij} = a_{p_{ij}}$.

Theorem 3.4. *If an absolutely convergent series $a_1 + a_2 + \cdots$ (consisting of elements of a normed space) is composed of an infinite number of convergent series*

$$s_1 = a_{11} + a_{12} + \cdots, \qquad s_2 = a_{21} + a_{22} + \cdots, \qquad \ldots,$$

such that the series $s_1 + s_2 + \cdots$ converges, then the series $a_1 + a_2 + \cdots$ converges itself, and

$$a_1 + a_2 + \cdots = s_1 + s_2 + \cdots.$$

Proof. Let (3.4) be the corresponding arrangement of positive integers and let $s_{in} = a_{p_{i1}} + \cdots + a_{p_{in}}$. Given any $\varepsilon > 0$, we first fix m such that

$$|a_{m+1}| + |a_{m+2}| + \cdots < \varepsilon$$

and choose r such that $p_{ij} > m$ for $i, j > r$ and that among the p_{ij} with $i, j \leq r$ there appear all the numbers $1, \ldots, m$. Then for $n > r$ the difference

$$(s_{1n} + \cdots + s_{nn}) - (a_1 + \cdots + a_n) \tag{3.5}$$

contains, after cancelling equal elements, only elements $a_{p_{ij}}$ with $p_{ij} > m$. Hence

$$|(s_{1n} + \cdots + s_{nn}) - (a_1 + \cdots + a_n)| < \varepsilon \quad \text{for} \quad n > r. \tag{3.6}$$

Similarly, for each i and $n > r$, the series

$$s_i - s_{in} = a_{p_{i,n+1}} + a_{p_{i,n+2}} + \cdots$$

contains only elements $a_{p_{ij}}$ with $p_{ij} > m$, and therefore, by Theorem 3.1,

$$|s_1 - s_{1n}| + \cdots + |s_n - s_{nn}| < \varepsilon \quad \text{for} \quad n > r. \tag{3.7}$$

From (3.6) and (3.7) it follows easily that

$$|(s_1 + \cdots + s_n) - (a_1 + \cdots + a_n)| < 2\varepsilon \quad \text{for} \quad n > r.$$

This shows that the difference (3.5) tends to 0, as $n \to \infty$. But, by hypothesis, the sequence $s_1 + \cdots + s_n$ is convergent, and so the assertion follows.

4. Banach space

The space of the complex numbers has such a property that every absolutely convergent series converges to a limit. Generally, a normed space where every absolutely convergent series converges to a limit is called a *complete normed space* or *Banach space*. The Banach space may also be defined, on talking of sequences instead of series. Thus a normed space is a Banach space, if every absolutely convergent sequence converges to a limit.

We say that a sequence of elements of a normed space $a_1, a_2, \ldots$ is a *Cauchy sequence*, if

$$\lim_{\substack{m \to \infty \\ n \to \infty}} |a_m - a_n| = 0, \tag{4.1}$$

i.e., if for every $\varepsilon > 0$ there is an index n_0, such that

$$|a_m - a_n| < \varepsilon \quad \text{for} \quad m > n_0, \quad n > n_0. \tag{4.2}$$

Theorem 4. (Riesz). *A normed space is complete if and only if every Cauchy sequence is convergent.*

Proof. Since $|a_m - a_n| \leq |a_{n+1} - a_n| + \cdots + |a_m - a_{m-1}|$, every absolutely convergent sequence is a Cauchy sequence. Thus, if every Cauchy sequence convergent, the space is complete.

Assume, now, that a normed space is complete and that a sequence a_1, $a_2, \ldots$ is a Cauchy sequence. We shall prove that the series is convergent. Let p_n be an increasing sequence of positive integers such that

$$|a_p - a_r| < \varepsilon_n \quad \text{for} \quad p, r > p_n, \tag{4.3}$$

where $\varepsilon_1 + \varepsilon_2 + \cdots < \infty$. Then

$$|a_{p_1}| + |a_{p_2} - a_{p_1}| + |a_{p_3} - a_{p_2}| + \cdots < \infty.$$

Since the space is complete, the sequence $a_{p_1}, a_{p_2}, \ldots$ must converge to a limit a, thus

$$|a_{p_n} - a| \to 0.$$

It follows from (4.3) in particular that

$$|a_p - a_{p_m}| < \varepsilon_n \quad \text{for} \quad p, p_m > p_n.$$

Thus the inequality

$$|a_p - a| \leq |a_p - a_{p_m}| + |a_{p_m} - a|$$

implies, as $m \to \infty$,

$$|a_p - a| < \varepsilon_n \quad \text{for} \quad p > p_n.$$

Hence, the sequence $a_1, a_2, \ldots$ converges to a.

The Cauchy sequences are mostly used, in the literature, just to define complete spaces. One says that *a space is complete, if every Cauchy sequence converges.* Theorem 4 shows that, in the case of normed spaces, both definitions are equivalent.

The condition (4.1) is equivalent to the following one:

$$a_{p_{n+1}} - a_{p_n} \to 0 \quad \text{for every subsequence } a_{p_n}. \tag{4.4}$$

In fact, if a_n satisfies (4.1) and a_{p_n} is any subsequence, then, for every $\varepsilon > 0$, there is an index n_0 such that $|a_{p_{n+1}} - a_{p_n}| < \varepsilon$ for $n > n_0$. This means that $a_{p_{n+1}} - a_{p_n} \to 0$. Suppose, now, that (4.1) does not hold. Then, there is a number $\varepsilon > 0$ and an increasing sequence of positive integers p_n such that $|a_{p_{2n}} - a_{p_{2n-1}}| \geq \varepsilon$, as $n = 1, 2, \ldots$ This implies that the subsequence a_{p_n} does not satisfy the condition $a_{p_{n+1}} - a_{p_n} \to 0$. In this way, the equivalence of (4.1) and (4.4) is proved.

Chapter III

The Bochner Integral

1. Vector valued step functions

By *brick functions* we will understand, exactly as in Chapter I, characteristic functions of bricks. By a *vector valued step function f* we mean a function which can be represented in the form

$$f = \lambda_1 f_1 + \cdots + \lambda_n f_n,$$

where $f_1, \ldots, f_n$ are brick functions and $\lambda_1, \ldots, \lambda_n$ are elements of a given normed space. (Note that we do not preserve the convention from Chapter I, concerning the meaning of Latin and Greek letters.)

The theory of step functions and of their integrals, sketched in sections 1 and 2 of Chapter I, is valid also in the present general case, with the only exception that the property $f \leq g$ implies $\int f \leq \int g$ has no meaning for vector valued functions and, therefore, must be omitted.

2. Bochner integrable functions

Given any function f from $\mathbf{R}^q$ to a given Banach space E (i.e., the arguments are in $\mathbf{R}^q$, the values are in E), we shall write

$$f \simeq \lambda_1 f_1 + \lambda_2 f_2 + \cdots, \tag{2.1}$$

where f_i are brick functions and λ_i are elements of E, if

$1°$ $|\lambda_1| \int f_1 + |\lambda_2| \int f_2 + \cdots < \infty$, *and*

$2°$ $f(x) = \lambda_1 f_1(x) + \lambda_2 f_2(x) + \cdots$ *at those points x at which the series converges absolutely.*

The functions satisfying (2.1) will be called *Bochner integrable*. By the integral $\int f$ we understand the sum

$$\int f = \lambda_1 \int f_1 + \lambda_2 \int f_2 + \cdots.$$

This definition is completely analogous to the definition of Lebesgue integrable functions. The only difference is that the symbols λ_i are now interpreted more generally. In particular, if E is the space of the real numbers, then Bochner integrable functions are Lebesgue integrable functions.

It follows directly from the definition that the product λf of a Bochner integrable function by any real number λ is also a Bochner integrable function. Moreover, the sum $f+g$ of two Bochner integrable functions f and g is again a Bochner integrable function. Thus the set of Bochner integrable functions (whose values are in a common Banach space E) is a linear space.

3. The modulus of a Bochner integrable function

By the modulus $|f|$ of a vector valued function f we understand the function whose value at any point equals to the modulus (norm) of the value of f at that point. Thus, $|f|$ is always a real valued non-negative function.

Theorem 3.1. *The modulus $|f|$ of a Bochner integrable function*

$$f \simeq \lambda_1 f_1 + \lambda_2 f_2 + \cdots \tag{3.1}$$

is a Lebesgue integrable function. Moreover

$$\left| \lambda_1 \int f_1 + \lambda_2 \int f_2 + \cdots \right| \leq \int |f| \leq |\lambda_1| \int f_1 + |\lambda_2| \int f_2 + \cdots. \tag{3.2}$$

Proof. The equality

$$f = \lambda_1 f_1 + \lambda_2 f_2 + \cdots$$

holds at every point where the series converges absolutely. Denoting by Z the set of such points, we have

$$f = \lim_{n \to \infty} s_n \quad \text{for} \quad x \in Z,$$

where

$$s_n = \lambda_1 f_1 + \cdots + \lambda_n f_n. \tag{3.3}$$

This implies

$$|f| = \lim_{n \to \infty} |s_n| \quad \text{for} \quad x \in Z. \tag{3.4}$$

The sequence on the right side of (3.4) can be changed again into a series, on writing

$$|f| = |s_1| + (|s_2| - |s_1|) + (|s_3| - |s_2|) + \cdots. \tag{3.5}$$

Since all the terms on the right side are step functions, we can write

$$|s_1| = |\lambda_1| f_1 = \kappa_1 g_1, \tag{3.6}$$

$$|s_{n+1}| - |s_n| = \kappa_{p_n+1} g_{p_n+1} + \cdots + \kappa_{p_{n+1}} g_{p_{n+1}} \tag{3.7}$$

for $n = 1, 2, \ldots, p_1 = 1,$

where κ_i are real numbers, and g_i are brick functions. Moreover the simple functions g_i can be chosen, for every fixed n, so that their carriers have no common points. If this is done, then

$$|s_{n+1}| - |s_n| = |\kappa_{p_{n+1}}| g_{p_{n+1}} + \cdots + |\kappa_{p_{n+1}}| g_{p_{n+1}} \quad \text{for} \quad n = 1, 2, \ldots$$

Hence, in view of

$$\left| |s_{n+1}| - |s_n| \right| \le |s_{n+1} - s_n| = |\lambda_{n+1} f_{n+1}| = |\lambda_{n+1}| f_{n+1},$$

we obtain

$$|\kappa_{p_{n+1}}| g_{p_{n+1}} + \cdots + |\kappa_{p_{n+1}}| g_{p_{n+1}} \le |\lambda_{n+1}| f_{n+1}.$$

On adding all these inequalities, for $n = 1, 2, \ldots$, to the obvious inequality $|\kappa_1| g_1 \le |\lambda_1| f_1$, we get

$$|\kappa_1| g_1 + |\kappa_2| g_2 + \cdots \le |\lambda_1| f_1 + |\lambda_2| f_2 + \cdots. \tag{3.8}$$

On the other hand, if we first integrate all these inequalities, and then sum them up, we get

$$|\kappa_1| \int g_1 + |\kappa_2| \int g_2 + \cdots \le |\lambda_1| \int f_1 + |\lambda_2| \int f_2 + \cdots. \tag{3.9}$$

By hypothesis, the series on the right side of (3.9) is convergent. Thus also the series on the left side is convergent. Consequently, there is a Lebesgue integrable function

$$g \simeq \kappa_1 g_1 + \kappa_2 g_2 + \cdots. \tag{3.10}$$

But it follows from (3.8) that the series in (3.10) converges absolutely on Z. Its sum on Z is $|f|$, which follows from (3.5) and (3.7). Thus $|f| = g$ at the points of Z. But we cannot write $|f| \simeq \kappa_1 g_1 + \kappa_2 g_2 + \cdots$, because the series may converge absolutely at some points outside Z. In order to get rid of the absolute convergence at those 'wrong' points, we write

$$|f| \simeq \kappa_1 g_1 + |\lambda_1| f_1 - |\lambda_1| f_1 + \kappa_2 g_2 + |\lambda_2| f_2 - |\lambda_2| f_2 + \cdots.$$

Thus $|f|$ is a Lebesgue integrable function, and according to the definition of the integral we have

$$\int |f| = \kappa_1 \int g_1 + |\lambda_1| \int f_1 - |\lambda_1| \int f_1 + \kappa_2 \int g_2 + |\lambda_2| \int f_2 - |\lambda_2| \int f_2 + \cdots,$$

or, on cancelling the unnecessary terms,

$$\int |f| = \kappa_1 \int g_1 + \kappa_2 \int g_2 + \cdots. \tag{3.11}$$

This implies, together with (3.9), the second of the inequalities in (3.2). In order to prove the first of the inequalities in (3.2), we add (3.6) and (3.7) for $n = 1, \ldots, m-1$, and obtain

$$|s_n| = \kappa_1 g_1 + \cdots + \kappa_{p_n} g_{p_n}.$$

Since s_m and $|s_m|$ are step functions, this implies that

$$\left|\lambda_1\int f_1+\cdots+\lambda_m\int f_m\right|=\left|\int s_m\right|\leqslant\int|s_m|\leqslant\kappa_1\int g_1+\cdots+\kappa_{p_m}\int g_{p_m}.$$

Letting $m\to\infty$, the required inequality follows, by (3.11).

It follows from Theorem 3.1 that every real valued non-negative function f, if Bochner integrable, is also Lebesgue integrable, for we may then write $|f|=f$. On the other hand, every real valued Bochner integrable function f is the difference $g-h$ of two non-negative Bochner integrable function g and h (it suffices to put $g=\frac{1}{2}(|f|+f)$ and $h=\frac{1}{2}(|f|-f)$). Consequently, every real valued Bochner integrable function is also Lebesgue integrable.

If f is a real valued Bochner integrable function, then its product by any element λ of the Banach space under consideration is also a Bochner integrable function. In fact, since f is then Lebesgue integrable, we can write $f\simeq\lambda_1f_1+\lambda_2f_2+\cdots$, where the coefficients λ_i are real. Hence $\lambda f\simeq(\lambda\lambda_1)f_1+(\lambda\lambda_2)f_2+\cdots$.

We can complete Theorem 3.1 as follows:

Theorem 3.2. *Given any Bochner integrable function f and any number $\varepsilon>0$, there exists an expansion $f\simeq\lambda_1f_1+\lambda_2f_2+\cdots$ such that $|\lambda_1|\int f_1+|\lambda_2|\int f_2+\cdots<\int|f|+\varepsilon$.*

Proof. Let us take, at first, an arbitrary expansion

$$f\simeq\kappa_1g_1+\kappa_2g_2+\cdots.\tag{3.12}$$

Thus the series $|\kappa_1|\int g_1+|\kappa_2|\int g_2+\cdots$ is convergent, and there exists an index p such that

$$|\kappa_{p+1}|\int g_{p+1}+|\kappa_{p+2}|\int g_{p+2}+\cdots<\frac{\varepsilon}{2}.\tag{3.13}$$

Let

$$s=\kappa_1g_1+\cdots+\kappa_pg_p;$$

then

$$f-s\simeq\kappa_{p+1}g_{p+1}+\kappa_{p+2}g_{p+2}+\cdots.\tag{3.14}$$

Since s is a step function, we may write

$$s=\lambda_1f_1+\cdots+\lambda_nf_n,\tag{3.15}$$

where $f_1,\ldots,f_n$ are brick functions with disjoint carriers. Thus

$$|s|=|\lambda_1|f_1+\cdots+|\lambda_n|f_n.\tag{3.16}$$

Replacing p initial terms in (3.12) by (3.15), we get another expansion of f,

$$f \simeq \lambda_1 f_1 + \cdots + \lambda_n f_n + \kappa_{p+1} g_{p+1} + \kappa_{p+2} g_{p+2} + \cdots.$$

We shall prove that the last series has the required property.
The inequality $|s| \leq |f| + |f - s|$ implies

$$\int |s| \leq \int |f| + \int |f - s|.$$

On applying Theorem 3.1 to the function (3.14) we obtain from the last inequality,

$$\int |s| \leq \int |f| + |\kappa_{p+1}| \int g_{p+1} + |\kappa_{p+2}| \int g_{p+2} + \cdots.$$

Hence we get, by (3.16) and (3.13),

$$|\lambda_1| \int f_1 + \cdots + |\lambda_n| \int f_n \leq \int |f| + \frac{\varepsilon}{2}.$$

If we add this inequality to (3.13), we obtain

$$|\lambda_1| \int f_1 + \cdots + |\lambda_n| \int f_n + |\kappa_{p+1}| \int g_{p+1} + |\kappa_{p+2}| \int g_{p+2} + \cdots \leq \int |f| + \varepsilon,$$

which was to be proved.

Theorem 3.3. *Every Bochner integrable function f such that $\int |f| = 0$ can be expanded into a series $f \simeq \lambda_1 f_1 + \lambda_2 f_2 + \cdots$ which converges to 0 at every point where it converges absolutely.*

Proof. Let $\varepsilon_1 + \varepsilon_2 + \cdots$ be any convergent series of positive numbers. By Theorem 3.2, there are expansions

$$f \simeq \kappa_{i1} g_{i1} + \kappa_{i2} g_{i2} + \cdots \qquad (i = 1, 2, \ldots) \tag{3.17}$$

such that

$$|\kappa_{i1}| \int g_{i1} + |\kappa_{i2}| \int g_{i2} + \cdots < \varepsilon_i.$$

Let us arrange all the double indices $i1, i2, \ldots$ $(i = 1, 2, \ldots)$ into a single infinite sequence $p_1, p_2, \ldots$ and put $\lambda_n = \kappa_{p_n}$, $f_n = g_{p_n}$. Then the series

$$\lambda_1 f_1 + \lambda_2 f_2 + \cdots, \tag{3.18}$$

is composed of all the series (3.17) (in the sense of section 3, Chapter II) and we have

$$|\lambda_1| \int f_1 + |\lambda_2| \int f_2 + \cdots < \varepsilon_1 + \varepsilon_2 + \cdots.$$

If the series (3.18) converges absolutely at a point x, then all the series (3.17) converge absolutely at the same point and have there the common sum $f(x)$. This implies that the sum of series (3.18) is $f(x)+f(x)+\cdots$, and consequently that $f(x)$ must vanish at that point. Thus the series (3.18) converges to 0 at any point where it converges absolutely, and the function f admits there the value 0. This means that $f \simeq \lambda_1 f_1 + \lambda_2 f_2 + \cdots$.

4. The Bochner integral

Recall that by an integral of a Bochner integrable function $f \simeq \lambda_1 f_1 + \lambda_2 f_2 + \cdots$ we mean

$$\int f = \lambda_1 \int f_1 + \lambda_2 \int f_2 + \cdots .$$

This definition has been given in section 2, however no use of it has been made till now. We shall first prove that the value of the integral is unique for every given function f. In fact, suppose that there is another expansion of the same function,

$$f \simeq \kappa_1 g_1 + \kappa_2 g_2 + \cdots .$$

Then the difference $f - f = 0$ can be expanded into the series

$$0 \simeq \lambda_1 f_1 - \kappa_1 g_1 + \lambda_2 f_2 - \kappa_2 g_2 + \cdots .$$

This implies, by Theorem 3.1,

$$\left| \lambda_1 \int f_1 - \kappa_1 \int g_1 + \lambda_2 \int f_2 - \kappa_2 \int g_2 + \cdots \right| \leq \int |0| = 0.$$

Hence

$$\lambda_1 \int f_1 - \kappa_1 \int g_1 + \lambda_2 \int f_2 - \kappa_2 \int g_2 + \cdots = 0,$$

i.e.,

$$\left(\lambda_1 \int f_1 + \lambda_2 \int f_2 + \cdots \right) - \left(\kappa_1 \int g_1 + \kappa_2 \int g_2 + \cdots \right) = 0.$$

This proves that the value of $\int f$ does not depend on the expansion of f, which means the consistency of the definition. As at the end of section 3, Chapter I, we easily see that property 1° implies that the series in 2° converges absolutely almost everywhere.

Directly from the definition we obtain the formulae:

$$\int (\lambda f) = \lambda \int f \quad \text{for any real number } \lambda, \tag{4.1}$$

$$\int (f + g) = \int f + \int g. \tag{4.2}$$

The first inequality from Theorem 3.1 may be written in the form

$$\left| \int f \right| \leqslant \int |f|.$$

(4.3)

Note also that, if f is real valued Bochner integrable function and λ any element of the proper Banach space, then

$$\int (\lambda f) = \lambda \int f.$$

(4.4)

In fact, this follows from the fact that f can be expanded into a sequence with real coefficients.

5. Series of Bochner integrable functions

Given a sequence of Bochner integrable functions $f_1, f_2, \ldots$, we shall write

$$f \simeq f_1 + f_2 + \cdots,$$

if

1° $\int |f_1| + \int |f_2| + \cdots < \infty,$ *and*

2° $f(x) = f_1(x) + f_2(x) + \cdots$ *at those points x at which the series converges absolutely.*

Theorem 5.1. *If f_1, $f_2, \ldots$ are Bochner integrable functions and $f \simeq f_1 + f_2 + \cdots$, then f is Bochner integrable and*

$$\int f = \int f_1 + \int f_2 + \cdots.$$

Proof. Let ε be an arbitrary fixed positive number and let $\varepsilon_1 + \varepsilon_2 + \cdots$ be a series of positive numbers whose sum is ε. By Theorem 3.2, we can choose expansions

$$f_i \simeq \lambda_{i1} f_{i1} + \lambda_{i2} f_{i2} + \cdots \qquad (i = 1, 2, \ldots),$$

(5.1)

where f_{ij} are brick functions such that

$$|\lambda_{i1}| \int f_{i1} + |\lambda_{i2}| \int f_{i2} + \cdots < \varepsilon_i + \int |f_i|.$$

(5.2)

Let

$$\kappa_1 g_1 + \kappa_2 g_2 + \cdots$$

(5.3)

be a series of brick functions which is composed (in the sense of section 3, Chapter II) of all the series (5.1). Then, in view of (5.2).

$$|\kappa_1|\int g_1+|\kappa_2|\int g_2+\cdots<\varepsilon_1+\varepsilon_2+\cdots+M, \tag{5.4}$$

where $M=\int|f_1|+\int|f_2|+\cdots$. Thus there is a function g such that $g\simeq\kappa_1 g_1+\kappa_2 g_2+\cdots$. If series (5.3) converges absolutely at a point, then each of series (5.1) converges absolutely at that point, and consequently the sum of (5.3) is there equal to the sum of $f_1+f_2+\cdots$. This proves that f is Bochner integrable and that

$$f\simeq\kappa_1 g_1+\kappa_2 g_2+\cdots.$$

Hence, we get

$$\int f=\kappa_1\int g_1+\kappa_2\int g_2+\cdots, \tag{5.5}$$

and from (5.1),

$$\int f_i=\lambda_{i1}\int f_{i1}+\lambda_{i2}\int f_{i2}\cdots \qquad (i=1,2,\ldots). \tag{5.6}$$

From (5.4) and (5.2) it follows that the series in (5.5) and (5.6) converge absolutely. But the series in (5.5) is composed of all the series in (5.6) (see section 3, Chapter II). This implies that $\int f=\int f_1+\int f_2+\cdots$.

Chapter IV

Axiomatic Theory of the Integral

It should be emphasized that no attempt will be made, in this chapter, to give an alternative definition of the Lebesgue or Bochner integral. Our main purpose is, at present, to develop the preceding theory. Only the method used in the sequel will be different. We shall select a few basic properties of the integral and found upon them the whole theory which follows.

1. Elementary axioms

The set of the complex numbers can be considered as a vector space with real coefficients, since all properties (1^+) to (3^+) and $(1^·)$ to $(4^·)$ in section 1, Chapter II, are satisfied, when interpreting Greek letters as real numbers, and Latin letters as complex numbers. This space has a particular property that its coefficients, i.e., real numbers, are also elements of the space. Similarly, the space of the real numbers can be considered as a vector space with real coefficients.

Let K be the Euclidean space of any number of dimensions and let E be a Banach space which includes all real numbers as its elements. Finally, let U be the space of the Bochner integrable functions from K to E.

The space U and the integral defined on it have the following properties:

> **H**   If $f \in U$ and $\lambda \in \mathbf{R}^1$, then $\lambda f \in U$ and $\int \lambda f = \lambda \int f$;
>
> **A**   If $f \in U$ and $g \in U$, then $f + g \in U$,   and $\int (f+g) = \int f + \int g$;
>
> **M**   If $f \in U$,   then

Properties **H** (Homogeneity) and **A** (Additivity) say that U is a vector space (because the set of all possible E-valued functions is a vector space) and that the integral is a linear functional on it. In **M** (Modulus property), the symbol $|f|$ denotes the function whose value at every point $x \in K$ equals to the modulus (norm in E) of $f(x)$ at that point. In what precedes, the restriction has been made that E includes real numbers. This restriction is needed because of axiom **M**, where the integral of a real valued function $|f|$ appears. However it is easy to see that this is no essential restriction, and that the theory can be applied, in various ways even, also when real numbers are not in E. In fact, we can choose an arbitrary element $a \in E$ with $|a| = 1$ and identify it with the number 1. Consequently we have also to identify λa with λ. Such an identification does not lead to any misunderstanding. We can also proceed in another way. It is known that the number 1, if does not belong to E, can always be adjoined as a new element. Then all real numbers are automatically adjoined. As an example, let us mention the space of the 3-dimensional geometrical vectors. Adjoining real numbers we get then the space of quaternions. Finally, note that the restriction on the space E can be omitted, provided we consider the theory in two interpretations simultaneously: for E and for $\mathbf{R}^1$. In fact, the space $\mathbf{R}^1$ (of real numbers) is a space in which all the axioms **HAM** are sensible. If, now, E is another Banach space, then we understand the integral $\int |f|$ in **M** as already defined by the first interpretation. For simplicity, the assumption that E includes real numbers is adopted further on.

There are notions and theorems which can be deduced from properties **HAM**, no matter how those properties have been proved, whether by means of step functions or by any other way. Thus, on constructing new notions and proving new theorems we can entirely forget what step functions are. The only properties **HAM** are used to develop the further theory. Therefore, it is quite irrelevant what the nature of elements of the set K is, we even need not make any hypothesis on the structure of K. In this way, the theory wins on generality.

On the other hand, we do assume that U is a vector space of functions from K to a Banach space E (including real numbers as elements) and that if $f \in U$ then also $|f| \in U$. For the integral $\int f$ we can take any operation which assigns elements of E to functions $f \in U$, provided the properties **HAM** are satisfied.

A theory founded upon a set of properties is called *axiomatic* and the basic properties are called *axioms*. In the sequel we admit **HAM** as axioms. The Lebesgue and the Bochner integrals are particular interpretations of the axiomatic theory. An axiomatic approach emphasizes what is substantial in the theory. Besides, it enables to transfer notions and theorems onto new interpretations.

2. Consequences of the elementary axioms

On letting $\lambda = 0$ in **H**, we get the equality

$$\int 0 = 0. \tag{2.1}$$

On the other hand, on letting $\lambda = -1$, we get

$$\int (-f) = -\int f. \tag{2.2}$$

If we replace, in **A**, f by λf and g by κg (λ and κ being real numbers), we obtain, in view of **H**,

$$\int (\lambda f + \kappa g) = \lambda \int f + \kappa \int g. \tag{2.3}$$

Conversely, from (2.3) it follows **H** by the substitution $\kappa = 0$, and also **A** by the substitution $\kappa = \lambda = 1$. Thus axioms **H** and **A** could be replaced by a single axiom, (2.3).

The equality (2.3) implies, for $\lambda = 1$ and $\kappa = -1$,

$$\int (f - g) = \int f - \int g. \tag{2.4}$$

Moreover, we obtain from (2.3), by induction,

$$\int (\lambda_1 f_1 + \cdots + \lambda_n f_n) = \lambda_1 \int f_1 + \cdots + \lambda_n \int f_n \tag{2.5}$$

for arbitrary functions $f_i \in U$ and arbitrary real numbers λ_i.

From **M** it follows that

$$\int |f| = 0 \quad \text{implies} \quad \int f = 0. \tag{2.6}$$

If $f \geq 0$, i.e., if f admits real non-negative values only, then $|f| = f$. Since anyway $|\int f| \geq 0$ holds, it follows from (2.6) that

$$f \geq 0 \quad \text{implies} \quad \int f \geq 0. \tag{2.7}$$

If f is any real valued function, we can write $f = f^+ + f^-$, where $f^+ = \frac{1}{2}(|f| + f)$ and $f^- = \frac{1}{2}(-|f| + f)$. From the equality $\int f = \int f^+ - \int (-f^-)$ it follows that $\int f$ is a real number. Thus the integral of a real valued function is a real number. This implies that, given any set U satisfying **HAM**, if we select from it all the real valued functions, we obtain a subset which also satisfies **HAM**.

If f and g are real valued and if $f \leq g$, then $g - f \geq 0$, which implies, by (2.7) that $\int (g - f) \geq 0$, i.e., $\int f \leq \int g$, in view of (2.4). Thus

$$f \leq g \quad \text{implies} \quad \int f \leq \int g. \tag{2.8}$$

Since $|f_1 + f_2| \leq |f_1| + |f_2|$ holds for any functions f_1 and f_2 from U, we obtain $\int |f_1 + f_2| \leq \int |f_1| + \int |f_2|$, by (2.8) and **A**. Hence, by **M**,

$$\left| \int (f_1 + f_2) \right| \leq \int |f_1| + \int |f_2|,$$

and by induction,

$$\left| \int (f_1 + \cdots + f_n) \right| \leq \int |f_1| + \cdots + \int |f_n|. \tag{2.9}$$

From (2.9) we can come back to **M**, on letting $f_2 = \cdots = f_n = 0$.

3. Union and intersection of functions

By the *union* of functions f and g whose values are in a given Banach space we mean the real valued function

$$f \cup g = \max (|f|, |g|);$$

the value of $f \cup g$ at a point is thus the greatest of the values of $|f|$ and $|g|$ at that point. This definition is thought so that the characteristic function of the union of sets is the union of their characteristic functions. Similarly, by the *intersection* of f and g we mean

$$f \cap g = \min (|f|, |g|).$$

More generally, by the union and intersection of functions $f_1, \ldots, f_n$ we mean the functions

$$f_1 \cup \cdots \cup f_n = \max (|f_1|, \ldots, |f_n|)$$

and

$$f_1 \cap \cdots \cap f_n = \min (|f_1|, \ldots, |f_n|).$$

It is easily seen that

$$\begin{aligned} f_1 \cup \cdots \cup f_{n+1} &= (f_1 \cup \cdots \cup f_n) \cup f_{n+1}, \\ f_1 \cap \cdots \cap f_{n+1} &= (f_1 \cap \cdots \cap f_n) \cap f_{n+1}. \end{aligned} \tag{3.1}$$

Theorem 3. *If $f_i \in U$ holds for $i = 1, \ldots, n$, then $f_1 \cup \cdots \cup f_n \in U$ and $f_1 \cap \cdots \cap f_n \in U$. In other words, the union and the intersection of a finite number of integrable functions are integrable.*

Proof. It is easy to check that

$$f \cup g = \tfrac{1}{2}(|f| + |g| + ||f| - |g||),$$

$$f \cap g = \tfrac{1}{2}(|f| + |g| - ||f| - |g||).$$

This implies that the union and the intersection of two integrable functions are integrable. The theorem follows hence by induction, on taking in account formulae (3.1).

4. Null functions and equivalent functions

A function $h \in U$ is called a *null function*, if $\int |h| = 0$. The function which vanishes identically is an example of a null function. There can exist null functions which do not vanish identically.

The set of the null functions is a vector space, since $\int |h| = 0$ implies

$$\int |\lambda h| = \int (|\lambda| \cdot |h|) \leq |\lambda| \int |h| = 0,$$

and $\int |h| = \int |k| = 0$ implies

$$\int |h+k| \le \int (|h| + |k|) = \int |h| + \int |k| = 0 + 0.$$

Moreover, it follows from the definition that the modulus $|h|$ of a null function h is again a null function.

Two arbitrary functions f and g from K to E are called *equivalent*, if their difference $f - g$ is a null function, i.e., if $f - g \in U$ and $\int |f - g| = 0$. We then write $f \sim g$. (We do not require that f and g should belong to U.) In particular for null functions h we have $h \sim 0$.

The relation $\sim$, introduced above, has three following properties:

(i) $f \sim f$ (reflexivity);
(ii)   if $f \sim g$, then $g \sim f$ (symmetry);
(iii)   if $f \sim g$ and $g \sim h$, then $f \sim h$ (transitivity).

Properties (i) and (ii) are obvious. In order to prove (iii) we start from the inequality $0 \le |f - h| \le |f - g| + |g - h|$. Hence we obtain $0 \le \int |f - h| \le \int |f - g| + \int |g - h|$. If $f \sim g$ and $g \sim h$, then both the last integrals vanish, which implies $\int |f - h| = 0$, i.e., $f \sim h$.

Beside (i)–(iii), the following properties hold:

(iv)   if $f \sim g$, then $\lambda f \sim \lambda g$ for any real number λ;
(v)   if $f_1 \sim g_1$ and $f_2 \sim g_2$, then $f_1 + f_2 \sim g_1 + g_2$;
(vi)   if $f \sim g \in U$, then $f \in U$ (functions equivalent to integrable functions are integrable themselves);
(vii)   if $f \sim g \in U$, then $|f| \sim |g|$.

In order to prove (iv) it suffices to remark that, if $\int |\lambda f - \lambda g| = |\lambda| \int |f - g| = 0$. To prove (v), it suffices to remark that, if $\int |f_1 - g_1| = 0$ and $\int |f_2 - g_2| = 0$, then $\int |(f_1 + f_2) - (g_1 + g_2)| = \int |(f_1 - g_1) + (f_2 - g_2)| \le \int |f_1 - g_1| + \int |f_2 - g_2| = 0$. Property (vi) follows from the equality $f = g + (f - g)$, for $f - g$ belongs to U, as a null function. Finally, in order to prove (vii), we start from the inequality $0 \le ||f| - |g|| \le |f - g|$. Since $f \sim g \in U$ implies that $|f| \in U$, $|g| \in U$ and $|f| - |g| \in U$, we conclude from the above inequality that $0 \le \int ||f| - |g|| \le \int |f - g|$. If the last integral vanishes, so must do the preceding one, and this proves (vii).

We shall still prove that

(viii) if $f \sim g \in U$, then $\int f = \int g$. (The integrals of equivalent functions are equal.)

In fact, $|\int f - \int g| = |\int (f - g)| \le \int |f - g|$. If $f \sim g$, the last integral vanishes, which implies $\int f - \int g = 0$. This proves (viii).

5. The space $\tilde{U}$

Let us denote generally by $\tilde{f}$ the class of all functions equivalent to f. By (i) we have $f \in \tilde{f}$. The equality $\tilde{f} = \tilde{g}$ means that the classes $\tilde{f}$ and $\tilde{g}$ are

identical, i.e., contain exactly the same elements. We are going to prove
that the equality $\tilde{f} = \tilde{g}$ holds if and only if $f \sim g$. In fact, assume at first,
that $\tilde{f} = \tilde{g}$ holds. From $f \in \tilde{f}$ it follows that also $g \in \tilde{f}$, for the classes f and g
are identical. Since all the functions which belong to $\tilde{f}$ are equivalent to f,
$g \sim f$ must hold, and this implies $f \sim g$, by (ii). Assume now, conversely,
that $f \sim g$. Every function equivalent to g is also equivalent to f, by (iii). In
other words, every element of class $\tilde{f}$ is an element of class $\tilde{g}$. Thus $\tilde{f}$ and
$\tilde{g}$ are equivalent.

Let $\tilde{U}$ denote the set of all the classes $\tilde{f}$ such that $f \in U$. One could say,
intuitively, that elements of $\tilde{U}$ are obtained, when equivalent elements of
U are stuck together. To each element of U there corresponds exactly
one element of $\tilde{U}$. However, to each element of $\tilde{U}$ there corresponds a
very class of elements of U.

In $\tilde{U}$, we define a multiplication by real number λ such that $\lambda \tilde{f}$ means the
class of elements equivalent to λf. Similarly, we define the sum $\tilde{f} + \tilde{g}$, on
assuming that this is the class of elements equivalent to $f + g$. It is easy to
prove the consistency of these definitions. Thus the set $\tilde{U}$ is a vector
space.

Let us introduce the notation

$$|\tilde{f}| = \int |f|.$$

If $\tilde{f} = \tilde{g}$, then $f \sim g$ and $|f| \sim |g|$, which implies $\int |f| = \int |g|$, i.e., $|\tilde{f}| = |\tilde{g}|$. This
proves the consistency of the definition of the symbol $|\tilde{f}|$.

The above definition implies that

$$|\lambda \tilde{f}| = |\lambda| \cdot |\tilde{f}|, \tag{5.1}$$

$$|\tilde{f} + \tilde{g}| \leq |\tilde{f}| + |\tilde{g}|, \tag{5.2}$$

$$|\tilde{f}| = 0 \quad \text{implies} \quad \tilde{f} = 0. \tag{5.3}$$

Properties (5.1) and (5.2) can be obtained on integrating the known
relations, $|\lambda f| = |\lambda| \cdot |f|$, $|f + g| \leq |f| + |g|$. Property (5.3) follows from the
fact that the equality $\int |f| = 0$ means $f \sim 0$, i.e., $\tilde{f} = 0$.

In view of (5.1) to (5.3), the entity $|\tilde{f}|$ can be considered as the modulus of
$\tilde{f}$, and $\tilde{U}$ as a normed space.

6. Norm convergence

The convergence $\tilde{f}_n \to \tilde{f}$ in $\tilde{U}$ means $|\tilde{f}_n - \tilde{f}| \to 0$, i.e., $\int |f_n - f| \to 0$. In that
case we will also say that the sequence of functions f_n *converges in norm*
to f, and we will write

$$f_n \to f \quad \text{i.n.}$$

All the four expressions: $\tilde{f}_n \to \tilde{f}$, $|\tilde{f}_n - \tilde{f}| \to 0$, $\int |f_n - f| \to 0$ and $f_n \to f$ i.n.
are equivalent. Note that a norm limit is not defined uniquely. If f is a

norm limit, so is every function equivalent to f, but no other function. In other words, a norm limit is defined up to equivalent functions.

General properties of sequences convergent in a normed space have their interpretation for norm convergence: $1°$ If $f_n \to f$ i.n. and $g_n \to g$ i.n., then $f_n + g_n \to f + g$ i.n. and $f_n - g_n \to f - g$ i.n.; $2°$ If λ_n is a sequence of real numbers convergent (in the usual sense) to λ and if $f_n \to f$ i.n., then $\lambda_n f_n \to \lambda f$ i.n.

Theorem 6.1. *If* $f_n \to f$ *i.n.* $(f_n, f \in U)$, *then* $\int f_n \to \int f$.

Proof. This is a direct consequence of the inequality

$$\left| \int f_n - \int f \right| = \left| \int (f_n - f) \right| \leq \int |f_n - f|.$$

A series of integrable functions $f_1 + f_2 + \cdots$ is said to *converge in norm* to f, if the sequence of its partial sums $f_1 + \cdots + f_n$ converges in norm to f. Then we write

$$f_1 + f_2 + \cdots = f \quad \text{i.n.}$$

For series, Theorem 6.1 takes the following form

Theorem 6.2. *If* $f_1 + f_2 + \cdots = f$ *i.n.* $(f_n, f \in U)$, *then* $\int f_1 + \int f_2 + \cdots = \int f$. *That is, a series which converges in norm can be integrated term by term.*

7. Expansion axiom

We write, according to section 5, Chapter III,

$$f \simeq f_1 + f_2 + \cdots \qquad (f_n \in U),$$

if

$1°$ $\int |f_1| + \int |f_2| + \cdots < \infty$, *and*

$2°$ $f(x) = f_1(x) + f_2(x) + \cdots$ *at those points x at which the series con-verges absolutely.*

If we mean by U the set of Bochner integrable functions, then Theorem 5 from Chapter III can be formulated as follows:

E If $f \simeq f_1 + f_2 + \cdots$ $(f_n \in U)$,   then $f \in U$ and $\int f = \int f_1 + \int f_2 + \cdots$.

This property can be verbally stated in the following way: If a function expands (in the above sense) into a series of integrable functions, then that function is integrable itself, and its integral equals to the sum of the integrals of the series.

Up to now, the whole theory of this chapter has been founded upon axioms **HAM** only. In the sequel, we join property **E** as another axiom. This axiom is sharper than **A**, and reduces to **A**, when assuming $f_3 = f_4 = \cdots = 0$. Thus on admitting **E**, we can cancel **A**. In what follows, our theory will be founded on **HEM**. Theorems obtained in this way will be true, in particular, for the Lebesgue and Bochner integrals.

If we select all real valued functions from a set U, satisfying **HEM**, we will obtain a subset which also satisfies **HEM**.

Remark. Axiom **E** is sensible only when $f_n \in U$ implies $|f_n| \in U$, and this is ensured by axiom **M**. Thus the natural way of ordering the axioms would be **HME**. However shall keep the **HEM** ordering, since axiom **E** has been introduced in the place of **A**, in **HAM**, and also for mnemonic reasons.

Theorem 7.1. *If h is a null function, and g is a function whose value is 0 at every point, at which the value of h is 0, then g is also a null function.*

Proof. Let $f_1 = f_2 = \cdots = |h|$. Then the series $f_1 + f_2 + \cdots$ converges absolutely at such points, exactly, where $h = 0$. Its sum is, at those points, equal to $|g|$. Thus $|g| \simeq f_1 + f_2 + \cdots$. Since $\int |f_n| = \int |h| = 0$, it follows that $\int |f_1| + \int |f_2| + \cdots = 0$, and by **E**, $\int |g| = 0$.

The above theorem asserts that, *in a null function, we may change arbitrarily its values which are different from 0, and the function remains still a null function.*

As before, let K denote the set on which the functions $f \in U$ are defined. A subset of K is called a null set, if its characteristic function is a null function. The empty set is always a null set.

Theorem 7.2. *A function is a null function, if and only if it vanishes almost everywhere, i.e., everywhere except for a null set.*

Proof. Given any null function f, let Z be the set of the points x at which $f(x) \neq 0$, and let g be the characteristic function of Z. By Theorem 7.1, g is a null function and hence Z is a null set. Conversely, if Z is a null set and g is its characteristic function, then every function f which vanishes outside Z is a null function, by Theorem 7.1.

Theorem 7.3. *If $\int |f_1| + \int |f_2| + \cdots < \infty$ $(f_n \in U)$, then $f_1(x) + f_2(x) + \cdots$ converges absolutely almost everywhere, i.e., everywhere except for a null set.*

Proof. Let Z be the set of the points at which $f_1(x) + f_2(x) + \cdots$ does not converge absolutely, and let g be the characteristic function of Z. Then evidently $g \simeq f_1 - f_1 + f_2 - f_2 \cdots$. Hence $g = 0$, which proves the theorem.

Theorem 7.4. *If $f \simeq f_1 + f_2 + \cdots$, then $\int |f| \leq \int |f_1| + \int |f_2| + \cdots$.*

Proof. Let g be a function assuming the value $|f_1(x)|+|f_2(x)|+\cdots$ at every point x at which this series converges, and the value $|f(x)|$ at the remaining points. Then $|f| \leqslant g \simeq |f_1|+|f_2|+\cdots$. Hence we obtain, by (2.8) and **E**, $\int|f| \leqslant \int g = \int|f_1|+\int|f_2|+\cdots$.

Theorem 7.5. *If $f \simeq f_1+f_2+\cdots$ and $g \simeq f_1+f_2+\cdots$, then $f \sim g$.*

Proof. In fact, we then have $f - g \simeq f_1 - f_1 + f_2 - f_2 + \cdots$. This means that $\int|f_1|+\int|-f_1|+\int|f_2|+\int|-f_2|+\cdots<\infty$ and that the function $f-g$ admits the value 0 at every point x at which the series $f_1(x)-f_1(x)+f_2(x)-f_2(x)+\cdots$ converges absolutely. This implies, by Theorem 7.3 that $f - g \sim 0$, i.e, $f \sim g$.

8. Convergence almost everywhere

We say that a sequence of functions f_n *converges almost everywhere* to a function f, if it converges to f at every point except for a null set; we then write

$$f_n \to f \quad \text{a.e.}$$

The following theorem shows that convergence almost everywhere could also be defined without speaking of any sets.

Theorem 8.1. *A sequence f_n converges almost everywhere to f, if and only if there are functions $g_n \sim f_n$ such that the sequence g_n converges to f at every point.*

Proof. Assume first that $f_n \to f$ a.e. Let Z be the set of points at which f_n does not converge to f. Z is a null set. Let $g_n(x) = f(x)$ at the points $x \in Z$ and $g_n(x) = f_n(x)$ at the points $x \notin Z$. Then evidently $g_n \sim f_n$ and $g_n \to f$ everywhere.

Assume now, conversely, that $g_n \sim f_n$ and $g_n \to f$ everywhere. Then $\int|g_1 - f_1|+\int|g_2 - f_2|+\cdots = 0$. This implies, by Theorem 7.3, that the series $|g_1 - f_1|+|g_2 - f_2|+\cdots$ converges at every point except for a null set Z. Hence $g_n - f_n \to 0$ outside Z and, consequently, $f_n = g_n - (g_n - f_n) \to f - 0$ outside Z.

If a sequence converges at every point, then it also converges almost everywhere to the same limit; in other words, $f_n \to f$ implies $f_n \to f$ a.e. The converse implication does not hold. Thus, convergence almost everywhere is more general that the convergence at every point. Note that if a sequence converges almost everywhere, then each of its subsequences converges almost everywhere to the same limit. Like in the case of norm limit, also everywhere limit in not determined uniquely. Namely:

Theorem 8.2. *A limit of a sequence convergent almost everywhere is determined up to the class of equivalent functions.*

The proof will become easier, if we use the fact that *the union of two null sets is a null set.* (A more general statement will be given in Theorem 1, Chapter V.) In order to see this, denote by f and g the characteristic functions of given null sets X and Y and by h the characteristic function of their union $X \cup Y$. Then $h \leqslant f + g$ and hence $\int h \leqslant \int f + \int g = 0$.

Proof of Theorem 8.2. Assume that $f_n \to f$ a.e., i.e., $f_n \to f$ except for a null set X. Let $f \sim g$, i.e., $f = g$ except for a null set Y. Then $f_n \to g$ outside $X \cup Y$. This g is another limit almost everywhere.
Assume conversely that $f_n \to f$ except for X and $f_n \to g$ except for Y. Then $f = g$ except for $X \cup Y$.

Theorem 8.3. *If $f_n \to f$ a.e., then $\lambda f_n \to \lambda f$ for any real number λ. That is, the product by a number of a sequence convergent almost everywhere converges almost everywhere to the product of its limit by that number.*

Proof.   It follows from $f_n \sim g_n \to f$ that $\lambda f_n \sim \lambda g_n \to \lambda f$.

Theorem 8.4. *If $f_n \to f$ a.e. and $g_n \to g$ a.e., then $f_n + g_n \to f + g$ a.e. That is, the sum of sequences convergent almost everywhere converges to the sum of their limits.*

Proof. From $f_n \sim \bar{f}_n \to f$ and $g_n \sim \bar{g}_n \to g$ it follows that $f_n + g_n \sim \bar{f}_n + \bar{g}_n \to f + g$.

Theorem 8.5. *If $f_n \to f$ a.e., then $|f_n| \to |f|$ a.e. That is, the modulus of a sequence convergent almost everywhere converges to the modulus of its limit.*

Proof.   From $f_n \sim g_n \to f$ it follows that $|f_n| \sim |g_n| \to |f|$.

Theorem 8.6. *If $f \approx f_1 + f_2 + \cdots$ $(f_n \in U)$, then $f = f_1 + f_2 + \cdots$ i.n. and $f = f_1 + f_2 + \cdots$ a.e.*

Proof.   Given any $\varepsilon > 0$, we can choose an index n_0 such that

$$\int |f_{n+1}| + \int |f_{n+2}| + \cdots < \varepsilon \quad \text{for} \quad n > n_0.$$

Since $f_{n+1} + f_{n+2} + \cdots = f - f_1 - \cdots - f_n$ holds at any point, at which the series converges absolutely, we obtain, $\int |f - f_1 - \cdots - f_n| < \varepsilon$ for $n > n_0$, which proves the first part of the assertion.
On the other hand, by Theorem 7.3, the series $f_1 + f_2 + \cdots$ converges absolutely at every point except for a null set Z. Evidently, outside Z, the limit must be equal to f, which proves the second part of the assertion.

Theorem 8.7. *If $\int |f_1| + \int |f_2| + \cdots < \infty$, then the equality $f = f_1 + f_2 + \cdots$ i.n. implies $f = f_1 + f_2 + \cdots$ a.e., and conversely.*

Proof. Let g be any function which equals to $f_1 + f_2 + \cdots$ at every point, where the series converges absolutely. In other words, let

$$g \simeq f_1 + f_2 + \cdots.$$

Then both $g = f_1 + f_2 + \cdots$ i.n. and $g = f_1 + f_2 + \cdots$ a.e., hold by Theorem 7.4. If $f = f_1 + f_2 + \cdots$ i.n., then $f \sim g$, since the norm limit is determined up to equivalent functions. Since the limit almost everywhere is also determined up to equivalent functions, we have $f = f_1 + f_2 + \cdots$ a.e. The proof in the converse direction is similar.

Remark. The proofs of Theorems 8.3, 8.4, and 8.5 do not make use of axiom **E** (axioms **HAM** are sufficient).

9. A few theorems referred to by name

In this section, we are going to prove some theorems due to Riesz, Beppo Levi and Lebesgue. It should be emphasized that the role of axiom **E** will be, here, essential.

Theorem 9.1 (Riesz). *The space $\tilde{U}$ is complete. In other words, if $f_n \in U$ and $f_{p_{n+1}} - f_{p_n} \to 0$ i.n. for each increasing sequence of indices $p_1, p_2, \ldots$, then there is a function $f \in U$ such that $f_n \to f$ i.n.*

Proof. The absolute convergence of a series $\tilde{f}_1 + \tilde{f}_2 + \cdots (\tilde{f}_n \in \tilde{U})$ means that $|\tilde{f}_1| + |\tilde{f}_2| + \cdots < \infty$, i.e., $\int |f_1| + \int |f_2| + \cdots < \infty$. Let $f \simeq f_1 + f_2 + \cdots$. Then $f = f_1 + f_2 + \cdots$ i.n., by Theorem 8.6. Consequently, the series $\tilde{f}_1 + \tilde{f}_2 + \cdots$ converges to $\tilde{f}$. Thus the completeness of $\tilde{U}$ is proved. The second formulation of the theorem follows from Theorem 4, Chapter II, on using the fact that the expression $f_n \to f$ i.n. is equivalent to $\tilde{f}_n \to \tilde{f}$.

Theorem 9.2 (Riesz). *If a sequence f_n ($f_n \in U$) converges in norm to f, then $f \in U$ and there is a subsequence which converges to f almost everywhere.*

Proof. We have $\int |f_m - f_n| \leqslant \int |f_m - f| + \int |f_n - f|$. By hypothesis, both the integrals on the right side tend to 0, as $m \to \infty$ and $n \to \infty$. Hence

$$\lim_{\substack{m \to \infty \\ n \to \infty}} |\tilde{f}_m - \tilde{f}_n| = 0,$$

which means that $\tilde{f}_n$ is a Cauchy sequence. Since the space $\tilde{U}$ is complete, the sequence $\tilde{f}_n$ converges to an element $\tilde{g} \in \tilde{U}$, by Theorem 4, Chapter II. In other words, we have $f_n \to g$ i.n. with $g \in U$. Since $f_n \to f$ i.n., we have $f \sim g$, which implies that $f \in U$.

Instead of $f_n \to f$ i.n. we may equivalently write $\tilde{f}_n \to \tilde{f}$. By Theorem 3.2, Chapter II, there is a subsequence $\tilde{f}_{p_n}$ which converges absolutely, i.e., $|\tilde{f}_{p_1}| + |\tilde{f}_{p_2} - \tilde{f}_{p_1}| + |\tilde{f}_{p_3} - \tilde{f}_{p_2}| + \cdots < \infty$. Hence $\int |f_{p_1}| + \int |f_{p_2} - f_{p_1}| + \int |f_{p_3} - f_{p_2}| + \cdots < \infty$. The sequence f_{p_n} converges to f, thus $f_{p_n} \to f$ i.n. We may also write

$$f = f_{p_1} + (f_{p_2} - f_{p_1}) + (f_{p_3} - f_{p_2}) + \cdots \text{ i.n.},$$

which implies, by Theorem 8.7,

$$f = f_{p_1} + (f_{p_2} - f_{p_1}) + (f_{p_3} - f_{p_2}) + \cdots \text{ a.e.}$$

But the last equality is equivalent to $f_{p_n} \to f$ a.e., which proves the theorem.

As a complement of Theorem 9.2 we can consider

Theorem 9.3. *If a sequence f_n ($f_n \in U$) converges in norm, then there is a subsequence f_{p_n} which is bounded almost everywhere by a non-negative function $r \in U$, i.e., we have $|f_{p_n}| \leq r$ everywhere except for a null set.*

Proof. We select a sequence f_{p_n} as in the preceding proof. There is a non-negative function r such that $r \approx |f_{p_1}| + |f_{p_2} - f_{p_1}| + |f_{p_3} - f_{p_2}| + \cdots$. Then we evidently have $|f_{p_n}| \leq r$ at every point at which the last series converges absolutely, i.e., everywhere except for a null set.

Theorem 9.4 (Beppo Levi) (monotone convergence theorem). *If $f_1, f_2, \ldots$ is a monotone sequence of real valued functions such that $f_n \in U$ and $|\int f_n| \leq M$, then there exists a function $f \in U$ such that $f_n \to f$ i.n. and $f_n \to f$ a.e.*

Proof. We may assume that the sequence f_n is non-negative and non-decreasing (otherwise we would consider $f_n - f_1$ or $f_1 - f_n$). Then $\int |f_1| + \int |f_2 - f_1| + \cdots + \int |f_n - f_{n-1}| = |\int f_n| \leq M$ and, letting $n \to \infty$, $\int |f_1| + \int |f_2 - f_1| + \cdots \leq M < \infty$. Let f be any function such that $f(x) = f_1(x) + [f_2(x) - f_1(x)] + \cdots$ holds at all points at which the series converges absolutely, we have $f \approx f_1 + (f_2 - f_1) + \cdots$. By **E** and Theorem 8.6, we hence get $f \in U$ and $f = f_1 + (f_2 - f_1) + \cdots$ i.n. and a.e. This is, in fact our statement.

Given a sequence of functions $f_1, f_2, \ldots$ whose values are in a Banach space, the intersection

$$f_1 \cap f_2 \cap \cdots = \lim_{n \to \infty} f_1 \cap \cdots \cap f_n$$

always exists and represents a non-negative function, because the sequence $f_1 \cap \cdots \cap f_n$ is non-negative and non-decreasing. If all f_n are bounded in common by a non-negative function r, i.e., $|f_n| \leq r$, then also the union

$$f_1 \cup f_2 \cup \cdots = \lim_{n \to \infty} f_1 \cup \cdots \cup f_n$$

exists and is bounded by r.

Theorem 9.5. (a) *If $g = f_1 \cap f_2 \cap \cdots$, $f_n \in U$, then $g \in U$ and $0 \leq g \leq |f_n|$.*
(b) *If $h = f_1 \cup f_2 \cup \cdots$, $f_n \in U$, $|f_n| \leq r \in U$, then $h \in U$ and $|f_n| \leq h$.*

Proof. The sequence $g_n = f_1 \cap \cdots \cap f_n$ is non-increasing and we have $g_n \in U$, $0 \le g_n \le |f_1| \in U$, $\int g_n \le \int |f_1|$, which implies $g \in U$, by Theorem 9.4. Similarly, the sequence $h_n = f_1 \cup \cdots \cup f_n$ is non-decreasing and we have $h_n \in U$, $0 \le h_n \le r$, $\int h_n \le \int r$. This implies $h \in U$, again by Theorem 9.4. The inequalities are obvious.

Theorem 9.6 (Lebesgue) (dominated convergence theorem). *If $f_n \in U$, $f_n \to f$ a.e. and $|f_n| \le r \in U$, then $f_n \to f$ i.n., and therefore $\int f_n \to \int f$.*

Proof. The unions $k_n = f_n \cup f_{n+1} \cup \cdots$ are, by Theorem 9.5, non-negative integrable functions. Moreover, the sequence $k_1, k_2, \ldots$ is non-decreasing and therefore converges to a non-negative limit k. By Theorem 9.4, we have $\int k_n \to \int k$.

Assume first that $f \equiv 0$. Then $f_n \to 0$ a.e. and also $k_n \to 0$ a.e. Hence $k \sim 0$ and therefore $\int k_n \to 0$.

Assume now that $f \not\equiv 0$ and let p_n be an arbitrary increasing sequence of positive integers. Then $h_n = f_{p_{n+1}} - f_{p_n} \to 0$ a.e. and $|h_n| \le 2r$. By what we just proved it follows that $h_n \to 0$ i.n. By Theorem 9.1, it thus exists a function $g \in U$ such that $f_n \to g$ i.n. By Theorem 9.2, we can select from f_n a subsequence f_{q_n} such that $f_{q_n} \to g$ a.e. But $f_n \to f$ a.e., thus also $f_{q_n} \to f$ a.e., which implies $f \sim g$. Hence the assertion $f_n \to f \in U$ follows.

The above Lebesgue theorem can be generalized, while replacing $|f_n| \le r \in U$ by a weaker condition. Also the condition $f_n \to f$ a.e. can be relaxed, on introducing the concept of an *asymptotic convergence*. We are going to discuss this matter in the next section.

10. Asymptotic convergence

The ordinary convergence of numbers satisfies the following

Urysohn's condition L*. *If from each subsequence of a given sequence a_n we can select a subsequence which converges to a, then a_n converges to a.* This can be equivalently formulated as follows: *If a_n does not converge to a, then it contains a subsequence whose no subsequence converges to a.*

We shall prove that *the convergence in any Banach space satisfies Urysohn's condition.* In fact, assume that a_n does not converge to a. This means that there is a number $\varepsilon > 0$ such that the inequality $|a_n - a| < \varepsilon$ does not hold for all n. There is thus a subsequence b_n of a_n such that $|b_n - a| \ge \varepsilon$. This implies that no subsequence of b_n converges to a.

It is interesting to remark that *the almost everywhere convergence does not satisfy Urysohn's condition.* In fact, let us consider a sequence of intervals $[\alpha_n, \beta_n]$ such that $\beta_n - \alpha_n \to 0$ and each point of the real line is covered infinitely many times by those intervals. Then the sequence f_n of characteristic functions of $[\alpha_n, \beta_n]$ does not converge to 0 a.e., because at each point x the sequence $f_n(x)$ admits the value 1 infinitely many times.

However, from each subsequence g_n of f_n we can select a subsequence h_n which converges to 0 almost everywhere. This is trivial, if g_n converges itself to 0 almost everywhere, because we then take $h_n = g_n$. If it does not, there is a point x_0 such that the sequence $g_n(x_0)$ does not converge to 0. Since $g_n(x_0)$ admits values 0 and 1 only, there is a subsequence h_n of g_n such that $h_n(x_0) = 1$ for all n. The sequence h_n converges to 0 everywhere, except for $x = x_0$, because the lengths of intervals $[\alpha_n, \beta_n]$ decrease to 0. This proves that Urysohn's condition is not satisfied.

The lack of property L* can be considered as a defect of the convergence. However this defect can always be removed, by generalizing properly the convergence. If we do this for almost everywhere convergence, we obtain the so called asymptotic convergence.

We say that a sequence of functions $f_1, f_2, \ldots$ *converges asymptotically* to f and we write $f_n \to f$ as., if from each its subsequence it is possible to select a subsequence which converges to f almost everywhere. Evidently, every sequence which converges almost everywhere to f, converges asymptotically to f, because each subsequence of it converges to f almost everywhere. This implies, in turn, that the asymptotic convergence satisfies condition L*.

Asymptotic convergence is also a generalization of convergence in norm, i.e., *if a sequence converges in norm, then it converges asymptotically to the same limit.* In fact, if $f_n \to f$ i.n., then also $g_n \to f$ i.n. for every subsequence g_n of f_n. In turn, from g_n we can select, by Theorem 9.2, a subsequence which converges to f almost everywhere. This means that $f_n \to f$ as.

Theorem 10 (generalized theorem on dominated convergence). *If $f_n \in U$, $f_n \to f$ as. and $|f_n| \leq g_n \in U$, $g_n \to g$ i.n. then $f_n \to f$ i.n., and therefore $\int f_n \to \int f$, $\int |f| \leq \int g$.*

Proof. Let f_{i_n} be any subsequence of f_n. Then $f_{i_n} \to f$ as. By the definition of the asymptotic convergence, there is a subsequence f_{j_n} of f_{i_n} such that $f_{j_n} \to f$, except for a null set Z_1. We have $g_{j_n} \to g$ i.n., and thus $g \in U$, by Theorem 9.2. Moreover, by Theorem 9.3, there is a subsequence g_{k_n} of g_{j_n} and a non-negative function $r \in U$ such that $g_{k_n} \to r$ except for a null set Z_2. Let h_n be functions such that $h_n(x) = 0$ on the null set $Z = Z_1 \cup Z_2$ and $h_n(x) = f_{k_n}$ outside Z. Then $|h_n| \leq g_{k_n} \leq r$ holds everywhere and $h_n \to f$ a.e., because h_n is a subsequence of f_{j_n}. Hence $h_n \to f$ i.n., by Theorem 9.6, and consequently $f_{k_n} \to f$ i.n., because $h_n \sim f_{k_n}$. The obtained result can be now formulated as follows: from every subsequence a_{j_n} of the sequence $a_n = \int |f_n - f|$ we can select a subsequence a_{k_n} which converges to 0. Since the elements a_n are in a Banach space and the Urysohn condition is there satisfied, it follows that $a_n \to 0$. And this means that $f_n \to f$ i.n.

Chapter V

Applications to Set Theory

1. Characteristic functions of sets

Given any subset Z of K, one often denotes by χ_Z or by 1_Z the function whose value is 1 at every point of Z, and 0 at the remaining points of K. This function is called the *characteristic function* of the set Z.

A function f (defined on K) which admits values 0 and 1 only will be called a *zero-one function*. There is a one-to-one correspondence between sets and zero-one functions. It is easy to list relations for sets and the corresponding relations for zero-one functions.

Sets	*Zero-one functions*
$x \in Z$	$g(x) = 1$
$x \notin Z$	$g(x) = 0$
$Y \subset Z$	$f \leq g$
$Y \cap Z$	fg
$Y \cup Z$	$f - fg + g$
$Y \backslash Z$	$f - fg$
$K \backslash Z$	$1 - g$
$Z_1 \cap ... \cap Z_n$	$g_1 ... g_n$
$Z_1 \cup ... \cup Z_n$	$1 - (1 - g_1) ... (1 - g_n)$

Every statement concerning sets and involving relations on the left side of the above table has its equivalent statement in terms of zero-one functions. By means of this equivalence, several definitions and theorems, stated at first for functions, can be translated into the language of sets. We shall thus say that a set Z is *integrable*, if its characteristic function is integrable. Traditionally, the integral of this function is called the *measure* of the set and is denoted by $\mu(Z)$. Thus $\mu(Z) = \int \chi_Z$. Instead of $\mu(Z)$ we may simply write $\int Z$. Some authors do the converse. They call the integral of a function the measure of that function, and denote it by $\mu(f)$, even if f is not a zero-one function. If $\mu(Z) = 0$, the set Z is called, traditionally, a *set of measure zero* or a *null set* (see section 8, Chapter IV).

Various theorems concerned with the integral of functions are transformed automatically into theorems concerning sets. The formulation of such theorems would be, as a matter of fact, no mathematical activity; rather it would be like expressing the same things in another language. The simplest way to avoid such a redundancy is to identify sets with their characteristic functions. This means, in practical computations, that the equality $Z = \chi_Z$

is assumed. But then the symbol χ_Z becomes superfluous. After the identification, the symbol Z may denote both a set and a function, and the set theory becomes the theory of zero-one functions. Furthermore, the empty set can be denoted by 0, and the basic set K by 1.

For zero-one functions (or for sets) the following equations hold:

$$Z_1 \cup Z_2 = Z_1 - Z_1 Z_2 + Z_2 = 1 - (1 - Z_1)(1 - Z_2),$$

$$Z_1 \cap Z_2 = Z_1 Z_2, \qquad Z_1 \setminus Z_2 = Z_1 - Z_1 Z_2,$$

$$ZZ = Z, \qquad Z_1 \cap ... \cap Z_n = Z_1 ... Z_n,$$

$$Z_1 \cup ... \cup Z_n = 1 - (1 - Z_1)...(1 - Z_n), \qquad Z' = 1 - Z.$$

In the algebra of sets, various identities are being proved. The proofs are often boring and consist in the following general method. One proves that, if an element belongs to the set presented by the left hand side of the identity to be proved, then it also belongs to the right hand side, and conversely. In contrast, when dealing with zero-one functions, we entirely avoid this type of argument and reduce proofs to mechanical calculations like in the ordinary algebra to which we have been used since the primary school. For instance, the de Morgan formulae

$$(Z_1 \cup Z_2)' = Z_1' \cap Z_2',$$

$$(Z_1 \cap Z_2)' = Z_1' \cup Z_2'$$

reduce to the following algebraic identities

$$1 - (Z_1 - Z_1 Z_2 + Z_2) = (1 - Z_1)(1 - Z_2),$$

$$1 - Z_1 Z_2 = (1 - Z_1) - (1 - Z_1)(1 - Z_2) + (1 - Z_2).$$

On verifying these identities, one simultaneously proves the de Morgan formulae.

Interpreting sets as functions we also can prove the following theorem on null sets:

Theorem 1. *The union of a countable sequence of null sets is a null set.*

Proof. If $Z_1, Z_2, ...$ are null sets, i.e., if $\int Z_n = 0$ ($n = 1, 2, ...$), then $\int Z_1 + \int Z_2 + \cdots = 0$. Let $f = Z_1 + Z_2 + \cdots$ hold at every point at which the series converges, and let $f = 1$ at the remaining points. Then $f \approx Z_1 + Z_2 + \cdots$, which implies, by axiom **E**, that $\int f = 0$. If $Z = Z_1 \cup Z_2 \cup \cdots$, then $0 \leqslant Z \leqslant f$ and this implies $0 \leqslant \int Z \leqslant \int f = 0$. Hence the required equation $\int Z = 0$ follows.

From a logical point of view, a set and a zero-one function are entirely different notions. Their identification is allowed under the condition that we are concerned with relations which are equivalent for functions and for sets.

2. Convergence in measure

We say that a sequence f_n converges in measure to f and we write $f_n \to f$ i.m., if the following condition is satisfied:

C1. *For any $\varepsilon > 0$ and $\eta > 0$ there are integrable sets Z_n and an index p such that, for $n > p$, we have $|f_n - f| < \varepsilon$ outside Z_n and $\int Z_n < \eta$.*

We shall show that C1 is equivalent to the condition

C2. *There is a sequence of integrable sets Z_n such that $\int Z_n \to 0$, a sequence of positive numbers ε_n tending to 0, and an index p such that, for $n > p$, we have $|f_n - f| < \varepsilon_n$ outside Z_n.*

In fact, assume that C2 holds. Let $\varepsilon > 0$ and $\eta > 0$ be given. There is an index n_1 such that $\int Z_n < \eta$ for $n > n_1$. There is also an index n_2 such that, for $n > n_2$, we have $|f_n - f| < \varepsilon$ outside Z_n. Talking $p = \max(n_1, n_2)$ we fulfil C1.

Assume now that C1 holds. Let $\bar{\varepsilon}_m$ and $\bar{\eta}_m$ be arbitrary sequences of positive numbers which decrease monotonically to 0. According to C1, there are integrable sets $\bar{Z}_{mn}$ and indices p_n such that, for $n > p_m$, we have $|f_n - f| < \bar{\varepsilon}_m$ outside $\bar{Z}_{mn}$ and $\int \bar{Z}_{mn} = \bar{\eta}_m$ ($p = 1, 2, \ldots$). We obviously may assume that the sequence p_m is increasing. Put $\varepsilon_n = \bar{\varepsilon}_m$, $\eta_n = \bar{\eta}_m$ for $p_m < n < p_{m+1}$ and $Z_n = \bar{Z}_{nn}$. Then for $n > p = p_1$ we have $|f_n - f| < \varepsilon_n$ outside Z_n and $\int Z_n = \eta_n$. This proves that C2 holds.

It is evident that, if $f_n \to f$ a.e., then $f_n \to f$ i.m. On the other hand, we have

Theorem 2. *If $f_n \to f$ i.m., then $f_n \to f$ as.*

Proof. Let f_{i_n} be any subsequence of f_n and let Z_n and ε_n be sequences like in C2. Given any subsequence f_{i_n} of f_n, it is possible to select, by Theorem 9.2, Chapter IV, a subsequence f_{j_n} of f_{i_n} which converges to 0 everywhere except for a null set Z. We shall show that $f_{j_n} \to 0$ a.e. In fact, given any point $x \notin Z$, there is an index $n_1 \geq p$ such that $x \notin Z_{j_n}$ for $j_n \geq n_1$. Hence $|f_{j_n}(x) - f(x)| < \varepsilon_{j_n}$ for $j_n \geq n_1$. This proves that $f_{j_n} \to f$ a.e. Thus, from every subsequence f_{i_n} of f_n we can select a subsequence f_{j_n} which converges to f almost everywhere. This means that $f_n \to f$ as.

It is easily seen that the sequence $f_n(x) = x/n$ ($x \in \mathbf{R}^1$) converges asymptotically, but does not in measure. This example, together with Theorem 2, shows that asymptotic convergence is essentially more general than convergence in measure.

Chapter VI

Measurable Functions

1. Retracts of functions

Each vector a of a Banach space E can be represented in the form

$$a = e_a |a|,$$

where e_a is the *directional factor* of a and $|a|$ is the *length* of a. Instead of *length* also the words *modulus* or *norm* can be used. We evidently have $|e_a| = 1$, whenever $a \neq 0$. If $a = 0$, the directional factor is undetermined; we then admit, by convention, that $e_a = 0$. Instead of e_a we can equivalently use the symbol $a/|a|$ (whose meaning is $(1/|a|)a$, if $a \neq 0$, and 0, if $a = 0$).

The expression

$$h = \frac{f}{|f|} (f \cap g)$$

will be of importance in this chapter. It represents a function whose directional factor is, at each point, the same as that of the function f; thus, $e_h = e_f$. Also the length of h equals to the length of f, $|h| = |f|$, but only at the points at which $|f| \leqslant |g|$. At the remaining points, where $|f| > |g|$, we have $|h| = |g|$. We can say that the function h is obtained from f, on preserving the directional factors and *retracting* the lengths to $|g|$ at points where $|f| > |g|$. We say that h is the *retract of f by the function g*. In practice, the use of the symbol $(f/|f|)$ $(f \cap g)$ is somewhat cumbersome, we therefore shall abbreviate it to

$$f . \cap g.$$

The point . at f is to recall that the directional coefficient of $f . \cap g$ is that of f. The operation $.\cap$ is asymmetric, i.e., we have $f . \cap g \neq g . \cap f$ in general. The reader can easily check the following properties of the retract:

$$f . \cap g = f . \cap |g|,$$
$$|f . \cap g| = f \cap g,$$
$$|f| \leqslant g \quad \text{implies} \quad f . \cap g = f,$$
$$f . \cap (g . \cap h) = (f . \cap g) . \cap h.$$

The last property, the associativity of $.\cap$, allows us to write $f . \cap g . \cap h$ instead of the expressions on any side of the above equation. We further have

$$|f . \cap g . \cap h| = f \cap g \cap h,$$

$$f(g . \cap h) = fg . \cap |f| \, h, \quad \text{if } f \text{ or } g \text{ is real valued.}$$

If $f_n \to f$ and $g_n \to g$ everywhere (on the set K on which the functions are defined), then $f_n . \cap g_n \to f . \cap g$ everywhere. The same inclusion remains true, if we replace *everywhere* by *almost everywhere*. Note finally that, if the functions $f_1, \dots, f_n$ have disjoint carriers, i.e., if at every point at most one of functions is different from 0, then

$$(f_1 + \cdots + f_n) . \cap g = f_1 . \cap g + \cdots + f_n . \cap g.$$

2. Measurable functions. The preserving axiom

A function f from K to E is called *measurable*, if its retract by any integrable function is integrable, i.e., if

$$g \in U \quad \text{implies} \quad f . \cap g \in U. \tag{2.1}$$

Since $f . \cap g = f . \cap |g|$, we may assume, in the above definition, that g is non-negative.

P Every integrable function is measurable.

This property follows from **HEM** in two particular cases:

1°   for real valued functions;
2°   for Bochner integrable functions.

In case 1° the basic set K is quite arbitrary, but we assume that $E = \mathbf{R}^1$. In case 2° the Banach space E is quite arbitrary, but we assume that $K = \mathbf{R}^q$. Proof of **P** in case 1°. If $f \geq 0$, then (2.1) follows trivially, because $f . \cap g = f \cap g$. If f is an arbitrary real valued function, we write $f = f^+ - (-f^-)$, where the functions

$$f^+ = \tfrac{1}{2}(|f| + f) \quad \text{and} \quad -f^- = \tfrac{1}{2}(|f| - f)$$

are non-negative, integrable, and have disjoint carriers. Thus, $f . \cap g = f \cap g - f^- \cap g$ and hence the integrability of $f . \cap g$ follows.

Proof of **P** in case 2°. Remark first that, if $\lambda \in E$ and f is a brick function, then the product λf is measurable. In fact, this is trivial for $\lambda = 0$. If $\lambda \neq 0$, then

$$\lambda f . \cap g = \lambda f . \cap |\lambda| \frac{|g|}{|\lambda|} = \lambda \left\{ f . \cap \frac{|g|}{|\lambda|} \right\},$$

and the assertion is also evident, because the functions in the last parentheses are non-negative.

Suppose now that

$$f = \lambda_1 f_1 + \cdots + \lambda_n f_n,$$

where $\lambda_1, \ldots, \lambda_n$ are elements of E, and $f_1, \ldots, f_n$ are brick functions. Then we can write

$$f = \kappa_1 h_1 + \cdots + \kappa_p h_p,$$

where the $\kappa_1, \ldots, \kappa_p$ are elements of E, and the $h_1, \ldots, h_p$ are brick functions with disjoint carriers. Hence

$$f . \cap g = (\kappa_1 h_1) . \cap g + \cdots + (\kappa_p h_p) . \cap g.$$

Since all the terms on the right side are integrable, so is their sum $f . \cap g$. Finally, let f be an arbitrary Bochner integrable function. Then it can be expanded into a series of brick functions

$$f \simeq \lambda_1 f_1 + \lambda_2 f_2 + \cdots.$$

The sequence $s_n = \lambda_1 f_1 + \cdots + \lambda_n f_n$ converges to f at every point, except for a null set Z. The sequence $s_n . \cap g$ converges at the same points to $f . \cap g$, thus $s_n . \cap g \to f . \cap g$ a.e. But the functions $s_n . \cap g$ are bounded by the integrable function g and they are themselves integrable, by the preceding argument. Thus their limit $f . \cap g$ is integrable, by the Lebesgue dominated convergence theorem.

We thus have proved that, under any of additional hypotheses 1° or 2°, property **P** follows from **HEM**.

However, if we do not make additional assumptions on the set U, property **P** does not follow from **HEM**. Thus, if we want to base the general theory on property **P**, we must accept this property as a further axiom. The theory based on **HEMP** will be true, in particular, for any real valued functions satisfying **HEM**, and also for the Bochner integrable functions.

3. Elementary properties of measurable functions

Theorem 3.1. *A measurable function, bounded by an integrable function, is integrable.*

Proof. Let f be measurable, g integrable, and let $|f| \leq g$. Then by definition $f . \cap g$ is integrable. But the inequality $|f| \leq g$ implies $f . \cap g = f$, thus f is integrable.

Theorem 3.2. *If a sequence of measurable functions converges almost everywhere, its limit is measurable.*

Proof. Let $f_1, f_2, \ldots$ be measurable functions and let $f_n \to f$ a.e. Given any function g, we also have $f_n . \cap g \to f . \cap g$ a.e. and the functions $f_n . \cap g$ are bounded by g. If g is integrable, then the $f_n . \cap g$ so are in view of **P**, and, by the Lebesgue theorem, the limit $f \cap g$ is integrable. This proves the measurability of f.

The last theorem can be generalized as follows:

Theorem 3.3. *If a sequence of measurable functions converges asymptotically, its limit is measurable.*

Proof. If $f_n \to f$ as., then we can select from it a subsequence g_n such that $g_n \to f$ a.e. Thus f is measurable in view of Theorem 3.2.

Theorem 3.4. *The set of measurable functions is a linear space.*

Proof. If f is measurable, g integrable, and if λ is a real number, then $(\lambda f) \cap g = \lambda (f \cap (|g|/|\lambda|))$, which implies that the function $(\lambda f) \cap g$ is integrable. Thus the product of a measurable function by a real number is measurable.

Now, let f and g be measurable functions and h an integrable function. Remark that

$$h_n = (f \cap nh + g \cap nh) \cap h \to (f+g) \cap h. \tag{3.1}$$

In fact, this is trivial at points, where $h = 0$. If, at a point, $h \neq 0$, then $n|h| \to \infty$ and therefore $f \cap nh = f \cap n|h| \to f$ and, similarly, $g \cap nh \to g$. Thus, (3.1) holds everywhere. But the measurability of f and g implies the integrability of $f \cap nh$ and $g \cap nh$. Hence by **P** the integrability of h_n follows. Since the sequence h_n is bounded by the integrable function h, its limit $(f+g) \cap h$ is integrable, by the Lebesgue theorem. This means that the sum $f + g$ is measurable, and the proof is complete.

Theorem 3.5. *The modulus of a measurable function is measurable.*

Proof. This follows from the equality $|f| \cap g = |f \cap g|$.

Theorem 3.6. *The intersection and the union of two measurable functions are measurable.*

Proof. It suffices to remark that $f \cap g = \frac{1}{2}(|f| + |g| - ||f| - |g||)$ and $f \cup g = \frac{1}{2}(|f| + |g| + ||f| - |g||)$ and then to apply Theorems 3.5 and 3.4.

Theorem 3.7. *The retract of a measurable function by another measurable function is measurable. In other words, if f and g are measurable, then $f \cap g$ is measurable.*

Proof. If h is integrable, then $g \cap h$ is integrable and, consequently, $f \cap (g \cap h)$ so is. But the last function equals to $(f \cap g) \cap h$, which proves our assertion.

Theorem 3.8. *If f and g are measurable functions and one of them is real valued, then the function $\frac{f}{|f|}g$ is measurable.*

Proof. Suppose first that $g \geqslant 0$. Then

$$nf . \cap g = \frac{f}{|f|} \min (n|f|, g),$$

which implies that $nf . \cap g \rightarrow \frac{f}{|f|} g$. The function nf is measurable, by Theorem 3.4; $nf . \cap g$ is measurable by Theorem 3.7; finally, $\frac{f}{|f|} g$ is measurable by Theorem 3.2.

Suppose now that g is real, but not necessarily non-negative. Then the assertion follows from the equality $\frac{f}{|f|} g = \frac{f}{|f|} g^+ - \frac{f}{|f|} (-g^-)$

and the preceding result.

Finally, let f be real and g arbitrary. Then the assertion follows from the identity

$$\frac{f}{|f|} g = \frac{g}{|g|} \left(\frac{f}{|f|} |g| \right)$$

by what we have proved above.

The proof of the following theorem will make use of measurable functions:

Theorem 3.9 (*Fatou*). *If $f_n \in U$, $f_n \rightarrow f$ as. and $\int |f_n| \leqslant M$, then $f \in U$ and $\int |f| \leqslant M$.*

Proof. Letting $k_n = f_n \cap f_{n+1} \cap \cdots$, we have $k_n \leqslant |f_n|$, $\int k_n \leqslant M$. Since the sequence k_n is non-decreasing, there is a function $k \in U$ such that $k_n \rightarrow k$ i.n. and a.e., by the Beppo Levi theorem. Note that if k_n converges at some point, then $|f_n|$ converges to the same limit at that point. This implies that $|f| \sim k$, and hence $|f| \in U$. But f is measurable, by Theorem 3.3, it is thus integrable, by Theorem 3.1, i.e., $f \in U$. We also can write $k_n \rightarrow |f|$ i.n., which implies $\int k_n \rightarrow \int |f|$ and, in consequence, $\int |f| \leqslant M$, because $\int k_n \leqslant M$.

4. Measurable sets

A set is called *measurable*, if its characteristic function is measurable. The intersection $Y \cap Z$ of two measurable sets Y and Z is measurable, by Theorem 3.5, because $Y \cap Z = Y . \cap Z$. Also the union $Y \cup Z$ and the set difference $Y \backslash Z$ are measurable, since we can write $Y \cap Z = YZ$, $Y \cup Z = Y - YZ + Z$ and $Y \backslash Z = Y - YZ$. It follows by induction that *the union* $Z_1 \cup \cdots \cup Z_n$ *and the intersection* $Z_1 \cap \cdots \cap Z_n$ *of n measurable sets are measurable sets.* Hence by Theorem 3.2, also the sets $Z_1 \cup Z_2 \cup \cdots = \lim_{n \to \infty} Z_1 \cup \cdots \cup Z_n$ and $Z_1 \cap Z_2 \cap \cdots = \lim_{n \to \infty} Z_1 \cap \cdots \cap Z_n$ are measurable,

whenever $Z_1, Z_2, \ldots$ are measurable. In other words, *the union and the intersection of an infinite sequence of measurable sets are measurable.*

5. Integrals on arbitrary sets

On identifying the set Z with its characteristic function, we may write

$$Z = \frac{Z}{|Z|}.$$

Hence, it follows by Theorem 3.8 that, if f is a measurable function and Z is a measurable set, then the function fZ is measurable.

If a function f is integrable and a set Z is measurable, then the function fZ is integrable, for it is bounded by $|f|$. Traditionally, the integral $\int fZ$ is written in the form

$$\int_Z f,$$

and is called the *integral of f on the set Z.* Thus the integral of an integrable function exists on every measurable set. In other words, *an integrable function f is integrable on every measurable set.* However, in general, in order that f should be integrable on a set Z, we need assume neither the integrability of f nor the measurability of Z; it suffices that the product fZ should be integrable.

Theorem 5.1. *If a function is integrable on a given set, then it is also integrable on the intersection of this set with any measurable set.*

Proof. In fact, if the product fZ is integrable, then the product $fZ \cdot Y$ is integrable for any measurable set Y. Since this product is equal to $f \cdot (Z \cap Y)$, this means that f is integrable on the intersection $Z \cap Y$.

Theorem 5.2. *If f is integrable on each of the sets Z_1 and Z_2, then it is also integrable on $Z_1 \cap Z_2$ and on $Z_1 \cup Z_2$.*

Proof. It is assumed that $fZ_1 \in U$ and $fZ_2 \in U$. Hence

$$f(Z_1 \cap Z_2) = fZ_1 Z_2 = |fZ_1| \cdot \frac{f}{|f|} Z_2 = |fZ_1| \cdot \frac{fZ_2}{|fZ_2|} \in U,$$

by Theorem 3.6. On the other hand,

$$f(Z_1 \cup Z_2) = f(Z_1 - Z_1 Z_2 + Z_2) = fZ_1 - fZ_1 Z_2 + fZ_2 \in U.$$

Theorem 5.3. If f is integrable on each of the sets Z_1, Z_2, and if these sets are disjoint, then

$$\int_{Z_1 \cup Z_2} f = \int_{Z_1} f + \int_{Z_2} f.$$

Proof.   Since $Z_1 Z_2 = 0$, we have $Z_1 \cup Z_2 = Z_1 + Z_2$ and, consequently,

$$\int_{Z_1 \cup Z_2} f = \int f(Z_1 + Z_2) = \int fZ_1 + \int fZ_2 = \int_{Z_1} f + \int_{Z_2} f,$$

and the proof is complete.

In the particular case, when the function f is defined on the real axis, and the set Z is an interval $\alpha \leqslant x < \beta$, then the integral $\int_Z f$ (in the sense of Lebesgue or Bochner) is usually written in the form

$$\int_\alpha^\beta f. \tag{5.1}$$

It follows from Theorem 5.3 that, if $\alpha < \beta < \gamma$, then

$$\int_\alpha^\gamma f = \int_\alpha^\beta f + \int_\beta^\gamma f, \tag{5.2}$$

when assuming that f is integrable on the intervals $\alpha \leqslant x < \beta$ and $\beta \leqslant x < \gamma$. Instead of this assumption, we may also assume, owing to Theorem 5.1, that f is integrable on $\alpha \leqslant x < \gamma$.

In the case of the Lebesgue or Bochner integrals, it is irrelevant, whether the integral (5.1) is interpreted as on the interval $\alpha \leqslant x < \beta$, $\alpha < x \leqslant \beta$, $\alpha < x < \beta$, or $\alpha \leqslant x \leqslant \beta$. This follows from the fact that the integral $\int f$ on the set Z consisting of a single point is equal to 0 (for $fZ \sim 0$).

If we adopt the supplementary definition

$$\int_\beta^\alpha f = - \int_\alpha^\beta f \quad \text{for} \quad \alpha \leqslant \beta, \tag{5.3}$$

then (5.2) holds for arbitrary numbers α, β, γ. Of course, we must then assume that $\int_\alpha^\alpha f = 0$.

6. The Stone axiom

The set of axioms **HEMP** will be now completed by

S   Every constant function f such that $|f| \equiv 1$ is measurable.

This axiom was primarily stated by M. H. Stone for real valued functions in the form: *the function $f \equiv 1$ is measurable*. Our axiom **S** is an adaptation of Stone's axiom to vector valued functions. It can also be formulated as follows: if $c \in E$ and $h \in U$, then $c \,.\cap\, h \in U$. Property **S** holds in particular, when U is the set of Bochner (or Lebesgue) integrable functions. In fact, let f_n be brick functions whose carriers increase with n so as to cover the whole space $\mathbf{R}^q$. Then the sequence cf_n tends, at every point, to c. Since the functions cf_n are Bochner integrable, the limit c is a measurable function, by Theorem 3.2.

Theorem 6.1. *Each constant function is measurable.*

Proof.   Let c be an arbitrary element of the Banach space E and let $f \equiv c$. If $c = 0$, then f is integrable, thus measurable. If $c \neq 0$, then the function $f_1 = \dfrac{c}{|c|}$ is measurable, by **S**. We have $f . \cap g = |c| \left(f_1 . \cap \dfrac{g}{|c|} \right)$. Since $g/|c| \in U$, this implies by **P** that $f_1 . \cap g$ is integrable, whenever g is integrable. Then also $f . \cap g$ is integrable, by **H**. This proves the measurability of f.

Theorem 6.2. *If $f \in U$, then for any given number $\varepsilon > 0$, we can find a number $\delta > 0$ such that $\int |f| < \varepsilon$ holds for each integrable set Z with $\int Z < \delta$.*

Proof.   The sequence $f_n = n \cap f$ is non-decreasing and converges to the integrable function $|f|$. By Theorems 6.1 and 3.6 we have $f_n \in U$ and thus $\int(|f| - f_n) \to 0$. Thus, there is an index n_0 such that $\int(|f| - f_{n_0}) < \frac{1}{2}\varepsilon$. It is easy to see that the number $\delta = \varepsilon/2n_0$ has required property. In fact, if $\int Z < \delta$, then

$$\int_Z |f| = \int_Z (|f| - f_{n_0}) + \int_Z f_{n_0}.$$

Since $|f| - f_{n_0} \geqslant 0$, the first integral on the right side is less than or equal to the same integral extended over the whole set K. Thus it is less than or equal to $\dfrac{\varepsilon}{2}$. Since $|f_{n_0}| \leqslant n_0$, the second integral on the right side is less than or equal to $n_0 \int Z$, and thus less than or equal to $\dfrac{\varepsilon}{2}$. This implies that $\int_Z |f| < \varepsilon$.

Theorem 6.3. *A real valued function f is measurable if and only if, for any real number α, the set Z_α of points, where $f > \alpha$, is measurable.*

Proof. Let f be a measurable function. Then the function $(f - \alpha)^+ = \frac{1}{2}(|f - \alpha| + (f - \alpha))$ is measurable, by Theorems 3.5 and 3.4. In view of **S** and Theorems 3.4 and 3.6 also the functions $g_n = 1 \cap n(f - \alpha)^+$ are measurable. Evidently, $g_n \to Z_\alpha$ so that Z_α is measurable, by Theorem 3.2. Assume now, conversely, that the sets Z_α are measurable for every real α. If $\alpha < \beta$, then $Z_\beta \leqslant Z_\alpha$ and the set of points at which $\alpha < f \leqslant \beta$ is $Z_\alpha - Z_\beta$. We plainly have

$$0 \leqslant \beta(Z_\alpha - Z_\beta) f < \beta - \alpha \tag{6.1}$$

for points x, where $Z_\alpha(x) - Z_\beta(x) = 1$, i.e., for points of the set $Z_\alpha - Z_\beta$. Consider the sum

$$f_\varepsilon = \sum_{m=-\infty}^{+\infty} \varepsilon m (Z_{\varepsilon(m-1)} - Z_{\varepsilon m}), \tag{6.2}$$

where ε is any positive number. Since $Z_{\varepsilon(m-1)} - Z_{\varepsilon m}$ is the set of points, where $\varepsilon(m-1) < f \leqslant \varepsilon m$, all such differences are disjoint sets. Therefore, at any fixed point $x \in K$, the sum (6.2) consists, in fact, of one term only. More precisely, we have $f_\varepsilon = \varepsilon m (Z_{\varepsilon(m-1)} - Z_{\varepsilon m}) = \varepsilon m$ at the points of $Z_{\varepsilon(m-1)} - Z_{\varepsilon m}$. Applying the general inequality (6.1), we thus obtain

$$0 \leqslant f_\varepsilon - f < \varepsilon \tag{6.3}$$

for points of $Z_{\varepsilon(m-1)} - Z_{\varepsilon m}$. Since the union of all the sets $Z_{\varepsilon(m-1)} - Z_{\varepsilon m}$ is K, inequalities (6.3) hold everywhere on K. Remark also that, since the sets $Z_{\varepsilon m}$ are measurable, so is the function f_ε, being the sum of a series of measurable functions.

Now, let $\varepsilon_1, \varepsilon_2, \ldots$ be any sequence of positive numbers convergent to 0. Then inequalities (6.3) imply that the sequence $f_{\varepsilon_1}, f_{\varepsilon_2}, \ldots$ converges to f. Thus f is measurable, which completes the proof.

Theorem 6.3 suggests, for real valued functions, the following alternative definition of being measurable: *a function f is measurable, if the set Z, where $f > \alpha$, is measurable for every real number α.* In fact, this definition is usually given in text books. Remark however that it requires a former definition of measurable sets. Besides, it applies only to real valued functions.

7. Superposition of a continuous and a measurable function

A function $g(x)$ from a Banach space F to another Banach space E is said to be continuous at $x_0 \in F$, if, given any number $\varepsilon > 0$, there is a number $\delta > 0$ such that the inequality $|x - x_0| < \delta$ $(x \in F)$ implies $|g(x) - g(x_0)| < \varepsilon$. This definition is like that of Classical Analysis, but its interpretation is more general. The sign of modulus denotes here the modulus (norm) of that Banach space to which the element under the sign of modulus belongs. In the following theorem we assume that $F = \mathbf{R}$.

Theorem 7. *If g is a continuous function from $\mathbf{R}$ to a Banach space E, and if f is a real valued measurable function, defined on K, then the function $h(x) = g(f(x))$ is measurable.*

Proof. We introduce the function f_ε, defined by (6.2). Such a function admits the value εm on the set $Z_{\varepsilon(m-1)} - Z_{\varepsilon m}$. Consequently, the function $h_\varepsilon(x) = g(f_\varepsilon(x))$ admits the value $g(\varepsilon m)$ on that set, and we may write

$$h_\varepsilon(x) = \sum_{m=-\infty}^{+\infty} g(\varepsilon m)(Z_{\varepsilon(m-1)} - Z_{\varepsilon m}).$$

By Theorem 6.1, the constants $g(\varepsilon m)$ are measurable and, consequently, the products under the summation sign are measurable (see the remark at the beginning of section 5). Thus the function h_ε is measurable, being the limit of a series of measurable functions. Now, if ε_1, ε_2, ... is any sequence of positive numbers convergent to 0, then $f_{\varepsilon_n} \to f$, as in the proof of Theorem 6.3. Since g is continuous, this implies that $h_{\varepsilon_n}(x) = g(f_{\varepsilon_n}(x)) \to h(x)$. Thus $h(x)$ is measurable, being a limit of a sequence of measurable functions.

Theorem 7 can be generalized in various ways, however we will not need such generalizations.

From Theorem 7 it follows, in particular, that the product λf of a real valued measurable function f by an element $\lambda \in E$ is measurable. If, moreover, f is integrable, then also the product λf is integrable, for it is bounded by the integrable function $|\lambda| \cdot |f|$.

8. The product of measurable functions

Applying Theorem 7 we can prove

Theorem 8.1. *If the functions f and g are measurable, one of them being real valued, then the product fg is a measurable function.*

Proof. Assume first that the functions f and g are identical and admit real values. Thus their product is f^2 and may be considered as a superposition $k(f(x))$, where $k(x) = x^2$. Since $k(x)$ is continuous, the superposition $k(f(x)) = f^2$ is measurable, by Theorem 7.

If f and g are arbitrary real valued measurable functions, the measurability of their product follows by the following identity

$$fg = \tfrac{1}{4}((f+g)^2 - (f-g)^2).$$

If, finally, one of the functions, let us say g, is real valued, while the other one admits arbitrary values (from the Banach space under consideration), we write

$$fg = \frac{f}{|f|} (g \cdot |f|).$$

The function $g \cdot |f|$ is measurable, for both factors g and $|f|$ are measurable and real valued. The product of that function by $\frac{f}{|f|}$ is also measurable, by Theorem 3.8. Since it equals fg, the proof is complete.

Theorem 8.1 is not true, when replacing measurable functions by integrable ones. That is, the product of two integrable functions may be not integrable. However, the following theorem holds:

Theorem 8.2. *If f is a measurable bounded function and g is integrable on a set Z, one of the functions being real valued, then the product fg is integrable on Z.*

Proof. The integrability of g on Z means that the product gZ is integrable. Hence the product fgZ is measurable, by Theorem 8.1. Since we have by hypothesis $|f| \le M$ (M a number), the inequality $|fgZ| \le M|gZ|$ follows. This means that the product fgZ is bounded by an integrable function. Thus it is integrable itself, by Theorem 3.1.

If, in particular, f is measurable and real valued with $m \le f \le M$ and g is integrable on Z and non-negative, then the inequalities $mgZ \le fgZ \le MgZ$ imply

$$m \int_Z g \le \int_Z fg \le M \int_Z g.$$

Consequently, there exists a number ξ with $m \le \xi \le M$ such that

$$\int_Z fg = \xi \int_Z g.$$

In text books, this equality is usually called the *mean value theorem*.

9. Local convergence in measure. Axiom Y

We say that a sequence of functions f_n *converges locally in measure* to f and write $f_n \to f$ l.i.m., if, for each integrable set Y, we have $f_n Y \to fY$ i.m. The reader can easily check that, if $f_n \to f$ i.m., then $f_n \to f$ l.i.m. If the basic set K which the functions are defined on is integrable, then also, conversely, $f_n \to f$ l.i.m. implies $f_n \to f$ i.m., both types of convergence are thus equivalent. However, if K is not integrable, local convergence in measure is essentially more general than convergence in measure. For example, if $K = \mathbf{R}^1$ (and the measure is meant in the Lebesgue sense), then the sequence $f_n = \dfrac{x}{n}$ converges to 0 locally in measure, but does not converge in measure.

In section 2 we have considered asymptotic convergence which is also more general than convergence in measure. There is at first no connection between asymptotic convergence and local convergence in measure, i.e., none of them is more general. However, asymptotic convergence turns out to be more general, if we assume the following axiom:

Y The basic set K is a union of a countable sequence of integrable subsets.

Axiom **Y** is stronger than **S**. In fact, if **Y** holds, we can write $K = \lim_{n \to \infty} (Y_1 \cup \cdots \cup Y_n)$, where Y_n are integrable sets. This implies, by Theorems 3.4 and 3.2, that K is measurable, which means that **S** holds. Consequently, all what has been proved so far under axioms **HEMPS** remains true under axioms **HEMPY**.

Axiom **Y** is satisfied, in particular, in the theory of the Lebesgue and the Bochner integral. To see this, it suffices to decompose $\mathbf{R}^q$ into bricks and note that bricks are integrable sets.

Under axioms **HEMPY** the following theorem holds:

Theorem 9.1. *If $f_n \to f$ l.i.m., then $f_n \to f$ as. In other words, asymptotic convergence is more general than local convergence in measure.*

Proof. Let $K = Y_1 \cup Y_2 \cup \cdots$, where Y_n are integrable sets. Then $f_n Y_m \to f Y_m$ i.m., and, consequently, $f_n Y_m \to f Y_m$ as. for each fixed m. Let g_n be any subsequence of f_n. There is a subsequence g_{1n} of g_n such that $g_{1n} Y_1 \to f Y_1$ a.e., which means everywhere except for a null set Z_1. There also exists a subsequence g_{2n} of g_{1n} such that $g_{2n} Y_2 \to f Y_2$ except for a null set Z_2. We may of course assume that $g_{21} = g_{11}$. Further, there is a subsequence g_{3n} of g_{2n} such that $g_{3n} Y_3 \to f Y_3$ except for a null set Z_3. We may assume that $g_{31} = g_{21}$, $g_{32} = g_{22}$. Continuing so, we obtain infinitely many subsequences

$$g_{i1}, g_{i2}, \ldots \qquad (i = 1, 2, \ldots) \tag{9.1}$$

such that the $(i+1)$th sequence is a subsequence of the ith sequence and we have $g_{(i+1)1} = g_{i1}, \ldots, g_{(i+1)i} = g_{ii}$. Moreover, we have $g_{in} Y_i \to f Y_i$ outside a null set Z_i. Now, the sequence $g_{11}, g_{22}, \ldots$ converges to f outside the union $Z = Z_1 \cup Z_2 \cup \cdots$. But Z is a null set, thus $g_{nn} \to f$ a.e. Now, g_{nn} is a subsequence of g_n which has been taken as an arbitrary subsequence of f_n. This proves that $f_n \to f$ as.

The preceding theorem can be completed, still under **HEMPY**, by

Theorem 9.2. *If f_n are measurable functions, then $f_n \to f$ l.i.m. implies $f_n \to f$ as., and conversely. In other words, in the class of measurable*

functions local convergence in measure is equivalent to asymptotic convergence.

Proof. Assume that f_n does not converge locally in measure to f. It then exists an integrable set Y such that the relation $f_n Y \to fY$ i.m. does not hold. There is thus a number $\varepsilon > 0$ such that, if Z_n denotes the set on which $|f_n Y - fY| \geq \varepsilon$, then $\int Z_n$ does not converge to 0. (The symbol $\int Z_n$ is meaningful, because the measurability of f_n implies the measurability of f and that of the sets Z_n. Since $Z_n \subset Y$, the sets Z_n are integrable.) Thus there is a subsequence Z_{p_n} such that $\int Z_{p_n} \geq \eta > 0$. Let $g_n = (f_n Y - fY) \cap 1$. Then $g_n \geq \varepsilon$ on Z_n and

$$\int g_{p_n} \geq \int \varepsilon Z_{p_n} \geq \varepsilon \eta > 0. \tag{9.2}$$

Assume that $f_n \to f$ as. Then we can select from f_{p_n} a subsequence f_{q_n} such that $f_{q_n} \to f$ a.e. This implies that $g_{q_n} \to 0$ a.e. But $0 \leq g_{q_n} \leq Y \in U$, thus $\int g_{p_n} \to 0$, by the Lebesgue theorem. This is in contradiction with (9.2) and proves that the relation $f_n \to f$ as. does not hold.

In this way we have proved that $f_n \to f$ as. implies $f_n \to f$ l.i.m. This is, together with the converse implication, stated in Theorem 9.1, our assertion.

Under **HEMPY** we also have

Theorem 9.3. *A function is measurable, if and only if it is a limit of a sequence of integrable functions.*

Proof. Let f be a measurable function and let $K = Y_1 \cup Y_2 \cup \cdots$, where the Y_n are integrable sets. Then

$$f = \lim_{n \to \infty} (Z_n f. \cap n)$$

with $Z_n = Y_1 \cup \cdots \cup Y_n$. But the function $Z_n f$ is measurable, by Theorem 3.7, because we may write $Z_n f = \dfrac{Z_n}{|Z_n|} f$. Moreover, the function $Z_n f. \cap n$ is integrable, because it is measurable and bounded by the integrable function nZ_n. We thus have proved that each integrable function is a limit of a sequence of integrable functions. The converse implication was stated earlier, in Theorem 3.2.

The above theorem says that, under axioms **HEMPY**, measurable functions can be defined as limits of sequences of integrable functions. Such a definition is somewhat simpler than the former one, because no concept of a retract is then necessary.

Chapter VII

Examples and Counterexamples

This chapter contains examples which illustrate and complete the theory presented so far. The chapter is not indispensable for understanding the subsequent parts of this book.
We first show, for a few particular integrable functions, what their expansions in brick functions look like. We also give examples which show to what extent axioms **HAEMPSY** are independent. Furthermore, examples of non-measurable sets are considered. At this opportunity, the role of the Axiom of Choice is discussed. Finally, we produce examples showing the differences between some types of convergence considered in the preceding chapters.

1. Examples of expansions of Lebesgue integrable functions

According to the definition given in Chapter I, a function f is integrable, if it can be expanded into a series

$$f \simeq \lambda_1 f_1 + \lambda_2 f_2 + \cdots, \tag{1.1}$$

where the f_n are brick functions. We want to show, at present, how such expansions look in particular cases. We restrict ourselves to functions of a single real variable. Then each brick is determined by two real numbers: the initial point α of the brick and its terminal point β. Such a brick can be denoted by $b_{\alpha,\beta}(x)$; its diagram is shown in Figure 5. For graphical reasons it is more convenient to write $b(\alpha, \beta; x)$ or, when no confusion occurs, by $b(\alpha, \beta)$. This notation will be used in the sequel.

Example 1. The continuous function whose diagram is seen in Figure 6 can be analytically defined by the equations

$$f(x) = \begin{cases} 1+x & \text{for } -1 \le x < 0, \\ 1-x & \text{for } 0 \le x < 1, \\ 0 & \text{elsewhere.} \end{cases}$$

This function is integrable, because it can be expanded as follows:

$$f \simeq \tfrac{1}{2}b(-\tfrac{1}{2}, \tfrac{1}{2}) + \tfrac{1}{4}b(-\tfrac{3}{4}, -\tfrac{2}{4}) + \tfrac{1}{4}b(-\tfrac{1}{4}, \tfrac{1}{4}) + \tfrac{1}{2}b(\tfrac{2}{4}, \tfrac{3}{4})$$

$$+ \tfrac{1}{8}b(-\tfrac{7}{8}, -\tfrac{6}{8}) + \tfrac{1}{8}b(-\tfrac{5}{8}, -\tfrac{4}{8}) + \tfrac{1}{8}b(-\tfrac{3}{8}, -\tfrac{2}{8}) + \tfrac{1}{8}b(-\tfrac{1}{8}, \tfrac{1}{8})$$

$$+ \tfrac{1}{8}b(\tfrac{2}{8}, \tfrac{3}{8}) + \tfrac{1}{8}b(\tfrac{4}{8}, \tfrac{5}{8}) + \tfrac{1}{8}b(\tfrac{6}{8}, \tfrac{7}{8}) + \cdots$$

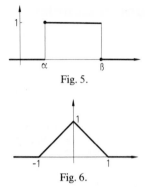

Fig. 5.

Fig. 6.

The Figures 7–9 represent partial sums of the series, consisting of one, four and eleven terms. According to the definition of the integral we have

$$\int f = \tfrac{1}{2} + (\tfrac{1}{16} + \tfrac{1}{8} + \tfrac{1}{16}) + (\tfrac{1}{64} + \tfrac{1}{64} + \tfrac{1}{64} + \tfrac{1}{32} + \tfrac{1}{64} + \tfrac{1}{64} + \tfrac{1}{64}) + \cdots$$

$$= \tfrac{1}{2} + \tfrac{1}{4} + \tfrac{1}{8} + \cdots = 1.$$

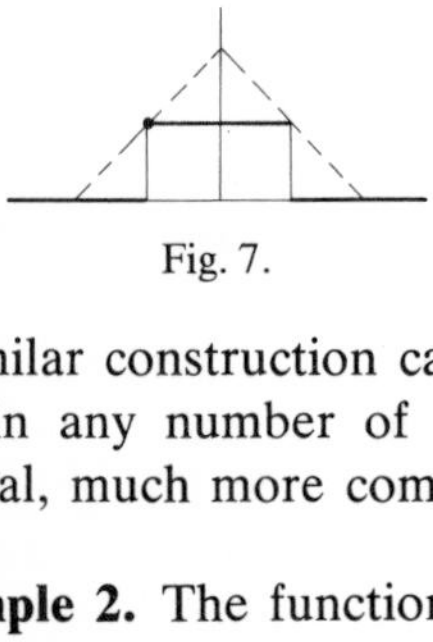

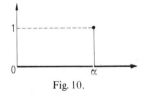

Fig. 7. 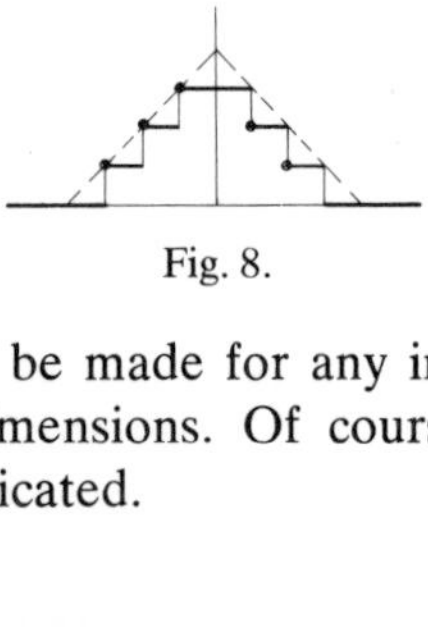   Fig. 8. 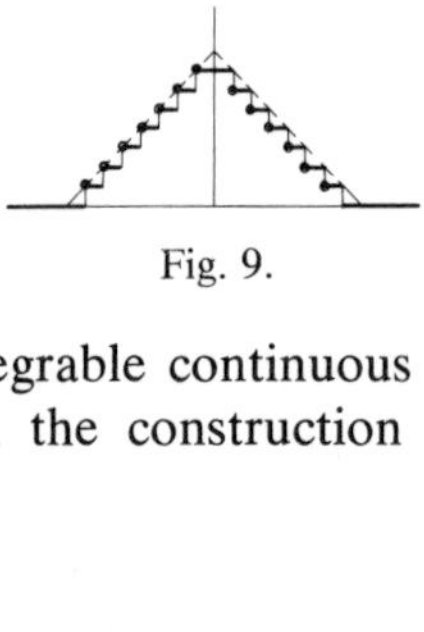   Fig. 9.

A similar construction can be made for any integrable continuous function in any number of dimensions. Of course, the construction is, in general, much more complicated.

Example 2. The function

$$f_\alpha(x) = \begin{cases} 1 & \text{for} \quad x = \alpha, \\ 0 & \text{for} \quad x \neq \alpha, \end{cases}$$

is an example of an integrable discontinuous function. Its diagram is shown in Figure 10. It is easy to construct an expansion (1.1) which converges

Fig. 10.

absolutely to f_α at every point. In fact, let β_n be any sequence of numbers decreasing to α; then

$$f_\alpha \simeq b(\alpha, \beta_1) - b(\beta_2, \beta_1) - b(\beta_3, \beta_2) - \cdots.$$

According to the definition, we have

$$\int f_\alpha = (\beta_1 - \alpha) - (\beta_2 - \beta_1) - (\beta_3 - \beta_2) - \cdots = 0.$$

It follows from this example that the characteristic functions of bounded intervals: open, closed or half-closed $\alpha < x < \beta$, $\alpha \leqslant x \leqslant \beta$, $\alpha < x \leqslant \beta$ are integrable. In fact, they can be represented in the shapes $b(\alpha, \beta) - f_\alpha$, $b(\alpha, \beta) - f_\beta$, $b(\alpha, \beta) - f_\alpha + f_\beta$, respectively.

Example 3. The Dirichlet function

$$d(x) = \begin{cases} 1 & \text{for rational } x, \\ 0 & \text{for irrational } x, \end{cases}$$

is integrable. In order to prove it, we arrange all the rational numbers in a sequence $\alpha_1, \alpha_2, \ldots$ and represent $d(x)$ as an infinite series $d(x) = f_{\alpha_1} + f_{\alpha_2} + \cdots$, where the functions f_{α_i} are defined as in Example 2. We expand each of functions f_{α_i} into a series

$$f_{\alpha_i} = b(\alpha_i, \beta_{i1}) - b(\beta_{i1}, \beta_{i2}) - \cdots, \tag{1.2}$$

as in Example 2, but we additionally assume that

$$\int b(\alpha_i, \beta_{i1}) + \int b(\beta_{i2}, \beta_{i1}) + \cdots = \frac{1}{2^i}, \tag{1.3}$$

which can be achieved on letting $\beta_{i1} - \alpha_i = \dfrac{1}{2^i}$. Let us consider now a sequence

$$\lambda_1 g_1 + \lambda_2 g_2 + \cdots \tag{1.4}$$

which is composed (see section 3, Chapter I) of all the series (1.2). The elements of this series are thus brick functions with coefficients 1 or -1. It follows from (1.3) that $\int g_1 + \int g_2 + \cdots = 1$, and this proves that (1.4) is an expansion of an integrable function.

Series (1.4) consists, for each fixed x, of numbers 1, -1 or 0, only. If $x = \alpha_i$, then the first element in (1.4) is 1, and all the following elements are 0. If $x \neq \alpha_i$, then either all elements are 0, or else the first element is 1 and one (but only one) of the following elements is -1, and all the remaining ones are 0. Obviously, the composed series (1.4) admits also only 1, -1, or 0 for its elements. Consequently, if it converges at some point x, at most a finite number of its elements can be different from 0 at that point, and the convergence is, plainly, absolute. From the construction of series (1.2) it follows that, for each fixed x, the number of elements equal to 1 is, in series (1.4) greater by one than or equal to the number of the -1, according to whether x is rational or irrational. Hence the limit of series (1.4) is, at each point of absolute convergence, equal to $d(x)$. This proves that $d(x) \simeq \lambda_1 g_1 + \lambda_2 g_2 + \cdots$ and that the function $d(x)$ is integrable.

In view of the fact that the series of integrals corresponding to series (1.2) converges to 0, it is easy to conclude that also $\lambda_1 \int g_1 + \lambda_2 \int g_2 + \cdots = 0$, which proves that $\int d = 0$. This result is interesting not only because $d(x)$ takes the value 1 at infinitely many points, but because these points lie densely on the real line and, in spite of this, the integral is 0. Note that, if one is not interested in having an explicit brick functions expansion for the function $d(x)$, but one wishes to know only whether the function is integrable and what its integral is, one can apply the Beppo Levi theorem to the sequence $f_{\alpha_1} + \cdots + f_{\alpha_n}$, and the answer follows immediately.

2. Relations between the integration axioms

If a set of axioms is given, then always the questions arise, whether the axioms are consistent and whether they are independent. If a set of axioms is not consistent, the axioms are contradictory and they are never satisfied in any interpretation. Such a set is therefore of no interest. However, in the case of our axioms **HAEMPSY** we have two interpretations, the Lebesgue and the Bochner integrals. This proves the consistency of **HAEMPSY**. The consistency can also be proved in a simpler way, on considering other interpretations. For instance, let $U = E$ and $\int a = a$ for $a \in U$. Then it is almost trivial to check that the **HAEMPSY** are satisfied.

The next question concerns the independence of axioms. As we have seen, axiom **S** follows from **HEMPY**. If $E = \mathbf{R}^1$, then also **P** follows from **HEM**. In this section we are going to look for further relations between the axioms. Note first that the axiom

E *If* $f \simeq f_1 + f_2 + \cdots (f_n \in U)$, *then* $f \in U$ *and* $\displaystyle\int f = \int f_1 + \int f_2 + \cdots$

is meaningful, only when $f \in U$ implies $|f| \in U$. In fact, the first condition in the definition of $f \simeq f_1 + f_2 + \cdots$ is $\int |f_1| + \int |f_2| + \cdots < \infty$ and therefore the assumption of the integrability of the moduli $|f_1|, |f_2|, \ldots$ is necessary. Furthermore, the last inequality is used to express the fact that the series of integrals is convergent. We thus should suppose that all the terms of the series are non-negative. Hence, if we take **E** under consideration, we always have to assume additionally that

M' *If* $f \in U$, *then* $|f| \in U$ *and* $\displaystyle\int |f| \geq 0$.

This property follows trivially from the former condition

M *If* $f \in U$, *then* $|f| \in U$ *and* $\displaystyle\left| \int f \right| \leq \int |f|$.

Hence, if we assume that both the axioms **E** and **M** are satisfied, we do not need to assume **M'**. However, if we do not assume that **M** holds, we always have to consider **E** together with **M'**, because otherwise **E** would be senseless.

It is easily seen that **A** follows from **EM'**; of course, **A** also follows from **EM**.

Axiom **M** *is independent of* **HAEM'PSY**. In fact, suppose that K consists of a single point a and that E is the set of complex numbers. If $f(a) = u + iv$, we define $\int f = u + 2v$. Thus, the value of the integral is always real. It is easy to check that all the axioms **HAEM'PSY** are satisfied. However **M** is not, because, if $f(a) = i$, then $|\int f| = |2i| = 2$ and $\int |f| = |i| = 1$.

Axioms **HA** say that U is a linear space and the integral is a linear operation on it. The same conclusion follows from **HEM'**, because **EM'** implies **A**. It can be noted that, in **HEM'**, the axiom

H *If* $f \in U$ *and* $\lambda \in \mathbf{R}^1$, *then* $\lambda f \in U$ *and* $\displaystyle\int (\lambda f) = \lambda \int f$,

can be replaced by the following weaker condition:

H$_{-1/2}$ *If* $f \in U$, *then* $-\frac{1}{2}f \in U$.

In other words, we assert that:

Axiom **H** *follows from* **H**$_{-1/2}$**EM**. In fact, it follows by induction from **H**$_{-1/2}$ that, if $f \in U$, then $(-\frac{1}{2})^p f \in U$ for each positive integer p. From **EM'** it follows that, if $f \in U$, then $mf \in U$ for each positive integer m. Combining both results, we see that, if $f \in U$, then $\dfrac{m}{2^p} f \in U$ for each integer m and positive integer p. Now, given any number λ, we can expand it into a convergent series $\lambda = \lambda_0 + \lambda_1 + \cdots$, where all the numbers λ_i are of the form $\dfrac{m}{2^p}$, and $\lambda_i \geqslant 0$ for $i > 0$. By what we have proved, we find

$$\int |\lambda_0 f| + \int |\lambda_1 f| + \cdots = (|\lambda_0| + \lambda_1 + \lambda_2 + \cdots) \int |f| < \infty.$$

Moreover, $\lambda f(x) = \lambda_0 f(x) + \lambda_1 f(x) + \cdots$ at each point $x \in K$, the convergence being absolute. We thus may write $\lambda f \simeq \lambda_0 f + \lambda_1 f + \cdots$. By **E**, it follows that $\lambda f \in U$ and $\int(\lambda f) = \int(\lambda_0 f) + \int(\lambda_1 f) + \cdots = (\lambda_0 + \lambda_1 + \cdots)\int f = \lambda \int f$, which proves **H**.

The above result proves that **HEM** can be replaced **H**$_{-1/2}$**EM**. Consequently, in the set **HAEMPSY** the axiom **H** can be replaced by the weaker condition **H**$_{-1/2}$. However, this axiom cannot be cancelled entirely. In other words:

Axiom **H** *is independent of* **AEMPSY**. In fact, suppose that K consists of a single point a and let $E = \mathbf{R}^1$. For U we take all the functions, whose values are integers. (Of course, U is then not a linear space.) We define

$\int f = f(a)$. Then all the axioms **AEMPSY** are satisfied. However, **H** is not, because if $f = 1$, then $\frac{1}{2}f \notin U$. This proves our assertion.

*Axiom **E** is independent of **HAMPSY**.* This statement is intuitively obvious, because **E** is the only axiom in which infinite series are involved. In spite of this, an adequate example showing the independence of **E** is not elementary. Let K be the real interval $-1 \leqslant x \leqslant 1$ and U the set of continuous real valued functions on it. The integral is assumed to be the Lebesgue integral. The essential difference with respect to the general theory developed earlier is that U is at present the set of continuous functions which are considered as the only integrable functions. (In this particular case the integral can be equivalently defined as in a primary course on integration.) Then axioms **HAMPSY** are plainly satisfied, but **E** is not. In fact, let f_n be continuous functions which are positive in $(0, 1]$ and negative in $[-1, 0)$ and such that

$$f(x) = f_1(x) + f_2(x) + \cdots = \begin{cases} 1 & \text{for } 0 < x \leqslant 1, \\ 0 & \text{for } x = 0, \\ -1 & \text{for } -1 \leqslant x < 0 \end{cases}$$

$\left(\text{we can take, e.g., } f_n(x) = \dfrac{2}{\pi} \arctan \dfrac{x}{n^2 + n - 1} \right).$ Then evidently, $f \simeq f_1 + f_2 + \cdots$. But $f \notin U$, because f is discontinuous at 0. Thus, **E** is not satisfied.

We have shown that the axiom **S** does depend on **HEMPY**. However:

*Axiom **S** is independent of **HAEMP**.* Let K consist of two points a, b and let $E = \mathbf{R}^1$. For U we take the set of all real valued functions f such that $2f(a) = f(b)$ and we define $\int f = f(a)$. Then axioms **HAEMP** are satisfied. Now, **S** tells us that $h = 1. \cap f \in U$, if $f \in U$. Let $f(a) = 1$, $f(b) = 2$. Then $h(a) = 1$, $h(b) = 1$, and consequently $h \notin U$. Thus **S** does not hold.

*Axiom **Y** is independent of **HAEMPS**.* In fact, let $K = \mathbf{R}^1$. For U we take the space l_1 consisting of all real functions f which vanish everywhere on $\mathbf{R}^1$ except for a countable set of points and such that $\sum_{x \in \mathbf{R}^1} |f(x)| < \infty$. Then we define $\int f = \sum_{x \in \mathbf{R}^1} f(x)$. (In these sums the summation is to be carried out over all the points x at which $f(x) \neq 0$.) It can be checked that all the axioms **HAEMPS** are satisfied. However **Y** is not, because the only integrable sets are finite subsets of $\mathbf{R}^1$. Thus $K = \mathbf{R}^1$ is not a union of a countable number of integrable sets. (It is plain that the example can be modified on taking for K any uncountable set.)

*Axiom **P** is independent of **HAEMSY**.* We suppose that E is the space l_1 considered in the preceding example and we define the norm of a E as

$$|a| = \sum_{x \in \mathbf{R}^1} |a(x)|.$$

Then E is a Banach space. In particular, we denote by a_0 the function whose value is 1 at the origin and 0 elsewhere. Then $a_0(x-t)$ is a function of t which has the value 1 at the point $t = x$ and 0 elsewhere. This function is plainly an element of E.

Now, we suppose that $K = \mathbf{R}^1$ and that the set U consists of all functions of the form

$$f(x) = a + \lambda A(x), \qquad (2.1)$$

where $a \in E$, $\lambda \in \mathbf{R}^1$ and $A(x) = \{a_0(t-x)\}$. Thus, if $\lambda = 0$, then $f(x)$ does not depend on x. The representation of $f \in U$ in the form (2.1) is unique. By the integral of (2.1) we mean

$$\int f = \sum_{t \in R^1} a(t) + \lambda.$$

The reader will easily check that the axioms **HAEMSY** are satisfied. In order to show that **P** is not satisfied, we observe that the retract $A . \cap a$, where $a = a(t)$ is different from 0 at least at two different points t, is not of the form (2.1). Thus $A . \cap a \notin U$, which proves the assertion.

3. Examples of non-measurable sets

In this section we are going to give examples of sets in $\mathbf{R}^q$ which are not measurable (in the sense of Lebesgue theory). To this end, we divide $\mathbf{R}^q$ into subsets X such that two points x, y of $\mathbf{R}^q$ belong to the same X, if and only if the difference $x - y$ is a rational point of $\mathbf{R}^q$ (i.e., a point whose all coordinates are rational numbers). It is easy to see that all the sets X are disjoint. We select, from every X, an arbitrary point and denote by G the set consisting of all the selected points. Thus, G has exactly one point in common with each of sets X. We shall show that G is not measurable. Moreover, each measurable subset of G is a null set.

The proof of this fact will not be quite simple. We shall give, afterwards, another example for which the proof will be simpler, but the definition of the function slightly more sophisticated.

Note first that, if a is a rational point of $\mathbf{R}^q$, different from 0, then the set G_a consisting of the points $a + x$ with $x \in G$ is disjoint from G. In fact, if we had an element y belonging to G and G_a simultaneously, we would have $y = a + x$ for some $x \in G$. The difference $y - x$ would then be rational, and both the points x, y would belong to a common set X. But this is impossible, for G and X have only one point in common. Similarly we see that, if a and b are two different rational points, then G_a and G_b are disjoint. Moreover, the union of all G_a with rational a is the whole space $\mathbf{R}^q$. In other words, if we denote by Q the set of all rational points of $\mathbf{R}^q$, we have

$$\bigcup_{a \in Q} G_a = \mathbf{R}^q. \qquad (3.1)$$

Let H denote the q-dimensional brick whose initial point lies at 0, and the terminal point has all its coordinates 1. Thus if $x = (\xi_1, \ldots, \xi_q) \in \mathbf{R}^q$, then H is the set of the points x such that $0 \leqslant \xi_j \leqslant 1$ $(j = 1, \ldots, q)$. Let H_a denote the translated brick consisting of the points $a + x$ with $x \in H$. If B is the set of all integral points of $\mathbf{R}^q$ (i.e., of points whose all coordinates are integers), then, for each $a \in Q$,

$$\bigcup_{m \in B} H_{a+m} = \mathbf{R}^q.$$

We have $GH_a = (G_{-a}H)_a$ for each $a \in \mathbf{R}^q$ (we generally use, for sets, the notation YZ equivalently with $Y \cap Z$, as in section 1, Chapter V).

Let F be a measurable subset of G. Then the sets $FH_{a+m} = F \cap H_{a+m}$ are integrable and we have $\int FH_{a+m} = \int F_{-a-m}H$, because the Lebesgue integral is translation invariant (see Theorem 3.3, Chapter I). If B_n is any finite subset of B, then

$$\int \left(F \bigcup_{m \in B_n} H_{a+m} \right) = \int \left(\bigcup_{m \in B_n} F_{-a-m} \right) H \leqslant \int H = 1.$$

If B_n is a non-decreasing sequence exhausting $\mathbf{R}^q$, then also the sequences under the integral signs are non-decreasing and, by the Beppo Levi theorem, we get $\int F = \int J_a H$, where $J_a = \bigcup_{m \in B} F_{-a-m}$. If we take n rational points $a_1, \ldots, a_n$, different one from another and all belonging to the interval $[0, 1)$, then the sets $J_{a_1}, \ldots, J_{a_n}$ are disjoint and we thus have

$$n \int F = \int \left(\bigcup_{\nu=1}^{n} J_{a_\nu} H \right) \leqslant \int H = 1.$$

Letting $n \to \infty$, we hence get $\int F = 0$.

In this way we have proved that each measurable subset of G is a null set. In particular, G is a subset of itself. Hence, if it were measurable, we would have $\int G = 0$ and, consequently, also $\int G_a = 0$ for each $a \in \mathbf{R}^q$. Since the set Q of all rational points is countable, it would follow from (3.1) that $\mathbf{R}^q$ is of measure 0. This nonsensical result shows that G is not measurable.

In modifying the preceding example we shall restrict ourselves to the real line $\mathbf{R}^1$. We shall use the same notation, by assuming that $q = 1$. Then Q is the set of rational numbers, B is the set of integers and $H = [0, 1)$. Let $F = \bigcup_{m \in B} G_m$. Then F is periodical, i.e., the set F_n consisting of points $n + x$ with $x \in F$ is, for each $n \in B$, identical with F. Moreover, all the F_a with rational a satisfying $0 \leqslant a < 1$ are disjoint and their union is the whole real line. In symbols,

$$\bigcup_{a \in I} F_a = \mathbf{R}^1, \tag{3.2}$$

where $I = Q \cap H$.

Assume that F is measurable. Then the retract $F . \cap H_{-a} = FH_{-a}$ is integrable for each $a \in \mathbf{R}^q$ and, since the Lebesgue integral is translation invariant, we can easily prove that

$$\int F_a H = \int FH_{-a} = \int FH. \tag{3.3}$$

From (3.2) we get $\bigcup_{a \in I} F_a H = H$ and hence $\sum_{a \in I} \int F_a H = 1$, which is not compatible with (3.3). Thus F is not measurable.

Evidently, examples of non-measurable sets are, simultaneously, examples of non-measurable functions, their characteristic functions.

The existence of non-measurable sets and functions was first shown by G. Vitali, in 1905, by giving examples similar to ours. In spite of this, H. Lebesgue, the very creator of the theory, still claimed that no non-measurable sets existed and he objected to Vitali that his argument was not convincing. Such an opinion of Lebesgue was probably influenced by his wish to have all possible functions embraced by his theory. He rejected, as logically unjustified, the possibility of choosing one point from each set (of a given family of sets) and to form a new set out of them. This objection gave rise to ardent discussions for long years. E. Zermelo formulated explicitly the following principle:

For any family of non-void sets there exists a set which has exactly one element in common with each set of the given family.

This principle is called *Zermelo's axiom* or *Axiom of Choice*. Any form of this axiom is fairly plausible, and it might seem even paradoxal to contradict it. In spite of this intuitive evidence, the axiom was accepted by mathematicians with much skepticism. The source of doubts lies in various paradoxes which are a logic consequence of the axiom. The most famous is the Banach-Tarski paradox that tells us that a 3-dimensional ball can be decomposed into a finite number of parts (non-measurable sets) from which, after proper translations and rotations, two complete balls can be reconstructed.

However, blaming the Axiom of Choice seems rather unjust, because, when taken alone, it does not lead to any paradoxes. Only, if we consider it together with other axioms of Set Theory, the so called paradoxes arise. On the other hand, paradoxes leave off being paradoxes, as time goes on and we get used to them. For instance, the ancient paradox of Zeno arouses no inquietude nowadays. In fact, it was proved by Gödel that the system of axioms which is adopted in the Set Theory and which includes the Axiom of Choice will never lead to a logical contradiction.

4. The outer and the inner cover of a set

If $G \subset \mathbf{R}^q$ is a non-measurable (Lebesgue) set, then for each measurable set $Y \supset G$ there is another measurable set $Z \neq Y$ such that $G \subset Z \subset Y$. In fact, since Y is measurable and $G \subset Y$ non-measurable, there is a point $x_0 \in Y$ which does not belong to G. If we remove x_0 from Y, we obtain a set Z with required property. Thus, among all measurable sets including a given non-measurable set G there exists no smallest one. However, there do exist some which are the smallest in measure. More precisely, we have the following theorem which is true generally under axioms **HEMPY**.

Theorem 4.1. *For every set $G \subset K$ there is a measurable set $Y \supset G$ such that, for each measurable $Z \supset G$, the set $Y \backslash Z$ is of measure* 0.

Proof. Let T be an integrable set and let a_T be the greatest lower bound of $\int S$ for all integrable $S \supset GT$. Of course $0 \leqslant a_T \leqslant \int T$. Let S_n ($n = 1, 2, \ldots$) be integrable sets such that $GT \subset S_n \subset T$ and $\int S_n \to a_T$. The intersection V of all S_n is integrable and we have $GT \subset V \subset T$, $\int V = a_T$. Moreover, for each measurable set $Z \supset G$, we have $\int (V \backslash Z) = \int V - \int ZV \leqslant a_T - a_T = 0$, because $ZV \supset GT$. Thus, for each integrable set T_n we can find an integrable set V_n such that $GT_n \subset V_n \subset T_n$ and $\int (V_n \backslash ZT_n) = 0$. If for T_n we take integrable sets such that their sequence tends monotonically to K, then the union Y of the corresponding V_n is measurable and has the required property. In fact, given any measurable $Z \supset G$, the set $Y \backslash Z$ is the union of the sets $V_1 \backslash Z$, $V_2 \backslash Z$, ... which are of measure 0. In consequence, $Y \backslash Z$ is itself of measure 0.

The set Y which appears in Theorem 4.1 can be called *outer cover* of X. All the outer covers of a given set X are equivalent one with another. In fact, if Y and Z are outer covers of X, then $Y \backslash Z$ and $Z \backslash Y$ are of measure 0. Thus, from $|Y - Z| = (Y - Z)^2 = (Y - YZ) + (Z - YZ) = (Y \backslash Z) + (Z \backslash Y)$ (see section 1, Chapter V) it follows that $\int |Y - Z| = \int (Y \backslash Z) + \int (Z \backslash Y) = 0$.
The following dual theorem also holds under **HAMPY**.

Theorem 4.2. *For every $G \subset K$ there is a measurable set $X \subset G$ such that, for each measurable $Z \subset G$, the set $Z \backslash X$ is of measure* 0.

Proof. One can use a direct argument, like in the proof of Theorem 4.1. Or else, one can use the result already obtained in Theorem 4.1 and apply it to the complement of G. In fact, there is a measurable set $Y \supset 1 - G$ such that, for each measurable $Z \subset G$, i.e., for $1 - Z \supset 1 - G$, the set $Y \backslash (1 - Z)$ is of measure 0. Letting $X = 1 - Y$, we have $Y \backslash (1 - Z) = (1 - X) - (1 - X)(1 - Z) = Z - XZ = Z \backslash X$. Thus, $Z \backslash X$ is of measure 0.

The set X which appears in Theorem 4.2 can be called an *inner cover* of G. If G is any set and X and Y are its inner and upper covers, respectively, then $X \subset G \subset Y$. If $\int (Y - X) = 0$, then G is measurable. If $\int (Y - X) > 0$, then G is non-measurable. The difference of the covers $Y - X$ expresses the degree of non-measurability of G.

5. Norm convergence and pointwise convergence

There is no link between both types of convergence. There exist sequences which converge in norm and pointwise; there exist pointwise convergent sequences which do not converge in norm; finally, there exist sequences which converge in norm, but do not pointwise. All the three cases will be illustrated by the following examples (concerning real valued functions).

Example 1.   The sequence $f_n = \dfrac{1}{n}\, g$, where g is an integrable function, converges in norm and pointwise (at each point).

Example 2.   The sequence $f_n = \dfrac{n}{1+(x-n)^2}$ converges to 0 at every point. However, it does not converge in norm (with the Lebesgue integral), because we have, for each integrable function f, $\int |f_n - f| \geqslant \int |f_n| - \int |f| = n\pi - \int |f| \to \infty$.

Example 3.   Figure 11 represents diagrams of brick functions $f_1, f_2, \ldots$ defined as follows. The carrier of f_1 is $[-1, 1)$. Evidently we have $\int f_1 = 2$. Next we have four functions $f_2, \ldots, f_5$ such that $\int f_2 = \cdots = \int f_5 = 1$ and the union of the carriers is $[-2, 2)$. The third group consists of nine

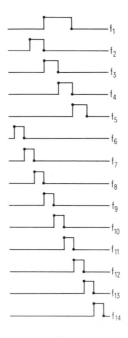

Fig. 11.

functions $f_6, \ldots, f_{14}$ such that $\int f_6 = \cdots = \int f_{14} = \frac{1}{2}$ and the union of the carriers is $[-3, 3)$. The nth successive group will contain functions whose integrals are 2^{-n-1}, and the union of carriers is $[-n, n)$.

Then $\int f_n \to 0$ and, because the functions are non-negative, this proves that $f_n \to 0$ i.n. However the sequence does not converge pointwise, because, at each point of the real line, it admits infinitely many times the value 1 and infinitely many times the value 0.

Examples 2 and 3 also show that neither convergence almost everywhere implies convergence in norm, nor conversely.

6. Local convergence in measure and asymptotic convergence

In section 9, Chapter VI, we have proved that, under axioms **HEMPY**, asymptotic convergence is at least as general as the local convergence in measure. We are going to give an example which shows that it is substantially more general, i.e., *there are sequences which converge asymptotically, but do not locally in measure*. Since the axioms **HEMPY** are satisfied, in particular, by the Lebesgue integral, it suffices to restrict oneself to that case.

Let g be a zero-one function such that

$$\sum_{a \in Q} g(x + a) = 1 \quad \text{for each} \quad x \in \mathbf{R}^q$$

and $g(x + a)g(x + b) = 0$, if $a \neq b$, $a, b \in Q$, where Q is the set of all rational points of $\mathbf{R}^q$. The existence of such a function follows from section 3: g is the characteristic function of the set G considered there and is a non-measurable function. Let us order the elements of Q into a sequence $a_1, a_2, \ldots$ and put $f_n(x) = g(x + a_1) + \cdots + g(x + a_n)$. Then $f_n \to 1$ at each point $x \in \mathbf{R}^q$, thus also $f_n \to 1$ as.

However f_n does not converge locally in measure. In fact, assume, conversely, that it does. Then it follows from Theorem 9.1, Chapter VI, that the limit is 1. Suppose that Y_n is a zero-one measurable function such that $Y_n \geq 1 - f_n$. Then $Y_n(x) \geq g(x + a_{n+1})$. Hence $Y_n(x - a_n) \geq g(x)$ and, because the Lebesgue integral is translation invariant, $\int Y_n \geq \int Y$, where Y is the outer cover of g. But $\int Y > 0$, for the function g is non-measurable. Thus, $\int Y_n$ does not converge to 0. This proves that f_n does not converge locally in measure to 1 and, therefore, to any other limit.

In this way we have shown that, in the domain of arbitrary functions, the local convergence in measure is not general enough as to embrace all sequences that converge asymptotically. Let us recall that, in the class of all measurable functions, both types of convergence are equivalent, provided axioms **HEMPY** hold (Theorem 9.2, Chapter VI).

Chapter VIII

The Upper Integral and Some Traditional Approaches to Integration

This chapter has a more historical character and its main purpose is to show what is the relation of the matter presented in this book to the integrals of Riemann, of Daniell and the integral generated by a σ-measure. We state the following facts. The Riemann integral is the Lebesgue integral restricted to the class of functions which are continuous almost everywhere. The Daniell integral is nothing else, but the **HEM** integral in the domain of real functions. Finally, the integral generated by a σ-measure is a **HEMPS** integral in the domain of real functions. This in particular implies that measure theory is not an adequate tool to construct the Daniell integral, nor the general **HEM** integral, because both of them are of an essentially wider extent.

Although, simplicity was thought as one of devices in preparing this book, this device cannot be kept in the present chapter, because of the complexity of concepts with which we make the comparison. However, the insertion of a few sections on upper integrals facilitates preserving the self-containedness of the book and presenting the matter in a possibly uniform way.

The reader who is not interested in subtle nuances between various approaches to integration can safely omit this chapter, without any loss in understanding the remaining part of the book.

1. The upper and the lower integrals

By the *upper integral* $\overline{\int} f$ of a real valued function f we mean the greatest lower bound of the set S_f of values $\int g$ with $g \geq f$, $g \in U$. If S_f is unbounded from below, we write $\overline{\int} f = -\infty$. If S_f is empty, we write $\overline{\int} f = +\infty$. Similarly, by the *lower integral* $\underline{\int} f$ of f we mean the least upper bound of the set T_f of values $\int g$ with $g \leq f$, $g \in U$. If T_f is unbounded from above, we write $\underline{\int} f = +\infty$. If T_f is empty, we write $\underline{\int} f = -\infty$. According to these definitions the symbols $\overline{\int} f$ and $\underline{\int} f$ are meaningful for every real valued function f (defined on the considered set K). The following properties are obtained easily, under **HAM**:

1° $\underline{\int} f \leq \overline{\int} f$;

2° $\underline{\int} f = -\overline{\int}(-f)$;

3°   If $f \in U$, then $\underline{\int} f = \int f = \overline{\int} f$.

By 2°, we see that all properties of the lower integral $\underline{\int} f$ can be described by properties of the upper integral $\overline{\int} f$. We can therefore restrict our considerations to the upper integral. We have:

4° $\overline{\int} \lambda f = \lambda \overline{\int} f$ for each non-negative number λ;

5° $f \leqslant g$ implies $\overline{\int} f \leqslant \overline{\int} g$;

6°   If $\overline{\int} f < \infty$, then $\overline{\int} f^+ < \infty$ and $\overline{\int} f = \overline{\int} f^+ + \overline{\int} f^-$.

Properties 4° and 5° follow immediately from the definition of the upper integral. To prove 6°, note that if $\overline{\int} f < \infty$, then there are integrable functions $g \geqslant f$. Since $g^+ \geqslant f^+$ and $g^- \geqslant f^-$, and g^+, g^- are integrable as well, we get $\overline{\int} f^+ \leqslant \int g^+ = \int g - \int g^- < \infty$. Moreover $\int g = \int g^+ + \int g^- \geqslant \overline{\int} f^+ + \overline{\int} f^-$. Since this holds for each integrable $g \geqslant f$, it follows that $\overline{\int} f \geqslant \overline{\int} f^+ + \overline{\int} f^-$. To prove the converse inequality, we take arbitrary integrable functions $g \geqslant f^+$ and $h \geqslant f^-$. Then $f \leqslant g + h$, $\overline{\int} f \leqslant \int (g + h) = \int g + \int h$. Hence $\overline{\int} f \leqslant \overline{\int} f^+ + \overline{\int} f^-$, which completes the proof of 6°.

Under **HEM** we shall prove

Theorem 1.1. *If* $\overline{\int} f_1^+ + \overline{\int} f_2^+ + \cdots < \infty$ *and if* $f \leqslant f_1 + f_2 + \cdots$ *holds at every point at which* $f_1^+ + f_2^+ + \cdots < \infty$, *then* $\overline{\int} f \leqslant \overline{\int} f_1 + \overline{\int} f_2 + \cdots$.

Proof. Let $\varepsilon_1 + \varepsilon_2 + \cdots = \varepsilon < \infty$, $\varepsilon_n > 0$. There are functions $g_n \in U$ such that $g_n \geqslant f_n^+$ and $\int g_n \leqslant \varepsilon_n + \overline{\int} f_n^+$. Since $\int g_1 + \int g_2 + \cdots \leqslant \varepsilon + \overline{\int} f_1^+ + \overline{\int} f_2^+ + \cdots < \infty$, it follows that the series $g_1 + g_2 + \cdots$ converges everywhere outside a set Z of measure 0. Consequently $f_1^+ + f_2^+ + \cdots$ converges outside Z and we have $f \leqslant f_1 + f_2 + \cdots$ outside Z. We consider 3 cases.

Case 1. $\overline{\int} f_p^- = -\infty$ for some p. Then $f \leqslant f_p^- + f_1^+ + f_2^+ + \cdots$ outside Z. For each $n = 1, 2, \ldots$ there is an integrable function $h_n \geqslant f_p^-$ such that $\int h_n < -n$. Let $k_n = h_n + g_1 + g_2 + \cdots$ outside Z and $k_n = f$ on Z. Then the functions k_n are integrable and $\int k_n < -n + \varepsilon + M$, $k_n \geqslant f$ everywhere. This implies that $\overline{\int} f = -\infty$, and the wished inequality is fulfilled trivially.

Case 2. $\overline{\int} f_p^- > -\infty$ for each $p = 1, 2, \ldots$ and $\overline{\int} f_1^- + \overline{\int} f_2^- + \cdots = -\infty$. For each $n = 1, 2, \ldots$ there is an index p_n such that $\overline{\int} f_1^- + \cdots + \overline{\int} f_{p_n}^- < -n$. There exist functions $h_n \in U$ such that $f_n^- \leqslant h_n \leqslant 0$ and $\int h_n \leqslant \varepsilon_n + \overline{\int} f_n^-$. Let $k_n = h_1 + \cdots + h_{p_n} + g_1 + g_2 + \cdots$ outside Z and $k_n = f$ on Z. The functions k_n are integrable and $\int k_n < -n + 2\varepsilon + M$. But $k_n \geqslant f$, thus $\overline{\int} f = -\infty$, and again the inequality is fulfilled trivially.

Case 3. $\overline{\int} f_1^- + \overline{\int} f_2^- + \cdots > -\infty$. As before we take functions $h_n \in U$ such that $f_n^- \leqslant h_n \leqslant 0$ and $\int h_n \leqslant \varepsilon_n + \overline{\int} f_n^-$. Then $\int h_1 + \int h_2 + \cdots > -\infty$ which implies that $h_1 + h_2 + \cdots$ converges everywhere except for a set Y of measure 0. Let $k = (g_1 + g_2 + \cdots) + (h_1 + h_2 + \cdots)$ outside the set $Y \cup Z$ and $k = f$ on $Y \cup Z$. Then k is integrable and $k \geqslant f$. Hence $\overline{\int} f \leqslant \int k \leqslant (\varepsilon + \overline{\int} f_1^+ + \overline{\int} f_2^+ + \cdots) + (\varepsilon + \overline{\int} f_1^- + \overline{\int} f_2^- + \cdots) = 2\varepsilon + \overline{\int} f_1 + \overline{\int} f_2 + \cdots$. Since ε is arbitrary, the required inequality follows.

Under **HEM** we also have

Theorem 1.2. *A function f is integrable, if and only if $-\infty < \underline{\int} f = \overline{\int} f < +\infty$.*

Proof. By 3° it suffices to show that if $-\infty < \underline{\int} f = \overline{\int} f < +\infty$, then $f \in U$. There are functions $f_n, k_n \in U$ such that $f_n \leqslant f \leqslant k_n$ and $\int f_n \to \underline{\int} f, \int k_n \to \overline{\int} f$. Let $g_n = \max(f_1, \ldots, f_n)$ and $h_n = \min(k_1, \ldots, k_n)$. Then $g_n, h_n \in U$. Moreover, the sequence $g_1, g_2, \ldots$ is non-decreasing, the sequence $k_1, k_2, \ldots$ is non-increasing and we have $f_n \leqslant g_n \leqslant h_n \leqslant k_n$. Hence $\int f_n \leqslant \int g_n \leqslant \int h_n \leqslant \int k_n$. Since $\underline{\int} f = \overline{\int} f$, we hence conclude that $\int g_n$ and $\int h_n$ converge to the same limit. But the functions $g = \lim g_n$ and $h = \lim h_n$ are integrable, thus $g \sim h$. Since $g \leqslant f \leqslant h$, the function f must be integrable itself.

2. Defining integrable functions by means of an upper integral

In what precedes, the upper integral $\overline{\int} f$ was defined by means of the integral $\int f$. In this section, we shall show that the converse way is also possible. Namely, one first introduces the concept of an upper integral and then one uses it to define the integral $\int f$.

Let $\overline{\int} f$ be a functional defined on all functions f from a given set K to $\mathbf{R}^1$. We assume that the values of $\overline{\int} f$ are real numbers or $+\infty$ or $-\infty$, but not exclusively $+\infty$ or $-\infty$; in other words we assume that the values of $\int f$ are finite for some functions f. Moreover, we assume that the following properties hold:

H̄ $\overline{\int} \lambda f = \lambda \overline{\int} f$ for $\lambda \geqslant 0$;

Ē If $\overline{\int} f_1^+ + \overline{\int} f_2^+ + \cdots < \infty$ and if $f \leqslant f_1 + f_2 + \cdots$ holds at every point at which $f_1^+ + f_2^+ + \cdots < \infty$, then $\overline{\int} f \leqslant \overline{\int} f_1 + \overline{\int} f_2 + \cdots$;

M̄ If $\overline{\int} f < \infty$, then $\overline{\int} f^+ < \infty$ and $\overline{\int} f = \overline{\int} f^+ + \overline{\int} f^-$.

(These properties were considered already, in section 1, as 4°, Theorem 1.1 and 6°.) We define the class U of integrable functions, on assuming that $f \in U$, if and only if

$$-\infty < \underline{\int} f = \overline{\int} f < \infty, \tag{2.1}$$

where $\underline{\int} f = -\overline{\int}(-f)$. In other words, a function f is said to be integrable, if its lower and its upper integrals coincide and are finite. Their common value is called the integral of f and denoted by $\int f$. Thus $\underline{\int} f = \int f = \overline{\int} f$. From the definition it follows easily that if $f \in U$, then $-f \in U$ and $\int(-f) = -\int f$. In fact, (2.1) implies $-\infty < -\overline{\int} f = -\underline{\int} f < \infty$, i.e., $-\infty < \underline{\int}(-f) = \overline{\int}(-f) < \infty$.

We shall prove that the integral f, defined as above, satisfies **HEM**. First of all let us note a few properties of the upper integral which follow from $\overline{\mathbf{H}\overline{\mathbf{E}}\overline{\mathbf{M}}}$. By hypothesis, there is a function f such that the value of $\overline{\int} f$ is finite. Letting $\lambda = 0$, we thus find from $\overline{\mathbf{H}}$ that

$$\overline{\int} 0 = 0. \tag{2.2}$$

Next we show that

$$f \leqslant g \text{ implies } \overline{\int} f \leqslant \overline{\int} g. \tag{2.3}$$

In fact, this is trivial, if $\overline{\int} g = +\infty$. If $\overline{\int} g < \infty$, then also $\overline{\int} g^+ < \infty$, by $\overline{\mathbf{M}}$. Letting $f_1 = g$ and $f_2 = f_3 = \cdots = 0$ and using (2.2), we obtain (2.3) from $\overline{\mathbf{E}}$. From (2.2) and (2.3) it follows that

$$0 \leqslant g \quad \text{implies} \quad 0 \leqslant \overline{\int} g, \tag{2.4}$$

$$f \leqslant 0 \quad \text{implies} \quad \overline{\int} f \leqslant 0. \tag{2.5}$$

We now show that

$$\overline{\int} (f+g) \leqslant \overline{\int} f + \overline{\int} g, \quad \text{if} \quad \overline{\int} f < \infty \quad \text{and} \quad \overline{\int} g < \infty. \tag{2.6}$$

In fact, by $\overline{\mathbf{M}}$ we have $\overline{\int} f^+ < \infty$ and $\overline{\int} g^+ < \infty$. Replacing, in $\overline{\mathbf{E}}$, f by $f+g$ and letting $f_1 = f$, $f_2 = g$, $f_3 = f_4 = \cdots = 0$, we get (2.6).
Setting $\underline{\int} f = -\overline{\int} (-f)$, we have

$$\underline{\int} f \leqslant \overline{\int} f. \tag{2.7}$$

In fact, this is trivially true, if $\underline{\int} f = -\infty$ or $\overline{\int} f = +\infty$. If $\underline{\int} f > -\infty$ and $\overline{\int} f < \infty$, then by (2.2) and (2.6) we get $0 = \overline{\int} [f+(-f)] \leqslant \overline{\int} f + \overline{\int} (-f)$, because $\overline{\int} (-f) = -\underline{\int} f < \infty$. Hence (2.7) follows.
If $\lambda \geqslant 0$, then by $\overline{\mathbf{H}}$ we have $\overline{\int} (-\lambda f) = \lambda \overline{\int} (-f)$ which implies $\underline{\int} \lambda f = \lambda \underline{\int} f$. If $f \in U$, then $\underline{\int} f = \overline{\int} f$ and hence $\underline{\int} \lambda f = \overline{\int} \lambda f$, i.e., $\lambda f \in U$. Moreover, $\int \lambda f = \lambda \int f$. If $\lambda \leqslant 0$, then $-\lambda \int f = \int (-\lambda f) = \overline{\int} (-\lambda f) = -\underline{\int} \lambda f$ and $-\lambda \int f = \underline{\int} (-\lambda f) = -\overline{\int} \lambda f$. Thus $\underline{\int} \lambda f = \lambda \int f = \overline{\int} \lambda f$, which means that $\lambda f \in U$ and $\int \lambda f = \lambda \int f$. This proves that the integral $\int f$ satisfies $\mathbf{H}$.
From (2.6) we easily obtain

$$\underline{\int} f + \underline{\int} g \leqslant \underline{\int} (f+g), \quad \text{if} \quad \underline{\int} f > -\infty \quad \text{and} \quad \underline{\int} g > -\infty. \tag{2.8}$$

If $f \in U$ and $g \in U$, then we can apply both (2.6) and (2.8) and we thus get, in view of the general inequality (2.7),

$$\underline{\int} f + \underline{\int} g \leqslant \underline{\int} (f+g) \leqslant \overline{\int} (f+g) \leqslant \overline{\int} f + \overline{\int} g.$$

This implies that $f + g \in U$ and

$$\int (f + g) = \int f + \int g.$$

To prove **M**, note that $f \in U$ implies $-\infty < \underline{\int} f = \overline{\int} f < \infty$ and, by (2.4) and $\overline{\textbf{M}}$, $0 \leqslant \overline{\int} f^+ < \infty$, $\overline{\int} f = \overline{\int} f^+ + \overline{\int} f^-$. Symmetrically, we have $-\infty < \underline{\int} f \leqslant 0$ and $\underline{\int} f = \underline{\int} f^+ + \underline{\int} f^-$. Consequently, $\overline{\int} f^+ + \overline{\int} f^- = \underline{\int} f^+ - \underline{\int} f^-$ and hence $(\overline{\int} f^+ - \underline{\int} f^+) + (\overline{\int} f^- - \underline{\int} f^-) = 0$. Since the differences in the parentheses are non-negative, it follows that $\underline{\int} f^+ = \overline{\int} f^+$ and $\underline{\int} f^- = \overline{\int} f^-$. This proves that $f^+ \in U$ and $f^- \in U$. Hence $|f| = f^+ + (-1)f^- \in U$ and also $-|f| \in U$. But $-|f| \leqslant f \leqslant |f|$, we thus get $-\int |f| \leqslant \int f \leqslant \int |f|$, which proves **M**.

A function h defined on K is called a *null function*, if $\overline{\int} |h| = 0$. The set of null functions is a linear space, i.e., the product of a null function by any number is a null function, and the sum of two null functions is a null function. Easy proofs are left to the reader.

If h is a null function, and g is a function whose value is 0 at every point at which the value of h is 0, then g is also a null function. In fact, let $f_1 = f_2 = \cdots = |h|$. Then $\overline{\int} f_1^+ + \overline{\int} f_2^+ + \cdots = 0$, and the series $f_1^+ + f_2^+ + \cdots$ converges exactly at those points where $h = 0$, and we have $|g| = f_1 + f_2 + \cdots$ there. Hence $\overline{\int} |g| \leqslant \overline{\int} f_1 + \overline{\int} f_2 + \cdots = 0$, proving the assertion. Consequently, *we may arbitrarily change, in a null function, the values which are $\neq 0$, and the function still remains a null function.*

We shall prove that, *if $\overline{\int} |f_1| + \overline{\int} |f_2| + \cdots < \infty$, then $f_1 + f_2 + \cdots$ converges absolutely outside a null set.* In fact, let Z be the set of points at which $|f_1| + |f_2| + \cdots = \infty$. Let M be an arbitrary positive number and let $g_n = (|f_1| + \cdots + |f_n|) \cap M$, $h_1 = g_1$, $h_{n+1} = g_{n+1} - g_n$. Then $0 \leqslant h_n \leqslant f_n \cap M \leqslant |f_n|$, and hence $\overline{\int} h_1 + \overline{\int} h_2 + \cdots \leqslant N = \overline{\int} |f_1| + \overline{\int} |f_2| + \cdots$. Consequently also $\overline{\int} (h_1 Z)^+ + \overline{\int} (h_2 Z)^+ + \cdots \leqslant N$. On the other hand, $MZ = h_1 Z + h_2 Z + \cdots$ holds everywhere, so, by $\overline{\textbf{H}}$ and $\overline{\textbf{E}}$, it follows that $M \overline{\int} Z \leqslant \overline{\int} h_1 Z + \overline{\int} h_2 Z + \cdots \leqslant N$. Since M can be taken arbitrarily large, and N is fixed, it follows that $\int Z = 0$, i.e., Z is a null set.

We now are in a position to prove **E**. We assume that

1° $\int |f_1| + \int |f_2| + \cdots < \infty$, $f_n \in U$, and

2° $f = f_1 + f_2 + \cdots$ at every point at which the series converges absolutely.

Since $\overline{\int} |f_n| = \int |f_n|$, we also have $\overline{\int} |f_1| + \overline{\int} |f_2| + \cdots < \infty$ and, consequently, the set Z on which $f = f_1 + f_2 + \cdots$ does not hold is a null set. We put $g = g_1 = g_2 = \cdots = 0$ on Z, and $g = f$, $g_n = f_n$ outside Z. Then $g = g_1 + g_2 + \cdots$ holds everywhere. Moreover, $\overline{\int} g_1^+ + \overline{\int} g_2^+ + \cdots < \infty$, because $\overline{\int} g_n^+ \leqslant \overline{\int} f_n^+ \leqslant \overline{\int} |f_n|$. We thus may apply $\overline{\textbf{E}}$ and we so find $\overline{\int} g \leqslant \overline{\int} g_1 + \overline{\int} g_2 + \cdots$. But $\overline{\int} |f - g| = 0$, $\overline{\int} |f_n - g_n| = 0$, and this easily implies that $\overline{\int} g = \overline{\int} f$, $\overline{\int} g_n = \overline{\int} f_n$. Hence, $\overline{\int} f \leqslant \int f_1 + \int f_2 + \cdots$. Applying the same argument to functions $-f$ and $-f_n$, we obtain the inequality $\overline{\int} (-f) \leqslant \int (-f_1) + \int (-f_2) + \cdots$. This implies $\underline{\int} f \geqslant \int f_1 + \int f_2 + \cdots$, proving the assertion.

3. Further relations between the integral and the upper integral

In section 1 we have constructed an operation A which assigns an upper integral $\bar{\int} = A \int$ (satisfying $\mathbf{H\bar{E}M}$) to every integral $\int$ (satisfying $\mathbf{HEM}$). In section 2 we have constructed an operation B which, conversely, assigns an integral $\int = B\bar{\int}$ (satisfying $\mathbf{HEM}$) to every upper integral (satisfying $\mathbf{H\bar{E}M}$). The question arises, whether $BA\int = \int$. The answer is positive. In other words, if we apply operation A to an integral $\int$ and then apply operation B to the resulting upper integral, then we come back to the original integral $\int$.

To prove this, assume that $f \in U$. Then $A\int f = \int f$ and $A\int(-f) = -\int f$. Thus $-A\int(-f) = \int f = A\int f$. This means that f is integrable in the new sense, say $f \in BAU$, and that $BA\int f = \int f$. Assume now that $f \notin U$. Then $-A\int(-f) < A\int f$, by Theorem 1.2. This implies that $f \notin BAU$. Thus we have proved that $BAU = U$ and $BA\int f = \int f$. This means that the operation B is inverse to A.

One can also ask, if the operation A is inverse to B, i.e., if $AB\bar{\int} f = \bar{\int} f$. In this case the answer is negative, as the following example shows. We assume that the set K the functions are defined on consists of a single point a. We write $\bar{\int} f = f(a)$, if $f(a) > 0$, and $\bar{\int} f = 0$, if $f(a) \leq 0$. Then the only integrable function is $f = 0$ and, of course, $B\bar{\int} 0 = 0$. Thus, if $0 < f(a) < \infty$, there is no integrable function g satisfying $g \geq f$. This means that $AB\bar{\int} f = +\infty$, and we therefore have $AB\bar{\int} f \neq \bar{\int} f$.

4. Riemann integrable functions

In this section, we shall be concerned with real valued functions, defined on $\mathbf{R}^q$. We shall write $f \in V$, if and only if f expands in a series of brick functions

$$f \simeq \lambda_1 f_1 + \lambda_2 f_2 + \cdots,$$

where the coefficients λ_n are real and almost all (i.e., all except for a finite number of them) are ≥ 0, and the series is convergent for each point $x \in \mathbf{R}^q$. We thus have $\lambda_1 \int f_1 + \lambda_2 \int f_2 + \cdots < \infty$, and $f = \lambda_1 f_1 + \lambda_2 f_2 + \cdots$ everywhere in $\mathbf{R}^q$. Evidently, V is a particular class of Lebesgue integrable functions. Let Z be the set of the boundary points of the carriers of all $f_1, f_2, \ldots$. We shall prove that

$$f(x) \leq f_*(x) = \liminf_{t \to x} f(t)$$

for each x outside Z. In fact, let x be fixed outside Z. Then all the functions f_n are continuous at x. Denote by A the set of all indices n such that $\lambda_n < 0$ or $f_n(x) = 1$ and by B the set of indices n such that $\lambda_n \geq 0$ and $f_n(x) = 0$. We decompose f into a sum of two functions a and b such that

$$a = \sum_{n \in A} \lambda_n f_n, \qquad b = \sum_{n \in B} \lambda_n f_n.$$

Since the number of negative λ_n is finite and the numerical series $\sum\limits_{n \in A} \lambda_n$ is convergent, it follows that the series representing the function a converges uniformly. Since all the f_n are continuous at x, it follows that also a is continuous at x, i.e., $a(x) = \lim\limits_{t \to x} a(t)$. On the other hand, we have $b(x) = 0$ and $b \geq 0$ everywhere. This implies that $b(x) \leq \lim\limits_{t \to x} \inf b(t)$. Hence, the required inequality follows. Since Z is of measure 0, we can say that the inequality $f \leq f_*$ is satisfied almost everywhere for each function $f \in V$.

By $-V$ we denote the class of functions h such that $-h \in V$. We thus have, in particular, $h = \kappa_1 h_1 + \kappa_2 h_2 + \cdots$ everywhere in $\mathbf{R}^q$, where almost all the coefficients are ≤ 0. Each function $h \in -V$ satisfies $h(x) \geq h^*(x) = \lim\limits_{t \to x} \sup h(t)$ for each x outside Z.

A real function g (defined on $\mathbf{R}^q$) is called *Riemann integrable*, or shortly, *R-integrable*, if there are functions $f \in V$ and $h \in -V$ such that $f \leq g \leq h$ and $\int f = \int h$, where

$$\int f = \lambda_1 \int f_1 + \lambda_2 \int f_2 + \cdots \quad \text{and} \quad \int h = \kappa_1 \int h_1 + \kappa_2 \int h_2 + \cdots,$$

i.e., $\int f$ and $\int g$ are Lebesgue integrals. Evidently, g is then also Lebesgue integrable. The integral corresponds, in this particular case, to the *Riemann integral*. This name is, in fact, superfluous, because the Riemann integral always is the Lebesgue integral, only the class of functions it is applied to is narrower. The traditional definition of the Riemann integral is formally different, but a reader acquainted with its theory will easily recognize the equivalence with ours. The following few remarks can be helpful to elucidate the situation.

The inequality $f \leq g \leq h$ means that

$$\lambda_1 f_1 + \lambda_2 f_2 + \cdots \leq g \leq \kappa_1 h_1 + \kappa_2 h_2 + \cdots. \tag{4.1}$$

There is an index m such that $\lambda_n \geq 0$ and $\kappa_n \leq 0$ for $n > m$. Thus

$$\lambda_1 f_1 + \cdots + \lambda_m f_m \leq g \leq \kappa_1 h_1 + \cdots + \kappa_m h_m.$$

This implies that the function g vanishes outside a bounded interval and there is a number M such that $|g| < M$. In other words, each R-integrable function has a bounded carrier and is bounded. The sums $\underline{s}_n = \lambda_1 f_1 + \cdots + \lambda_n f_n$ $(n = m, m+1, \ldots)$ are step functions which approximate g from below, and $\bar{s}_n = \kappa_1 h_1 + \cdots + \kappa_n h_n$ $(n = m, m+1, \ldots)$ are step functions approximating g from above. By definitions we have

$$\lim \int \underline{s}_n = \int g = \lim \int \bar{s}_n.$$

The class of R-integrable functions can also be characterized by the following

Theorem 4.1. *A function g is R-integrable, if and only if g has a bounded carrier, is bounded and continuous a.e., i.e., continuous everywhere except for a set of Lebesgue measure 0.*

Proof.   Assume that g vanishes outside a brick I_1 and is bounded by M, i.e., $|g| \le M$. We denote by f_1 the characteristic function of I_1 and put $\lambda_1 = -M$. We divide I_1 into 2^q equal bricks $I_2, \ldots, I_{p_1}$ ($p_1 = 2^q + 1$) each of which has one of its vertices in the middle of I_1, and we denote by $f_2, \ldots, f_{p_1}$ their characteristic functions. Let $\lambda_2, \ldots, \lambda_{p_1}$ be the greatest numbers such that $\lambda_1 f_1 + \lambda_2 f_2 + \cdots + \lambda_{p_1} f_{p_1} \le g$. Evidently, all these numbers are non-negative. We divide each of bricks $I_2, \ldots, I_{p_1}$ into 2^q bricks in the same way as the brick I_1 was divided. One actually obtains 2^{2q} bricks $I_{p_1+1}, \ldots, I_{p_2}$ ($p_2 = 2^{2q} + 2^q + 1$) and denote by $f_{p_1+1}, \ldots, f_{p_2}$ their characteristic functions. Then we denote by $\lambda_{p_1+1}, \ldots, \lambda_{p_2}$ the greatest numbers such that $\lambda_1 f_1 + \cdots + \lambda_{p_1+1} f_{p_1+1} + \cdots + \lambda_{p_2} f_{p_2} \le g$. Continuing so, we obtain an infinite series $\lambda_1 f_1 + \lambda_2 f_2 + \cdots$ whose all the coefficients, except for the first, are ≥ 0. It is easy to see that the limit f of the series belongs to V and that $f \le g$. Assuming that g is continuous almost everywhere, we shall show that $f \sim g$. In fact, let Z_1 be the set of discontinuity points of g, and let Z_2 be the set of boundary points of intervals $I_1, I_2, \ldots$. Both the sets Z_1 and Z_2 are null sets and so is their union $Z = Z_1 \cup Z_2$. Let x be an arbitrary fixed point of Z. Given any $\varepsilon > 0$, there is a neighbourhood T of x such that $|g(x) - g(t)| < \varepsilon$ for $t \in T$. There is an index m such that $I_m \subset T$. This implies that $\underline{s}_m = \lambda_1 f_1 + \cdots + \lambda_m f_m \ge g - \varepsilon$ in I_m. Since $\underline{s}_m \le g$ everywhere, we thus have, in particular, $g(x) - \varepsilon \le \underline{s}_m(x) \le g(x)$. We also have $g(x) - \varepsilon \le \underline{s}_n(x) \le g(x)$ for each $n > m$, because the sequence $\underline{s}_n(x)$ is non-decreasing and bounded by $g(x)$. This proves that $f(x) = \lim_{n \to \infty} \underline{s}_n = g(x)$. Since this holds for each x not belonging to the null set Z, we have $f \sim g$. In a similar way, we construct a function $h \in -V$ such that $h \sim g$ and $h \ge g$. Hence $\int f = \int h$, which proves that g is R-integrable.

We now assume that g is discontinuous on a set X of positive measure and that $f \le g \le h$, where $f \in V$, $h \in -V$. If g is discontinuous at a point x, the either $g_*(x) < g(x)$ or $g(x) < g^*(x)$. But $f \le g \le h$ implies $f_*(x) \le g_*(x)$ and $g^*(x) \le h^*(x)$. Hence $f_*(x) < h^*(x)$. We thus have $f < h$ on X. Since $f \le f_*$ and $h^* \le h$ outside a set Z of measure 0, we obtain $f < h$ on the set $X \setminus Z$ which is of positive measure. This proves that g is not R-integrable.

The following three functions are examples of functions on $\mathbf{R}^q$ which are Lebesgue integrable, but are not Riemann integrable.

$$h_1(x) = \frac{1}{1 + x^2};$$

$$h_2(x) = \begin{cases} \log|x| & \text{for} \quad 0 < |x| < 1, \\ 0 & \text{elsewhere;} \end{cases}$$

$$h_3(x) = \begin{cases} 1 & \text{for rational } x \text{ satisfying } 0 < x < 1, \\ 0 & \text{elsewhere.} \end{cases}$$

The function h_1 is not R-integrable, because its carrier is not bounded. The carrier of h_2 is bounded, but the function itself is not bounded, it therefore is not R-integrable. Finally, h_3 is bounded and its carrier is bounded, but the function is discontinuous in the whole interval $(0, 1)$. It thus is not R-integrable.

From Theorem 4.1 it follows immediately that R-integrable functions satisfy axioms **HAM** (where U is then to be meant as the set of R-integrable functions). However, they do not satisfy axiom **E**. In fact, observe first that the function

$$g(x - \alpha) = \begin{cases} 1 & \text{for} \quad x = \alpha, \\ 0 & \text{for} \quad x \neq \alpha, \end{cases}$$

is R-integrable, by Theorem 4.1. We order all rational satisfying $0 < x < 1$ into a sequence $\alpha_1, \alpha_2, \ldots$ and put $f_n(x) = g(x - \alpha_n)$. Letting $f = f_1 + f_2 + \cdots$, we plainly have $f \simeq f_1 + f_2 + \cdots$, but f is not R-integrable. Thus **E** does not hold, if U is the set of R-integrable functions. This fact shows a great superiority of the Lebesgue theory, because many important theorems are based on **E**, and they fail for R-integrable functions. The only reason why **E** does not hold for R-integrable functions is that one cannot assert that the function f which appears in **E** is R-integrable. Hence **E** will become true also for R-integrable functions, if we transfer '$f \in U$' from the assertion to the hypothesis. Explicitly:

> **E₁** *If* $f \simeq f_1 + f_2 + \cdots$ *and* $f \in U$, $f_n \in U$, *then* $\int f = \int f_1 + \int f_2 + \cdots$.

It is also useful to remark the following corollary of **E₁**:

> **E₀** *If* $f_1, f_2, \ldots$ *is a non-increasing sequence of functions in* U, *which converges at every point to* 0, *then* $\int f_n \to 0$.

The theory of Riemann's integration was prior to the Lebesgue theory which was founded, later on, in a quite different way. However, P. Daniell has shown that it is possible to obtain the Lebesgue integral from the Riemann integral by a proper construction. His method continues to apply in a more general case which will be discussed in the next section.

5. The Daniell integral

We assume that a set U of real valued functions on a set K is given, as well as an integral $\int$ satisfying:

> **H** *If* $f \in U$ *and* $\lambda \in \mathbf{R}^1$, *then* $\lambda f \in U$ *and* $\int \lambda f = \lambda \int f$;

A *If $f \in U$ and $g \in U$, then $f + g \in U$, and $\int (f + g) = \int f + \int g$;*

M *If $f \in U$, then $|f| \in U$ and $\left| \int f \right| \leq \int |f|$;*

E₀ *If $f_1, f_2, \ldots$ is a non-increasing sequence of functions in U, which converges at every point to 0, then $\int f_n \to 0$.*

Properties **HAME₀** are satisfied in particular, if U is the set of R-integrable functions. Or else, if U is the set of all continuous functions vanishing outside a common interval, or if U is the set of step functions vanishing outside a common interval. In these particular cases, the integral is meant to be the Lebesgue integral, but restricted to special classes of functions. Simpler alternative definitions can be given, according to the considered case.

Let W be the class of functions which are limits of non-decreasing sequences of functions in U. Obviously, W includes U. Although the functions in U admit only finite values, $+\infty$ will be allowed as a possible value for functions in W.

Lemma 1. *If the sequences $f_1, f_2, \ldots$ and $g_1, g_2, \ldots$ ($f_n, g_n \in U$) are non-decreasing and $\lim f_n \leq \lim g_n$, then $\lim \int f_n \leq \lim \int g_n$.*

Proof. We first note that if $k \in U$ and $\lim g_n \geq k$, then $\lim \int g_n \geq \int k$. In fact, we have $g_n \geq k_n$, where $k_n = \min (g_n, k)$ and $k - k_n$ tends monotonically to 0. Hence $\int k - \int k_n \to 0$, by **E₀**, i.e., $\int k_n \to \int k$. But $\int g_n \geq \int k_n$, thus $\lim \int g_n \geq \int k$.

Taking $k = f_m$ and passing to the limit as $m \to \infty$, we get $\lim\limits_{m \to \infty} f_m \leq \lim\limits_{n \to \infty} g_n$.

We extend the definition of $\int f$ onto functions $f \in W$, letting $\int f = \lim \int f_n$ for $f_n \uparrow f$ (i.e., if $f_1, f_2, \ldots$ is non-decreasing and tends to f at each point), $f_n \in U$, where again $+\infty$ is allowed as a value of $\int f$. It is plain that the new definition agrees with the old in the case $f \in U$; the consistency of this definition follows by Lemma 1.

Evidently, if $f \leq g$, f, $g \in W$, then $\int f \leq \int g$. In particular, $\int f \geq 0$ for $f \geq 0$ and $\int f \leq 0$ for $f \leq 0$, $f \in W$. Furthermore, if $f \in W$, then $f^+ \in W$, $f^- \in W$ and $\int f^+ \geq 0$, $\int f^- \leq 0$, $\int f = \int f^+ + \int f^-$. If $f, g \in W$, then $\min (f, g) \in W$, $\max (f, g) \in W$ and $f + g \in W$, $\int (f + g) = \int f + \int g$. Moreover, we have

$$\int \lambda f = \lambda \int f \quad \text{for} \quad f \in W, \quad \lambda \geq 0. \tag{5.1}$$

In fact, if $f_n \uparrow f$, then also $\lambda f_n \uparrow \lambda f$, and the equation follows. (This argument would fail, if $\lambda < 0$.)

Lemma 2. *If the sequence $f_1, f_2, \ldots$ ($f_n \in W$) is non-decreasing and $f_n \to f$, then $f \in W$ and $\int f_n \to \int f$.*

Proof. There are functions $f_{mn} \in U$ such that $f_{mn} \leq f_{m+1,n}$ and $\lim_{m \to \infty} f_{mn} = f_n$. Let $g_m = \max (f_{m1}, \ldots, f_{mm})$. Then $g_m \in U$ and the sequence $g_1, g_2, \ldots$ is non-decreasing. Also $f_{mn} \leq g_m \leq f_m$ for $m \geq n$. If we pass to the limit first with respect to m and then with respect to n, then we get $f \leq \lim_{m \to \infty} g_m \leq f$. Doing the same with the inequality $\int f_{mn} \leq \int g_m \leq \int f_m$, we get $\lim \int f_m \leq \int f \leq \lim \int f_m$, and the assertion follows.

By means of the integral, extended to W, we now define an upper integral $\bar{\int} f$ for each real valued function f (defined on K). We namely denote by $\bar{\int} f$ the greatest lower bound of the set S_f of values $\int g$ with $g \geq f$, $g \in W$. The set S_f is not empty. If it is unbounded from below, we write $\bar{\int} f = -\infty$. Evidently, $\bar{\int} f = \int f$, if $f \in U$. It is to emphasize that the integral $\bar{\int} f$ is defined for quite arbitrary real valued functions f, but the values $-\infty$ and $+\infty$ are admitted for f, in no point of K. In contrast, the functions in W are not arbitrary, being limits of non-decreasing functions from U, but the value $+\infty$ is allowed at some or all points of K. We shall show that $\bar{\int} f$ has properties $\bar{\mathbf{H}}\bar{\mathbf{E}}\bar{\mathbf{M}}$.

In fact, $\bar{\mathbf{H}}$ follows from (5.1). To prove $\bar{\mathbf{M}}$, note that if $\bar{\int} f < \infty$, then there is a function $g \geq f$, $g \in W$, such that $\bar{\int} g < \infty$. Hence $\bar{\int} g^+ < \infty$. Since $f^+ \leq g^+$, it follows that $\bar{\int} f^+ \leq \int g^+$. We thus have proved that $\bar{\int} f < \infty$ implies $\bar{\int} f^+ < \infty$. Since also $f^- \leq g^-$, we have $\bar{\int} f^- \leq \int g^-$ and, consequently, $\int g = \int g^+ + \int g^- \geq \bar{\int} f^+ + \bar{\int} f^-$ for each $g \in W$ such that $g \geq f$. Hence $\bar{\int} f \geq \bar{\int} f^+ + \bar{\int} f^-$. On the other hand, if g and h are arbitrary functions in W such that $g \geq f^+$, $h \geq f^-$, then $f \leq g + h$, $\bar{\int} f \leq \int (g+h) = \int g + \int h$. Hence $\bar{\int} f \leq \bar{\int} f^+ + \bar{\int} f^-$, which completes the proof of $\bar{\mathbf{M}}$.

It remains to prove $\bar{\mathbf{E}}$. The proof will be similar to that of Theorem 1.1. Let $\varepsilon_1 + \varepsilon_2 + \cdots = \varepsilon < \infty$, $\varepsilon_n > 0$. There are functions $g_n \in W$ such that $\int g_n \leq \varepsilon_n + f_n^+$. We consider 3 cases.

Case 1. $\bar{\int} f_p^- = -\infty$ for some p. Then for each $n = 1, 2, \ldots$ there is a function $h_n \geq f_p^-$, $h_n \in W$, such that $\int h_n < -n$. This implies $\bar{\int} f = -\infty$, and the required inequality holds trivially.

Case 2. $\bar{\int} f_p^- > -\infty$ for each $p = 1, 2, \ldots$ and $\bar{\int} f_1^- + \bar{\int} f_2^- + \cdots = -\infty$. For each $n = 1, 2, \ldots$ there is an index p_n such that $\bar{\int} f_1^- + \cdots + \bar{\int} f_{p_n}^- < -n$. There exist functions $h_n \in W$ such that $f_n^- \leq h_n \leq 0$ and $\int h_n \leq \varepsilon_n + \bar{\int} f_n^-$. Let $k_n = h_1 + \cdots + h_{p_n} + g_1 + g_2 + \cdots$. Then $k_n \geq f$, $k_n \in W$ and $\int k_n < -n + 2\varepsilon$. This implies $\bar{\int} f = -\infty$ and the wished inequality.

Case 3. $\bar{\int} f_1^- + \bar{\int} f_2^- + \cdots > -\infty$. There is an index p such that $\bar{\int} f_{p+1}^- + \bar{\int} f_{p+2}^- + \cdots > -\varepsilon$. As before, we take functions $h_n \in W$ such that $f_n^- \leq h_n \leq 0$ and $\int h_n \leq \varepsilon_n + \bar{\int} f_n^-$. Let $k = h_1 + \cdots + h_p + g_1 + g_2 + \cdots$. Then $k \in W$ and $k \geq f$. Hence $\bar{\int} f \leq \int k \leq (\varepsilon + \bar{\int} f_1^- + \cdots + \bar{\int} f_p^-) + (\varepsilon + \bar{\int} f_1^+ + \bar{\int} f_2^+ + \cdots) \leq 3\varepsilon + \bar{\int} f_1 + \bar{\int} f_2 + \cdots$. Since ε is arbitrary, the required inequality follows.

We have shown that, starting from any integral $\int f$ defined on a set U of real functions and satisfying $\mathbf{HAME}_0$, one can construct an upper integral $\bar{\int} f$ satisfying $\mathbf{H\bar{E}M}$ and such that $\bar{\int} f = \int f$ for $f \in U$. Since $f \in U$ implies $-f \in U$, we also have $\bar{\int} (-f) = -\int f$, i.e., $\underline{\int} f = \int f$. Hence, $\underline{\int} f = \bar{\int} f$ for $f \in U$. Let V be the set of all real functions f such that $\underline{\int} f = \bar{\int} f$. Evidently, $U \subset V$. We put by definition $\int f = \bar{\int} f$ for $f \in V$. This extension of the integral from U to V is called the *Daniell integral*. According to section 3, it satisfies axioms $\mathbf{HEM}$. Thus, the extension is certainly essential, if the original integral, defined on U, does not satisfy $\mathbf{HEM}$, as the Riemann integral, for instance. In such a case, U is a proper part of V. However, if the original integral defined on U satisfies $\mathbf{HEM}$, then, according to section 3, we have $V = U$ and the new integral coincides with the old. In such a case, the whole construction presented in this section does not yield anything new and leads back to the original integral.

Generally, we say that an integral is an extension of an integral $\int$ defined on U, if it is defined on a set $T \supset U$ and agrees on U with $\int$. By the *smallest extension* of $\int$ we mean an extension $\hat{\int}$ such that every extension of $\int$ is an extension of $\hat{\int}$.

Theorem 5.1. *Given an integral defined on a set U of real functions and satisfying $\mathbf{HAME}_0$, there exists its smallest extension to an integral satisfying $\mathbf{HEM}$. This smallest extension is the Daniell integral.*

Proof.   Assume that T is a set of functions including U and that $\tilde{\int}$ is an integral defined on T, satisfying $\mathbf{HEM}$, such that $\tilde{\int} f = \int f$ for $f \in U$. We have to show that $V \subset T$ and $\tilde{\int} f = \hat{\int} f$ for $f \in V$, where $\hat{\int}$ denotes the Daniell integral.

Let g be a given function in V. Then $\underline{\int} g = \hat{\int} g = \bar{\int} g$. There are functions $k_1, k_2, \ldots$ in W such that $k_n \geq g$ and $\lim \int k_n = \hat{\int} g$. Let $h_n = \min(k_1, \ldots, k_n)$. Then $h_n \in W$, $g \leq h_n \leq k_n$ and $\lim \int h_n = \hat{\int} g$. Moreover, the sequence $h_1, h_2, \ldots$ is non-increasing. On the other hand, each element h_n is the limit of a non-decreasing sequence of functions in U, which implies, by $\mathbf{E}$, that $h_n \in T$ and $\tilde{\int} h_n = \int h_n$. Since $g \in V$ implies $-g \in V$, there is also a non-increasing sequence $f_1, f_2, \ldots$ such that $f_n \in W$, $f_n \geq -g$, $\lim \int f_n = -\hat{\int} g$, $f_n \in T$ and $\tilde{\int} f_n = \int f_n$. We thus have $-f_n \leq h_n$. Since the sequence $-f_1, -f_2, \ldots$ is non-decreasing and the sequence $h_1, h_2, \ldots$ is non-increasing, they converge to some limits $-f \in T$ and $h \in T$, respectively. Moreover, $\tilde{\int} h = \lim \tilde{\int} h_n = \lim \int h_n = \hat{\int} g$ and, similarly, $\tilde{\int} (-f) = \hat{\int} g$. Thus, $\tilde{\int} (-f) = \hat{\int} g \leq \tilde{\int} h$. Since $-f \leq g \leq h$, it follows that $g \in T$ and $\tilde{\int} g = \hat{\int} g$.

We shall say that U is a dense subset of the space V on which the integral is defined, if for each $f \in V$ there is a sequence of functions in U that converges in norm to f. As a complement of Theorem 5.1 we have

Theorem 5.2. *Under hypothesis of Theorem 5.1, the set U is dense in the space V the Daniell integral is defined on.*

Proof. Let $g \in V$. As in Theorem 5.1, there is a non-increasing sequence $h_1, h_2, \ldots$ such that $h_n \in W$, $h_n \geqslant g$ and $\lim \int h_n = \hat{\int} g$. We may assume that

$$\hat{\int} g \leqslant \int h_n \leqslant \hat{\int} g + \frac{1}{n}.$$

Since each h_n is the limit of a non-decreasing sequence of functions in U, there are functions $l_n \in U$ such that $l_n \leqslant h_n$,

$$\underline{\int} h_n - \frac{1}{n} \leqslant \int l_n \leqslant \underline{\int} h_n.$$

Hence

$$\hat{\int} |l_n - g| = \overline{\int} |l_n - g| \leqslant \overline{\int} (h_n - l_n) + \overline{\int} (h_n - g)$$

$$\leqslant \overline{\int} h_n + \overline{\int} (-l_n) + \overline{\int} h_n + \overline{\int} (-g) = \int h_n - \int l_n + \int h_n - \hat{\int} g \leqslant \frac{2}{n},$$

which proves that $l_n \to g$ i.n.

For different integrals $\int$ and $\hat{\int}$, the classes of null sets may happen to be different. We therefore shall use the names '$\int$-null set' and '$\hat{\int}$-null set' whose meanings are obvious.

Theorem 5.3. *Let $\int$ be a **HEM** integral defined on V and let U be a dense subset of V such that the restriction of $\int$ to U satisfies **HAME**$_0$. By $\hat{\int}$ we denote the Daniell integral for this restriction. We assert that the family $\hat{V}$ of $\hat{\int}$-integrable functions coincides with V, if and only if the family of $\hat{\int}$-null sets coincides with the family of $\int$-null sets.*

Proof. The necessity of the condition being obvious, it remains to prove its sufficiency. We evidently have

$$U \subset \hat{V} \subset V. \tag{5.2}$$

Suppose that $g \in V$. There exist functions $g_n \in U$ such that $g_n \to g$ i.n. and $g_n \to g$ at each point outside a set Z such that $\int Z = 0$. We have $g_n^+ \in U$, $\int g_n^+ \to \int g^+$ and $g_n^+ \to g^+$ outside Z. We have $f_{np} = g_n^+ \cap \cdots \cap g_p^+ \in U$ for $p \geqslant n$ and $f_{np} \downarrow f_n = g_n \cap g_{n+1} \cap \cdots \in \hat{V}$, as $p \to \infty$. The sequence f_n is non-decreasing and $f_n \to g^+$ outside Z. By the assumption on null sets, we have $\hat{\int} Z = 0$ and this implies that $g^+ \in \hat{V}$. Applying the same argument to $-g$, we obtain as result, $g^- \in \hat{V}$. Hence $g = g^+ + g^- \in \hat{V}$, which proves, together with (5.2), that $\hat{V} = V$. By Theorem 5.1, the Daniell integral $\hat{\int}$ is the smallest tension of the integral $\int$ restricted to U, which implies that $\hat{\int}$ and $\int$ coincide on V.

It is easy to see that the Lebesgue integral and the Daniell integral constructed from the set of step functions have the same family of null sets, they therefore coincide, by Theorem 5.3. For the same reason, the

Lebesgue integral is obtained as a Daniell integral, when starting from the set of continuous functions or from the set of Riemann integrable functions.

Let us finally note that the Daniell method applies to real functions only, whereas the **HEM** theory applies to vector functions as well, and is therefore more general.

6. Integrals generated by σ-measures

A non-void family Σ of subsets of a given set K is called a σ-*algebra*, if it has the following properties:

1° $X \in \Sigma$ implies $K \backslash X \in \Sigma$;

2°   If $X_1, X_2, \ldots$ belong to Σ, then $X_1 \cup X_2 \cup \cdots$ also belongs to Σ.

It is easy to show that the empty set and the set K always belong to Σ. Also, if $X_1, X_2, \ldots$ belong to Σ, then $X_1 \cap X_2 \cap \cdots$ belongs to Σ.

By a σ-*measure* μ on Σ we mean a function which assigns, to each $X \in \Sigma$ a non-negative number μX, finite or infinite, so that

C.   If $X_1, X_2, \ldots$ are disjoint, $X_n \in \Sigma$, then $\mu(X_1 \cup X_2 \cup \cdots) = \mu X_1 + \mu X_2 + \cdots$.

Property C is called *countable additivity* of the measure. It is equivalent to the property

C'.   If a sequence $Y_1, Y_2, \ldots, Y_n \in \Sigma$, tends monotonically to the empty set, then $\mu Y_n \to 0$.

We shall say that a set $X \in \Sigma$ has a finite measure or is of finite measure, if $\mu X < \infty$. Let us denote by U_Σ the set of functions of the form

$$s = \lambda_1 f_1 + \cdots + \lambda_p f_p, \tag{6.1}$$

where $\lambda_i \in \mathbf{R}^1$ and the f_i are characteristic functions of sets X_i of finite measure. U_Σ is evidently a linear space. Each function in U_Σ admits only a finite number of values ($+\infty$ is not allowed), each on a set belonging to Σ. Each function in U_Σ is bounded and its carrier is of finite measure. We may evidently assume, if necessary, that the carriers of $f_1, \ldots, f_p$ in (6.1) are disjoint. It is easy to prove that

$$s \in U_\Sigma \quad \text{implies} \quad s. \cap X \in U_\Sigma \text{ for each } X \in \Sigma. \tag{6.2}$$

We shall say that an integral $\int$ is *generated* by a σ-measure μ, if it satisfies **HEM** and

(i)   each set $X \in \Sigma$ such that $\mu X < \infty$ is integrable and $\int X = \mu X$;

(ii)   each integral satisfying **HEM** and (i) is an extension of $\int$.

Theorem 6.1. *Each σ-measure μ on a σ-algebra Σ generates an integral $\int$ on a set U of real functions. This integral satisfies, beside* **HEM**, *also* **P** *and* **S**. *Moreover, each set in Σ is measurable with respect to $\int$. The generated integral $\int$ is determined uniquely for each given σ-measure μ.*

Proof. U must evidently include U_Σ and the integral of (6.1) is

$$\int s = \lambda_1 \mu X_1 + \cdots + \lambda_p \mu X_p.$$

It is not difficult to prove the consistency of this definition (for $s \in U_\Sigma$) and that the integral $\int$ has, on U_Σ, properties **HAM**. We shall show that it also satisfies $\textbf{E}_0$. In fact, let $s_1, s_2, \ldots$ be a sequence of non-negative functions in U_Σ, tending monotonically to 0. There is a number M such that $s_1 \leqslant M$ and a set $X \in \Sigma$ such that $\mu X < \infty$ and $s_1 = 0$ outside X. Let ε be any positive number. Denote by X_n the set on which $s_n > \varepsilon M$. Since X_n tends monotonically to the empty set, we have $\mu X_n \to 0$, by C'. Since $s_n \leqslant M$, this implies that $\int s_n X_n \leqslant M \int X_n = M \mu X_n$, and hence $\int s_n X_n \to 0$. But $\int s_n = \int s_n X_n + \int s_n (X - X_n)$ and $\int s_n (X - X_n) \leqslant \int \varepsilon M (X - X_n) \leqslant \varepsilon M \int X = \varepsilon M \mu X$. We thus get $\lim \int s_n \leqslant \varepsilon M \mu X$. Since ε is arbitrary and $\int X < \infty$, it follows that $\lim \int s_n = 0$. This proves that the integral on U_Σ satisfies $\textbf{E}_0$.

We extend $\int$ to the least integral satisfying **HEM**, which is possible in view of Theorem 5.1. This extended integral satisfies (i) and (ii), and therefore is the integral generated by $\int$. Since the considered functions are real valued, property **P** is fulfilled automatically. Also **S** is fulfilled. In fact, since the functions are real valued, it suffices to prove that $f \in U$ implies $f . \cap 1 \in U$. But the set U is dense in U, there thus exist functions $s_n \in U_\Sigma$ such that $s_n \to f$ i.n. Because $s_n . \cap 1 \in U_\Sigma$, by (6.2), and $s_n . \cap 1 \to f . \cap 1$ i.n., it follows that $f . \cap 1 \in U$. Hence $1 . \cap f = |f . \cap 1| \in U$, which proves **S**.

Now, let $X \in \Sigma$, $f \in U$. By Theorem 5.1, the set U_Σ is dense in U, there thus exist functions $s_n \in U_\Sigma$ such that $s_n \to f$ i.n. Hence $s_n . \cap X \to f . \cap X$ i.n., which proves, by (6.2) and Theorem 9.2, Chapter IV, that $f . \cap X \in U$. Consequently, $X . \cap f = |f . \cap X| \in U$, which proves that X is measurable.

To see the uniqueness of the generated integral assume that there exist another integral with properties **HEM** and (i), (ii). Then each of the integrals is an extension of the other, so that both coincide. This statement completes the proof.

In particular, if we take, for Σ, the family of Lebesgue measurable sets, then for the generated integral we obtain just the Lebesgue integral. Throughout this section, Σ will always denote a σ-algebra, μ a σ-measure defined on it, and $\int$ the integral generated by μ. If we say *integrable* or *measurable*, this is always meant with respect to the integral $\int$. We carefully have to distinguish integrable sets (i.e., sets with integrable characteristic functions) from sets of finite measure. Similarly, we have to distinguish measurable sets from sets in Σ.

Theorem 6.2. *For each integrable set X there is a set $Z \in \Sigma$ such that $X \subset Z$ and $\int X = \mu Z$.*

Proof. Let W be the set of limits of non-decreasing sequences $f_1, f_2, \ldots$, where $f_n \in U_\Sigma$, and let $\int \lim f_n = \lim \int f_n$. Since the characteristic function of X is integrable, there exists, for each fixed number $\varepsilon > 0$, a function $h \in W$ such that $h \geqslant (1 + \varepsilon)g$ and $\int h \leqslant \int (1 + \varepsilon)g + \varepsilon$, where g is the characteristic function of X. There are functions $h_n \in U_\Sigma$ such that $h_n \uparrow h$. Let X_n denote the set on which $h_n \geqslant 1$. Then $X_n \in \Sigma$, $X_n \uparrow Y_\varepsilon \in \Sigma$, $X \subset Y_\varepsilon$ and $\mu Y_\varepsilon = \int Y_\varepsilon \leqslant \int h \leqslant \int g + \varepsilon(\int g + 1)$. Now, let ε_n be a sequence of positive numbers tending to 0, and let $Z_n = Y_{\varepsilon_1} \cap \cdots \cap Y_{\varepsilon_n}$. Then $Z_n \in \Sigma$, $Z_n \downarrow Z \in \Sigma$, $X \subset Z$ and $\mu Z_n \leqslant \int X + \varepsilon_n(\int X + 1)$. Letting $n \to \infty$, we get $\mu Z \leqslant \int X < \infty$. Hence $\int Z = \mu Z$, by (i). But $X \subset Z$ implies $\int X \leqslant \int Z$, thus $\int X \leqslant \mu Z$, which yields, together with the preceding inequality, $\int X = \mu Z$.

Theorem 6.3. *If a set X is integrable and belongs to Σ, then its measure is finite and $\int X = \mu X$.*

Proof. By the preceding theorem, there exists a set $Z \in \Sigma$ such that $X \subset Z$ and $\mu Z = \int X < \infty$. But $\mu X \leqslant \mu Z$, thus $\mu X < \infty$ and, by (i), we have $\mu X = \int X$.

According to (i), each set of finite measure is integrable. The converse is not true. The following example shows a little more, namely, that there are integrable sets which do not belong to Σ. In fact, let Σ be the family of sets on the real line $\mathbf{R}^1$ which are Lebesgue measurable. But we assume that the measure defined on is not the Lebesgue measure. Instead, we put by definition $\mu X = \lambda(J \cap X)$, where λ is the Lebesgue measure and J is the set of all non-negative numbers. Then Σ is a σ-algebra and μ is a σ-measure defined on it. The set I consisting of all negative numbers belongs to Σ and, consequently, to the family of measurable sets. Moreover, $\int I = 0$. We hence also have $\int Z = 0$ for each $Z \subset I$, i.e., for each set of negative numbers. But there exist sets of negative numbers which are not Lebesgue measurable. Such sets do not belong to Σ, though they are integrable in the sense of the generated integral $\int$.

The above example shows, together with property (i), that the class of integrable sets exceeds, in general, the class of sets of finite measure. However, both the classes coincide for σ-measures μ satisfying the condition

$3°$ If $X \subset Z \in \Sigma$ and $\mu Z = 0$, then $X \in \Sigma$.

The measures satisfying $3°$ are traditionally called *complete*.

Theorem 6.4. *A σ-measure is complete, if and only if the family of integrable sets coincides with the family of sets whose measure is finite.*

Proof. If a set X is integrable, there is, by Theorem 6.2, a set $Z \in \Sigma$ such that $X \subset Z$ and $\int X = \mu Z$. Also $\int Z = \mu Z$, by (i). Hence $\int (Z \setminus X) = 0$. Again by Theorem 6.2, there is a set $Y \in \Sigma$ such that $Z \setminus X \subset Y$ and

$\mu Y = 0$. This implies $Z \setminus X \in \Sigma$, by the completeness of μ. Hence $X = Z \setminus (Z \setminus X) \in \Sigma$. This proves, together with Theorem 6.3, that the completeness of μ implies the equality of the families of integrable sets and of those of finite measure.

The converse implication can be proved under a slightly weaker assumption that each null set belongs to Σ. In fact, if $X \subset Z \in \Sigma$ and $\mu Z = 0$, then $\int Z = 0$, by (i), and hence $\int X = 0$. Thus, X is a null set and belongs therefore to Σ. This proves the completeness of μ.

The following example shows that the completeness of a σ-measure does not imply that the family of measurable sets should coincide with Σ. Assume that Σ consists of countable sets of points on the real line $\mathbf{R}^1$ and of their complements. Then Σ is a σ-algebra. For the measure μX we take the number of points of X, if the set X is finite, and $+\infty$, if it is infinite. Then μ is a σ-measure on Σ. It is easy to see that the interval $[0, 1]$ is measurable, but does not belong to Σ.

We shall say that a measure μ is *bi-complete*, if it is complete and, moreover, has the following property:

4°   Each set $X \subset K$ such that $X \cap Y \in \Sigma$ for $Y \in \Sigma$ and $\mu Y < \infty$ belongs to Σ.

Theorem 6.5. *If a σ-measure on a σ-algebra is bi-complete, then each measurable set belongs to Σ.*

Proof. Let X be a measurable set and let $Y \in \Sigma$, $\mu Y < \infty$. By (i), Y is integrable and, consequently, $X \cap Y = X . \cap Y$ is integrable. By Theorem 6.4, we have $X \cap Y \in \Sigma$. By 4°, this implies that $X \in \Sigma$.

A measure μ is called *half-finite* or *σ-finite*, if it satisfies the condition

5°   There exist sets $X_n \in \Sigma$ such that $\mu X_n < \infty$ $(n = 1, 2, \ldots)$ and $K = X_1 \cup X_2 \cup \cdots$.

Property 5° turns out to be stronger than 4°, which can be expressed by

Theorem 6.6. *Each half-finite measure satisfies* 4°.

Proof. Let $X \subset K$ be a set such that $X \cap Y \in \Sigma$. whenever $Y \in \Sigma$ and $\mu Y < \infty$. Then, in view of condition 5°, $X \cap X_n \in \Sigma$. Hence $X = X \cap K = X \cap (X_1 \cup X_2 \cup \cdots) = (X \cap X_1) \cup (X \cap X_2) \cup \cdots \in \Sigma$, which proves 4° and the theorem.

As an immediate corollary we obtain

Theorem 6.7. *Each half-finite complete measure is bi-complete.*

A bi-complete σ-measure need not be half finite. In order to see it, we can take, for Σ, the set of all subsets of $\mathbf{R}$ and define μX as the number of points of X; if this number is infinite, we put $\mu X = +\infty$.

Let U be a set of functions defined on K and $\int$ an integral defined on U. We assume that axioms **HEMPS** are satisfied. Let Σ be the family of measurable sets. It is easy to show that Σ is a σ-algebra. We define a measure on Σ, on letting $\mu X = \int X$ for integrable sets X and $\mu X = +\infty$, if X is measurable, but not integrable. The measure μ will be called *induced* by the integral $\int$.

Theorem 6.8. *If an integral $\int$ satisfies* **HEMPS**, *then the induced measure μ is a bi-complete σ-measure.*

The proof consists in checking properties $1°$–$4°$, which is a quite easy and elementary task.

Theorem 6.9. *Each σ-measure μ defined on a σ-algebra Σ is a restriction to Σ of a bi-complete σ-measure defined on a σ-algebra including Σ.*

Proof. Let $\int$ be the integral generated by μ, and let $\bar{\mu}$ be the measure induced by $\int$. The family of measurable sets is a σ-algebra, by Theorem 6.8. That algebra includes Σ, by Theorem 6.1. The measure $\bar{\mu}$ is a bicomplete σ-measure, by Theorem 6.8, which agrees with μ on Σ.

The last theorem shows that bi-complete σ-measures have a distinguished position and it is a risk of redundancy to discuss in detail various σ-measures. The more types of them, the more theorems, but rather cheap and not very interesting ones. Nowadays, when the number of new concepts and definitions increases in mathematics like an avalanche, it becomes important to make some selection of old concepts.

In view of Theorem 6.8 and 6.9, theory of σ-measures is embraced by the theory of the **HEMPS** integral. It is worthwhile to recall here that the Daniell integral is the **HEM** integral, restricted to real functions. It satisfies automatically **P**, but need not satisfy **S**. It therefore is more general than integrals generated by σ-measures. Still more general is the **HEM** integral for vector functions, because then **P** need not be satisfied either. Consequently, the Daniell integral and the general **HEM** integral escape from measure theoretical treatment.

However, under some natural assumptions, there is a way to reduce the **HEM** integral to the **HEMS** or **HEMPS** integral, as will be shown in the next chapter.

Chapter IX

Defining New Integrals by Given Ones

An integral having properties **HEM** will be called a **HEM**-integral. Similarly, we shall use the names **HEMS**-integral and **HEMPS**-integral whose meaning is obvious. By means of a given **HEM**-integral one can define new **HEM**-integrals by proper operations. We discuss four methods: 1° restriction of the set on which the integrands are defined; 2° substitution; 3° multiplication of the integrand by a positive factor; 4° sticking given integrals together. We also discuss the question how and when a **HEM**-integral can be expressed by a **HEMPS**-integral.

1. Restriction to a subset

In section 5, Chapter VI, we have considered integrals $\int f = \int_Z fZ$, where Z is a subset of the set K the functions f are defined on. It is evident that $\int_Z f$ does not depend on the values of f outside Z and can therefore be interpreted as an integral defined on functions whose domain is Z. However the integral $\int fZ$ looses then its sense and the following modification of the definition of $\int_Z f$ is needed. We say that a function f, defined on Z, is $\int_Z$-integrable, or belongs to U_Z, if there is a function $g \in U$ such that $f(x) = g(x)$ for $x \in Z$ and $g(x) = 0$ for $x \in K \setminus Z$. We then write $\int_Z f = \int g$. The new integral $\int_Z$ will be called the *restriction* of $\int$ to the set Z. It is defined for all $f \in U_Z$.

Theorem 1.1. *If $\int$ is a **HEM**-integral on a family U of functions defined on a set K, and Z is a fixed subset of K, then the restriction $\int_Z$ of $\int$ to Z is a **HEM**-integral on U_Z. Moreover, if $\int$ satisfies **P** or **S**, then so does $\int_Z$.*

There is no problem to prove Theorem 1.1 directly. However, it will be useful to introduce, in this connection, a general concept of *hemmorphic* integrals.

2. Hemmorphic integrals

An integral $\int_0$ on a family U_0 of functions defined on a set K_0 will be called *hemmorphic* to an integral $\int$ on a family U of functions defined on a set K, if there is a map $\bigwedge$ from U_0 into U such that $\int_0 f = \int \bigwedge f$ and

(h)　　If $\lambda \in \mathbf{R}^1$ and $f \in U_0$, then $\lambda f \in U_0$ and $\bigwedge \lambda f = \lambda \bigwedge f$;

(e)　　If $f_n \in U_0$ $(n = 1, 2, \ldots)$, $\int_0 |f_1| + \int_0 |f_2| + \cdots < \infty$ and $f = f_1 + f_2 + \cdots$ holds at points of absolute convergence, then $f \in U_0$ and the equation $\bigwedge f = \bigwedge f_1 + \bigwedge f_2 + \cdots$ holds at the points of absolute convergence;

(m)　　$f \in U_0$ implies $|f| \in U_0$ and $\bigwedge |f| = |\bigwedge f|$.

Note that, in the above definition, it is unnecessary to assume that any of integrals $\int_0$ or $\int$ satisfies **HEM**. The word 'integral' is thus synonymously to the word 'operation', because no further properties are postulated. One only assumes that $\int_0$ maps U_0 into a given Banach space and $\int$ maps U into the another Banach space.

Theorem 2.1. *Each integral hemmorphic to a* **HEM***-integral is a* **HEM***-integral.*

Proof. Let $\int$ be a given **HEM**-integral on U and $\int_0$ an integral on U_0, hemmorphic to $\int$. By (h) we have $\int_0 \lambda f = \int \bigwedge \lambda f = \int \lambda \bigwedge f = \lambda \int \bigwedge f = \lambda \int_0 f$, proving that $\int_0$ satisfies **H**. By (m) we have $|\int_0 f| = |\int \bigwedge f| \leqslant \int |\bigwedge f| = \int \bigwedge |f| = \int_0 |f|$, proving that $\int_0$ satisfies **M**. Assume that $f_n \in U_0$ $(n = 1, 2, \ldots)$, $\int_0 |f_1| + \int_0 |f_2| + \cdots < \infty$ and $f = f_1 + f_2 + \cdots$ at each point of absolute convergence. We then also have $\int |\bigwedge f_1| + \int |\bigwedge f_2| + \cdots < \infty$ and, by (e), $f \in U_0$ and $\bigwedge f = \bigwedge f_1 + \bigwedge f_2 + \cdots$ at the points of absolute convergence. Since $\int$ satisfies **E**, it follows that $\int \bigwedge f = \int \bigwedge f_1 + \int \bigwedge f_2 + \cdots$, i.e., $\int_0 f = \int_0 f_1 + \int_0 f_2 + \cdots$, proving that $\int_0$ satisfies **E**.

Proof of Theorem 1.1. It is easy to check that, letting $\int_0 = \int\limits_Z$ and $U_0 = U_Z$, the integral $\int\limits_Z$ is hemmorphic to $\int$. It thus satisfies **HEM**, in view of Theorem 2.1. Moreover, if $f, g \in U_Z$ and $\bigwedge f, \bigwedge g$ are the restrictions of the functions f, g to the domain Z, then $f . \cap g = \bigwedge f . \cap \bigwedge g$ on Z. If $\int$ satisfies **P**, then $\bigwedge f . \cap \bigwedge g \in U$ and hence $f . \cap g \in U_Z$. This proves that $\int\limits_Z$ satisfies **P**. Finally, let $f = a \in X$, $|a| = 1$, $g \in U_Z$. Then $f . \cap g = a . \cap g = a . \cap \bigwedge g$ on Z. If $\int$ satisfies **S**, then $a . \cap \bigwedge g \in U$, which implies that $f . \cap g \in U_Z$. Thus, $\int\limits_Z$ satisfies **S**.

3. Substitution

The restriction of an integral gives one of possible examples of hemmorphic integrals. We are going to consider two further examples which are obtained by *substitution* and by *multiplication of the integrand*.
If we substitute, in a function $f(y)$, the variable y by another function

$\varphi(x)$, we obtain the composition $f[\varphi(x)]$ which is a third function. From the logical point of view, $f(y)$ is the value of the function f at the point y, and $\varphi(x)$ is the value of the function φ at the point x. Finally, $f[\varphi(x)]$ is the value of the composition at x. For the composition itself, which is also a function, the symbol $f \circ \varphi$ is often used in modern books. Then we consequently may write $(f \circ \varphi)(x) = f[\varphi(x)]$. If φ is a function from K onto K_0 and f is a function from K_0 into a Banach space E, then $f \circ \varphi$ is a function from K into E. No further assumption on φ is needed. The following formulae are easily deduced from the definition of $f \circ \varphi$:

$$\lambda(f \circ \varphi) = (\lambda f) \circ \varphi \qquad (\lambda \in \mathbf{R}^1),$$
$$|f| \circ \varphi = |f \circ \varphi|.$$

Theorem 3.1. *Let $\int$ be a* **HEM**-*integral on a family U of functions defined on K and let φ be a map from K onto a set K_0. By U_0 we denote the family of all functions f on K_0 such that $f \circ \varphi \in U$. Then the integral $\int_0$ on U_0 defined by the equation $\int_0 f = \int (f \circ \varphi)$ is also a* **HEM**-*integral.*

Proof. By Theorem 1.1, it suffices to prove that $\int_0$ is hemmorphic to $\int$. In fact, let $\bigwedge f = f \circ \varphi$. If $\lambda \in \mathbf{R}^1$ and $f \in U_0$, then $f \circ \varphi \in U$ and also $(\lambda f) \circ \varphi = \lambda(f \circ \varphi) \in U$, by **H**. This implies that $\lambda f \in U_0$ and $\bigwedge \lambda f = \lambda \bigwedge f$. Thus, property (h) holds. We also have, for $f \in U_0$, $|f| \circ \varphi = |f \circ \varphi| \in U$, which implies that $|f| \in U_0$ and $\bigwedge \lambda f = \lambda \bigwedge f$. Thus, (m) holds. Finally, assume that $f_n \in U_0$ $(n = 1, 2, \ldots)$,

$$\int_0 |f_1| + \int_0 |f_2| + \cdots < \infty, \tag{3.1}$$

and $f = f_1 + f_2 + \cdots$ holds on the set of all points $y \in K_0$ at which the last series converges absolutely. Let X be the set of all the points $x \in K$ such that $\varphi(x) \in Y$. Then the equation

$$f \circ \varphi = f_1 \circ \varphi + f_2 \circ \varphi + \cdots \tag{3.2}$$

holds on X, and X is the set of all the points $x \in K$ at which the series in (3.2) converges absolutely. But (3.1) implies $\int |f_1 \circ \varphi| + \int |f_2 \circ \varphi| + \cdots < \infty$, and we therefore have $f \circ \varphi \in U$, because $\int$ satisfies **E**. Hence $f \in U_0$ which, together with (3.2), proves (e).

4. Multiplication of the integrand

Another way to obtain new **HEM**-integrals is given by

Theorem 4.1. *Let $\int$ be a* **HEM**-*integral on a family U of functions defined on K and let h be an arbitrary fixed non-negative function on K (which may not belong to U). By U_0 we denote the family of all functions f on K such that $fh \in U$. Then the integral $\int_0$ defined on U_0 by the equation*

$\int_0 f = \int fh$ is a **HEM**-*integral. Moreover, if f is a function on K such that the product fh is $\int$-measurable, then f is $\int_0$-measurable.*

Proof. Letting $\bigwedge f = fh$, it is easily checked that properties (h), (e), (m) hold. The integral is thus hemmorphic to $\int$ and satisfies **HEM**, by Theorem 2.1. Assume that fh is $\int$-measurable and $g_0 \in U_0$. Then $(f \cdot \cap g)h = fh \cdot \cap gh \in U$ and this implies that $f \cdot \cap g \in U_0$. Thus, f is $\int_0$-measurable, which completes the proof.

One cannot assert, in Theorem 4.1, that conversely, if f is $\int_0$-measurable, then fh is $\int$-measurable, as it is shown by the following example, given by CZESŁAW KLIŚ. Let U be the family of Lebesgue integrable functions on $\mathbf{R}^1$. For h we take the characteristic function of a non-measurable set whose each measurable subset is a null set. If $f \in U_0$. then $fh \in U$ and, consequently, $\int fh = 0$. We put $\int_0 f = \int fh \ (= 0)$ for $f \in U_0$. The function h is $\int_0$-measurable, because $h \cdot \cap g \in U_0$, whenever $g \in U_0$. On the other hand, the product hh is not $\int$-measurable, because it equals to h everywhere. However the situation changes, when we assume that $h > 0$ on K. We namely have

Theorem 4.2. *If the hypothesis of Theorem 4.1 is satisfied and, moreover, $h > 0$ holds everywhere on K, then f is $\int_0$-measurable, if and only if fh is $\int$-measurable.*

Proof. Let $h_0 = \dfrac{1}{h}$. Then U coincides with the family of functions such that $fh_0 \in U$ and we have $\int f = \int_0 fh_0$. Applying Theorem 4.1 with the converse roles of $\int$ and $\int_0$ we find that, if fh_0 is $\int_0$-measurable, then f is $\int$-measurable. It turns out on the same to say that if f is $\int_0$-measurable, then fh is $\int$-measurable. The implication in the converse direction has already been stated in Theorem 4.1.

5. Sticking integrals together

Let $\Re$ be a collection (finite, countable or uncountable) of disjoint sets K. On each $K \in \Re$ there is defined a family U_K of functions whose values are in a given Banach space E. On each set U_K there is defined a **HEM**-integral $\int_K$. Let K_0 be the union of all $K \in \Re$. Our aim is to define the family U_0 of functions which are integrable on the whole set K_0 and whose restriction f_K to any $K \in \Re$ belongs to U_K. If the collection $\Re$ consists of a finite number of sets K, then each function f with the above property is to be taken as an element of U_K. The integral $\int_0$ on K_0 is then defined by the equation

$$\int_0 f = \sum_{K \in \Re} \int_K f_K. \tag{5.1}$$

However, if the collection $\mathfrak{K}$ contains infinitely many sets K, then we have to take care of the convergence (absolute) of the sum in (5.1). We therefore say that $f \in U_0$, iff $\int_K |f_K|$ different from zero for at most a countable subcollection $\mathfrak{J} \subset \mathfrak{K}$ of sets K and $\sum_{K \in \mathfrak{J}} \int_K |f_K| < \infty$. We then write

$$\int_0 f = \sum_{K \in \mathfrak{J}} \int_K f_K.$$

The collection $\mathfrak{J}$ depends on the function f, it is therefore more convenient to use the notation (5.1) also in the general case, provided we mean that the summation is stretched only on terms $\int_K f_K$ which are $\neq 0$.

We shall show that the new integral $\int_0$ is a **HEM**-integral on U_0. In fact, if $f \in U_0$ and $\lambda \in \mathbf{R}^1$, then $\lambda f \in U_0$ and $\int_0 f = \sum_{K \in \mathfrak{K}} \int_K \lambda f_K = \lambda \sum_{K \in \mathfrak{K}} \int_K f_K = \lambda \int_0 f$, proving that $\int_0$ satisfies **H**. Moreover, if $f \in U_0$, then $|f| \in U_0$ and $|\int_0 f| = |\sum_{K \in \mathfrak{K}} \int_K f_K| \leq \sum_{K \in \mathfrak{K}} \int_K |f_K| = \int_0 |f|$, proving **M**. Finally, assume that $f_n \in U_0$ $(n = 1, 2, \ldots)$, $\int_0 |f_1| + \int_0 |f_2| + \cdots < \infty$ and $f = f_1 + f_2 + \cdots$ at points of absolute convergence. If f_{nK} denotes the restriction of f_n to K, then of course $f_K = f_{1K} + f_{2K} + \cdots$ at points of absolute convergence. Moreover, since $\int_K |f_{nK}| \leq \int_0 |f_n|$, we have $\int_K |f_{1K}| + \int_K |f_{2K}| + \cdots < \infty$. Because the integral $\int$ satisfies **E**, this implies that $f_K \in U_K$ and $\int_K f_K = \int_K f_{1K} + \int_K f_{2K} + \cdots$. We thus have proved that the restriction f_K of f to K belongs to U_K. In order to prove that $f \in U_0$, we have still to show that $\sum_{K \in \mathfrak{K}} \int_K |f_K| < \infty$. But $\int_K |f_K| \leq \sum_{n=1}^{\infty} \int_K |f_{nK}|$, thus

$$\sum_{K \in \mathfrak{K}} \int_K |f_K| \leq \sum_{K \in \mathfrak{K}} \sum_{n=1}^{\infty} \int_K |f_{nK}| = \sum_{n=1}^{\infty} \sum_{K \in \mathfrak{K}} \int_K |f_{nK}| = \sum_{n=1}^{\infty} \int_0 |f_n|,$$

which is $< \infty$, by hypothesis. This proves that $f \in U_0$. Moreover, we have

$$\int_0 f = \sum_{K \in \mathfrak{K}} \int_K f_K = \sum_{K \in \mathfrak{K}} \sum_{n=1}^{\infty} \int_K f_{nK} = \sum_{n=1}^{\infty} \sum_{K \in \mathfrak{K}} \int_K f_{nK} = \sum_{n=1}^{\infty} \int_0 f_n,$$

which completes the proof of property **E** for the integral $\int_0$.

In order to formulate briefly the obtained result, let is call the integrals *disjoint*, if the corresponding integrable functions are defined on disjoint sets. The integral $\int_0$, 'sticked together' from disjoint integrals, as described above, can be called the *global integral*. Then our result may be formulated as

Theorem 5.1. *The global integral for a collection of disjoint* **HEM**-*integrals is a* **HEM**-*integral.*

6. An example

Let K_0 be the sphere $|x| = 1$ in $\mathbf{R}^3$, i.e., the set of points $x = (\xi, \eta, \zeta)$ such that $\xi^2 + \eta^2 + \zeta^2 = 1$. This sphere can be decomposed into 3 parts:

$$K_1: \quad \sqrt{1 - \xi^2 - \eta^2} > 0 \quad \text{(upper open hemisphere)},$$

$$K_2: \quad -\sqrt{1 - \xi^2 - \eta^2} < 0 \quad \text{(lower open hemisphere)},$$

$$K_3: \quad \sqrt{1 - \xi^2 - \eta^2} = 0 \quad \text{(circumference between } K_1 \text{ and } K_2).$$

We define families U_1, U_2, U_3 of integrable functions on K_1, K_2, K_3 respectively. A function $f = f(\xi, \eta, \zeta)$ from K_1 to a given Banach space E is said to belong to U_1, if the Bochner integral $\int$ restricted to the circle C: $\xi^2 + \eta^2 < 1$ is sensible for the function $f_1 = f_1(\xi, \eta) = f(\xi, \eta, \sqrt{1 - \xi^2 - \eta^2})/\sqrt{1 - \xi^2 - \eta^2}$. Then we put by definition $\int_1 f = \int f_1$. Similarly, a function $f = f(\xi, \eta, \zeta)$ belongs to U_2, if the Bochner integral $\int$ restricted to the same circle C exists for the function $f_2 = f_2(\xi, \eta) = f(\xi, \eta, -\sqrt{1 - \xi^2 - \eta^2})/\sqrt{1 - \xi^2 - \eta^2}$. Then we put by definition $\int_2 f = \int f_2$. Finally, the family U_3 consists of all possible functions from K_3 to E, and we put, by definition, $\int_3 f = 0$ for each $f \in U_3$. We shall show that the global integral

$$\int_0 f = \int_1 f + \int_2 f + \int_3 f,$$

defined on the whole sphere K_0, is a **HEM**-integral. By Theorem 5.1, it suffices to show that each of integrals $\int_1, \int_2, \int_3$ is a **HEM**-integral. This is trivially true for $\int_3$. Because of symmetry, it now suffices to show that $\int_1$ is a **HEM**-integral.

In fact, the Bochner integral satisfies **HEM**. Also its restriction $\int_C$ to the circle C satisfies **HEM**, by Theorem 1.1. Now, the function f_1 is obtained from the function f by a proper substitution and then multiplication by the factor $h = 1/\sqrt{1 - \xi^2 - \eta^2}$. This implies, by Theorems 3.1 and 4.1, that the integral $\int_1 f = \int_C f_1$ satisfies **HEM**.

In the above reasoning, the formal application of Theorem 3.1 may present some difficulty because of different notation used there and in our example. The function φ actually maps the circle C onto the hemisphere K_1 which is a part of the 3-dimensional space $\mathbf{R}^3$. If we denote by $\varphi_1, \varphi_2, \varphi_3$ the coordinates of φ, then we have $\varphi_1 = \xi$, $\varphi_2 = \eta$, $\varphi_3 = \sqrt{1 - \xi^2 - v^2}$, and these three equations are to be considered as the definition of the map φ, in our example.

Remark. It can be proved that the integral $\int_0$ defined on the sphere K_0, as shown above, is rotation invariant.

7. Defining HEM-integrals by HEMS-integrals

In this section we discuss the question, when a **HEM**-integral $\int_0$ reduces to a **HEMS**-integral $\int$ by means of the equation $\int_0 f = \int fh$. We first consider the case of real valued functions. Then the axiom **P** is satisfied automatically and therefore each **HEMS**-integral is a **HEMPS**-integral.

Theorem 7.1. *Let U_0 be a family of real valued functions on a set K and $\int_0$ a **HEM**-integral on U_0. A necessary and sufficient condition for the existence of a representation $\int_0 f = \int fh$, where $h \geq 0$ and $\int$ is a **HEMS**-integral, is that there should exist a $\int_0$-measurable function, positive everywhere on K.*

Proof. Assume that g is such a function. For U we then take the family of all functions f such that $fg \in U_0$ and we put $\int f = \int_0 fg$. Applying Theorem 4.1 (with interchanged roles of $\int_0$ and $\int$, and with g instead of h), we conclude that $\int$ is a **HEM**-integral. Moreover, since the function $1 \cdot g$ is $\int_0$-measurable, it follows that 1 is $\int$-measurable, i.e., $\int$ satisfies **S**. Letting $h = \dfrac{1}{g}$, we evidently have $\int_0 f = \int fh$ with $h > 0$.

Assume now, conversely, that $h \geq 0$ and $\int$ is a **HEMS**-integral such that $\int_0 f = \int fh$. Let k be a function on K such that $k = \dfrac{1}{h}$ at points at which $h > 0$ and $k = 1$ elsewhere. We shall prove that k is $\int_0$-measurable. In fact, let $g \in U_0$. Then $(k . \cap g)h = kh . \cap gh = 1 . \cap gh$, because $kh = 1$ at each point at which $gh \neq 0$. Since 1 is $\int$-measurable and $gh \in U$, it follows that $1 . \cap gh \in U$, i.e., $(k . \cap g)h \in U$. This implies $k . \cap g \in U_0$ and $\int_0$-measurability of k.

In all known interpretations of the **HEM**-integrals (i.e., of the Daniell integrals) the condition which appears in Theorem 7.1 is always satisfied. There thus arises the question whether it really can happen that the condition is not satisfied. In other words, does there exist a **HEM**-integral $\int_0$ such that each $\int_0$-measurable function vanishes at some points? – A positive answer was recently given by KLIŚ and NARDZEWSKI in [13].

If we consider vector valued functions, i.e., functions from K to a Banach space E, then Theorem 7.1 fails to hold, as the following counter-example shows.

Counter-example. Let K consist of two points 0 and 1 and let E be the set of complex numbers. By U we mean the family of all functions f such that the value $f(0)$ is real and $f(1)$ is complex. We put $\int f = f(0) + f(1)$. Then condition **HEM** hold. The function $h \equiv 1$ (i.e., such that

$f(0) = f(1) = 1$) belongs to U, it is thus measurable and positive on K. However **S** does not hold, because the constant function $f \equiv i$ (imaginary unit) is not measurable.

In the case of vector valued functions Theorem 7.1 regains its truthfulness, provided we complete the condition in it by the assumption that the product af of any $a \in E$ by a real function $f \in U$ still belongs to U.

Chapter X

The Fubini Theorem

The Fubini theorem belongs to the most powerful tools in Analysis. It is very useful in practical calculations and, besides, plays a striking role in proving several important theorems on integration. The Fubini theorem establishes a connection between the so called double integrals and repeated integrals. The proofs given in text books are usually difficult. Using our definitions of the Lebesgue or the Bochner integrals, the proof becomes surprisingly simple and reduces in fact to various interpretations of the same definition.

In this chapter, we also discuss the general case, when the partial integrals are **HEM** (or Daniell) integrals. Defining properly the functional $\iint$, the proof remains as simple as before. However, we know at first very little on the functional $\iint$ and, if we wish to obtain it as another **HEM**-integral, we must make some further assumptions. Then the proof that $\iint$ satisfies **HEM** is more difficult than the proof of the Fubini equation itself.

At the beginning of this chapter we have to settle some preliminaries about the Cartesian products which are necessary to understand the theorem.

1. Cartesian products

The system

$$x = (\xi_1, \ldots, \xi_q), \tag{1.1}$$

of q real numbers $\xi_1, \ldots, \xi_q$ is called a point of Euclidean q-dimensional space $\mathbf{R}^q$. Each of numbers ξ_i may be considered as a point of the one-dimensional Euclidean space $\mathbf{R}$. One often says that $\mathbf{R}^q$ is the *Cartesian product* of q one-dimensional spaces $\mathbf{R}$.

If $K_1, \ldots, K_q$ are arbitrary subsets of $\mathbf{R}$, then by their Cartesian product

$$K = K_1 \times \cdots \times K_q$$

we understand the set of all points (1.1) such that $\xi_i \in K_i$. For instance, if $K_1, \ldots, K_q$ are one dimensional intervals, then their Cartesian product is a q-dimensional interval.

Now, if $K_1, \ldots, K_q$ are arbitrary sets of arbitrary elements, then by their Cartesian product $K = K_1 \times \cdots \times K_q$ we understand the set of all systems

$$u = (x_1, \ldots, x_q)$$

such that $x_i \in K_i$. The points $x_1, \ldots, x_q$ may be considered a coordinates of the point u.

If $X = \mathbf{R}^p$ and $Y = \mathbf{R}^r$, then $X \times Y = \mathbf{R}^{p+r}$. Thus a function $f(x, y)$ of two variables $x \in X$ and $y \in Y$ may be considered as a function defined on $X \times Y$. The integrability of f can be considered on $X \times Y$ or else, when one of variabiles y or x is fixed, on X or Y, respectively. There arises the question, how should we distinguish, in notation, the integrals over $X \times Y$, X, or Y?

The traditional notation, due to Leibnitz, seems to be helpful. Thus the symbols

$$\int f \, dx, \quad \int f \, dy, \quad \text{and} \quad \int\int f \, dx \, dy$$

or, more precisely,

$$\int_X f \, dx, \quad \int_Y f \, dy, \quad \text{and} \quad \int\int_{X \times Y} f \, dx \, dy$$

will denote the integrals on X, Y, or $X \times Y$, respectively.

If the integral $\int f \, dy$ exists for every $x \in X$, i.e., if f is integrable over Y for every fixed x, then the symbol $\int f \, dy$ represents a function of x, defined on X. This function may happen to be integrable on X. Then its integral should be consequently written in the form $\int(\int f \, dy) \, dx$. To avoid parentheses, we shall instead use the symbol

$$\int dx \int f \, dy, \tag{1.2}$$

according to the traditional notation.

It is convenient to use the symbol (1.2) also if the function $g(x) = \int f \, dy$ is defined almost everywhere in X (not necessarily for all $x \in X$). In fact, if we assign arbitrary values at points at which g is not defined, then it becomes either an integrable or a non-integrable function, independently of the choice of the new adopted values. Moreover, the value of the integral $\int g = \int dx \int f \, dy$, if exists, does not depend on that choice. So far, we considered only functions which were defined everywhere. Nevertheless, in the formulation of the theorem of Fubini (in the next section), it is useful to admit also functions which are defined almost everywhere. The meaning of the statement that such a function is integrable is obvious. It is also obvious that the value of the integral is determined uniquely.

The integral $\int dx \int f \, dy$ is called sometimes an *iterated* or a *repeated integral*, in order to distinguish it from the *double integral* $\int\int f \, dx \, dy$.

2. The Fubini theorem

Let X and Y be Euclidean spaces of any number of dimensions, and $X \times Y$ their Cartesian product.

Theorem 2 (Fubini). *If $f(x, y)$ is a Bochner integrable function on $X \times Y$, then the function $\int f\,dy$ (of x) is determined almost everywhere on X and is Bochner integrable on X. Similarly, the function $\int f\,dx$ (of y) is determined almost everywhere on Y and is Bochner integrable on Y. Moreover,*

$$\iint f\,dx\,dy = \int dx \int f\,dy = \int dy \int f\,dx. \tag{2.1}$$

Proof. By the definition of the double integral in $X \times Y$, there exists an expansion

$$f(x, y) \simeq \lambda_1 g_1(x)h_1(y) + \lambda_2 g_2(x)h_2(y) + \cdots, \tag{2.2}$$

where $g_n(x)$ and $h_n(y)$ are brick functions in X and Y, respectively, and the products $g_n(x)h_n(y)$ are brick functions in $X \times Y$. Furthermore

$$\iint g_n(x)h_n(y)\,dx\,dy = \int g_n \int h_n. \tag{2.3}$$

Relation (2.2) means that the series in (2.2) converges to $f(x, y)$ at points where it converges absolutely, and that

$$|\lambda_1| \int g_1 \int h_1 + |\lambda_2| \int g_2 \int h_2 + \cdots < \infty.$$

But this implies, by the definition of the integral on X, that the series

$$\lambda_1 g_1(x) \int h_1 + \lambda_2 g_2(x) \int h_2 + \cdots \tag{2.4}$$

may be considered as an expansion of a function of x which is Bochner integrable on X.

Let x_0 be an arbitrary point at which the series (2.4) converges absolutely. Then the series

$$\lambda_1 g_1(x_0)h_1(y) + \lambda_2 g_2(x_0)h_2(y) + \cdots$$

may be considered as an expansion of a function of y which is Bochner integrable on Y. But this series converges to $f(x_0, y)$ at every point at which it converges absolutely. Thus, by the definition of the integral on Y, we can write

$$\int f(x_0, y)\,dy = \lambda_1 g_1(x_0) \int h_1 + \lambda_2 g_2(x_0) \int h_2 + \cdots.$$

Since this equation holds for every x_0, where series (2.4) converges absolutely, the function $k(x) = \int f(x, y)\,dy$ is determined almost everywhere in X, and (2.4) is its expansion.

Thus, according to the definition of the integral in X, we have

$$\int k(x)\,dx = \lambda_1 \int g_1 \int h_1 + \lambda_2 \int g_2 \int h_2 + \cdots.$$

But, by the definition of the integral in X, we obtain from (2.2),

$$\int\int f(x,y)\,dx\,dy = \lambda_1\int\int g_1(x)h_1(y)\,dx\,dy + \lambda_2\int\int g_2(x)h_2(y)\,dx\,dy + \cdots .$$

In view of (2.3), the last two equations imply $\int\int f(x,y)\,dx\,dy = \int k(x)\,dx$, which is equivalent to the first equality in (2.1). The second equality in (2.1) can be obtained in a similar way, when interchanging the role of x and y.

3. A generalization of the Fubini theorem

Let X and Y be arbitrary sets (not necessarily Euclidean) and let V and W be families of integrable functions on X and Y, respectively. We assume that the functions belonging to V and W take their values in a Banach space E. Integrals on V and W are supposed to satisfy **HEM**, and both will be denoted by the same sign $\int$.

Let G be a family of functions defined on the Cartesian product $X \times Y$ such that the modulus of each function in G also belongs to G. We assume that $f(x,y) \in G$ implies $f(x_0, y) \in W$ for each element $x_0 \in X$ and that $\int f(x,y)\,dy \in V$. (Functions from G are here a substitute of brick functions.) By means of G we define a family U of functions on $X \times Y$ such that f belongs to U, iff there are functions $f_n \in G$ $(n = 1, 2, \ldots)$ satisfying two following conditions:

1° $\int dx \int |f_1|\,dy + \int dx \int |f_2|\,dy + \cdots < \infty$;

2° $f(x,y) = f_1(x,y) + f_2(x,y) + \cdots$ *holds at those points (x,y) at which the series converges absolutely.*

We then write

$$f \simeq f_1 + f_2 + \cdots .$$

We define on U an E valued functional $\int\int$ such that

$$\int\int f = \int\int f\,dx\,dy = \int dx\int f_1\,dy + \int dx\int f_2\,dy + \cdots . \qquad (3.1)$$

The consistency of this definition follows from

Theorem 3.1. *If $f \in U$, then the function $\int f\,dy$ is determined almost everywhere on X and belongs to V. Moreover,*

$$\int\int f\,dx\,dy = \int dx\int f\,dy. \qquad (3.2)$$

Proof. Inequality 1° implies, by Theorem 7.3, Chapter IV, that the series

$$\int |f_1|\,dy + \int |f_2|\,dy + \cdots \qquad (3.3)$$

converges for almost every $x \in X$. Let x_0 be a point at which (3.3) converges absolutely, i.e.,

$$\int |f_1(x_0, y)| \, dy + \int |f_2(x_0, y)| \, dy + \cdots < \infty.$$

Again by Theorem 7.3, Chapter IV, applied now to X, we conclude that the series

$$f_1(x_0, y) + f_2(x_0, y) + \cdots$$

converges almost everywhere in Y. Since, at each point of its absolute convergence, the series converges to $f(x_0, y)$, by definition of f, we have,

$$f(x_0, y) \simeq f_1(x_0, y) + f_2(x_0, y) + \cdots \quad \text{in } W.$$

Thus, by **E**, we have $f(x_0, y) \in W$ and

$$\int f(x_0, y) \, dy = \int f_1(x_0, y) \, dy + \int f_2(x_0, y) \, dy + \cdots.$$

This equation holds for all $x_0 \in X$ except for a null set. We thus may write

$$\int f(x, y) \, dy = \int f_1(x, y) \, dy + \int f_2(x, y) \, dy + \cdots \quad \text{a.e. in } X. \tag{3.4}$$

Since $|\int f_n \, dy| \leqslant \int |f_n| \, dy$, we have by 1°,

$$\int \left| \int f_1 \, dy \right| dx + \int \left| \int f_2 \, dy \right| dx + \cdots < \infty. \tag{3.5}$$

From (3.4) and (3.5) it follows that the series in (3.4) converges in norm to $\int f(x, y) \, dy$ (Theorem 8.7, Chapter IV). It can therefore be integrated term by term (Theorem 6.2, Chapter IV). So we get

$$\int dx \int f(x, y) \, dy = \int dx \int f_1 \, dy + \int dx \int f_2 \, dy + \cdots.$$

In view of (3.1) we hence obtain the wanted equality (3.2).

Remark. Theorem 3.1 is a generalization of Theorem 2. In fact, assume that X and Y are Euclidean spaces, $X \times Y$ their Cartesian product, and V, W, U families of Bochner integrable functions on X, Y, and $X \times Y$, respectively. The integrals $\int$ on V and W are Bochner integrals and so is the integral $\iint$ on U. For G we take the family of products λf of elements $\lambda \in E$ by brick functions f in $X \times Y$. Then Theorem 2 follows immediately from Theorem 3.1. (The second equality in (2.1) also follows, because the role of V and W is symmetric.)

Theorem 3.2. *If* $f_i \in U$ $(i = 1, \ldots, k)$, *then* $f_1 + \cdots + f_k \in U$ *and* $\iint (f_1 + \cdots + f_k) = \iint f_1 + \cdots + \iint f_k$.

Proof.   If $f_1 \in U$ and $f_2 \in U$, then $f_1 \simeq f_{11} + f_{12} + \cdots (f_{1n} \in G)$ and $f_2 \simeq f_{21} + f_{22} + \cdots (f_{2n} \in G)$. Hence

$$f_1 + f_2 \simeq f_{11} + f_{21} + f_{12} + f_{22} + f_{13} + f_{23} + \cdots .$$

This proves that $f_1 + f_2 \in U$. By induction, it follows that, if $f_i \in U$ $(i = 1, \ldots, k)$, then $f_1 + \cdots + f_k \in U$. Now, in view of Theorem 3.1, we have

$$\int\int (f_1 + \cdots + f_k) = \int dx \int (f_1 + \cdots + f_k)\, dy$$

$$= \int dx \left(\int f_1\, dy + \cdots + \int f_k\, dy \right)$$

$$= \int dx \int f_1\, dy + \cdots + \int dx \int f_k\, dy = \int\int f_1 + \cdots + \int\int f_k.$$

Theorem 3.3.   *If the functions* $f, g \in U$ *are real valued and* $f \leq g$, *then* $\int\int f \leq \int\int g$.

Proof.   By Theorem 3.1, the functions $\int f\, dy$ and $\int g\, dy$ are defined almost everywhere on X. This implies that $\int f\, dy \leq \int g\, dy$ holds almost everywhere on X, and we hence obtain $\int dx \int f\, dy \leq \int dx \int g\, dy$, which is the required inequality.

4. The double integral as a HEM-integral

Very little can be said on the functional $\int\int$ defined by (3.1), unless additional assumptions on the family G are made. We therefore introduce the following conditions:

(h)   *If* $f \in G$ *and* $\lambda \in \mathbf{R}^1$, *the* $\lambda f \in G$;
(em)   *For each system* $f_1, \ldots, f_k$ *of functions from* G, *there exists in* G *another system of functions* $g_1, \ldots, g_p$, *having disjoint carriers* (*i.e.,* $g_i g_j = 0$ *for* $i \neq j$), *such that* $f_1 + \cdots + f_k = g_1 + \cdots + g_p$.

The disjointness of carriers of the g_i implies that $|f_1 + \cdots + f_k| = h_1 + \cdots + h_p$, where $h_i = |g_i| \in G$.
The following theorem states that, under conditions (h), (em), $\int\int$ is a **HEM**-integral. This theorem will however not be used in the sequel and can therefore be skipped as well as its proof. The reader can pass directly to section 5.

Theorem 4.1.   *If family* G *satisfies additional conditions* (h) *and* (em), *then the functional* $\int\int$ *defined by (3.1) is a* **HEM**-*integral.*

Proof.   Using (h), it is easily checked that $\int\int$ satisfies **H**.
In order to prove that $\int\int$ satisfies **M**, assume that $f \simeq f_1 + f_2 + \cdots (f_i \in G)$.

Then the equation $f = f_1 + f_2 + \cdots$ holds at every point of $X \times Y$ at which the series converges absolutely. Denoting by $Z \subset X \times Y$ the set of such points, and letting

$$s_n = f_1 + \cdots + f_n,$$

we have $f = \lim s_n$ for points of Z. This implies that $|f| = \lim |s_n|$, i.e.,

$$|f| = |s_1| + (|s_2| - |s_1|) + (|s_3| - |s_2|) + \cdots \quad \text{on } Z. \tag{4.1}$$

We can write

$$|s_1| = g_1,$$

$$|s_{n+1}| - |s_n| = g_{p_n+1} + \cdots + g_{p_{n+1}} \quad \text{for} \quad n = 1, 2, \ldots, \tag{4.2}$$

where $g_i \in G$. Since $\left| |s_{n+1}| - |s_n| \right| \leq |s_{n+1} - s_n| = |f_{n+1}|$, we have

$$|g_{p_n+1}| + \cdots + |g_{p_{n+1}}| \leq |f_{n+1}| \quad (n = 1, 2, \ldots). \tag{4.3}$$

Summing all these inequalities and adding $|g_1| = |f_1|$, we get

$$|g_1| + |g_2| + \cdots \leq |f_1| + |f_2| + \cdots \quad \text{on } Z. \tag{4.4}$$

On the other hand, by Theorems 3.2 and 3.3, we get from (4.3),

$$\int\int |g_{p_n+1}| + \cdots + \int\int |g_{p_{n+1}}| \leq \int\int |f_{n+1}| \quad (n = 1, 2, \ldots).$$

Summing all these inequalities and adding $\int\int |g_1| = \int\int |f_1|$, we get

$$\int\int |g_1| + \int\int |g_2| + \cdots \leq \int\int |f_1| + \int\int |f_2| + \cdots. \tag{4.5}$$

From (4.1) and (4.2) it follows that

$$|f| = g_1 + g_2 + \cdots \quad \text{on } Z. \tag{4.6}$$

From (4.4) it follows that the series in (4.6) converges absolutely on Z. It may also happen to converge absolutely at some points outside Z and not necessarily to $|f|$. To avoid this situation, we write

$$|f| = g_1 + f_1 - f_1 + g_2 + f_2 - f_2 + \cdots$$

and the last series converges absolutely on and only on Z. But the assumption $f \approx f_1 + f_2 + \cdots$ implies that the series on the right side of (4.5) is convergent. Consequently,

$$\int\int |g_1| + \int\int |f_1| + \int\int |f_1| + \int\int |g_2| + \int\int |f_2| + \int\int |f_2| + \cdots < \infty.$$

The last inequality together with the preceding equation mean that

$$|f| \approx g_1 + f_1 - f_1 + g_2 + f_2 - f_2 \cdots,$$

which proves that $|f| \in U$.

Moreover, by Theorems 4.1 and 3.3, we have

$$\left|\iint f\right| = \left|\iint f\,dx\,dy\right| = \left|\int dx \int f\,dy\right| \leq \int dx \left|\int f\,dy\right| \leq \int dx \int |f|\,dy = \iint |f|,$$

which completes the proof of **M**.
It still remains to prove **E**. We shall first establish two lemmas.

Lemma 1. If $f \simeq f_1 + f_2 + \cdots$ $(f_i \in G)$, then $\iint |f| \leq \iint |f_1| + \iint |f_2| + \cdots$.

Proof. From (4.6) and (4.5) it follows that

$$\iint |f| = \iint g_1 + \iint g_2 + \cdots \leq \left|\iint g_1\right| + \left|\iint g_2\right| + \cdots$$
$$\leq \iint |f_1| + \iint |f_2| + \cdots.$$

Lemma 2. If $f \in U$, then for each $\varepsilon > 0$ there is an expansion $f \simeq f_1 + f_2 + \cdots$ $(f_i \in G)$ such that $\iint |f_1| + \iint |f_2| + \cdots < \iint |f| + \varepsilon$.

Proof. We take an arbitrary expansion $f \simeq g_1 + g_2 + \cdots$ $(g_i \in G)$. Since $\iint |g_1| + \iint |g_2| + \cdots < \infty$, there is an index p such that

$$\iint |g_{p+1}| + \iint |g_{p+2}| + \cdots < \frac{\varepsilon}{2}. \tag{4.7}$$

There are functions $f_1, \ldots, f_p \in G$, having disjoint carriers, such that

$$s = g_1 + \cdots + g_p = f_1 + \cdots + f_p.$$

Letting $f_i = g_i$ for $i > p$, we shall show that $f \simeq f_1 + f_2 + \cdots$ is the required expansion. In fact, by (4.7) we have

$$\iint |f_1| + \iint |f_2| + \cdots \leq \iint |f_1| + \cdots + \iint |f_p| + \frac{\varepsilon}{2}. \tag{4.8}$$

Since the carriers of $f_1, \ldots, f_p$ are disjoint, we have

$$\iint |f_1| + \cdots + \iint |f_p| = \iint |s| \leq \iint |f| + \iint |f - s|. \tag{4.9}$$

But $f - s \simeq f_{p+1} + f_{p+2} + \cdots$, and hence, by Lemma 1,

$$\iint |f - s| \leq \iint |g_{p+1}| + \iint |g_{p+2}| + \cdots. \tag{4.10}$$

Relations (4.8), (4.9), (4.10) now imply the required inequality.

Proof of Theorem 4.1, continued. To prove **E**, we assume that

$$f \simeq f_1 + f_2 + \cdots,$$

where $f_i \in U$, and we then show that there exist $g_i \in G$ such that

$$f \simeq g_1 + g_2 + \cdots. \tag{4.11}$$

Let $\varepsilon_1 + \varepsilon_2 + \cdots$ be a convergent series of positive numbers. By Lemma 2, we can choose expansions

$$f_i \simeq f_{i1} + f_{i2} + \cdots \qquad (i = 1, 2, \ldots), \tag{4.12}$$

where $f_{ij} \in G$, such that

$$\iint |f_{i1}| + \iint |f_{i2}| + \cdots < \varepsilon_i + \iint |f_i|. \tag{4.13}$$

Let $g_1 + g_2 + \cdots$ be a series composed (see section 3, Chaper II) of all the series (4.12). Then, in view of (4.13).

$$\iint |g_1| + \iint |g_2| + \cdots < \varepsilon_1 + \varepsilon_2 + \cdots + M, \tag{4.14}$$

where $M = \iint |f_1| + \iint |f_2| \cdots$. Thus, there is a function g such that $g \simeq g_1 + g_2 + \cdots$. If $g_1 + g_2 + \cdots$ converges absolutely at a point, then each of series (4.12) converges absolutely at the same point, and we have $g_1 + g_2 + \cdots = f_1 + f_2 + \cdots$. This proves that $f \in U$ and that (4.11) holds. From (4.11) we get

$$\iint f = \iint g_1 + \iint g_2 + \cdots \tag{4.15}$$

and from (4.12),

$$\iint f_i = \iint f_{i1} + \iint f_{i2} + \cdots \qquad (i = 1, 2, \ldots). \tag{4.16}$$

But inequalities (4.13) and (4.14) imply that series (4.15) and (4.16) converge absolutely. Since series (4.15) is composed of all the series (4.16), it follows that

$$\iint f = \iint f_1 + \iint f_2 + \cdots.$$

This completes the proof of **E**.

5. Corollaries of the Fubini theorem

The principal domain of applications of the Fubini theorem are Lebesgue and Bochner integrable functions, and in the sequel we restrict ourselves to this particular case. We recall that a vector function is Bochner measurable, if its retract by any integrable function is Bochner integrable. If the functions are real valued, then Bochner measurable functions are Lebesgue measurable.

Theorem 5.1. *If a function $f(x, y)$ is Bochner measurable on the Cartesian product $X \times Y$ of Euclidean spaces X and Y, then for every $x_0 \in X$, except for a null set, the function $f(x_0, y)$ is Bochner measurable on Y.*

Proof. Let $g_n(x, y)$ be brick functions (i.e., characteristic functions of intervals in $X \times Y$) such that $g_n(x, y) \to 1$ at every point of $X \times Y$. Then the functions $f_n = f \cap ng_n$ are Bochner integrable on $X \times Y$ and tend to f, as $n \to \infty$. By Theorem 2, the function $f_n(x_0, y)$ is Bochner integrable on Y for every x_0, except for a null set $Z_n \subset X$. Thus, if x_0 does not belong to $Z = \bigcup_n Z_n$, each of functions $f_n(x_0, y)$ is Bochner integrable on Y. This implies, by Theorem 3.2, Chapter V, that the limit $f(x_0, y)$ is Bochner measurable on Y. Since Z is a null set, the assertion follows.

Note that the converse of Theorem 4.1 is not true, i.e., the measurability of $f(x_0, y)$ on Y does not imply the measurability of $f(x, y)$ on $X \times Y$. (W. SIERPIŃSKI has constructed a function $f(x, y)$ which is measurable on each straight line, but is not measurable on the plane.)
In practical calculations we often have to change the order of integration, $\int dx \int f \, dy = \int dy \int f \, dx$, which is not allowed without special circumspection. In such cases, it is convenient to use the following theorem which is a simple consequence of the Fubini theorem, but does not postulate the existence of the double integral.

Theorem 5.2 (Tonelli). *If $f(x, y)$ is Bochner measurable on $X \times Y$, and the repeated integral $\int dx \int |f| \, dy$ exists, then there also exist the three integrals in the equation*

$$\iint f \, dx \, dy = \int dx \int f \, dy = \int dy \int f \, dx,$$

and the equation holds.

Proof. Let $g_n(x, y)$ be brick functions whose carriers increase and cover the whole space $X \times Y$, as $n \to \infty$. Then the functions $h_n = \min(ng_n, |f|)$ are integrable, and we have, by the Fubini theorem, $\iint h_n \, dx \, dy = \int dx \int h_n \, dy$. But $h_n \leq |f|$ and $\int |f| \, dy$ is, by hypothesis, an integrable function on X. Hence $\iint h_n \, dx \, dy \leq \int dx \int |f| \, dy$. Since the sequence h_n is non decreasing it follows that its limit $|f|$ is integrable on $X \times Y$, by Theorem 9.4, Chapter IV. Because the function f is measurable and bounded by $|f|$, it is integrable, by Theorem 3.1, Chapter VI. Hence the assertion follows, by the Fubini theorem.

Theorem 5.3. *If a function f is Bochner measurable in a Euclidean space X and if Y is another Euclidean space, then the function $f(x, y) = f(x)$ (which is constant with respect to $y \in Y$) is measurable in $X \times Y$.*

Proof.   Assume first that f is Bochner integrable in X and

$$f \simeq \lambda_1 f_1 + \lambda_2 f_2 + \cdots \quad \text{in } X,$$

where f_n are brick functions in X. Let g be a brick function in Y. Then $f_n g$ are brick functions in $X \times Y$ and

$$fg \simeq \lambda_1 f_1 g + \lambda_2 f_2 g + \cdots \quad \text{in } X \times Y.$$

The product fg is thus Bochner integrable in $X \times Y$.

Now, if f is Bochner measurable in X, then f is a limit of a sequence of integrable functions f_n, by Theorem 9.3, Chapter V. Let g_n be a non-decreasing sequence of brick functions, converging to 1 in Y. By what we have just proved the functions $f_n g_n$ are integrable in $X \times Y$, and we evidently have $f_n(x) g_n(y) \rightarrow f(x, y)$. This proves that $f(x, y)$ is measurable in $X \times Y$, by the same Theorem 9.3, Chapter V.

Theorem 5.4. *If f and g are Bochner measurable functions in Euclidean spaces X and Y respectively (one of them being real valued), then the product $f(x)g(y)$ is Bochner measurable in $X \times Y$.*

Proof.   By Theorem 5.3, the function $f(x)$ is measurable in $X \times Y$ and so is $g(y)$, owing to symmetry. Hence the product $f(x)g(y)$ is measurable, according to the result in section 7, Chapter V.

Theorem 5.5. *If the functions $f_1, \ldots, f_r$ are Bochner integrable on $\mathbf{R}^{p_1}, \ldots, \mathbf{R}^{p_r}$ respectively and all of them except for at most one are real valued, then the product $f(x) = f_1(x_1) \cdots f_r(x_r)$ is Bochner integrable on $\mathbf{R}^{p_1} \times \cdots \times \mathbf{R}^{p_r}$. Moreover,*

$$\int f = \int f_1 \cdots \int f_r.$$

Proof.   We have

$$\int |f_1(x_1)| \, dx_1 \cdot \int |f_2(x_2)| \, dx_2 = \int \left(|f_1(x_1)| \int |f_2(x_2)| \, dx_2 \right) dx_1$$

$$= \int dx_1 \int |f_1(x_1)f_2(x_2)| \, dx_2.$$

This ensures the existence of the last integral. We thus may apply the Tonelli theorem, which implies

$$\iint f(x_1)f(x_2) \, dx_1 \, dx_2 = \int dx_1 \int f_1(x_1)f_2(x_2) \, dx_2$$

$$= \int f_1(x_1) \, dx_1 \cdot \int f_2(x_2) \, dx_2.$$

This proves the validity of the theorem for $r = 2$. The general assertion follows by induction.

6. A generalization of the Tonelli theorem

It looks a little awkward to postulate, in Theorems 5.3 and 5.4, that only one of the factors may admit vectors for its values, and it would be nice to have a more symmetric formulation. To this aim, we introduce the concept of a product of two or more vectors. Such products are often introduced in mathematics.

Examples

1°   The inner product $x \cdot y$ of two vectors $x = (\xi_1, \xi_2, \xi_3)$, $y = (\eta_1, \eta_2, \eta_3)$ is defined by the equation $x \cdot y = \xi_1 \eta_1 + \xi_2 \eta_2 + \xi_3 \eta_3$. Here x and y belong to $\mathbf{R}^3$ and the product $x \cdot y$ belongs to $\mathbf{R}^1$.

2°   The vector product $x \times y$ of vectors $x, y \in \mathbf{R}^3$ is defined by $x \times y = (\xi_2 \eta_3 - \xi_3 \eta_2, \xi_3 \eta_1 - \xi_1 \eta_3, \xi_1 \eta_2 - \xi_2 \eta_1)$. Here x, y and the product $x \times y$ belong to $\mathbf{R}^3$.

3°   The tensor product $x \otimes y$ is defined by the matrix

$$x \otimes y = \begin{pmatrix} \xi_1 \eta_1 & \xi_1 \eta_2 & \xi_1 \eta_3 \\ \xi_2 \eta_1 & \xi_2 \eta_2 & \xi_2 \eta_3 \\ \xi_3 \eta_1 & \xi_3 \eta_2 & \xi_3 \eta_3 \end{pmatrix}.$$

Here $x, y \in \mathbf{R}^3$ and $x \otimes y \in \mathbf{R}^9$.

Similar examples can be given for any number of dimensions. There are also many other examples in which multiplication is defined for more general Banach spaces or for other linear spaces. For our purposes, it will suffice to consider the case when the factors and the value of the product belong to Banach spaces. We thus are concerned with 3 Banach spaces (which may be different) A, B and C. We shall assume that $x \in A$, $y \in B$, $xy \in C$ and that the following properties hold:

$$\left.\begin{aligned} &(\lambda x)y = x(\lambda y) \quad \text{for each } \lambda \in \mathbf{R}^1, \\ &(x + y)z = xz + yz, \\ &x(y + z) = xy + xz, \\ &|xy| \leqslant |x| |y|; \end{aligned}\right\} \tag{6.1}$$

in the last inequality, the modulus signs denote the norms in the corresponding Banach spaces. It is easy to check that all these properties hold in the case of examples given above. In the sequel, when we speak of products, we always assume that at least properties (6.1) are satisfied. If any of spaces A, B, or C happens to be the space of real or complex numbers, then by the norm in that space we always shall mean the absolute value of the number.

If nothing is said explicitly, no commutativity and no associativity of the products is assumed. An example of a non-commutative product is the vector product $x \times y$. Non-associativity occurs, e.g., in the composition $x \times (y \times z)$.

Theorem 6.1. *If $a_n \to a$, $b_n \to b$, then $a_n b_n \to ab$.*

Proof. We have

$$a_n b_n - ab = (a_n - a)(b_n - b) + (a_n - a)b + a(a - b),$$

and hence

$$|a_n b_n - ab| \leqslant |(a_n - a)(b_n - b)| + |(a_n - a)b| + |a(b_n - b)|$$
$$\leqslant |a_n - a| \, |b_n - b| + |a_n - a| \, |b| + |a| \, |b_n - b|.$$

Since $|a_n - a| \to 0$ and $|b_n - b| \to 0$, this implies that $|a_n b_n - ab| \to 0$.

From Theorem 6.1 it follows, in particular, that $ab_n \to ab$ as $b_n \to b$. Letting $b_n = c_1 + \cdots + c_n$ we hence get

$$ac_1 + ac_2 + \cdots = a(c_1 + c_2 + \cdots),$$

whenever the series on the right side converges.

Products of more than two factors can be easily defined by iteration of products of two factors. However, the order of multiplication must be then indicated, unless the associativity is assumed.

In the following two theorems we restrict ourselves to Bochner integrals.

Theorem 6.2. *If f is a Bochner integrable function and a is an element of a Banach space, then the product af is Bochner integrable and we have $\int af = a \int f$.*

Proof. Since f is Bochner integrable, there are brick functions f_n and elements λ_n of the corresponding Banach space such that

$$|\lambda_1| \int f_1 + |\lambda_2| \int f_2 + \cdots < \infty$$

and

$$f = \lambda_1 f_1 + \lambda_2 f_2 + \cdots \quad \text{a.e.}$$

Since $|a\lambda_n| \leqslant |a| \, |\lambda_n|$, it follows that

$$|a\lambda_1| \int f_1 + |a\lambda_2| \int f_2 + \cdots < \infty$$

and

$$af = a\lambda_1 f_1 + a\lambda_2 f_2 + \cdots \quad \text{a.e.}$$

This implies that af is Bochner integrable and

$$af = a\lambda_1 f_1 + a\lambda_2 f_2 + \cdots \quad \text{i.n.,}$$

by Theorem 8.7, Chapter IV. Consequently

$$\int af = a\lambda_1 \int f_1 + a\lambda_2 \int f_2 + \cdots,$$

by Theorem 6.1, Chapter IV. The equation, together with

$$\int f = \lambda_1 \int f_1 + \lambda_2 \int f_2 + \cdots,$$

implies $\int af = a \int f$, what has been to be shown.

Remarks. In the particular case a $\mathbf{R}^1$, Theorem 6.2 reduces to formula (4.1), Chapter III. Let us also note that, if the product fa is defined, then we have $\int fa = \int f \cdot a$, which is obvious by reasons of symmetry. It has been proved earlier (Theorem 8.1, Chapter V) that the product of two measurable functions is measurable, provided at least one of the factors is assumed to be real valued. This restriction will be released, now.

Theorem 6.3. *The product fg of two measurable vector functions f and g is measurable.*

Proof. We first assume that f and g are integrable. Then

$$f \approx \lambda_1 f_1 + \lambda_2 f_2 + \cdots, \qquad g \approx \kappa_1 g_1 + \kappa_2 g_2 + \cdots,$$

where $\lambda_i \in A$, $\kappa_i \in B$, and f_i, g_i are brick functions. Let

$$s_n = \lambda_1 f_1 + \cdots + \lambda_n f_n, \qquad t_n = \kappa_1 g_1 + \cdots + \kappa_n g_n.$$

Then

$$s_n t_n = \sum_{i,j=1}^{n} \lambda_i \kappa_j f_i g_j,$$

where $\lambda_i \kappa_j \in C$ and $f_i g_j$ are brick functions. Since $s_n \to f$ a.e. and $t_n \to g$ a.e., it follows that $s_n t_n \to fg$ a.e. The product fg is thus measurable, by Theorem 3.2, Chapter V.

Now, let f and g be arbitrary measurable functions. By Theorem 9.3, Chapter V, there are integrable functions f_n, g_n such that $f_n \to f$ and $g_n \to g$ everywhere. Hence, $f_n g_n \to fg$. Since the products $f_n g_n$ are measurable, by what we have just established, the measurability of fg follows by any of theorems quoted above.

Theorem 6.4. *If $f(x)$ is measurable on X, $g(x, y)$ is measurable on the Cartesian product $X \times Y$, and the repeated integral*

$$\int |f(x)| \, dx \int |g(x, y)| \, dy \tag{6.2}$$

exists, then there exist all the integrals in

$$\iint f(x)g(x, y)\, dx\, dy = \int f(x)\, dx \int g(x, y)\, dy \tag{6.3}$$

and the equation holds.

Proof. The integral (6.2) can be written as $\int dx \int |f(x)|\, |g(x, y)|\,'dy$. Its existence implies, by Theorem 5.2, the existence of the double integral $\iint |f(x)|\, |g(x, y)|\, dx\, dy$, which means that the function $|f(x)|\, |g(x, y)|$ is integrable on $X \times Y$.

The function $f(x)$, defined on X, can also be considered as a function on $X \times Y$ which is constant with respect to $y \in Y$. The measurability of $f(x)$ on X implies the measurability of $f(x)$ on $X \times Y$ (see the remark at the end of section 5). Since $g(x, y)$ is also measurable on $X \times Y$, so is the product $f(x)g(x, y)$, by Theorem 6.3. But this product is bounded by the integrable function $|f(x)|\, |g(x, y)|$, it is thus integrable itself. We therefore have, by Theorem 3.1,

$$\iint f(x)g(x, y)\, dx\, dy = \int dx \int f(x)g(x, y)\, dy. \tag{6.4}$$

The existence of the repeated integral (6.2) assumes, implicitly, that $\int |g(x, y)|\, dy$ exists a.e. in X, i.e., $|g(x, y)|$ is integrable in Y for almost every $x \in X$. Since $g(x, y)$ is measurable, it is measurable in Y for almost every $x \in X$, by Theorem 5.1. Consequently, $g(x, y)$ is integrable in Y for almost every $x \in X$. We thus have $\int f(x)g(x, y)\, dy = f(x) \int g(x, y)\, dy$ a.e. in X, by Theorem 6.3. Combining this with (6.4), we obtain the wished equation (6.3).

Evidently, Theorem 6.4 is a generalization of Tonelli's theorem 5.2 and reduces to it on assuming that $f(x) \equiv 1$. Note that a similar generalization of the Fubini theorem fails, because the integrability of the integrand $f(x)g(x, y)$ is not sufficient to ensure (6.3). In fact, if $f(x) = a$, $g(x, y) = b \neq 0$ and $ab = 0$, then the left side of (6.3) is 0, but the right side does not make sense, since the integral $\int g(x, y)\, dy$ does not exist.

Chapter XI

Complements on Functions and Sets in the Euclidean q-Space

The aim of this chapter is to state a few elementary facts concerning functions and sets in the particular case: $K = \mathbf{R}^q$. Those facts do not follow from the general theory (with arbitrary K), because properties of the space $\mathbf{R}^q$ must be taken in account. We are going to discuss locally integrable functions, continuous functions, closed and open sets on $\mathbf{R}^q$ and relations between them.

1. Locally integrable functions

We say that a function f is *Bochner locally integrable* or simply *locally integrable* if the integral $\int f$ exists on every interval J: $a \leq x < b$. Evidently, a measurable function which is bounded on every interval J, is locally integrable. We can also say that f is locally integrable if its product fJ by any brick function J (we use the same symbol J for the interval J and for its characteristic function) is integrable (more exactly: Bochner integrable). Every integrable function f is locally integrable, for the product fJ is measurable and bounded by the function $|f|$, which is integrable. Thus the class of locally integrable functions is wider than the class of integrable functions. If f is locally integrable, then also every function g, equivalent to f, is locally integrable. It is easy to verify that the class of locally integrable functions is a linear space. Moreover, if f is locally integrable, then also its modulus $|f|$ is locally integrable. Note finally that the class of locally integrable functions is contained in the class of measurable functions; this follows from the equality $fJ = \lim_{n \to \infty} f . \cap nJ$.

Theorem 1. *If f is a locally integrable function and J is a given interval, then for every number $\varepsilon > 0$ we can find a number $\delta > 0$ such that the inequality $\int_Z |f| < \varepsilon$ holds for every measurable set $Z \subset J$ with $\int Z < \delta$.*

Proof. We have $\int_Z |f| = \int |f|Z = \int |f|JZ = \int_Z |f|J$. Since $|f|J$ is integrable, the assertion follows from Theorem 6.1, Chapter VI.

2. Local convergence

We say that a sequence of functions f_n *converges locally* to f, and we write

$$f_n \to f \text{ loc.,}$$

if, given any brick function J, the sequence $f_n J$ converges in norm to fJ, i.e., if $\int |f_n J - fJ| \to 0$. If functions f_n are locally integrable, then also the limit f is locally integrable, which easily follows from the first part of Theorem 10, Chapter IV.

The local limit, if exists, is determined up to equivalent functions. In fact, it is obvious that, if f is a local limit of f_n, then every function equivalent to f is also a limit of f_n. Moreover, if f and g are local limits of the same sequence f_n, then $\int |(f-g)J| \leq \int |f_n J - fJ| + \int |f_n J - gJ| \to 0$. This implies that $(f-g)J$ is a null function. If J_n is a sequence of brick functions, convergent everywhere to 1, then $(f-g)J_n$ converges everywhere to $f-g$, which implies that $f-g$ is a null function. Thus f and g are equivalent. It is easy to see that local convergence is more general than norm convergence. If a sequence of integrable functions converges locally, its limit is a locally integrable function, but not necessarily integrable.

Theorem 2. *If $f_n \to f$ loc., then there is a subsequence f_{p_n} such that $f_{p_n} \to f$ a.e.*

Proof. Let J_p be a sequence of intervals whose limit is the whole space $\mathbf{R}^q$. By the Riesz theorem we can select from f_n a subsequence f_{1n} which converges to f almost everywhere in J_1. Similarly, we can select from f_{1n} a subsequence f_{2n} which converges to f almost everywhere in J_2. And so on. Then the diagonal sequence f_{nn} converges almost everywhere in each of intervals J_p, and consequently almost everywhere in $\mathbf{R}^q$.

From Theorem 2 we immediately obtain.

Theorem 3. *If $f_n \to f$ loc. and $f_n \to g$ a.e., then $f = g$ a.e.*

3. Continuous functions

One of the most important subspaces of locally integrable functions is the space of *continuous functions*.

A function f from $\mathbf{R}^q$ to a Banach space E is called *continuous* at $x_0 \in \mathbf{R}^q$ if, given any number $\varepsilon > 0$, there exists a number $\delta > 0$ such that $|x - x_0| < \delta$ implies $|f(x) - f(x_0)| < \varepsilon$. Here, the modulus $|x - x_0|$ denotes the distance between the points x and x_0, and the modulus $|f(x) - f(x_0)|$ denotes the norm of $f(x) - f(x_0)$ in E. The function f is called continuous in $\mathbf{R}^q$, if it is continuous at every point $x_0 \in \mathbf{R}^q$.

In order to prove that continuous functions in $\mathbf{R}^q$ are locally integrable in $\mathbf{R}^q$, we will first introduce some auxiliary notation. Assuming that the number q of dimensions is fixed, we shall denote by $J_{\tau,m}$ the q-dimensional interval $\tau m \leq x < \tau(m+1)$, where τ is a positive number, m is an entire point of $\mathbf{R}^q$ (i.e., a point whose all the coordinates are entire numbers), and $m+1$ is the point whose coordinates are greater by 1 than the coordinates of m.

Now, let f be a given function, continuous in $\mathbf{R}^q$, and let k_τ be a function whose value is, on every interval $J_{\tau,m}$, constant and equal to some value of f in that interval. It is easy to see that the function k_τ is measurable (even locally integrable) for every fixed $\tau > 0$. On the other hand, we have $k_{\tau_n} \to f$, as $\tau_n \to 0$. Thus f is measurable, being a limit of a sequence of measurable functions. But f is bounded on every bounded interval, since f is continuous in the whole space $\mathbf{R}^q$. Thus f is locally integrable.

We say that a sequence of functions f_n, defined in $\mathbf{R}^q$, converges to f *almost uniformly* in $\mathbf{R}^q$ if it converges to f uniformly on every bounded interval J. It is known that if the functions f_n are continuous, then also the limit is a continuous function.

If a sequence of measurable functions f_n converges almost uniformly to f, then it converges also locally to f. In fact, given any brick function J, the almost uniform convergence of f_n implies that there is a sequence of positive numbers ε_n, convergent to 0, such that $|f_n J - f J| < \varepsilon_n$. Of course we also have $|f_n J - f J| < \varepsilon_n J$, and hence $\int |f_n J - f J| \leq \varepsilon_n \int J$. This implies that $\int |f_n J - f J| \to 0$. Thus f_n converges locally to f.

We can also say that local convergence is more general than almost uniform convergence.

The following alternative definition of continuous functions is occasionally useful:

A function f from $\mathbf{R}^q$ to E is called continuous at $x_0 \in \mathbf{R}^q$, if for any sequence of points $x_n \in \mathbf{R}^q$ converging to x_0 we have $f(x_n) \to f(x_0)$.

It is known that this definition is equivalent to the previous one. The easy proof runs exactly like for real valued functions and is left to the reader. Some authors emphasize that the Axiom of Choice is used in the proof.

4. Closed sets

We say that a set $Z \subset \mathbf{R}^q$ is *closed*, if the limit of any convergent sequence of points x_n of Z belongs to Z. Remark that an interval is a closed set if and only if it is of the form $a \leq x \leq b$. Any set consisting of a single point or of a finite number of points is closed.

The limit of a convergent sequence of points of Z is said a *limit point* of Z. Thus we can also say that a set Z is closed if it contains all its limit points. Evidently, the whole space $\mathbf{R}^q$ is a closed set. It is also convenient to consider the empty set as a closed set.

It follows directly from the definition that the intersection of any number (finite or infinite) of closed sets is a closed set. It is also easy to see that the union of a finite number of closed sets is a closed set. (However, the union of an infinite number of closed sets need not be a closed set.)

If f is a real valued continuous function in $\mathbf{R}^q$, then the set Z of points where $f \leq 0$ holds, is closed. In fact, if $x_n \in Z$ and $x_n \to x_0$, then $f(x_n) \leq 0$ and $f(x_n) \to f(x_0)$. This implies that $f(x_0) \leq 0$. Hence $x_0 \in Z$, which proves that Z is closed.

In the next section, we shall prove that, for every closed set Z, there is a continuous function f such that $f=0$ holds on Z, and $f>0$ holds for points which do not belong to Z. As f we will take the distance of x from the set Z.

5. The distance of a point from a set

If Z is a given non-empty set of points of $\mathbf{R}^q$, and x is an arbitrary point of $\mathbf{R}^q$, then by the distance of the point x from Z we understand

$$\rho(x, Z) = \inf_{z \in Z} |x - z|.$$

Evidently, if $x \in Z$, then $\rho(x, Z) = 0$. It is easy to prove that

$$|\rho(x_1, Z) - \rho(x_2, Z)| \leq |x_1 - x_2|. \tag{5.1}$$

In fact, from the inequality $|x_1 - z| \leq |x_1 - x_2| + |x_2 - z|$ we obtain

$$\inf_{z \in Z} |x_1 - z| \leq |x_1 - x_2| + \inf_{z \in Z} |x_2 - z|,$$

and hence

$$\rho(x_1, Z) - \rho(x_2, Z) \leq |x_1 - x_2|.$$

On interchanging the role of the points x_1 and x_2, we obtain similarly

$$\rho(x_2, Z) - \rho(x_1, Z) \leq |x_1 - x_2|.$$

The both inequalities imply (5.1).

In particular, it follows from (5.1) that, for fixed Z, the function $\rho(x, Z)$ is a continuous function of x. This function is null on the set Z and non-negative outside it.

Now, it is easy to show that if Z is a closed set, then the equality $\rho(x, Z) = 0$ implies that $x \in Z$. In fact, since $\inf_{z \in Z} |x - z| = 0$, there is a sequence $z_n \in Z$ such that $|x - z_n| \to 0$, i.e., $z_n \to x$. Thus $x \in Z$, for Z is closed.

6. Open sets

A set Q is called *open*, if its complement $Z = C(Q) = \mathbf{R}^q \setminus Q$ is a closed set.

By the previous result, *Q is open if and only if there is a function $\phi(x)$, continuous in $\mathbf{R}^q$, which is positive for $x \in Q$, and null for $x \notin Q$.* This implies, by Theorem 6.3, Chapter VI, that *every open set is measurable*. Consequently, also *every closed set is measurable*, being the complement of an open set.

From the continuity of ρ it follows that every point x at which $\rho > 0$, is contained in an open interval $a < x < b$ in which $\rho > 0$. In other words, every point $x \in Q$ is contained in an open interval $J \subset Q$. This property is characteristic for open sets.

In fact, if a point x belongs to an open interval $J \subset Q$, then its distance $\rho(x, Z)$, where $Z = C(Q)$, is positive. If every point x of Q belongs to an open interval $J \subset Q$, then $\rho(x, Z) > 0$ for $x \in Q$, i.e., for $x \notin Z$. Hence the set Z is closed and the set Q is open, being its complement.

Thus, *a set Q is open if and only if every point $x \in Q$ belongs to an open interval $J \subset Q$.* This property can also be proved directly, without using the distance function ρ.

Remark that an open interval is an open set if and only if it is open in the sense used before, i.e., if it is of the form $a < x < b$.

From the last property of open sets, it follows easily that the union of any number (finite or infinite) of open sets is an open set. The intersection of a finite number of open sets is an open set. This might be also deduced from mutual properties of closed sets, by means of de Morgan formulas.

In the following theorem, by a *half-closed cube* we mean a brick whose all edges are equal.

Theorem 6.1. *Every open set $Q \subset \mathbf{R}^q$ is a union $Q = J_1 \cup J_2 \cup \cdots$ of disjoint half-closed cubes J_n inside Q.*

Proof. As in section 3, Chapter VII, let $J_{\tau,m}$ denote the q-dimensional brick $\tau m \leqslant x < \tau(m+1)$. We subtract from Q all the bricks $J_{1,m}$ which are inside Q. Let Q_1 be the set of the remaining points of Q. In turn, we subtract from Q_1 all the bricks $J_{1/2,m} \subset Q_1$ which are inside Q, and denote by Q_2 the set of remaining points. We proceed similarly with bricks $J_{1/4,m}$, $J_{1/8,m}, \ldots$. The set of all selected bricks can be ordered in a sequence J_1, $J_2, \ldots$. Every point of Q belongs to some brick J_n. Since the bricks J_n are contained in Q, this implies that $Q = J_1 \cup J_2 \cup \cdots$.

From Theorem 6.1, it follows, in particular, that every open set is measurable. This result has been obtained in another way at the beginning of this section.

Theorem 6.2. *Given any set Z inside an open bounded set Q, there is a finite number of disjoint intervals $J_1, \ldots, J_n$ inside Q such that $Z \subset J_1 + \cdots + J_n$.*

Proof. We subtract from Q all the intervals $J_{1,m}$ which are inside Q and which contain at least one point of Z. Let Q_1 be the set of the remaining points of Q. In turn, we subtract from Q_1 all the intervals $J_{1/2,m} \subset Q_1$ which are inside Q and contain at least one point of Z. After a finite number of similar steps, all the points of Z will be subtracted. In fact, if there were infinitely many subtracted intervals $J_{2^{-n},m}$ then the distance of points of $J_{2^{-n},m}$ from the complement of Q would decrease to 0. Thus, for sufficiently large n, those intervals could not contain points of Z.

Theorem 6.3. *For every integrable set $Z \subset \mathbf{R}^q$, there is a sequence of integrable open sets $Q_n \subset \mathbf{R}^q$ such that $Z \subset Q_{n+1} \subset Q_n$ $(n = 1, 2, \ldots)$ and $\int Q_n \to \int Z$.*

Proof. By Theorem 3.2, Chapter III, there is, for any given $\varepsilon > 0$, an expansion into brick functions

$$Z \simeq \lambda_1 f_1 + \lambda_2 f_2 + \cdots \qquad (6.1)$$

such that

$$|\lambda_1| \int f_1 + |\lambda_2| \int f_2 + \cdots \leq \int Z + \frac{\varepsilon}{2}.$$

The brick functions f_n are characteristic functions of half-closed intervals $a_n \leq x < b_n$. However, we can replace those intervals by slightly larger open intervals whose characteristic functions g_n satisfy the inequality

$$|\lambda_1| \int g_1 + |\lambda_2| \int g_2 + \cdots \leq \int Z + \varepsilon. \qquad (6.2)$$

Let Z_n denote the set of points x such that $|\lambda_1| g_1(x) + \cdots + |\lambda_n| g_n(x) > \frac{1}{2}$. It is easy to see that the sets Z_n are open and that $Z_n \subset Z_{n+1}$. Since the series (6.1) has the sum 1 at every point x of Z at which this series converges absolutely, and since $g_n \geq f_n$, every point of Z must belong to some Z_n.

Hence we obtain $Z \subset Y = \bigcup_n Z_n$, where Y is an open set. Since $\int Z_n \leq |\lambda_1| \int g_1 + \cdots + |\lambda_n| \int g_n$, we have, $\int Y \leq \int Z + \varepsilon$, by (6.2).

Now, let ε_n be a sequence of positive numbers, convergent to 0. For every ε_n there is an open set Y_n such that $Z \subset Y_n$ and $\int Y_n \leq \int Z + \varepsilon_n$. Let $Q_n = Y_1 \cdots Y_n$. Then $Z \subset Q_{n+1} \subset Q_n$ $(n = 1, 2, \ldots)$. Moreover

$$\int Z \leq \int Q_n \leq \int Z + \varepsilon_n,$$

which proves that $\int Q_n \to \int Z$. Thus the sets Q_n have the required properties.

Corollary 6.1. *For every measurable set $Z \subset \mathbf{R}^q$ and every $\varepsilon > 0$ there is an open set $Q \subset \mathbf{R}^q$ including Z such that $\int (Q - Z) < \varepsilon$.*

Proof. Let $P_n \subset \mathbf{R}^q$ be disjoint integrable sets such that $\bigcup_n P_n = \mathbf{R}^q$. Then the intersections $P_n Z$ are integrable and such that $\bigcup_n P_n Z = Z$. Let $\varepsilon_n > 0$ $\varepsilon_1 + \varepsilon_2 + \cdots < \varepsilon$. By Theorem 6.3 there are open sets $Q_n \supset P_n Z$ such that $\int (Q_n - P_n Z) < \varepsilon_n$. Then the set $Q = \bigcup_n Q_n$ is open and we have $Q \supset Z$ and

$$\int (Q - Z) = \int \bigcup_n (Q_n - P_n Z) \leq \sum_n \int (Q_n - P_n Z) < \varepsilon.$$

Theorem 6.4. *For every integrable set $Z \subset \mathbf{R}^q$ there is a sequence of bounded closed sets $Y_n \subset \mathbf{R}^q$ such that $Y_n \subset Y_{n+1} \subset Z$ $(n = 1, 2, \ldots)$ and $\int Y_n \to \int Z$.*

Proof. By Theorem 6.3 there is an open integrable set Q containing Z. The set $Q - Z$ is integrable and, by Theorem 6.3, there are open sets Q_n such that $Q - Z \subset Q_{n+1} \subset Q_n$ and $\int Q_n \to \int Q - \int Z$. Let $J_1, J_2, \ldots$ be an increasing sequence of bounded closed intervals which cover the whole space $\mathbf{R}^q$. We shall show that the sequence $Y_n = (Z \backslash Q_n) \cap J_n$ has the required properties. Evidently, the sets Y_n are bounded and closed. Moreover, considering Q, Z, Q_n, J_n and Y_n as zero-one functions, we can write $Y_n = Z(1 - Q_n)J_n$, $0 \leq Q_{n+1} \leq Q_n$ and $0 \leq J_n \leq J_{n+1} \to 1$. Hence $Z(1 - Q_n)J_n \leq Z(1 - Q_{n+1})J_{n+1}$, which means that $Y_n \leq Y_{n+1}$, or $Y_n \subset Y_{n+1}$. Furthermore, $0 \leq Z - Y_n = Z(1 - J_n) + ZJ_nQ_n$. But

$$ZQ_nJ_n \leq ZQ_n \leq ZQ_n + (1 - Q)Q_n = (Z + Q_n - Q)Q_n \leq Z + Q_n - Q$$

so that

$$0 \leq \int Z - \int Y_n \leq \int Z(1 - J_n) + \int Z + \int Q_n - \int Q \to 0$$

and, consequently $\int Y_n \to \int Z$.

7. The integral of a continuous function on a compact set

By a *compact set* we understand a closed and bounded set of points of $\mathbf{R}^q$. Every compact set is integrable, since it is measurable and contained in a bounded interval.

If f is a function defined and continuous in $\mathbf{R}^q$, and Z is a compact set, then the product fZ is measurable. Since every function continuous in $\mathbf{R}^q$ is bounded on any bounded set, we have $|fZ| \leq M$, where M is a number. We can also write $|fZ| \leq MZ$. Since the product fZ is measurable and bounded by MZ, it is integrable. This means that the integral $\int f$ exists. Thus, a *continuous function is integrable on every compact set.* Z

Remark that, in the integral $\int f$, the values of f outside Z play no role. This suggests a stronger formulation of the result just obtained. We will say that a function f is *relatively continuous* on a set $Z \subset \mathbf{R}^q$ if it is defined at least on Z (i.e., if the domain of f contains Z) and if, given any point $x_0 \in Z$ and any number $\varepsilon > 0$, there is a number $\delta > 0$ such that $|f(x) - f(x_0)| < \varepsilon$ holds for all the points $x \in Z$ satisfying the inequality $|x - x_0| < \delta$. (If we replaced, in this definition, '$x \in Z$' by '$x \in \mathbf{R}^q$', we would obtain the usual definition of continuity of f on Z.)

Theorem 7. *If a function is relatively continuous on a compact set, then it is integrable on that compact set.*

Remark. There is a theorem which says that for every relatively continuous function f on a closed set Z, there is a function g, continuous in $\mathbf{R}^q$ such that $fZ = gZ$. Hence Theorem 7 follows, according to the previous result. However, the proof that such a function g exists is rather tedious. We will therefore give another proof.

Proof. Let f be relatively continuous on a compact set Z. For each positive number τ we define a function k_τ in the following way. We assume that k_τ is constant on every interval $J_{\tau,m}$, defined as in section 6, and that its value is equal to some value which f admits on the intersection $J_{\tau,m}Z$, if this intersection is not empty. Otherwise, if $J_{\tau,m}Z = 0$, we assume that $k_\tau = 0$ on $J_{\tau,m}$. Then function k_τ is measurable (even locally integrable). It is easy to verify, taking into account the relative continuity of f, that $k_{\tau_n} \to fZ$, as $\tau_n \to 0$. Thus the function fZ is measurable, being a limit of a sequence of measurable functions. But fZ is also bounded by the integrable function MZ, where M is the maximum of f on the set Z. Thus fZ is integrable, i.e., f is integrable on the set Z.

Chapter XII

Changing Variables in Integrals

The main purpose of this chapter is to establish the formula

$$(*) \qquad \int_{\varphi(X)} f = \int_{X} |\det \varphi'| \, f[\varphi(x)] \, dx,$$

where φ is a map of a set $X \subset \mathbf{R}^q$ into $\mathbf{R}^q$, $\det \varphi'$ is the Jacobian of φ, and f is a vector valued function, integrable on the image $\varphi(X)$ of X.

In most text books, the above formula is proved under the hypothesis that X is an open set and φ is a *diffeomorphism* on it, i.e., φ is invertible on X, has all its derivatives continuous and, moreover, $\det \varphi' \neq 0$ on X. Sometimes it is assumed that X is a closed domain. Those hypotheses are however, as it is easily seen even in quite simple examples, much too strong and they can be relaxed in various directions (see Rado-Reichelderfer [22]).

In this chapter, we present a new way so that quite arbitrary measurable sets X are admitted. Also the class of admissible functions φ is extended, by introducing the concept of fully derivable functions. This concept is almost as simple as that of partial derivatives, but fits better to any sort of applications.

We prove equation (*) under the hypothesis that φ is fully derivable on X, whereas the Jacobian $\det \varphi'$ is allowed to vanish on arbitrary subsets of X. All we require is that the function φ should be invertible on the subset of X on which the Jacobian does not vanish. This restriction is quite natural and necessary (i.e., equation (*) fails, if it is not satisfied). All these hypotheses are easily understandable and applicable in practical calculations. The only new concept to get familiar with is the full derivative. The reader will note, in the sequel, that its theory is more elegant and simpler than the theory of traditional partial derivatives.

In spite of simplicity of the main result (Theorem 19), its proof is rather difficult and requires introducing special tools. First of all, algebraic and geometric questions arise when considering the linear transformation. These questions are discussed in sections 1–9. In order to pass from the linear to the general case, we need the geometric concepts of aureoles and antiaureoles which are the subject of sections 10 and 11. Sections 12–16 are devoted to full derivatives. The Vitali covering theorem is formulated and proved in section 17. It is then applied, in section 18, in the proof of the Jacobian Theorem which is a particular case of the main Substitution Theorem, stated in section 19. Finally, section 20 contains a few examples and remarks.

1. Translation

The simplest transformation of the Euclidean space $\mathbf{R}^q$ is

$$y = x + c \tag{1.1}$$

where $y \in \mathbf{R}^q$, $x \in \mathbf{R}^q$ and $c \in \mathbf{R}^q$. Using the coordinates, $y = (\eta_1, \ldots, \eta_q)$, $x = (\xi_1, \ldots, \xi_q)$, $c = (\gamma_1, \ldots, \gamma_q)$, we can write, instead of (1.1)

$$\eta_1 = \xi_1 + \gamma_1, \ldots, \eta_q = \xi_q + \gamma_q.$$

By convention, x is the point before the transformation and y the corresponding point after the transformation. One says that y is the *image* of x. The transformation (1.1) is established, whenever the point c is given. Instead of 'point' one often uses equivalently the word 'vector'. Both, a point in $\mathbf{R}^q$ and a vector in $\mathbf{R}^q$ are determined by q real numbers, their coordinates. Mathematically, it turns out on the same to say that they are systems of q real numbers. The transformation (1.1) is called a *translation* by the vector c.

Theorem 1.1. *The Bochner integral is translation invariant, i.e., for each vector c, we have*

$$\int f(x + c) \, dx = \int f(y) \, dy. \tag{1.2}$$

More exactly, if one of the above integrals exist, then also the other exists and the equality holds.

Proof. We first prove the theorem in the one-dimensional case, $q = 1$, while f is a brick function, i.e., a characteristic function of an interval $\alpha \leq \eta < \beta$. Then $f(\xi + \gamma)$ is the characteristic function of the interval $\alpha - \gamma \leq \xi < \beta - \gamma$ and we have

$$\int f(\xi + \gamma) \, d\xi = (\beta - \gamma) - (\alpha - \gamma) = \beta - \alpha = \int f(\eta) \, d\eta,$$

so that (1.2) holds.
Assume now that f is a brick function in $\mathbf{R}^q$, i.e.,

$$f(y) = f_1(\eta_1) \cdots f_q(\eta_q),$$

where the f_j are one-dimensional brick-functions. Then

$$f(x + c) = f_1(\xi_1 + \gamma_1) \cdots f_q(\xi_q + \gamma_q)$$

and we arrive to equality (1.2), on using the preceding result and Theorem 5.3, Chapter X.
Finally, if f is an arbitrary Bochner integrable function, we can write

$$f(y) \simeq \lambda_1 f_1(y) + \lambda_2 f_2(y) + \cdots.$$

This relation means that

$$|\lambda_1| \int f_1(y) \, dy + |\lambda_2| \int f_2(y) \, dy + \cdots < \infty$$

and

$$f(y) = \lambda_1 f_1(y) + \lambda_2 f_2(y) + \cdots \text{ at points } y \text{ of absolute convergence.}$$

By what we have already proved we obtain

$$|\lambda_1| \int f_1(x+c) \, dx + |\lambda_2| \int f_2(x+c) \, dx + \cdots < \infty.$$

We also trivially have

$$f(x+c) = \lambda_1 f_1(x+c) + \lambda_2 f_2(x+c) + \cdots$$

at points x of absolute convergence. This means that

$$f(x+c) \simeq \lambda_1 f_1(x+c) + \lambda_2 f_2(x+c) + \cdots.$$

The function $f(x+c)$ is thus Bochner integrable and equality (1.2) follows.

2. Linear substitution in one-dimensional case

In this section we prove two theorems which have rather an auxiliary character. They will be used in the sequel to prove more general theorems.

Theorem 2.1. *If $f(\xi)$ is a Bochner integrable function on the real line and α, β are real numbers, $\alpha \neq 0$, then $f(\alpha\xi + \beta)$ is Bochner integrable and we have*

$$|\alpha| \int f(\alpha\xi + \beta) \, d\xi = \int f(\xi) \, d\xi. \tag{2.1}$$

Proof. We first assume that f is a brick function, i.e., a characteristic function of a brick: $\xi_1 \leq \xi < \xi_2$. If $\alpha > 0$, then $f(\alpha\xi + \beta)$ is the characteristic function of the brick $(\xi_1 - \beta)/\alpha \leq \xi < (\xi_2 - \beta)/\alpha$ and, according to the definition of the integral of a brick function, we have

$$\int f(\alpha\xi + \beta) \, d\xi = \frac{\xi_2 - \beta}{\alpha} - \frac{\xi_1 - \beta}{\alpha} = \frac{\xi_2 - \xi_1}{\alpha}.$$

On the other hand,

$$\int f(\xi) \, d\xi = \xi_2 - \xi_1, \tag{2.2}$$

and the equation (2.1) follows.

If $\alpha < 0$, then $f(\alpha\xi + \beta)$ is the characteristic function of the interval $(\xi_2 - \beta)/\alpha < \xi \leq (\xi_1 - \beta)/\alpha$. If we replace $f(\alpha\xi + \beta)$ by the characteristic function of the brick $(\xi_2 - \beta)/\alpha \leq \xi < (\xi_1 - \beta)/\alpha$, we change its values at two points only and this will not affect the value of the integral. Thus,

$$\int f(\alpha\xi + \beta)d\xi = \frac{\xi_1 - \beta}{\alpha} - \frac{\xi_2 - \beta}{\alpha} = \frac{\xi_1 - \xi_2}{\alpha} = \frac{\xi_2 - \xi_1}{|\alpha|}.$$

In view of (2.2), equation (2.1) follows. If f is not a brick function, but integrable function, then the proof follows by its expansion into a series of brick functions.

Formula (2.1) is concerned with linear substitution of the argument in the integrand. Now, we are going to establish a similar formula for the measure of sets. Let X be an integrable subset of $\mathbf{R}^1$ (real line). By $\alpha X + \beta$ we mean the set of points $\alpha x + \beta$ such that $x \in X$. By $\int X$ we mean the Lebesgue measure of X and by $\int(\alpha X + \beta)$ the Lebesgue measure of $\alpha X + \beta$.

Theorem 2.2. *If X is a Lebesgue integrable subset of $\mathbf{R}^1$ and α, β are real numbers, then*

$$\int(\alpha X + \beta) = |\alpha| \int X. \tag{2.3}$$

Before we give the proof, let us call the attention to the fact that, in equations (2.1) and (2.3), the factor $|\alpha|$ stands on different sides. It is also important to note that formula (2.3) holds without any restrictions on α. In fact, if $\alpha = 0$, the right side of (2.3) is trivially 0. On the left side we then obtain the set $0X + \beta = (0) + \beta = (\beta)$. This small calculus needs an explanation. We must not write $0X = 0$, because $0X$ is the set which consists of the single point 0. Such a set is denoted by (0) and is to be distinguished from the point 0 itself. Now, $(0) + \beta$ is the set of all points $x + \beta$ such that $x \in (0)$, it thus consists of the single point (β). Its measure $\int(\beta)$ is 0, because the Lebesgue measure of any single point set is 0. We thus have shown that formula (2.3) holds for $\alpha = 0$.

In contrast, in (2.1) the value $\alpha = 0$ can be admitted only under artificial and trivial assumptions that $f(\beta) = 0$ and $\int f(\xi) \, d\xi = 0$.

Proof of Theorem 2.2. For $\alpha = 0$, the theorem has been already proved. We thus may assume that $\alpha \neq 0$. If we use the symbol $(\alpha X + \beta)(\xi)$ for the characteristic function of the set $\alpha X + \beta$ and $X(\xi)$ for the characteristic function of X, then we have

$$(\alpha X + \beta)(\xi) = X\left(\frac{\xi - \beta}{\alpha}\right). \tag{2.4}$$

To justify this equation, we have to show that $\xi \in \alpha X + \beta$, iff $(\xi - \beta)/\alpha \in X$. In fact, if $\xi \in \alpha X + \beta$, then $\xi = \alpha\eta + \beta$ with $\eta \in X$, by definition of $\alpha X + \beta$.

Hence we find $\eta = (\xi - \beta)/\alpha \in X$. Conversely, if $\eta = (\xi - \beta)/\alpha \in X$, then $\xi = \alpha\eta + \beta \in \alpha X + \beta$.

Using (2.4), we find, by Theorem 2.1,

$$\int (\alpha X + \beta) = \int (\alpha X + \beta)(\xi)\, d\xi = \int X\left(\frac{\xi - \beta}{\alpha}\right) d\xi$$

and hence, by Theorem 2.1,

$$\int (\alpha X + \beta) = |\alpha| \int X(\xi)\, d\xi = |\alpha| \int X.$$

Remark. Equality (2.3) can equivalently be written as

$$\int_{\alpha X + \beta} 1\, d\xi = |\alpha| \int_X 1\, d\xi. \tag{2.5}$$

It is immediately seen that (2.1) and (2.5) are particular cases of the more general formula

$$\int_{\alpha X + \beta} f(\xi)\, d\xi = |\alpha| \int_X f(\alpha\xi + \beta)\, d\xi.$$

We shall not discuss it in detail, because a still more general formula will be stated, later on, for any number of dimensions.

3. A particular transformation in $\mathbf{R}^q$

In this section, we consider a linear transformation of a single coordinate in $\mathbf{R}^q$, while all the remaining coordinates are left unaltered. More precisely, if i is the index of the coordinate to be transformed, the transformation can be written as a system of q equations:

$$\eta_i = \alpha_{i1}\xi_1 + \cdots + \alpha_{iq}\xi_q,$$
$$\eta_j = \xi_j \quad \text{for} \quad j \neq i.$$

This transformation assigns, to each point $x = (\xi_1, \ldots, \xi_q) \in \mathbf{R}^q$ another point of $\mathbf{R}^q$ which will be denoted by $A_i x$. If X is an integrable subset of $\mathbf{R}^q$, then by $A_i X$ we mean the set of all points $A_i x$ with $x \in X$. We shall prove that

$$\int A_i X = |\alpha_{ii}| \int X. \tag{3.1}$$

In fact, by the Fubini theorem, we may write

$$\int X = \iint X\, dx_i\, d\xi_i = \int dx_i \int X\, d\xi_i,$$

where $\xi_i \in \mathbf{R}^1$ and $x_i \in \mathbf{R}^{q-1}$. If x_i is fixed, then X can be considered as a one-dimensional set (which depends on the choice of x_i) and we then have

$$A_i X = \alpha_{ii} X + \beta_i,$$

where $\beta_i = \sum_{j \neq i} \alpha_{ij} \xi_j$. By Theorem 2.2 we get

$$\int A_i X \, d\xi_i = |\alpha_{ii}| \int X \, d\xi_i.$$

Hence

$$\int dx_i \int A_i X \, d\xi_i = |\alpha_{ii}| \int dx_i \int X \, d\xi_i,$$

and by the Tonelli theorem we obtain

$$\iint A_i X \, dx_i \, d\xi_i = |\alpha_{ii}| \iint X \, dx_i \, d\xi_i.$$

The abreviated form of the last equation is (3.1).

4. Linear transformation in $\mathbf{R}^q$

In sections 4 and 5, we state a few purely algebraic facts which will be used in the sequel.

A linear transformation in $\mathbf{R}^q$ is given by the system of q equations

$$\eta_1 = \alpha_{11} \xi_1 + \cdots + \alpha_{1q} \xi_q,$$
$$\cdots\cdots\cdots\cdots\cdots$$
$$\eta_q = \alpha_{q1} \xi_1 + \cdots + \alpha_{qq} \xi_q.$$

Using the notation

$$y = \begin{pmatrix} \eta_1 \\ \cdot \\ \cdot \\ \cdot \\ \eta_q \end{pmatrix}, \qquad x = \begin{pmatrix} \xi_1 \\ \cdot \\ \cdot \\ \cdot \\ \xi_q \end{pmatrix}$$

and

$$A = \begin{pmatrix} \alpha_{11} \cdots \alpha_{1q} \\ \cdots\cdots\cdots \\ \alpha_{q1} \cdots \alpha_{qq} \end{pmatrix},$$

this transformation can be shortly written as

$$y = Ax,$$

where the multiplication is meant, as usually, 'rows by columns'.

Every linear transformation in $\mathbf{R}^q$ is determined by its matrix A. We therefore may use the letter A for both the transformation and the matrix.

By a composition of two transformations $y = Ax$ and $y = Bx$ we mean $y = A(Bx)$. This composition is another linear transformation and is usually denoted by $y = (AB)x$ or $y = ABx$. We thus have by definition

$$(AB)x = A(Bx). \tag{4.1}$$

The matrix AB is called the product of matrices A and B and is obtained on multiplying the rows of A by the colums of B.

Using equality (4.1), we get

$$((AB)C)x = (AB)(Cx) = A(B(Cx)) = A((BC)x) = (A(BC))x.$$

The transformations $y = ((AB)C)x$ and $y = (A(BC))x$ are thus identical and, consequently, their matrices so are,

$$(AB)C = A(BC). \tag{4.2}$$

This equation expresses the associativity law for matrices.

Identity (4.1) allows us to write ABx, without parantheses, in place of $(AB)x$ or $A(Bx)$. Similarly, (4.2) allows us to write simply $ABCx$. More generally, we may write $A_1 \cdots A_p x$ for the composition of any number p of linear operations.

5. A decomposition theorem

By the *unit matrix* we mean the matrix

$$I = \begin{pmatrix} 1 & \cdots & 0 \\ \cdot & \cdots & \cdot \\ 0 & \cdots & 1 \end{pmatrix}$$

in which all the diagonal elements are 1, and the remaining ones are 0. A characteristic property of this matrix is that $IA = AI = A$ holds for any matrix A.

By a *simple matrix* we mean a matrix which is obtained from the unit matrix on replacing one row by arbitrary numbers. Such a matrix corresponds to a particular linear transformation considered in the preceding section.

Theorem 5.1. *Every matrix decomposes into a product of a finite number of simple matrices.*

This theorem has an obvious interpretation in the theory of linear transformations. It tells us that each linear transformation can be decomposed into a finite number of simple transformations, each of them consisting of a linear substitution for a single variable.

In text books on algebra, the above theorem can be found but under a superfluous hypothesis that the given matrix is invertible. We therefore shall display the proof here, after a few preliminary remarks.

A trivial example of decomposition of a non-invertible matrix is

$$\begin{pmatrix} 0 & 0 \\ 0 & 0 \end{pmatrix} = \begin{pmatrix} 1 & 0 \\ 0 & 0 \end{pmatrix}\begin{pmatrix} 0 & 0 \\ 0 & 1 \end{pmatrix}.$$

A more interesting example of decomposition (of an invertible matrix) is

$$\begin{pmatrix} 0 & 1 \\ 1 & 0 \end{pmatrix} = \begin{pmatrix} 1 & 0 \\ 0 & -1 \end{pmatrix}\begin{pmatrix} 1 & 1 \\ 0 & 1 \end{pmatrix}\begin{pmatrix} 1 & 0 \\ -1 & 1 \end{pmatrix}\begin{pmatrix} 1 & 1 \\ 0 & 1 \end{pmatrix}.$$

The matrix on the left side of this equation can be called a *transposing matrix*, for, on multiplying by it any other given matrix, we obtain as result the transposition of rows or columns of the latter (depending on whether the transposing matrix stands on the left or on the right side):

$$\begin{pmatrix} 0 & 1 \\ 1 & 0 \end{pmatrix}\begin{pmatrix} a & b \\ c & d \end{pmatrix} = \begin{pmatrix} c & d \\ a & b \end{pmatrix}, \qquad \begin{pmatrix} a & b \\ c & d \end{pmatrix}\begin{pmatrix} 0 & 1 \\ 1 & 0 \end{pmatrix} = \begin{pmatrix} b & a \\ d & c \end{pmatrix}.$$

Generally, by a *transposing matrix* T_{ij} (of an arbitrary order) we mean the matrix obtained from the unit matrix, on transposing the ith row with the jth row or, which turns out to be the same, the ith column with the jth column. If a given matrix A is multiplied by T_{ij} from the left side, then the ith row of the matrix A permutes with its jth row. In other words, the matrix $T_{ij}A$ differs from A by the ith and jth rows which are transposed. A similar effect for columns is obtained by the right-hand multiplication, i.e., the matrices AT_{ij} and A differ from each other by their ith and jth columns which are transposed.

From the above remarks it follows that rows and columns in any given matrix A can be arbitrarily rearranged by multiplying the matrix by properly chosen transposing matrices. In particular, we can secure such an arrangement that each partial matrix which stands in the upper left corner of A is invertible, whenever its degree is less than or equal to the rank of A. A matrix with this property will be called an *ordered matrix*.

Each transposing matrix decomposes into four simple matrices, as in the above given example of a matrix of degree 2. Generally, the decomposition can be performed as follows:

$$\begin{pmatrix} 1 & & & \\ & 0 \cdots 1 & \\ & \vdots \ddots \vdots & \\ & 1 \cdots 0 & \\ & & & 1 \end{pmatrix} = \begin{pmatrix} 1 & & & \\ & 1 \cdots 0 & \\ & \vdots \ddots \vdots & \\ & 0 - 1 & \\ & & & 1 \end{pmatrix}\begin{pmatrix} 1 & & & \\ & 1 \cdots 1 & \\ & \vdots \ddots \vdots & \\ & 0 \cdots 1 & \\ & & & 1 \end{pmatrix}\begin{pmatrix} 1 & & & \\ & 1 \cdots 0 & \\ & \vdots \ddots \vdots & \\ & -1 \cdots 1 & \\ & & & 1 \end{pmatrix}\begin{pmatrix} 1 & & & \\ & 1 \cdots 1 & \\ & \vdots \ddots \vdots & \\ & 0 \cdots 1 & \\ & & & 1 \end{pmatrix}.$$

Obviously, the above picture is no proof, but it is suggestive enough (for readers acquainted with multiplication of matrices) so that a formal proof can be spared.

Proof of Theorem 5.1. From the above remarks it follows that we may assume at once that the given matrix

$$A = \begin{pmatrix} \alpha_{11}, & \ldots, & \alpha_{1q} \\ \cdots\cdots\cdots\cdots \\ \alpha_{q1}, & \ldots, & \alpha_{qq} \end{pmatrix}$$

is ordered. Suppose that its degree is q, its rank is m and that $1 \leq m \leq q$. (The case $m = 0$ will be discussed separately.) We shall show that then there exists a decomposition

$$A = A_q \cdots A_1,$$

where A_i is a simple matrix with a properly chosen ith row. As A_1 we take the matrix obtained from the unit matrix I on replacing the first row by the first row of the matrix A. Arguing by induction, we suppose that the matrix

$$B_k = A_k \cdots A_1 \qquad (1 \leq k < q)$$

is formally obtained from I on replacing the k initial rows by the corresponding rows of A. This supposition is fulfilled for $k = 1$, in view of the definition of A_1. In the inductive step we want to show that it is possible to choose a simple matrix A_{k+1} such that B_{k+1} is formally obtained from I, on replacing the $k + 1$ initial rows by the corresponding rows of A. It will then follow by induction that the simple matrices $A_1, \ldots, A_q$ can be chosen so that B_n is formally obtained from I on replacing all the rows by the corresponding rows of A, i.e., we have $B_q = A$. It remains to discuss the inductive step.

Let A_{k+1} be the matrix which is obtained from I on replacing the $(k+1)$th row by elements $\xi_1, \ldots, \xi_q$ which will be established in a while. The matrix $A_{k+1}B_k$ then differs from B_k by the $(k+1)$th row only. We write down the elements of this row one below another and make them equal to the corresponding elements of the $(k+1)$th row of A:

$$\begin{aligned}
\alpha_{11}\xi_1 + \cdots + \alpha_{k1}\xi_k &= \alpha_{k+1,1} \\
\cdots\cdots\cdots\cdots\cdots\cdots\cdots\cdots\cdots \\
\alpha_{1k}\xi_1 + \cdots + \alpha_{kk}\xi_k &= \alpha_{k+1,k} \\
\alpha_{1,k+1}\xi_1 + \cdots + \alpha_{k,k+1}\xi_k + \xi_{k+1} &= \alpha_{k+1,k+1} \\
\cdots\cdots\cdots\cdots\cdots\cdots\cdots\cdots\cdots \\
\alpha_{1q}\xi_1 + \cdots + \alpha_{kq}\xi_k + \xi_q &= \alpha_{k+1,q}.
\end{aligned}$$

Assume that $k \leq m$. Then the determinant of the above system of equations is different from zero and the unknown elements $\xi_1, \ldots, \xi_q$ are determined uniquely. Assume now that $k \geq m$. From the hypothesis that m is the rank of A it then follows that the vector consisting of elements on the right-hand side of the system of equations is linearly dependent on the vectors whose coordinates are the coefficients at $\xi_1, \ldots, \xi_k$, respectively. This means that the elements $\xi_1, \ldots, \xi_k$ can be chosen so as to fulfil the equations (with $\xi_{k+1} = \cdots = \xi_q = 0$). Thus, the system is solvable in both cases, which proves the assertion.

We still have to discuss the case when $m = 0$, i.e., the rank of A is 0. Then all the elements in A are 0 and A is equal to the product of matrices $A_q \cdots A_1$ such that A_i is obtained from the unit matrix I on replacing the ith row by nothing but zeros. This remark completes the proof.

6. Measure of a linearly transformed set

We are now going to generalize formula (3.1) to arbitrary linear transformations $y = Ax$ in $\mathbf{R}^q$. By det A we shall mean the determinant of the matrix A. In particular, for the matrix A_i considered in section 3 we have det $A_i = \alpha_{ii}$.

Theorem 6.1. *If A is any matrix (of order q) and X is a Lebesgue integrable subset of $\mathbf{R}^q$, then*

$$\int AX = |\det A| \int X. \tag{6.1}$$

Proof.   We shall first prove that if (6.1) holds for two matrices A_1 and A_2, then also

$$\int A_1 A_2 X = |\det A_1 A_2| \int X. \tag{6.2}$$

In fact,

$$\int A_1 A_2 X = \int A_1 (A_2 X) = |\det A_1| \int A_2 X = |\det A_1| |\det A_2| \int X.$$

But the product of determinants of two matrices is equal to the determinant of the product of matrices, so that (6.1) holds. By induction it follows that, if (6.1) holds for matrices $A_1, \ldots, A_n$, then

$$\int A_1 \cdots A_n X = |\det A_1 \cdots A_n| \int X.$$

Since (6.1) holds for simple matrices, as we have shown in section 2, and each matrix decomposes into a product of simple matrices, our assertion follows.

A linear transformation $y = Ax$ such that $|\det A| = 1$ is called *unimodular*. The last theorem implies, in particular, that *the Lebesgue measure is invariant under unimodular transformations*. Among unimodular transformations, the most important are rotations. A linear transformation $y = Ax$ is a *rotation*, if the matrix A is orthogonal, i.e., if the inner product of two different rows is 0 and the inner product of the row by itself is 1. Rotation and translation are called Euclidean transformations. Also the composition of a rotation and a translation is a Euclidean transformation.

From Theorems 1.1 and (6.1) we obtain

Corollary. *The Lebesgue measure is invariant under Euclidean transformations.*

In the three-dimensional Euclidean space, this corollary has an intuitive physical interpretation: *a rigid body does not change its volume under rotation and translation.*

7. Anisotropic dilatation

As a further example of a linear transformation we are going to consider dilatation in the direction of a given vector $a \in \mathbf{R}^q$. We assume that $|a| = 1$. If the ratio of the dilatation is λ, then for each vector $x \in \mathbf{R}^q$ the component parallel to a is multiplied by λ. The length of the component of x equals to the scalar product ax, and the component itself is $(ax)a$. The increment of x is thus $(\lambda - 1)(ax)a$ and the whole vector after dilatation is $y = x + (\lambda - 1)(ax)a$.

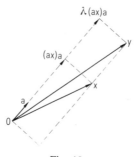

Fig. 12

In order to see that this equation determines a linear transformation, observe that

$$(ax)a = (a \otimes a)x,$$

where $a \otimes a$ is the tensor product of the vector $a = (\alpha_1, \ldots, \alpha_q)$ by itself,

$$a \otimes a = \begin{pmatrix} \alpha_1\alpha_1 & \cdots & \alpha_1\alpha_q \\ \cdots\cdots\cdots\cdots\cdots \\ \alpha_q\alpha_1 & \cdots & \alpha_q\alpha_q \end{pmatrix}.$$

Letting $\lambda - 1 = \mu$ for short, we thus have

$$I + \mu \cdot a \otimes a = \begin{pmatrix} 1 + \mu\alpha_1^2 & \mu\alpha_1\alpha_2 & \cdots & \mu\alpha_1\alpha_q \\ \mu\alpha_2\alpha_1 & 1 + \mu\alpha_2^2 & \cdots & \mu\alpha_2\alpha_q \\ \cdots\cdots\cdots\cdots\cdots\cdots\cdots\cdots\cdots\cdots \\ \mu\alpha_q\alpha_1 & \mu\alpha_q\alpha_2 & \cdots & 1 + \mu\alpha_q^2 \end{pmatrix}.$$

Denoting the last matrix by $D_{\lambda a}$, we can write

$$y = D_{\lambda a} x.$$

It is easy to show that det $D_{\lambda a} = \lambda$. In fact, let M_k denote the minor of order k of $D_{\lambda a}$ standing in the left upper corner. Evidently, det $M_1 = 1 + \mu \alpha_1^2$. Arguing by induction, assume that, for some $k < q$,

$$\det M_k = 1 + \mu \alpha_1^2 + \cdots + \mu \alpha_k^2.$$

We decompose M_{k+1} into the sum of two determinants

$$\det M_{k+1} = \begin{vmatrix} 1 + \mu \alpha_1^2 & \cdots & \mu \alpha_1 \alpha_k & 0 \\ \cdots\cdots\cdots\cdots\cdots\cdots\cdots\cdots \\ \mu \alpha_k \alpha_1 & \cdots & 1 + \mu \alpha_k^2 & 0 \\ \mu \alpha_{k+1} \alpha_1 & \cdots & \mu \alpha_{k+1} \alpha_k & 1 \end{vmatrix}$$

$$+ \begin{vmatrix} 1 + \mu \alpha_1^2 & \cdots & \mu \alpha_1 \alpha_k & \mu \alpha_1 \alpha_{k+1} \\ \cdots\cdots\cdots\cdots\cdots\cdots\cdots\cdots\cdots \\ \mu \alpha_k \alpha_1 & \cdots & 1 + \mu \alpha_k^2 & \mu \alpha_k \alpha_{k+1} \\ \mu \alpha_{k+1} \alpha_1 & \cdots & \mu \alpha_{k+1} \alpha_k & \mu \alpha_{k+1}^2 \end{vmatrix}.$$

From the last column of the second determinant we draw out the factor α_{k+1}. On multiplying then that column by α_i and subtracting from the ith column $(i = 1, \ldots k)$, we get

$$\alpha_{k+1} \begin{vmatrix} 1 & \cdots & 0 & \mu \alpha_1 \\ \cdots\cdots\cdots\cdots\cdots\cdots \\ 0 & \cdots & 1 & \mu \alpha_k \\ 0 & \cdots & 0 & \mu \alpha_{k+1} \end{vmatrix}.$$

Hence

$$\det M_{k+1} = M_k + \mu \alpha_{k+1}^2 = 1 + \mu \alpha_1^2 + \cdots + \mu \alpha_{k+1}^2.$$

By induction we thus have

$$\det D_{\lambda a} = \det M_q = 1 + \mu \alpha_1^2 + \cdots + \mu \alpha_q^2.$$

Since $\alpha_1^2 + \cdots + \alpha_q^2 = |a|^2 = 1$, we get det $D_{\lambda a} = 1 + \mu = \lambda$.
If X is any integrable set and $\int X$ is its measure, then, according to Theorem 6.1, the measure of $D_{\lambda a} X$ is $\lambda \int X$. This result is in agreement with intuition which tells us that the dilatation of a set in one direction by the factor λ implies the multiplication of its measure by λ.

8. Further properties of linear transformations

Evidently, if $A = (\alpha_{ij})$ is an arbitrary matrix of order q, $x \in \mathbf{R}^q$ and $\lambda \in \mathbf{R}^1$, then

$$A(\lambda x) = \lambda (Ax). \tag{8.1}$$

If $x, y \in \mathbf{R}^q$, then

$$A(x + y) = Ax + Ay. \qquad (8.2)$$

These properties justify the name 'linear transformation' and they often are used for definition.

Moreover

$$x_n \to x_0 \quad \text{implies} \quad Ax_n \to Ax_0. \qquad (8.3)$$

This relation means that any *linear transformation A is continuous.* One can equivalently say that, if a set X is closed, then so is its image AX.

If a set X is convex then also AX is convex. In fact, the convexity of X means that $x, y \in X$ implies that $\alpha x + \beta y \in X$ for $\alpha + \beta = 1$, $\alpha, \beta \geqslant 0$. Let Ax and Ay be any two points of AX. Then, by (8.1) and (8.2) we have $\alpha Ax + \beta Ay = A(\alpha x) + A(\beta y) = A(\alpha x + \beta y) \in AX$, which proves that AX is convex.

If a set X is symmetric with respect to the origin, then so is AX. In fact, the symmetry of the set X means that $x \in X$ implies $-x \in X$. Now, if Ax is any point of AX, then by (8.1) we have $-Ax = A(-x) \in X$, which proves that AX is symmetric with respect to 0.

Let $\|A\|$ denote the maximum of the moduli of elements of the matrix A:

$$\|A\| = \max_{ij} |\alpha_{ij}|.$$

From the definition of a determinant it then follows that

$$|\det A| \leqslant q! \, \|A\|^q. \qquad (8.4)$$

If

$$|A| = \left(\sum_{ij} \alpha_{ij}^2 \right)^{1/2},$$

then it is easy to show that

$$\|A\| \leqslant |A| \leqslant q \|A\|. \qquad (8.5)$$

Let $|x|$ generally denote the length of the vector $x = (\xi_1, \ldots, \xi_q) \in \mathbf{R}^q$, i.e., $|x| = \sqrt{\xi_1^2 + \cdots + \xi_q^2}$. Then we have

$$|Ax| \leqslant |A| \cdot |x|. \qquad (8.6)$$

In fact, if the vector a_i denotes the ith row of A, then

$$Ax = \begin{pmatrix} a_1 x \\ \cdot \\ \cdot \\ \cdot \\ a_q x \end{pmatrix},$$

where $a_i x$ denotes the inner product of vectors a_i and x. Since the absolute value of the inner product is always less than or equal to the product of the lengths of vectors, we have $|a_i x| \leqslant |a_i||x|$. Hence we obtain

$$(a_i x)^2 \leqslant a_i^2 x^2,$$

where the squares on the right side denote inner products of vectors by themselves. Consequently,

$$(Ax)^2 = (a_1 x)^2 + \cdots + (a_q x)^2 \leqslant (a_1^2 + \cdots + a_q^2)x^2 = |A|^2|x|^2,$$

which proves (8.6).

Let K_q denote the unit ball in $\mathbf{R}^q$, i.e., the set of points $x \in \mathbf{R}^q$ such that $|x| \leqslant 1$. For short, we shall also write K, if there is no confusion. Then by (8.6) we have

$$|Ax| \leqslant |A| \quad \text{for} \quad x \in K.$$

This inequality tells us that the image AK of the ball K is bounded.

If $\rho > 0$, then by ρK we denote the set points $x \in \mathbf{R}^q$ such that $|x| \leqslant \rho$. Thus, ρK is the q-dimensional ball of radius ρ and the center at the origin. We have

$$\int \rho K = \rho^q \int K, \tag{8.7}$$

because multiplication by ρ can be interpreted as multiplication by the matrix $\begin{pmatrix} \rho \cdot & 0 \\ 0 & \cdot \rho \end{pmatrix}$ which has ρ for the elements of its diagonal and 0 for the remaining elements. The determinant of such a matrix is ρ^q. The notation ρK will be used in the next section.

9. Invertible linear transformations

We first recall a few definitions and properties which are assumed to be known from the elementary course of algebra.

A linear transformation $y = Ax$ is called *invertible*, if the matrix A is *invertible*, i.e., there exists a matrix A^{-1} such that $AA^{-1} = I$. The last equation implies $A^{-1}A = I$ (though, in general, multiplication of matrices is not commutative). The matrix A^{-1} is called *inverse* to A and the transformation $y = A^{-1}x$ is called *inverse* to the transformation $y = Ax$. A matrix A is invertible, if and only if $\det A \neq 0$. We have $\det A^{-1} = (\det A)^{-1}$. An invertible linear operation maps the space $\mathbf{R}^q$ onto the whole space $\mathbf{R}^q$. This condition is also sufficient for a linear operation to be invertible.

Theorem 9.1. *A linear operation $y = Ax$ is invertible, iff there is a number $\rho > 0$ such that $|Ax| \geqslant \rho|x|$ for each $x \in \mathbf{R}^q$.*

Proof. If the linear operation is invertible, then the inverse matrix A^{-1} satisfies

$$|A^{-1}y| \leqslant |A^{-1}||y| \quad \text{for} \quad y \in \mathbf{R}^q,$$

which follows from (8.6) on replacing A by A^{-1} and x by y. For each $x \in \mathbf{R}^q$ there is a y such that $y = Ax$. Letting this in the above inequality, we get

$$|x| \leqslant |A^{-1}||Ax|.$$

Since $\det A^{-1} \neq 0$, we also have $|A^{-1}| \neq 0$ and the wished inequality follows with $\rho = |A^{-1}|^{-1}$.

Assume now, conversely, that $|Ax| \geqslant \rho|x|$ holds for some $\rho > 0$ and all $x \in \mathbf{R}^q$. Then the set AK contains the ball ρK and we have $|\det A| \int K = \int AK \geqslant \int \rho K = \rho^q \int K > 0$ (We evidently have $\int K > 0$, because the ball K contains the interval $-q^{-1/2} \leqslant \xi_i < q^{-1/2}$ $(i = 1, \ldots, q)$). Hence we get $\det A \neq 0$ and the invertibility of the transformation follows.

Given an invertible operation $y = Ax$, let ρ_A denote the greatest of numbers ρ such that $|Ax| \geqslant \rho|x|$ for each $x \in \mathbf{R}^q$. The number ρ_A is thus the radius of the ball $\rho_A K$ inscribed in AK. Hence $|\det A| \int K = \int AK \geqslant \int \rho_A K = \rho_A^q \int K$ and consequently $|\det A| \geqslant \rho_A^q$. Similarly, if σ_A is the radius of the ball $\sigma_A K$ described on AK, we find $|\det A| \leqslant \sigma_A^q$. Thus, $\rho_A^q \leqslant |\det A| \leqslant \sigma_A^q$. However, by a more subtle argument, sharper inequalities can be obtained. We namely have

Theorem 9.2. $\rho_A^{q-1} \sigma_A \leqslant |\det A| \leqslant \rho_A \sigma_A^{q-1}$.

Proof (sketch). The image AK of A is a q-dimensional ellipsoid whose greatest axis has the length $2\rho_A$ and the smallest $2\sigma_A$. Both axes are orthogonal. The ellipsoid AK has, in the whole, q orthogonal axes; their lengths will be denoted by $2\lambda_1, \ldots, 2\lambda_q$. The ellipsoid with such axes can be obtained from the ball K by an anisotropic dilatation by factors $\lambda_1, \ldots, \lambda_q$ in the directions indicated by the axes. Hence $\int AK = \lambda_1 \cdots \lambda_q \int K$. On the other side, we have $\int AK = |\det A| \int K$, which implies

$$|\det A| = \lambda_1 \cdots \lambda_q.$$

Since ρ_A is the smallest and σ_A the greatest of numbers $\lambda_1, \ldots, \lambda_q$, the wanted inequalities follow.

We shall still prove the inequalities

$$\|A\| \leqslant \sigma_A \leqslant q\|A\|. \tag{9.1}$$

In fact, if $A = (\alpha_{ij})$, then α_{ij} is the ith coordinate of the vector Ae_j, which implies that $|\alpha_{ij}| \leqslant \sigma_A$ and thus $\|A\| \leqslant \sigma_A$. If $x = (\xi_1, \ldots, \xi_q)$, then $Ax = (\alpha_{11}\xi_1 + \cdots + \alpha_{1q}\xi_q, \ldots, \alpha_{q1}\xi_1 + \cdots + \alpha_{qq}\xi_q)$. The length of Ax is

$$|Ax| = \sqrt{(\alpha_{11}\xi_1 + \cdots + \alpha_{1q}\xi_q)^2 + \cdots + (\alpha_{q1}\xi_1 + \cdots + \alpha_{qq}\xi_q)^2}.$$

Since $|\alpha_{ij}| \leqslant \|A\|$, we hence get

$$|Ax| \leqslant \|A\| \sqrt{q(|\xi_1| + \cdots + |\xi_q|)^2} = \sqrt{q} \|A\| (|\xi_1| + \cdots + |\xi_q|).$$

But $|\xi_1| + \cdots + |\xi_q| \leqslant \sqrt{q} |x|$ holds for each point $x \in \mathbf{R}^q$, thus $|Ax| \leqslant q\|A\| |x|$. This implies $\sigma_A \leqslant q\|A\|$.

10. Aureoles

Non-linear transformations are rather difficult and will therefore be approximated by linear transformations. To perform such an approximation a method of *aureoles* and *antiaureoles* will be used.

The set $X_\varepsilon = X + \varepsilon K$, where $\varepsilon > 0$ and K is the unit ball, consists of all sums $x + \varepsilon y$ with $x \in X$, $y \in K$ and will be called the ε-*aureole* of X. We can equivalently say that X consists of all sums $x + r$ such that $x \in X$ and $r \in \varepsilon K$. Since the concept of the unit ball K makes sense in any Banach space E, we need not assume in general that X is a subset of the Euclidean q-space. Also some elementary properties of the aureoles hold in arbitrary Banach spaces. Thus, if nothing is said explicitly, the sets considered below are subsets of any Banach space. By $\bar{X}$ we mean the closure of X, i.e., the set of all limits $\lim_{n \to \infty} x_n$, where $x_n \in X$. Of course $X \subset \bar{X}$. A set X is closed, iff $\bar{X} = X$.

The ε-aureole has the following properties:

(A1) $\bar{X} \subset X_\varepsilon$;
(A2) $X \subset Y$ implies $X_\varepsilon \subset Y_\varepsilon$;
(A3) $(\rho K)_\varepsilon = (\rho + \varepsilon)K$, $(\rho, \ \varepsilon > 0)$.

Properties (A1) and (A2) follow directly from the definition. To prove (A3), observe that $(\rho K)_\varepsilon$ is the set of points $x + r$ such that $|x| \leqslant \rho$ and $|r| \leqslant \varepsilon$. Subsequently, $|x + r| \leqslant \rho + \varepsilon$, which proves that $(\rho K)_\varepsilon \subset (\rho + \varepsilon)K$. If we assume, conversely, that $y \in (\rho + \varepsilon)K$, then $|y| \leqslant \rho + \varepsilon$. Writing $x = \rho y/(\rho + \varepsilon)$ and $r = \varepsilon y/(\rho + \varepsilon)$, we have $y = x + r$ and $|x| \leqslant \rho$, $|r| \leqslant \varepsilon$. Thus, $y \in (\rho K)_\varepsilon$, which proves that $(\rho + \varepsilon)K \subset (\rho K)_\varepsilon$, and completes the proof of (A3).

Properties (A1)–(A3) hold in any Banach space. In contrast, the two next properties will be proved for Euclidean spaces only.

(A4) *If* $X \subset \mathbf{R}^q$, *then* $\bar{X}_\varepsilon = (\bar{X})_\varepsilon$.

Proof. If $x \in (\bar{X})_\varepsilon$, then $x = y + r$, where $y \in \bar{X}$ and $r \in \varepsilon K$. There are points $y_n \in X$ such that $y = \lim y_n$. Since $y_n + r \in X + \varepsilon K = X_\varepsilon$, it follows that $x = \lim (y_n + r) \in \bar{X}_\varepsilon$.

Assume now that $x \in \bar{X}_\varepsilon$. This means that $x = \lim x_n$, $x_n \in X + \varepsilon K$. One may write $x_n = y_n + r_n$, where $y_n \in X$ and $r_n \in \varepsilon K$. Since the ball εK is a bounded set, the assumption $r_n \in \varepsilon K$ implies the existence of an increasing sequence of positive integers p_n such that the limit $r = \lim Ar_{p_n}$ exists (this

step would fail, if K were a ball in a Banach space). From $x = \lim x_n$ it
follows that $x = \lim x_{p_n}$, and hence $\lim y_{p_n} = \lim (x_{p_n} - r_{p_n}) = x - r \in \bar{X}$. Consequently, $x = (x - r) + r \in \bar{X} + \varepsilon K = (\bar{X})_\varepsilon$.

(A5) *In a Euclidean space, an aureole of a closed set is closed.*

Proof. If X is closed, then $\bar{X} = X$ and therefore, by (A4), $\bar{X}_\varepsilon = (\bar{X})_\varepsilon = X_\varepsilon$. This proves that X_ε is closed.

In the following propositions (A6)–(A8) we do not assume that X is a subset of $\mathbf{R}^q$; it can be a subset of any Banach space.
A set X in a Banach space is called *open*, iff for each point $x \in X$ there is a positive number ρ such that $x + \rho K \subset X$, where $x + \rho K$ denotes the set of all points $x + r$ with $r \in \rho K$.

(A6) *An aureole of an open set is open.*

Proof. If $x \in X_\varepsilon$, then $x = y + r$, where $y \in X$, $r \in \varepsilon K$. If X is open, there is a ball $x + \rho K \subset X$. Hence $(x + \rho K) + r \subset X + \varepsilon K$, i.e., $x + \rho K \subset X_\varepsilon$.

(A7) *An aureole of a convex set is convex.*

Proof. Let X be a convex set. If $x_1, x_2 \in X_\varepsilon$, then $x_1 = y_1 + r_1$, $x_2 = y_2 + r_2$, with $y_1, y_2 \in X$, $r_1, r_2 \in \varepsilon K$. Let $\alpha_1, \alpha_2 \geqslant 0$, $\alpha_1 + \alpha_2 = 1$. Since X and εK are convex sets, we have $y = \alpha_1 y_1 + \alpha_2 y_2 \in X$ and $r = \alpha_1 r_1 + \alpha_2 r_2 \in \varepsilon K$.

(A8) *If X is a convex set and τ is a positive number such that $\tau K \subset X$, then*

$$X_\varepsilon \subset \left(1 + \frac{\varepsilon}{\tau}\right) X.$$

Proof. $X_\varepsilon = X + \dfrac{\varepsilon}{\tau} \tau K \subset X + \dfrac{\varepsilon}{\tau} X = \left(1 + \dfrac{\varepsilon}{\tau}\right) X.$

The last equality is due to the following property of convex sets. *If X is convex, then $\lambda X + \mu X = (\lambda + \mu) X$ for any λ, $\mu > 0$.* In fact, if $x \in \lambda X + \mu X$,
then $x = y + z$ with $y \in \lambda X$, $z \in \mu X$. Hence $\dfrac{y}{\lambda} \in X$, $\dfrac{z}{\mu} \in X$ and, because of convexity,

$$\frac{\lambda}{\lambda + \mu} \frac{y}{\lambda} + \frac{\mu}{\lambda + \mu} \frac{z}{\mu} \in X.$$

This implies that $y + z \in (\lambda + \mu) X$ and proves the inclusion $\lambda X + \mu X \subset (\lambda + \mu) X$. If, conversely, $x \in (\lambda + \mu) X$, then $\dfrac{x}{\lambda + \mu} \in X$ and $\dfrac{\lambda x}{\lambda + \mu} \in \lambda X$, $\dfrac{\mu x}{\lambda + \mu} \in \mu X$. Hence $x \in \lambda X + \mu X$ and, consequently, $(\lambda + \mu) X \subset \lambda X + \mu X$

(this inclusion holds also for non-convex sets). From both inclusions, the equality follows.

(A9)   If X is a convex set in $\mathbf{R}^q$, $\tau K \subset X$ $(\tau > 0)$, A is a matrix, $\rho K \subset AK$ $(\rho > 0)$, then $(AX)_\varepsilon \subset \left(1 + \dfrac{\varepsilon}{\tau\rho}\right) AX.$

Proof.

$$(AX)_\varepsilon = AX + \frac{\varepsilon}{\rho} \rho K \subset AX + \frac{\varepsilon}{\rho} AK = A\left(X + \frac{\varepsilon}{\rho} K\right)$$

$$= AX_{\varepsilon/\rho} \subset A\left[\left(1 + \frac{\varepsilon}{\tau\rho}\right) X\right].$$

(The last inclusion follows by (A8).)

11. Antiaureoles

Given a subset X of a Banach space E and a number $\varepsilon > 0$, the set of all $x \in E$ such that $x + \varepsilon K \subset X$ will be denoted by $X_{-\varepsilon}$ and called the ε-antiaureole of X. Thus $X_{-\varepsilon}$ is the largest of sets Y satisfying $Y_\varepsilon \subset X$. In particular, $(X_{-\varepsilon})_\varepsilon \subset X$. The set of all x such that $x + \varepsilon K \subset X_\varepsilon$ can be denoted, consequently, by $(X_\varepsilon)_{-\varepsilon}$. On the other hand, if $x \in X$, then $x + \varepsilon K \subset X_\varepsilon$, according to the definition of an aureole. We thus have $X \subset (X_\varepsilon)_{-\varepsilon}$. Putting the obtained inclusions together, we can write

$$(X_{-\varepsilon})_\varepsilon \subset X \subset (X_\varepsilon)_{-\varepsilon}. \tag{11.1}$$

Example. If X is the set of all points x such that $|x| = \varepsilon > 0$, then $(X_{-\varepsilon})_\varepsilon = \emptyset$ (empty set), and $(X_\varepsilon)_{-\varepsilon}$ is the set of all points x such that $|x| \leq \varepsilon$.

We shall prove that an ε-antiaureole of X can be equivalently defined by the equation

$$X_{-\varepsilon} = E \setminus (E \setminus X)_\varepsilon. \tag{11.2}$$

In fact, if $x \notin X_{-\varepsilon}$, then there is an $r \in \varepsilon K$ such that $x + r \notin X$. Thus, $x + r \in E \setminus X$. Since $-r \in \varepsilon K$, we have $(x + r) - r \in (E \setminus X)_\varepsilon$. Hence $x \in (E \setminus X)_\varepsilon$ and $x \notin E \setminus (E \setminus X)_\varepsilon$. If $x \notin E \setminus (E \setminus X)_\varepsilon$, then $x \in (E \setminus X)_\varepsilon$, i.e., $x = y + r$ with $y \notin X$, $r \in \varepsilon K$. Hence $x - r \notin X$, which implies $x + \varepsilon K \not\subset X$, i.e., $x \notin X_{-\varepsilon}$. This proves the equivalence of both definitions.

By X° we shall denote the *interior* of X. We thus write $x \in X^\circ$, iff there is a number ρ such that $x + \rho K \subset X$. Evidently,

$$X^\circ \subset X.$$

Moreover,

$$\overline{E\backslash X} = E\backslash X^\circ, \qquad (E\backslash X)^\circ = E\backslash \bar{X}. \tag{11.3}$$

In fact, assume that $x \in \overline{E\backslash X}$. Then there are $x_n \in E\backslash X$ such that $x_n \to x$. Thus, $x_n \notin X$ and in each ball $x + \rho K$ there are elements x_n, not belonging to X. This proves that $x \notin X^\circ$, i.e., $x \in E\backslash X^\circ$. Assume now, conversely, that $x \in E\backslash X^\circ$. If $0 < \rho_n \to 0$, then in each ball $x + \rho_n K$ there is a point $x_n \in E\backslash X$, and we have $x_n \to x$. Hence $x \in \overline{E\backslash X}$ and the first of equations (11.3) is proved.

To prove the second of equations (11.3), assume that $x \notin (E\backslash X)^\circ$, i.e., there is a sequence of points $x_n \notin E\backslash X$, converging to x. Since $x_n \in X$, it follows that $x \in \bar{X}$, i.e., $x \notin E\backslash \bar{X}$. If $x \in (E\backslash X)^\circ$, then there is a ball $x + \rho K \subset E\backslash X$. Thus, if $x_n \to x$, then the points x_n are eventually in $E\backslash X$, i.e., $x_n \in X$ for large n. This proves that x cannot be a limit point of a sequence of points belonging to X, i.e., $x \notin \bar{X}$ and finally $x \in E\backslash \bar{X}$. This proves the second of equations (11.3).

Properties of antiaureoles are similar to those of aureoles, but occasionally additional assumptions are necessary. Everywhere we suppose that $\varepsilon > 0$.

(AA1) $X_{-\varepsilon} \subset X^\circ$.

Proof.   By (11.2), (A1) and (11.3) we have

$$X_{-\varepsilon} = E\backslash (E\backslash X)_\varepsilon \subset E\backslash \overline{E\backslash X} = E\backslash (E\backslash X^\circ) = X^\circ.$$

(AA2) $X \subset Y$ implies $X_{-\varepsilon} \subset Y_{-\varepsilon}$.

Proof.   By (A2) we have $(E\backslash Y)_\varepsilon \subset (E\backslash X)_\varepsilon$ and hence, by (11.2),

$$X_{-\varepsilon} = E\backslash (E\backslash X)_\varepsilon \subset E\backslash (E\backslash Y)_\varepsilon = Y_{-\varepsilon}.$$

(AA3) $(\rho K)_{-\varepsilon} = (\rho - \varepsilon)K \quad for \quad \rho > \varepsilon$.

Proof.   Let $Q = (\rho - \varepsilon)K$. Then by (A3) we can write $\rho K = Q_\varepsilon$. Hence $(\rho K)_{-\varepsilon} = (Q_\varepsilon)_{-\varepsilon} \supset Q$, in view of (11.1). On the other hand, if $x \in (\rho K)_{-\varepsilon}$, then we have by definition, $x + \varepsilon K \subset \rho K$. If $x \neq 0$, then we obtain successively $x + \varepsilon \dfrac{x}{|x|} \in \rho K$, $|x| + \varepsilon \leq \rho$, $|x| \leq \rho - \varepsilon$, $x \in Q$. Also, if $x = 0$, then trivially $x \in Q$. Thus, $(\rho K)_{-\varepsilon} \subset Q$, which completes the proof.

(AA4)   If $X \subset \mathbf{R}^q$, then $(X_{-\varepsilon})^\circ = (X^\circ)_{-\varepsilon}$.

Proof.   In the present case we have $E = \mathbf{R}^q$ and, by (11.2) and (11.3), we get

$$(X_{-\varepsilon})^\circ = [\mathbf{R}^q \backslash (\mathbf{R}^q \backslash X)_\varepsilon]^\circ = \mathbf{R}^q \backslash \overline{(\mathbf{R}^q \backslash X)_\varepsilon}.$$

Hence by (A4) and (11.3),

$$(X_{-\varepsilon})^\circ = \mathbf{R}^q \backslash \overline{(\mathbf{R}^q \backslash X)}_\varepsilon = \mathbf{R}^q \backslash (\mathbf{R}^q \backslash X^\circ)_\varepsilon = (X^\circ)_{-\varepsilon}.$$

(AA5)   *In a Euclidean space, the antiaureole of an open set is open.*

Proof.   If X is open, then $X^\circ = X$ and thus, by (AA4),

$$(X_{-\varepsilon})^\circ = (X^\circ)_{-\varepsilon} = X_{-\varepsilon},$$

which proves that $X_{-\varepsilon}$ is open.

In the following properties (AA6)–(AA8), X can be again a subset of any Banach space.

(AA6)   *An antiaureole of a closed set is closed.*

Proof.   If X is closed, then $E \backslash X$ is open, and so is $(E \backslash X)_\varepsilon$, by (A6). Hence $E \backslash (E \backslash X)_\varepsilon = E_{-\varepsilon}$ is closed.

(AA7)   *An antiaureole of a convex set is convex.*

Proof.   Let X be convex. If $x_1, x_2 \in X_{-\varepsilon}$, then $y_1 = x_1 + r \in X$, $y_2 = x_2 + r \in X$ for $r \in \varepsilon K$. If $\alpha_1, \alpha_2 \geqslant 0$, $\alpha_1 + \alpha_2 = 1$, then $\alpha_1 x_1 + \alpha_2 x_2 + r = \alpha_1 y_1 + \alpha_2 y_2 \in X$ for $r \in \varepsilon K$.

In propositions (AA8) and (AA9) which are analogous to (A8) and (A9) a stronger assumption on X will be needed. We shall say that a set X is *balanced* or *symmetric with respect to the origin*, if $x \in X$ implies $-x \in X$.

(AA8)   *If X is balanced and convex, and τ, ε are numbers such that*

$$0 < \varepsilon < \tau, \ \tau K \subset X, \ \text{then} \ \left(1 - \frac{\varepsilon}{\tau}\right) X \subset X_{-\varepsilon}.$$

In the proof we shall use the following

Lemma.   *If a set X is balanced and convex, then*

$$(E \backslash X) + \lambda X \subset E \backslash (1 - \lambda) X \quad \text{for} \quad 0 \leqslant \lambda < 1.$$

Proof of Lemma.   The case $\lambda = 0$ is trivial. We thus assume that $0 < \lambda < 1$. Let $x \in (E \backslash X) + \lambda X$. The $x = y + z$ with $y \notin X$, $z \in \lambda X$. Also $-z \in \lambda X$, because X is balanced. Assume that $x \notin E \backslash (1 - \lambda) X$, i.e., $y + z \in (1 - \lambda) X$. Then $\dfrac{-z}{\lambda} \in X$, $\dfrac{y + z}{1 - \lambda} \in X$. We have $\lambda \dfrac{-z}{\lambda} + (1 - \lambda) \dfrac{y + z}{1 - \lambda} \in X$, because X is convex. Hence $y \in X$. This contradiction proves Lemma.

Proof of (AA8). We have

$$(E\backslash X)_\varepsilon = (E\backslash X) + \varepsilon K \subset (E\backslash X) + \frac{\varepsilon}{\tau} X \subset E\backslash\left(1-\frac{\varepsilon}{\tau}\right)X,$$

by Lemma. Hence

$$X_{-\varepsilon} = E\backslash(E\backslash X)_\varepsilon \supset E\backslash\left(E\backslash\left(1-\frac{\varepsilon}{\tau}\right)X\right) = \left(1-\frac{\varepsilon}{\tau}\right)X.$$

(AA9)   *If X is a balanced and convex set in $\mathbf{R}^q$, A is a matrix, and ρ, ε, τ are numbers such that $0 < \varepsilon < \rho\tau$, $\rho K \subset AK$, $\tau K \subset X$, then*

$$\left(1-\frac{\varepsilon}{\rho\tau}\right)AX \subset (AX)_{-\varepsilon}.$$

Proof.   From $\rho K \subset AK$ it easily follows that $|Ax| \geqslant \rho|x|$ for each $x \in \mathbf{R}^q$. By Theorem 9.1, the matrix A is thus invertible and we have $A\mathbf{R}^q = \mathbf{R}^q$. Hence,

$$(\mathbf{R}^q\backslash AK)_\varepsilon = (\mathbf{R}^q\backslash AK) + \varepsilon K \subset (A\mathbf{R}^q\backslash AX) + \frac{\varepsilon}{\rho} AK$$

$$= A\left[(\mathbf{R}^q\backslash X) + \frac{\varepsilon}{\rho} K\right]$$

$$= A[(\mathbf{R}^q\backslash X)_{\varepsilon/\rho}].$$

Similarly,

$$(AX)_{-\varepsilon} = \mathbf{R}^q\backslash(\mathbf{R}^q\backslash AX)_\varepsilon = A\mathbf{R}^q\backslash A[(\mathbf{R}^q\backslash X)_{\varepsilon/\rho}].$$

$$= A[\mathbf{R}^q\backslash(\mathbf{R}^q\backslash X)_{\varepsilon/\rho}] = A(X_{-\varepsilon/\rho}) \supset \left(1-\frac{\varepsilon}{\rho\tau}\right)AX,$$

by (AA8).

12. Partial derivatives and full derivatives

In all transformations which are of practical use for changing variables in integrals, the type of differentiability plays a striking role. In most text books diffeomorphism is postulated. However, that hypothesis is much too strong and looks strange in the theory of the Lebesgue or the Bochner integral. On the other hand, if we assume only the existence of partial derivatives, various additional conditions are then necessary and make theorems unhandy in applications. Our aim is to provide a theory which is simple, general enough and ready to easy calculations. This end can be achieved on modifying the concept of a partial derivative.

The partial derivative of f with respect to the variable ξ_j is often denoted by $\partial f/\partial \xi_j$. Instead, we shall rather use the notation $f^{(e_j)}$ which is of advantage when writing down the value at a point x_0, viz. $f^{(e_j)}(x_0)$. This avoids the use of the complicated symbol $(\partial f/\partial \xi_j)_{x=x_0}$.

The traditional definition of a partial derivative $f^{(e_j)}$ at a point x_0 is

$$f^{(e_j)}(x_0) = \lim_{\lambda \to 0} \frac{f(x_0 + \lambda e_j) - f(x_0)}{\lambda},$$

where e_j has to be understood as the vector in $\mathbf{R}^q$ whose jth coordinate is 1, and all the remaining ones are 0. In this definition, the values of f only on the straight line passing through x_0 and parallel to the jth coordinate axis are taken into account. So is the partial derivative nothing else but an ordinary derivative of the function restricted to that line. Even if all the partial derivatives are given, we know very little on the behaviour of the function in the neighbourhood of the considered point. For instance, the existence of all the partial derivatives of f does not imply the existence of a differential nor yet the continuity of f.

The awkwardness of the concept of a partial derivative implies that no interesting proposition can be stated on assuming the existence of partial derivatives only, and some additional conditions are always necessary. Such inconveniences can be avoided by introducing the concept of a *full derivative* which is a slight modification of a partial derivative but is more suitable in applications.

The full derivative at x_0 is defined as the double limit

$$f^{(e_j)}(x_0) = \lim_{\substack{\lambda \to 0 \\ x \to x_0}} \frac{f(x + \lambda e_j) - f(x)}{\lambda}.$$

Evidently, if a full derivative exists, then also the corresponding partial derivative exists and both are equal. We therefore may use the same symbol $f^{(e_j)}$ for both. Note that, according to our definition, the existence of a full derivative of f at x_0 implies that f is defined in a full neighbourhood of x_0. This justifies the name 'full derivative'.

It is also useful to compare the definitions of a partial derivative and a full derivative in terms of neighbourhoods. By a neighbourhood of a point x_0 we mean any set containing a ball $x_0 + \rho K$, described round the point x_0. We say that u is the jth partial derivative of f at x_0, and we write $u = f^{(e_j)}(x_0)$, if for each $\varepsilon > 0$ there is a neighbourhood V of x_0 such that

$$\frac{|f(x) - f(x_0) - u e_j(x - x_0)|}{|x - x_0|} < \varepsilon,$$

for all $x \in V$ such that x and x_0 differ, from each other, by the jth coordinate, and only by that coordinate. In other words, the point x belongs to the intersection of V with the straight line passing through x_0 and parallel to the jth coordinate axis. The inner product $e_j(x - x_0)$ is equal to the difference of the jth coordinate of x and x_0.

On the other hand, we say that u is the jth full derivative of f at x_0, if for each $\varepsilon > 0$ there is a neighbourhood of x_0 such that

$$\frac{|f(x)-f(y)-ue_j(x-y)|}{|x-y|} < \varepsilon, \tag{12.1}$$

for $x, y \in V$ such that x and y differ, from each other, by the jth coordinate, and only by that coordinate. In other words, the points x and y belong to the intersection of V with the straight line parallel to the jth coordinate axis.

We see that, in the last definition, the points of the full neighbourhood V play a role, because the straight line which the points x and y lie on is not thought to pass necessarily through x_0. When speaking of a full derivative at a point we always shall tacitly assume that the function itself is defined in some neighbourhood of that point.

13. The one-dimensional case

The definition of a full derivative makes also sense in the case of one real variable. It turns out that also in this particular case the full derivative is not equivalent with the ordinary derivative. The difference arises from the fact that, in the definition of an ordinary derivative, beside x_0 there is only one variable point more under consideration, namely x. In contrast, in the definition of a full derivative two variable points x and y are involved. To show that this difference is essential let us first consider the function $r(x)$ whose diagram is

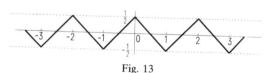

Fig. 13

Analytically, this function can be defined by the formula

$$r(x) = (-1)^k (x - k + \tfrac{1}{2}) \quad \text{for} \quad k - 1 \leqslant x < k, \quad k = 0, \pm 1, \pm 2, \ldots$$

Then the function

$$f(x) = \begin{cases} x^2 r(x^{-2}) & \text{for} \quad x \neq 0, \\ 0 & \text{for} \quad x = 0, \end{cases}$$

possesses at 0 the ordinary derivative equal to 0 and, nevertheless, the full derivative at 0 does not exist. In fact, from (12.1) it follows that

$$\frac{|f(x)-f(y)|}{|x-y|} \leqslant |u| + \varepsilon,$$

and in spite of this, for $x = n^{-(1/2)}$, $y = (n+1)^{-(1/2)}$ the left side of the above inequality is $(n + \tfrac{1}{2})(n^{-(1/2)} + (n+1)^{-(1/2)})$ and therefore is not bounded.

It is not much more difficult to show that, if in the definition of $f(x)$ the expression $x^2 r(x^{-2})$ is replaced by $x^3 r(x^{-2})$, then the full derivative does not exist either. In contrast, if we introduce the expression $x^4 r(x^{-2})$, then the full derivative at 0 will exist and its value will be 0 (as for the ordinary derivative).

14. Basic properties of full derivatives

We now list a few properties, theorems and comments concerning full derivatives. The functions considered here are defined on subsets of the q-dimensional Euclidean space $\mathbf{R}^q$; their values are real numbers or elements of any Banach space.

We say that a full derivative exists on a set $X \subset \mathbf{R}^q$, if it exists at every point of X.

Theorem 14.1. *If a full derivative $f^{(e_j)}$ exists on a set $X \subset \mathbf{R}^q$, then this derivative is continuous on X.*

Proof. If $x_0 \in X$, then for any $\varepsilon > 0$ there exists a ball $x_0 + \rho_0 K$ such that

$$|f(x) - f(y) - f^{(e_j)}(x_0) e_j (x - y)| < \frac{\varepsilon}{2} |x - y| \qquad (14.1)$$

for points $x, y \in x_0 + \rho_0 K$ which differ from each other by their jth coordinates only. Let $V = x_0 + \frac{1}{2}\rho_0 K$. Then for each point $z \in V \cap X$ there is a positive number $\rho \leqslant \frac{1}{2}\rho_0$ such that

$$|f(x) - f(y) - f^{(e_j)}(z) e_j (x - y)| < \frac{\varepsilon}{2} |x - y|$$

for points $x, y \in U = z + \rho K$ which differ from each other by their jth coordinates only. Since $U \subset x_0 + \rho_0 K$, we can take, in particular, z for the value of y and admit that x is any point of U which differs from z by the jth coordinate only. The above inequalities yield

$$|f^{(e_j)}(z)(x - z) - f^{(e_j)}(x_0)(x - z)| < \varepsilon |x - z|,$$

which implies that

$$|f^{(e_j)}(z) - f^{(e_j)}(x_0)| < \varepsilon. \qquad (14.2)$$

We have shown that for any $x_0 \in X$ and any $\varepsilon > 0$ there exists a neighbourhood V of x_0 such that (14.2) holds for each $z \in V \cap X$. This proves that, on the set X the function $f^{(e_j)}$ is continuous at x_0. Since x_0 is an arbitrary point of X, it follows that the function $f^{(e_j)}$ is continuous on the whole set X.

From the fact that a function possesses some full derivative on a set one cannot infer that the function itself is continuous. For instance, let $D(\xi)$

denote the Dirichlet function which equals to 1 at rational points ξ and vanishes for irrational ξ. Then the function $f(x) = D(\xi_q)$ has full derivatives $f^{(e_1)}, \ldots, f^{(e_{q-1})}$ at every point of $\mathbf{R}^q$, but is itself discontinuous everywhere in $\mathbf{R}^q$. The situation however changes, if all full derivatives $f^{(e_1)}, \ldots, f^{(e_q)}$ exist, as we shall see in Theorems 14.2 and 14.3.

We say that a function f satisfies *Lipschitz's condition* with the constant $k > 0$ at a point x_0, if there exists a neighbourhood V of x_0 such that the inequality

$$|f(x) - f(y)| < k|x - y|$$

holds for all points x and y of that neighbourhood.

From this definition it follows that if a function satisfies Lipschitz's condition with a constant k at a point x_0, then it satisfies it with the same constant k at all points of a neighbourhood of x_0 and is therefore continuous in that neighbourhood.

Theorem 14.2. *If all the full derivatives $f^{(e_1)}(x_0), \ldots, f^{(e_q)}(x_0)$ exist and are bounded by a number k, then for each $\varepsilon > 0$ there exists a neighbourhood of x_0 in which f satisfies the Lipschitz condition with the constant $\sqrt{q}\, k + \varepsilon$.*

Proof.   From the assumption that the full derivatives exist it follows that there exists a q-dimensional cube Q with its center at x_0, i.e., a set of points $x = (\xi_1, \ldots, \xi_q)$ satisfying $|\xi_j - \xi_{0j}| \le \rho$ with $x_0 = (\xi_{01}, \ldots, \xi_{0q})$, such that the inequality

$$\frac{|f(x) - f(y) - f^{(e_j)}(x_0)e_j(x - y)|}{|x - y|} < \frac{\varepsilon}{\sqrt{q}}$$

holds for points $x, y \in Q$ which differ by their jth coordinates only. Now, let x and y be quite arbitrary points of Q (which may differ by more than one coordinate). Then there are points $y_0, y_1, \ldots, y_{p-1}, y_p$ $(1 \le p \le q)$ such that $y_0 = x$, $y_p = y$ and the point $y_\varkappa$ differs from $y_{\varkappa - 1}$ by their $j_\varkappa$th coordinates only, and we have $j_\varkappa \ne j_\mu$ for $\varkappa \ne \mu$. From the hypothesis that Q is a cube it follows that all those points belong to Q. One may write

$$\frac{f(x) - f(y)}{|x - y|} = \sum_{\varkappa = 1}^{p} \frac{|y_{\varkappa - 1} - y_\varkappa|}{|x - y|} \frac{f(y_{\varkappa - 1}) - f(y_\varkappa) - f^{(e_{j\varkappa})}(x_0)e_j(y_{\varkappa - 1} - y_\varkappa)}{|y_{\varkappa - 1} - y_\varkappa|}$$

$$+ \sum_{\varkappa = 1}^{p} \frac{y_{\varkappa - 1} - y_\varkappa}{|x - y|} f^{(e_{j\varkappa})}(x_0).$$

By geometric inequality we have

$$\left(\sum_{\varkappa = 1}^{p} |y_{\varkappa - 1} - y_\varkappa| \right)^2 \le p \sum_{\varkappa = 1}^{p} |y_{\varkappa - 1} - y_\varkappa|^2 \le p|x - y|^2$$

and hence

$$\frac{|f(x)-f(y)|}{|x-y|}<\sqrt{p}\left(\frac{\varepsilon}{\sqrt{q}}+k\right)\leq\sqrt{q}k+\varepsilon.$$

From Theorem 14.2 it follows that *if f possesses all full derivatives at some point, then it is continuous at that point.* This implies furthermore that *if f has all its full derivatives on a set X, then it is continuous in an open set $\mathcal{O}$ including X* (but the derivatives need not be continuous in $\mathcal{O}$ and even they may not exist outside X). From these remarks and from Theorem 14.1 we get immediately

Theorem 14.3. *If f possesses all its full derivatives in an open set $X\subset\mathbf{R}^q$, then it is of class C^1 in X, i.e., the function itself and all its derivatives are continuous in X. The converse implication is also true.*

The above theorem shows that, in case of open sets, the concept of full derivatives does not yield anything new. However, a distinct difference arises, if the set X the function f has its full derivatives on is not open. This difference appears already in the case of a single real variable. We shall show it on a suitably constructed example.

Let, as in section 13,

$$r(x)=(-1)^k(x-k+\tfrac{1}{2})\quad\text{for}\quad k-1\leq x<k,\qquad k=0,\pm1,\pm2,\dots$$

Then for the function

$$f(x)=\sum_{n=1}^{\infty}6^{-n}r(2^nx)$$

the full derivative exists a.e. in $(0,\infty)$, viz., everywhere outside the set Y of points x having a finite diadic expansion

$$x=a_p2^p+\cdots+a_s2^s,$$

where p and s $(p>s)$ are integers (positive or negative), and the coefficients a_k are 1 or 0. The set Y is dense on the real axis, there thus exist, in each interval, points at which the full derivative does not exist. We shall show even more, namely, that the full derivative (which exists outside Y) cannot be extended continuously to any point of Y. This means that the points of Y are points of essential discontinuity of that derivative.

Before approaching the proof, let us remark that, if the role of numbers 6 and 2 appearing in the definition of $f(x)$ were changed, we would obtain a function which is derivable at no point (even in the ordinary sense).

Let now z be a point which does not expand in a finite diadic fraction and let ε be a positive number. We fix a positive integer p such that $3^{-p}<\varepsilon$ and then an integer m such that z belongs to the interval V defined by the inequalities $(m-1)2^{-p}<x<m\cdot2^{-p}$. Let

$$r'(x)=(-1)^k \quad \text{for} \quad k-1<x<k, \qquad k=0, \pm1, \pm2,\ldots$$

and

$$a=\sum_{n=1}^{\infty}3^{-n}r'(2^n z).$$

For $x,y\in V$ $(x\neq y)$ we then have

$$\frac{f(x)-f(y)-a(x-y)}{x-y}=\sum_{n=1}^{p}\left(3^{-n}\frac{r(2^n x)-r(2^n y)}{2^n x-2^n y}-3^{-n}r'(2^n z)\right)$$

$$+\sum_{n=p+1}^{\infty}3^{-n}\frac{r(2^n x)-r(2^n y)}{2^n x-2^n y}-\sum_{n=p+1}^{\infty}3^{-n}r'(2^n z).$$

But, in the first sum on the right side of the inequality, all summands are 0 and, in the second and the third sum, the terms are less than 3^{-n}. Hence

$$\frac{|f(x)-f(y)-a(x-y)|}{|x-y|}\leqslant 0+\tfrac{1}{2}3^{-p}+\tfrac{1}{2}3^{-p}<\varepsilon,$$

which proves that a is the full derivative of f at z.

Assume now that z has a finite diadic expansion. Then there exists an odd number m such that $z=m\cdot2^{-p}$. If $z<y<x<(m+1)2^{-p}$, then

$$\frac{f(x)-f(y)}{x-y}=S_{p-1}+3^{-p}(-1)^{(m+1)/2}+\sum_{n=p+1}^{\infty}3^{-n}\frac{r(2^n x)-r(2^n y)}{2^n x-2^n y},$$

where

$$S_{p-1}=\sum_{n=1}^{p-1}3^{-n}\frac{r(2^n x)-r(2^n y)}{2^n x-2^n y}=\sum_{n=1}^{p-1}3^{-n}r'(2^n z).$$

If $\tfrac{1}{2}(m+1)$ is odd, then

$$\frac{f(x)-f(y)}{x-y}\geqslant S_{p-1}+3^{-p}-\sum_{n=p+1}^{\infty}3^{-n}=S_{p-1}+\tfrac{1}{2}\cdot3^{-p}.$$

Similarly, we find for $(m-1)2^{-p}<y<x<z$,

$$\frac{f(x)-f(y)}{x-y}\leqslant S_{p-1}-\tfrac{1}{2}3^{-p}.$$

This implies that the full derivative does not exist at z. Moreover, it follows that at all points of the interval $((m-1)2^{-p}, z)$ at which the full derivative exists, this derivative is greater than or equal to $S_{p-1}+3^{-p}$, and at points of the interval $(z, (m+1)2^{-p})$ at which it exists is less than or equal to $S_{p-1}-3^{-p}$. This implies that the full derivative cannot be extended onto the point z so as to be continuous in it. A similar result is obtained, when $\tfrac{1}{2}(m+1)$ is an odd number, we only have to modify suitably the inequalities.

We are still going to consider a question which is not really connected with the substitution in integrals, but is interesting in itself. The question is whether the equation

$$(f^{(e_i)})^{(e_j)} = (f^{(e_j)})^{(e_i)}$$

holds for full derivatives. The question can be asked for a single given point, but to have it sensible, the inner derivatives are to be defined in some neighbourhood of that point. With this natural hypothesis, the answer is positive. We namely have

Theorem 14.4. *If the full derivatives* $f_i = f^{(e_i)}$ *and* $f_j = f^{(e_j)}$ *exist in the neighbourhood of a point* x_0 *and, moreover there exist, at* x_0, *the full derivatives* $f_i^{(e_j)}(x_0)$ *and* $f_j^{(e_i)}(x_0)$, *then they are equal.*

Proof. From Theorem 14.1 it follows that there is a neighbourhood U of x_0 in which the functions f_i and f_j are continuous. Let ε be any positive number. From the definition of the full derivative $f_i^{(e_j)}$ it follows that there is a neighbourhood V of x_0, contained in U, such that

$$\frac{|f_i(y) - f_i(z) - f_i^{(e_j)}(x_0)e_j(y-z)|}{|y-z|} < \tfrac{1}{2}\varepsilon \tag{14.3}$$

holds for points y, $z \in V$ which differ only by their jth coordinates. Let

$$A(x, \lambda, \varkappa) = \frac{f(x + e_i\lambda + e_j\varkappa) - f(x + e_i\lambda) - f(x + e_j\varkappa) + f(x)}{\lambda\varkappa}.$$

If the points $x + e_i\lambda + e_j\varkappa$, $x + e_i\lambda$, $x + e_j\varkappa$ and x belong to V, then the continuity of f_i implies that

$$A(x, \lambda, \varkappa) = \frac{f_i(x + e_i\theta\lambda + e_j\varkappa) - f_i(x + e_i\theta\lambda)}{\varkappa},$$

where $0 < \theta < 1$. Since the arguments of the function f_i in the numerator belong to V and differ only by their jth coordinates, it follows from (14.3) that

$$|A(x, \lambda, \varkappa) - f_i^{(e_j)}(x_0)| < \tfrac{1}{2}\varepsilon.$$

Similarly, changing the role of i and j we find

$$|A(x, \lambda, \varkappa) - f_j^{(e_i)}(x_0)| < \tfrac{1}{2}\varepsilon.$$

The two last inequalities imply

$$|f_i^{(e_j)}(x_0) - f_j^{(e_i)}(x_0)| < \varepsilon.$$

Since ε can be taken arbitrarily small, it follows that

$$f_i^{(e_j)}(x_0) = f_j^{(e_i)}(x_0).$$

The last theorem shows the elegancy and simplicity of the theory of full derivatives in comparison with the traditional partial derivatives (which are not commutative). This simplicity is still more remarkable, when considering the concept of a differential.

15. Differential

If

$$f^{(e_1)}(x_0) = a_1, \ldots, f^{(e_q)}(x_0) = a_q,$$

then the linear function of variables $\varkappa_1, \ldots, \varkappa_q$,

$$a_1\varkappa_1 + \cdots + a_q\varkappa_q, \tag{15.1}$$

will be called the *differential*. (Note that, traditionally, the function (15.1) is called the differential only when an additional condition, due to Stolz, is satisfied. See Remark at the end of this section.)
On introducing the vectorial notation $A = (a_1, \ldots, a_q)$, $h = (\varkappa_1, \ldots, \varkappa_q)$, the differential (15.1) can be shortly noted as the inner product Ah. Since h is an independent variable, the differential is entirely determined by the vector A, it thus mathematically turns out on the same to call the vector A itself a differential.

Theorem 15.1. *A function f has all its full derivatives at x_0, iff there is a vector $A = (a_1, \ldots, a_q)$ such that for any $\varepsilon > 0$ there is a neighbourhood V of x_0 in which*

$$\frac{|f(x) - f(y) - A(x - y)|}{|x - y|} < \varepsilon \tag{15.2}$$

holds for all pairs $x, y \in V (x \neq y)$. Then we have $f^{(e_j)}(x_0) = a_j$ $(j = 1, \ldots, q)$.

(Note that, in (15.2), $A(x - y)$ is the inner product of A and $x - y$.)

Proof. If x and y differ only by their jth coordinates, the equation (15.2) reduces to (12.1) with $u = a_j$. This implies that a_j is the full derivative. Conversely, if $a_1, \ldots, a_q$ are full derivatives, then there exists a q-dimensional cube Q with its center at x_0 such that

$$\frac{|f(x) - f(y) - a_j e_j(x - y)|}{|x - y|} < \frac{\varepsilon}{q}$$

for points $x, y \in Q$ which differ only by their jth coordinates.
Now, let x and y be two arbitrary different points in Q (which may differ by several coordinates). Then there exist points $y_0, y_1, \ldots, y_{p-1}, y_p$ $(1 \leq p \leq q)$ such that $y_0 = x$, $y_p = y$ and the point $y_\varkappa$ differs from $y_{\varkappa-1}$ only by its $j_\varkappa$-th coordinate $(j_\varkappa \neq j_\mu$ for $\varkappa \neq \mu)$. From the hypothesis that Q is a

cube it follows that all these points belong to Q. This implies that

$$I_\varkappa = \frac{|f(y_{\varkappa-1}) - f(y_\varkappa) - a_{j_\varkappa} e_{j_\varkappa}(y_{\varkappa-1} - y_\varkappa)|}{|y_{\varkappa-1} - y_\varkappa|} < \frac{\varepsilon}{q} \quad \text{for} \quad \varkappa = 1, \ldots p,$$

and furthermore

$$\frac{|f(x) - f(y) - A(x - y)|}{|x - y|} \leqslant I_1 + \cdots + I_p < \frac{p}{q} \varepsilon \leqslant \varepsilon,$$

because $|y_{\varkappa-1} - y_\varkappa| \leqslant |x - y|$.

In case $q = 1$ the vector A in Theorem 15.1 reduces to the single coordinate a_1 which equals to the derivative $f^{(e_1)}(x_0)$. In this case the derivative can be simply denoted by $f'(x_0)$ so that $A = f'(x_0)$. This notation can be transferred to any number of dimensions; then $f'(x_0)$ is the vector whose coordinates are $f^{(e_1)}(x_0), \ldots, f^{(e_q)}(x_0)$. Instead of saying that a function f has all its full derivatives, one can say that f if fully derivable or fully differentiable, and $f'(x_0)$ is its full differential.

Remark. The traditional condition for a differential is due to Stolz and can be written in the form

$$\frac{|f(x) - f(x_0) - A(x - x_0)|}{|x - x_0|} < \varepsilon. \tag{15.3}$$

It is evident that, if (15.2) holds for all $x, y \in V$, then (15.3) holds for $x \in V$. Our condition (15.2) is thus stronger than (15.3). In other words, the existence of all full derivatives implies that Stolz's condition is satisfied. In contrast, assuming that Stolz's condition holds, we cannot assert that the full derivatives exist.

16. Invertibility of a fully differentiable function

If the values of f are in a Banach space E, then also the coordinates of the vector $A = f'(x_0)$ are in E. The Euclidean space $\mathbf{R}^q$ is a particular Banach space. In this section we shall consider functions f whose arguments and values are in $\mathbf{R}^q$. Then the function $f(x)$ can be interpreted as a system of q functions of q variables

$$\varphi_1(\xi_1, \ldots, \xi_q), \ldots, \varphi_q(\xi_1, \ldots, \xi_q),$$

where $f = (\varphi_1, \ldots, \varphi_q)$ and $x = (\xi_1, \ldots, \xi_q)$. The differential $f'(x_0)$ is then a vector

$$f'(x_0) = \left(f^{(e_1)}(x_0), \ldots, f^{(e_q)}(x_0)\right)$$

whose each coordinate $f^{(e_j)}(x_0)$ is another vector

$$f^{(e_j)}(x_0) = \left(\varphi_1^{(e_j)}(x_0), \ldots, \varphi_q^{(e_j)}(x_0)\right).$$

In that case the differential can be interpreted as the square matrix

$$f'(x_0) = \begin{pmatrix} \varphi_1^{(e_1)}(x_0), & \ldots, & \varphi_1^{(e_q)}(x_0) \\ \cdots\cdots\cdots\cdots\cdots\cdots\cdots \\ \varphi_q^{(e_1)}(x_0), & \ldots, & \varphi_q^{(e_q)}(x_0) \end{pmatrix}.$$

The invertibility of the matrix $f'(x_0)$ is linked with the invertibility of the function f in the neighbourhood of x_0. We namely have

Theorem 16.1. *If a function f is fully derivable at x_0 and the matrix $f'(x_0)$ is invertible, then the function f is invertible in a neighbourhood of x_0. The inverse function g is fully derivable at the point $y_0 = f(x_0)$ and the matrix $g'(y_0)$ is inverse to $f'(x_0)$.*

The proof of this theorem will be preceded by a few comments. Full derivability in a point is a strong property and implies, in particular, that the considered function is defined in a neighbourhood and is there continuous (this follows directly from Theorem 14.2). The function f in Theorem 16.1 is thus continuous in a neighbourhood of x_0, and the function g is continuous in a neighbourhood of y_0. The most delicate point in the following proof is to show that the function g is defined in a neighbourhood of y_0. Only when having this ensured, we may approach the proof of full derivability of g.

Proof of Theorem 16.1. The invertibility of the matrix $A = f'(x_0)$ implies, by Theorem 9.1, that there is a number $m > 0$ such that $|Ax| \geqslant m|x|$ holds for all $x \in \mathbf{R}^q$. Let W be a neighbourhood of x_0 in which f is continuous. Then Theorem 15.1 implies that, for any $\varepsilon > 0$, there exists a closed ball $U_\varepsilon = x_0 + \rho_\varepsilon K$ contained in W such that

$$\frac{|f(x)-f(y)-A(x-y)|}{|x-y|} \leqslant \varepsilon \quad \text{for} \quad x, y \in U_\varepsilon, \qquad x \neq y.$$

The property of the number m implies that

$$|f(x)-f(y)-A(x-y)| \leqslant \frac{\varepsilon}{m}|A(x-y)| \quad \text{for} \quad x, y \in U_\varepsilon \qquad (16.1)$$

and

$$|f(x)-f(y)| \geqslant \left(1-\frac{\varepsilon}{m}\right)|A(x-y)| \geqslant (m-\varepsilon)|x-y| \quad \text{for} \quad x, y \in U_\varepsilon. \quad (16.2)$$

If $\varepsilon < m$, then the last inequality implies that f admits different values at different points, i.e., is invertible.

We shall show that, for each fixed $\varepsilon < \frac{1}{2}m$ the image $f(U_\varepsilon^0)$ of the interior of the ball U_ε is an open set. In fact, let $a \in U_\varepsilon^0$ and let $S = a + rK$ be a closed ball contained in U_ε^0. We shall show that the image $f(S)$ contains the ball $f(a) + pK$ with $p = \frac{1}{2}(m - \varepsilon)r$. To this end we fix a point b such that $|b - f(a)| < p$ and define

$$F(x) = |b - f(x)| \quad \text{for} \quad x \in S.$$

If $|x - a| = r$, then from (16.2) we get

$$2p \leqslant |f(x) - f(a)| \leqslant F(x) + F(a) < F(x) + p.$$

Hence

$$F(a) < p < F(x) \quad \text{for} \quad |x - a| \leqslant r. \tag{16.3}$$

Since the function f is continuous on the closed ball S, there is a point $c \in S$ such that $F(c) \leqslant F(x)$ for all $x \in S$. In view of (16.3), the point c belongs to the interior S^0 of S, because the equation $|x - a| = r$ means that x lies on the boundary of that ball.

Let $w = b - f(c)$. Since the matrix A is invertible, there is a point $h \in \mathbf{R}^q$ such that $Ah = w$. We select a number λ, $0 < \lambda < 1$, as small as to have $c + \lambda h \in S$. Then

$$|f(c) - b + A\lambda h| = (1 - \lambda)|w|.$$

But we have, by (16.1)

$$|f(c + \lambda h) - f(c) - A\lambda h| \leqslant \tfrac{1}{2}\lambda|w|.$$

Since $F(c + \lambda h)$ is the length of the sum of vectors which appear on the left sides of the two last formulae, we get

$$F(c + \lambda h) \leqslant (1 - \tfrac{1}{2}\lambda)F(c),$$

because $|w| = F(c)$. If we had $F(c) > 0$, it would follow $F(c + \lambda h) < F(c)$, which contradicts the definition of the point c. It thus remains the only possibility that $F(c) = 0$, i.e., $f(c) = b$.

We have proved that for each point $f(a)$ of the image $f(U^0)$ there exists a ball contained in $f(U_\varepsilon^0)$ whose center is at $f(a)$. The image $f(U_\varepsilon^0)$ is thus an open set containing the point $y_0 = f(x_0)$. Consequently, $f(U_\varepsilon)$ is a neighbourhood of y_0. Let us write

$$R(x, y) = \frac{f(x) - f(y) - A(x - y)}{|x - y|}. \tag{16.4}$$

Then $|R(x, y)| \leqslant \varepsilon$ for $x, y \in U_\varepsilon$, $x \neq y$, i.e., for $f(x), f(y) \in F(U_\varepsilon)$, $f(x) \neq f(y)$, in view of one-to-one mapping of U_ε onto $f(U_\varepsilon)$. Substituting $x = g(\bar{x})$, $y = g(\bar{y})$, we get

$$|R(g(\bar{x}), g(\bar{y}))| \leqslant \varepsilon \quad \text{for} \quad \bar{x}, \bar{y} \in f(U_\varepsilon), \qquad \bar{x} \neq \bar{y}.$$

If B denotes the matrix inverse to A, then (16.4) implies

$$BR(g(\bar{x}), g(\bar{y})) = \frac{B(\bar{x} - \bar{y}) - (g(\bar{x}) - g(\bar{y}))}{|g(\bar{x}) - g(\bar{y})|}.$$

Moreover, letting $0 < \varepsilon < \frac{1}{2}m$, we obtain from (16.2),

$$\frac{|g(\bar{x}) - g(\bar{y})|}{|\bar{x} - \bar{y}|} \leq \frac{2}{m}.$$

By the general formula (8.6), there is a number M such that $|Bx| \leq M|x|$ for $x \in \mathbf{R}^q$. Hence the last inequality implies that the expression

$$\frac{|g(\bar{x}) - g(\bar{y}) - B(\bar{x} - \bar{y})|}{|\bar{x} - \bar{y}|} \tag{16.5}$$

is not greater than

$$\frac{|g(\bar{x}) - g(\bar{y})|}{|\bar{x} - \bar{y}|} M |R(g(\bar{x}), g(\bar{y}))| \leq 2 \frac{M}{m} \varepsilon,$$

for $\bar{x}, \bar{y} \in f(U_\varepsilon)$, $\bar{x} \neq \bar{y}$.

We have proved that, for any ε satisfying $0 < \varepsilon < \frac{1}{2}m$, there exists a neighbourhood V of y_0 such that the expression (16.5) is not greater than $2(M/m)\varepsilon$ for $\bar{x}, \bar{y} \in V$, $\bar{x} \neq \bar{y}$. This easily implies that, for any $\bar{\varepsilon} > 0$ there exists a neighbourhood V of y_0 such that the expression (16.5) is not greater than $\bar{\varepsilon}$ for $\bar{x}, \bar{y} \in V$, $\bar{x} \neq \bar{y}$. This proves, in view of Theorem 15.1 that g has all its full derivatives at y_0. This completes the proof of Theorem 16.1.

17. The Vitali covering theorem

The theorem we are going to speak about is usually applied in the problem of differentiability, while we shall apply it, in this chapter, to obtain the integral substitution formula. The theorem in question was discovered and proved by G. Vitali in 1907 for the one-dimensional space $\mathbf{R}^1$ only. A generalization for arbitrary Euclidean spaces was given by H. Lebesgue in 1910. A simple and elegant proof was given by S. Banach in 1924. His proof is reproduced, without any substantial alteration, in most text books. However, when modifying it slightly, we are in a position, at the same amount of effort, to obtain a more general form of the theorem, as we shall show it in the sequel.

Let $Z \subset \mathbf{R}^q$ be a given set. We shall say that a *family* $\mathfrak{F}$ of closed sets X *covers* Z *in the Vitali sense*, if there is a fixed number $\mu \geq 1$ such that the following property holds: For each $x \in Z$ and each $\delta > 0$, there is a set $X \in \mathfrak{F}$ containing x, which is as small as to be included in a ball S_X of radius $\rho(S_X) < \delta$ such that $\mu \int X \geq \int S_X$.

Example 1. The family $\mathfrak{F}$ consists of balls X such that, for each $x \in Z$ and each $\delta > 0$ there is a ball $X \in \mathfrak{F}$ of radius $\rho(X) < \delta$ which contains x (in this case we have $S_X = X$).

Example 2. The family $\mathfrak{F}$ consists of q-dimensional cubes (i.e., q-dimensional intervals with equal lengths of edges) such that, for each $x \in Z$ and each $\delta > 0$ there is a cube of diametre 2δ, containing x.

Theorem 17 (Vitali). *If $\mathfrak{F}$ covers Z in the Vitali sense, then there exists a finite or infinite sequence of disjoint sets $X_n \in \mathfrak{F}$ that covers almost all points of Z.*

In the above theorem, the shape of closed sets is irrelevant, whereas in most text books, the sets X are assumed to be q-dimensional cubes. However, the same proof works in the general case, one only has to replace cubes by sets X or balls in a suitable way. Theorem 17 is susceptible of a further generalization, viz., it suffices to assume that the number μ appearing above may depend on the point x. This extent of generality is due already to Lebesgue (see SAKS [25], p. 111). If one restricts oneself to cubes, then one need not assume that they are closed, because open cubes differ from their closures by null sets only. The same remark applies to balls.

Proof of Theorem 17. We first suppose that the set Z is bounded, i.e., is contained in a bounded open interval J. We then may assume that all the sets $X \in \mathfrak{F}$ are contained in J; otherwise we could discard from $\mathfrak{F}$ all the sets which extend beyond J.

We construct the required sequence X_n in the following way. For X_1, we take an arbitrary set from $\mathfrak{F}$. The sets $X_2, X_3, \ldots$ will be determined successively by induction.

Let r_n be the least upper bound of $\rho(S_X)$ for all X such that S_X is disjoint from $X_1, \ldots, X_n$. We choose for X_{n+1} any set from $\mathfrak{F}$ such that

$$\rho(S_{X_{n+1}}) > \tfrac{1}{2} r_n. \tag{17.1}$$

Such a set X_{n+1} must exist, unless the sets $X_1, \ldots, X_n$ already cover the whole set Z, in which they constitute the sequence which was to be established. We may therefore suppose that induction can be continued indefinitely.

We are going to prove that the sequence $X_1, X_2, \ldots$ covers almost every point of Z.

Since we know that the sets $X_1, X_2, \ldots$ are disjoint and contained in J, we have $\int X_1 + \int X_2 + \cdots \leq \int J < \infty$. Since $\mu \int X_n \geq \int S_{X_n}$, it follows that

$$\int S_{X_1} + \int S_{X_2} + \cdots < \infty. \tag{17.2}$$

This implies that $\int S_{X_n} \to 0$ and therefore $\rho(S_{X_n}) \to 0$. Hence, by (17.1), we obtain

$$r_n \to 0. \tag{17.3}$$

Let T_n denote the ball concentric with S_{X_n} but of radius 5 times so large. Then $\int T_n = 5^q \int S_{X_n}$ and, by (17.2),

$$\int T_1 + \int T_2 + \cdots < \infty.$$

Let $V_n = T_{n+1} \cup T_{n+2} \cup \cdots$. Then the last inequality implies $\int V_n \to 0$. Thus if the set Y consisting of all points of Z which do not belong to any of sets $X_1, X_2, \ldots$ were contained in V_n for every n, it would be a null set. Thus, if we assume (in order to obtain a contradiction) that Y is not a null set, then there must exist a point $x \in Y$ which, for some N, does not belong to V_N. Since x does not belong to any of closed sets $X_1, \ldots, X_N$, it is in a set $X \in \mathfrak{F}$ such that S_X has no points in common with $X_1, \ldots, X_N$. This implies that $\rho(S_X) < r_N$. If the ball S_X also did not have points in common with X_{N+1}, we would also have $\rho(S_X) < r_{N+1}$. If it did not have points in common with any of sets $X_1, X_2, \ldots$, then we should have $\rho(S_X) < r_n$ for every n. But this is impossible, in view of (17.3).

Let P be the greatest of indices n such that S_X has no points in common with $X_1, \ldots, X_n$. Then $P \geqslant N$ and

$$\rho(S_X) < r_P, \tag{17.4}$$

by the definition of numbers r_n. Moreover, S_X has a point y in common with X_{P+1}.

Since $x \notin V_N$ and $T_{P+1} \subset V_N$, therefore x does not belong to T_{P+1} either. Thus, if c is the center of T_{P+1}, we must have

$$|x - c| > 5\rho(S_{X_{P+1}}).$$

On the other hand, since c is also the center of $S_{X_{P+1}}$, we have

$$|y - c| \leqslant \rho(S_{X_{P+1}}).$$

From both inequalities we obtain, by (17.1),

$$|x - y| > 4\rho(S_{X_{P+1}}) > 2r_P.$$

Since the points x and y belong to S_X, we have

$$\rho(S_X) \geqslant \tfrac{1}{2}|x - y|$$

and hence

$$\rho(S_X) > r_P.$$

But this is in a contradiction with (17.4). This contradiction proves that Y must be a null set and the proof is complete, under the additional hypothesis that Z is contained in a bounded interval J.

If Z is not bounded, denote by J_m the open interval $m < x < m + 1$, where $m \in \mathbf{R}^q$ and the coordinates of $m + 1 \in \mathbf{R}^q$ are those of m, but increased by 1. If $\mathbf{B}^q$ denotes the set of all integer points of $\mathbf{R}^q$ (i.e., points whose all coordinates are integers), then the union $\bigcup_{m \in \mathbf{B}^q} J_m$ covers $\mathbf{R}^q$ a.e. Consequently, the union $\bigcup_{m \in \mathbf{B}^q} (J_m \cap Z)$ covers Z a.e. By what we just proved, each of sets $J_m \cap Z$ is covered a.e. by disjoint sets $X \in \mathfrak{F}$ and we may assume, in addition, that all the x selected to cover $J_m \cap Z$ are contained in J_m. This assumption guarantees that the sets X which cover points belonging to different intervals J_m will be disjoint. Then all the sets X selected to cover all the $J_m \cap Z$, $m \in \mathbf{B}^q$, are disjoint and cover the set Z a.e.

18. Jacobian theorem

Let φ be a function which maps a set $X \subset \mathbf{R}^q$ into $\mathbf{R}^q$. Then we can represent φ as a vector

$$\varphi = (\varphi_1, \ldots, \varphi_q).$$

The determinant

$$\det \varphi' = \begin{vmatrix} \varphi_1^{(e_1)} & \cdots & \varphi_1^{(e_q)} \\ \cdots\cdots\cdots\cdots\cdots \\ \varphi_q^{(e_1)} & \cdots & \varphi_q^{(e_q)} \end{vmatrix}$$

is called the *Jacobian* of φ.
We are going to prove, now, the following Jacobian theorem:

Theorem 18. *If φ is fully derivable on a measurable set $X \subset \mathbf{R}^q$, then*

$$(J1) \qquad \int \varphi(X) \leqslant \int_X |\det \varphi'(x)| \, dx.$$

If, moreover, φ is invertible on X, then

$$(J2) \qquad \int \varphi(X) = \int_X |\det \varphi'(x)| \, dx.$$

Although the theorem is simple and, in order to understand it, it suffices to know what full derivability and what Jacobian are, the proof is rather laborious and consists in linearization of the problem.
We introduce the concept of a *slope* of a function. If φ is defined on a set $X \subset \mathbf{R}^q$ and its values are in $\mathbf{R}^q$ (or in any Banach space), then by a *slope* of φ on X we mean

$$s(\varphi, X) = \sup_{x, y \in X} \frac{|\varphi(x) - \varphi(y)|}{|x - y|}.$$

Evidently, the concept of a slope makes sense, if X contains at least 2 points. It is also evident that

$$X \subset Y \quad \text{implies} \quad s(\varphi, X) \leqslant s(\varphi, Y);$$
$$s(\lambda\varphi, X) = |\lambda| s(\varphi, X);$$
$$s(\varphi + \psi, X) \leqslant s(\varphi, X) + s(\psi, X).$$

Lemma 18.1. *If a function φ is fully derivable on a measurable set $X \subset \mathbf{R}^q$, then for each $\varepsilon > 0$ there exists a sequence of closed disjoint q-dimensional cubes (i.e., intervals with equal lengths of edges) $C_1, C_2, \ldots$ such that φ is defined on $Y = \bigcup_{n=1}^{\infty} C_n$, Y covers X a.e.,*

$$\int (Y \backslash X) < \varepsilon \tag{18.1}$$

and there is a function α which is linear on each of cubes C_n and satisfies

$$s(\varphi - \alpha, C_n) \leqslant \varepsilon \qquad (n = 1, 2, \ldots), \tag{18.2}$$
$$|\varphi^{(e_j)} - \alpha^{(e_j)}| \leqslant \varepsilon \quad \text{a.e.} \quad \text{on } X \qquad (j = 1, \ldots, q), \tag{18.3}$$
$$\text{for each } x \in Y \text{ there is a } z \in X \text{ such that } \alpha'(x) = \varphi'(z). \tag{18.4}$$

Moreover, if the values of φ are in $\mathbf{R}^q$ and $\det \varphi'(x) \neq 0$ for $x \in X$, then the cubes C_n can be chosen so that φ is a homeomorphism on each C_n, i.e., φ is continuous and invertible on C_n and the inverse function is continuous on the image $\varphi(C_n)$.

Proof. Let $\varepsilon > 0$ be given. There exists an open set $Q \supset X$ such that

$$\int (Q \backslash X) < \varepsilon, \tag{18.5}$$

by Corollary 6.1, Chapter XI. For each point $z \in X$ there is a neighbourhood V_z of z, contained in Q, such that

$$\frac{|\varphi(x) - \varphi(y) - \varphi'(z)(x - y)|}{|x - y|} < \varepsilon \tag{18.6}$$

for $x, y \in V_z$, and

$$|\varphi^{(e_j)}(x) - \varphi^{(e_j)}(y)| < \varepsilon \qquad (j = 1, \ldots, q) \tag{18.7}$$

for $x, y \in V_z \cap X$. Inequality (18.6) follows from the full derivability of φ, by Theorem 15.1, and (18.7) from the continuity of $\varphi^{(e_j)}$, according to Theorem 14.1. Moreover, if the values of φ are in $\mathbf{R}^q$ and $\varphi'(z) \neq 0$, we can choose the neighbourhood V_z so small, that φ is a homeomorphism on V_z, by Theorem 16.1.

By $\mathfrak{F}$ we denote the family of all closed q-dimensional cubes such that each of the cubes has its centre at a point $z \in X$ and is included in the neighbourhood V_z. By the Vitali covering theorem (Theorem 17), we can select from $\mathfrak{F}$ a sequence $C_1, C_2, \dots$ of disjoint cubes which cover almost every point of X. From (18.5) it follows that (18.1) holds. Let α be a function defined on Y which is linear on each cube C_n and such that

$$\alpha'(x) = \varphi'(z_n) \quad \text{on} \quad C_n, \tag{18.8}$$

where z_n is the centre of C_n. Then (18.6) implies that

$$\frac{|(\varphi(x) - \alpha(x)) - (\varphi(y) - \alpha(y))|}{|x - y|} < \varepsilon \quad \text{for} \quad x, y \in C_n,$$

and hence (18.2) follows. From (18.6) we also obtain

$$\frac{|[\varphi'(x_0) - \varphi'(z)](x - y)|}{|x - y|} < \varepsilon + \frac{|\varphi(x) - \varphi(y) - \varphi'(x_0)(x - y)|}{|x - y|}.$$

If x and y differ only by their jth coordinates, the left side of the above inequality becomes $|\varphi^{(e_j)}(x) - \varphi^{(e_j)}(z)|$. If $x_0 \in X \cap C_n$ and the points x, y move in $X \cap C_n$, tending to x_0, then the right side tends to ε, by Theorem 15.1. This implies that $|\varphi^{(e_j)}(x_0) - \varphi^{(e_j)}(z)| \leq \varepsilon$ for $x_0 \in X \cap C_n$. In view of (18.8), we have $\varphi^{(e_j)}(z) = \alpha^{(e_j)}(x_0)$, we thus can write $|\varphi^{(e_j)}(x_0) - \alpha^{(e_j)}(x_0)| \leq \varepsilon$ for $x_0 \in X \cap C_n$. Since this inequality holds for all n, and the union of the C_n covers X a.e., inequality (18.3) follows. Property (18.4) follows from the equation $Y = \bigcup_n C_n$ and from (18.8).

To complete the proof, it suffices to remark that, if φ is a homeomorphism on each of the V_z, then it is a homeomorphism on each C_n.

Lemma 18.2. *If a function φ whose values are in $\mathbf{R}^q$ satisfies, on an integrable set $X \subset \mathbf{R}^q$, the Lipschitz condition with a constant k, then the image $\varphi(X)$ is also integrable and we have $\int \varphi(X) \leq k^q \int X$.*

Proof. Assume first that X is a closed ball of centre x_0 and radius ρ, thus $X = x_0 + \rho K$. Then, $|\varphi(x) - \varphi(x_0)| \leq k|x - x_0| \leq k\rho$ for $x \in X$. This means that $\varphi(x) \in \varphi(x_0) + k\rho K$, i.e., $\varphi(X) \subset \varphi(x_0) + k\rho K$. Since the function φ is continuous and the set X is closed and bounded, it follows that the image $\varphi(X)$ is also closed and bounded, thus integrable. We therefore may write $\int \varphi(X) \leq \int (k\rho K) = (k\rho)^q \int K = k^q \int (x_0 + \rho K) = k^q \int X$, according to (8.7) and (2.3).

Assume now that X is a set of measure 0. Let ε be a given positive number. There is an open set Q such that $X \subset Q$ and $\int Q < \varepsilon$, by Corollary 6.1, Chapter XI. The set Q is a union $Q = J_1 \cup J_2 \cup \cdots$ of disjoint halfclosed cubes J_n inside Q, by Theorem 6.1, Chapter XI. Each cube J_n is contained in a ball B_n which is contained in the cube J_n^* concentric with J_n, but of the edge $\sqrt{q}$ times as large. Hence

$$\int J_n < \int B_n < (\sqrt{q})^q \int J_n.$$

Since $\varphi(X) \subset \bigcup_n \varphi(B_n)$, we have, by the just obtained result, $\int \varphi(X) \leqslant \sum_n \int \varphi(B_n) \leqslant \sum_n k^q \int B_n \leqslant (k\sqrt{q})^q \sum_n \int J_n = (k\sqrt{q})^q \int Q < (k\sqrt{q})^q \varepsilon$. Since the number ε is arbitrary, it follows that $\int \varphi(X) = 0$ so that the wanted inequality holds.

Let finally X be an arbitrary integrable set and ε any positive number. By Corollary 6.1, there is an open set $Q \supset X$ such that $\int Q < \int X + \varepsilon$. From the Vitali covering theorem it follows that there is a sequence of disjoint balls B_n in Q that covers X except for a set Y of measure 0, at most. We have $X \subset \bigcup_n B_n \cup Y$, and hence, $\varphi(X) \subset \bigcup_n \varphi(B_n) \cup \varphi(Y)$. Consequently, assuming that the set $\varphi(X)$ is integrable, we have

$$\int \varphi(X) \leqslant \sum_n \int \varphi(B_n) + \int \varphi(Y) \leqslant k^q \sum_n \int B_n + 0 \leqslant k^q \int Q < k^q \left(\int X + \varepsilon \right).$$

Since ε is arbitrary, the assertion follows.

It remains to show that integrability of X implies integrability of $\varphi(X)$. In fact, there is an increasing sequence of bounded closed sets Y_n such that $\int Y_n \to \int X$ (see Theorem 6.4, Chapter XI). We thus may write $X = \bigcup_n Y_n \cup Z$, where Z is a null set. Hence $\varphi(X) = \bigcup_n \varphi(Y_n) \cup \varphi(Z)$. But the images $\varphi(Y_n)$ are also bounded and closed, and $\varphi(Z)$ is a null set. This implies that the set $\varphi(X)$ is integrable.

Remark. If $\int X = 0$, then from Lemma 18.2 follows $\int \varphi(X) = 0$. In the sequel, only this particular case will be used so that, in fact, the third part of the last proof is unnecessary. A similar (but a little weaker) lemma is given in [24] (p. 337, Lemma 3).

We now are in a position to prove the inequality in Theorem 18. Assume at first that the set X is bounded and that all the full derivatives of φ are bounded on X by a number k. Let $\varepsilon > 0$ be given. In view of Lemma 18.1, there exists a sequence of closed disjoint cubes $C_1, C_2, \ldots$, covering X a.e., such that φ is defined on $Y = \bigcup_n C_n$ and (18.1) holds. Moreover there is a function α, linear on each C_n, such that (18.2)–(18.4) hold. Since $Y \subset X \cup (Y \setminus X)$, we have $\int Y \leqslant \int X + \varepsilon$. Let $X_0 = X \cap Y$. Evidently, X_0 is measurable. Moreover, $\int (X \setminus X_0) = \int (X \setminus Y) = 0$, because Y covers X a.e. Since all the full derivatives of φ are bounded on X by k, the function φ satisfies the Lipschitz condition on the set X and, consequently, on the set $X \setminus X_0$. But $\int (X \setminus X_0) = 0$, we thus have $\int \varphi(X \setminus X_0) = 0$, by Lemma 18.2. The inclusion $X_0 \subset X$ implies that $X = X_0 \cup (X \setminus X_0)$ and $\varphi(X) = \varphi(X_0) \cup \varphi(X \setminus X_0)$. Now the function φ is continuous on X which implies that the sets $\varphi(X)$ and $\varphi(X_0)$ are measurable and we have

$$\int \varphi(X) = \int \varphi(X_0).$$

From (18.2) it follows that, if C denotes any of cubes C_n and $x, y \in C$, we have

$$|\varphi(x) - \varphi(y) - A(x-y)| \leqslant \varepsilon |x-y|,$$

where A is the matrix such that $\alpha(x) = Ax$ for $x \in C$. Let $z = x - y$, $\psi(z) = \varphi(x) - \varphi(y)$. Then

$$|\psi(z) - Az| \leqslant \varepsilon |z| \leqslant 2\varepsilon\omega,$$

where ω is the radius of the ball described on C. Consequently, $\psi(C-y) \subset [A(C-y)]_{2\varepsilon\omega}$, where y is the centre of C. Hence by property (A9) of the aureoles we get

$$\psi(C-y) \subset \left(1 + \frac{2\varepsilon\omega}{\tau\rho_A}\right) A(C-y),$$

where τ is the radius of the ball inscribed in C, and ρ_A the radius of the ball inscribed in the image AK. But the ratio $\omega/\tau = \gamma$ of the radii of balls described on and inscribed in the same cube does not depend on the size of the cube, so that we can write

$$\psi(C-y) \subset \left(1 + \frac{2\varepsilon\gamma}{\rho_A}\right) A(C-y).$$

But the equality $\psi(x-y) = \varphi(x) - \varphi(y)$ implies that $\psi(C-y) = \varphi(C) - \varphi(y)$, thus

$$\varphi(C) - \varphi(y) \subset \left(1 + \frac{2\varepsilon\gamma}{\rho_A}\right)(AC - Ay).$$

Generally we have $\int (\lambda X) = \lambda^q \int X$ for $\lambda > 0$, we thus obtain from the last inclusion

$$\int \varphi(C) \leqslant \left(1 + \frac{2\varepsilon\gamma}{\rho_A}\right)^q \int AC = \left(1 + \frac{2\varepsilon\gamma}{\rho_A}\right)^q |\det A| \int C,$$

by Theorem 6.1. Hence, in view of Theorem 9.2,

$$\int \varphi(C) \leqslant |\det A| \int C + \beta_\varepsilon \rho_A \sigma_A^{q-1} \int C, \quad \text{where} \quad \beta_\varepsilon = \left(1 + \frac{2\varepsilon\gamma}{\rho_A}\right)^q - 1,$$

and σ_A is the radius of the ball described on AK. Since $Ax = \alpha(x)$ for $x \in C$, we have $\det A = \det \alpha'$ and get by (9.1),

$$\int_C \varphi(C) \leqslant \int_C |\det \alpha'| + \beta_\varepsilon \rho_A (kq)^{q-1} \int C,$$

because the boundedness of all full derivatives by k means that $\|A\| \leqslant k$.

Summing up the last inequality over all $C = C_n$ $(n = 1, 2, \ldots)$, we get

$$\int \varphi(Y) \leqslant \sum_n \int \varphi(C_n) \leqslant \int\limits_Y |\det \alpha'| + \beta_\varepsilon \rho_A (kq)^{q-1} \int Y,$$

because $\bigcup\limits_n \varphi(C_n) = \varphi(Y)$. Since $X \subset Y \cup (X \setminus Y)$, we have $\varphi(X) \subset$ $\varphi(Y) \cup \varphi(X \setminus Y)$. But $\int \varphi(X \setminus Y) = 0$, for φ satisfies the Lipschitz condition on X; thus, $\int \varphi(X) \leqslant \int \varphi(Y)$. Consequently,

$$\int \varphi(X) \leqslant \int\limits_{X_0} |\det \alpha'| + \int\limits_{Y \setminus X_0} |\det \alpha'| + \beta_\varepsilon \rho_A (kq)^{q-1} \int Y. \qquad (18.9)$$

Since all the elements of the matrix $\varphi'(z)$ are, for $z \in X$, bounded by k, it follows by (8.4) that $|\det \alpha'| \leqslant q! k^q$ for $x \in X$ and, consequently, for all $x \in Y$. Therefore

$$\int\limits_{Y \setminus X_0} |\det \alpha'| < \varepsilon q! k^q.$$

Moreover, from (18.3) it follows that

$$|\alpha^{(e_i)}| \leqslant |\varphi^{(e_i)}| + \varepsilon \quad \text{a.e. on } X,$$

and hence

$$|\det \alpha'| \leqslant |\det \varphi'| + \delta(\varepsilon) \quad \text{a.e. on } X, \qquad (18.10)$$

where $\delta(\varepsilon)$ depends on x, but tends uniformly on the set X to 0, because all the derivatives of φ are commonly bounded by k.

We now increase the right side of inequality (18.9) in the following way. We replace, in the first integral, the set X_0 by the greater set X. We replace the second integral by $\varepsilon q! k^q$ and we replace $\int Y$ by $\int X + \varepsilon$. Using then inequality (18.10), we obtain

$$\int \varphi(X) \leqslant \int\limits_X |\det \varphi'| + \int\limits_X |\delta(\varepsilon)| + \varepsilon q! k^q + \beta_\varepsilon \rho_A (qk)^{q-1} \left(\int X + \varepsilon \right).$$

Letting $\varepsilon \to 0$, we get the wanted inequality (J1).

If we release the condition that the set X is bounded and the derivatives are bounded, then we always can write $X = \bigcup\limits_{n=1}^{\infty} X_n$, where the sets X_n are integrable, pairwise disjoint, and such that, for each fixed n, all full derivatives $\varphi^{(e_i)}$ of φ are commonly bounded on X_n. By the preceding argument we have

$$\int \varphi(X_n) \leqslant \int\limits_{X_n} |\det \varphi'(x)| \, dx,$$

and the wished inequality (J1) follows by summation.

Before we approach the proof of the equality in Theorem 18, we shall state two further lemmas.

Lemma 18.3.   *If $P \subset \mathbf{R}^q$ is a convex neighbourhood of 0, and $x_0 \in P$, then $\lambda x_0 \in P^0$ (interior of P) for $0 \leqslant \lambda < 1$.*

Proof.   If $x_0 = 0$ or $\lambda = 0$, then the assertion is trivial. Let us thus assume that $x_0 \neq 0$ and $\lambda \neq 0$. Since $x_0 \in P$ and $0 \in P$, we also have $\lambda x_0 \in P$ by the convexity of P, because one can write $\lambda x_0 + (1 - \lambda)0$.
The hypothesis that P is a neighbourhood of 0 means that there is a ball $\rho K \subset P$ $(\rho > 0)$. It suffices to show that the ball $K_0 = \lambda x_0 + (1 - \lambda)\rho K$ is in P. In fact, for any $x \in K_0$ we can write

$$x = (1 - \lambda)y + \lambda x_0, \tag{18.11}$$

where $y = (x - \lambda x_0)/(1 - \lambda)$. The fact $x \in K_0$ means that $|x - \lambda x_0| \leqslant (1 - \lambda)\rho$. Hence $|y| \leqslant \rho$, i.e., $y \in \rho K \subset P$. Since also $\lambda x_0 \in P$, equation (18.11) implies that $x \in P$, by convexity of P. But x is an arbitrary point of K_0 so that $K_0 \subset P$, proving Lemma 18.3.

Before formulating next lemma we recall what is a homeomorphism. We say that a function φ is a *homeomorphism* on a set $P \subset \mathbf{R}^q$, if it is continuous and invertible on P and the inverse function is continuous on $\varphi(P)$. In this case, if x is an interior point of P, then $\varphi(x)$ is an interior point of $\varphi(P)$. In other words, $x \in P^0$ implies $\varphi(x) \in \varphi(P)^0$. If a point x lies on the boundary of P, then $\varphi(x)$ lies on the boundary of the image $\varphi(P)$.

Lemma 18.4.   *We assume that: 1° P is a balanced, closed and convex subset of $\mathbf{R}^q$ such that $\tau K \subset P$ for some $\tau > 0$, 2° φ is a homeomorphism from P into $\mathbf{R}^q$ such that $\varphi(0) = 0$, 3° A is a matrix such that $\rho K \subset AK$ for some $\rho > 0$ and $|\varphi(x) - Ax| \leqslant \varepsilon$ for $x \in P$ and some $\varepsilon < \tau\rho$. Then $(1 - (\varepsilon/\tau\rho))AP \subset \varphi(P)$.*

Proof.   Since $0 \in \tau K \subset P$, we have $0 \in P^0$. Consequently, $0 \subset \varphi(P)^0$. Let $z \in \mathbf{R}^q \setminus \varphi(P)$ and let λ_0 be the least upper bound of numbers λ such that $\varkappa z \in \varphi(P)$ for $0 \leqslant \varkappa \leqslant \lambda$. Since $0 \in \varphi(P)^0$, it follows that $\lambda_0 > 0$. The image $\varphi(P)$ is closed, because the function φ is continuous and P is closed. This implies that $\lambda_0 z \in \varphi(P)$ and, consequently, $\lambda_0 < 1$, because $z \notin \varphi(P)$. The point $\lambda_0 z$ lies on the boundary of $\varphi(P)$ and therefore the point $x_0 = \varphi^{-1}(\lambda_0 z)$ lies on the boundary B of P. Consequently Ax_0 lies on the boundary AB of AP (because the function $\psi(x) = Ax$ is also a homeomorphism). This implies that $\lambda_0 z \notin \mathbf{R}^q \setminus (AB)_\varepsilon \supset \mathbf{R}^q \setminus [\mathbf{R}^q \setminus (AP)^0]_{-\varepsilon} = (AP^0)_{-\varepsilon}$. By property (AA9) of antiaureoles it follows that $\lambda_0 z \notin (1 - (\varepsilon/\tau\rho))AP^0$.
Since P is a convex neighbourhood of 0, so is AP. Thus, if z were in $(1 - (\varepsilon/\tau\rho))AP$, we would have $\lambda_0 z \in (1 - (\varepsilon/\tau\rho))AP^0$, in view of Lemma

18.3. This contradiction proves that $z \notin (1-(\varepsilon/\tau\rho))AP$, which completes the proof.

In proving equation (J2), we first assume that X is bounded, all full derivatives of φ are bounded on X by a number k and there is a number $m > 0$ such that

$$|\det \varphi'(x)| \geq \frac{1}{m} \quad \text{for} \quad x \in X. \tag{18.12}$$

Let $0 < \varepsilon < (2m\sqrt{q})^{-1}(qk)^{-q+1}$. In view of Lemma 18.1, there is a sequence of closed disjoint cubes $C_1, C_2, \ldots$ such that φ is a homeomorphism on each C_n and (18.1) holds. Moreover, there exists a function α, linear on each C_n, such that (18.2)-(18.4) hold. As before we find

$$\int \varphi(X) = \int \varphi(X_0),$$

where $X_0 = X \cap Y$, $Y = \bigcup_n C_n$. Moreover, if C denotes any of cubes C_n and $x, y \in C$, we have

$$|\psi(z) - Az| \leq 2\varepsilon\omega,$$

where $z = x - y$, $\psi(z) = \varphi(x) - \varphi(y)$, $\alpha(x) = Ax$ for $x \in C$ and ω is the radius of the ball described on C. Since $\alpha'(x) = A$ for $x \in C$, it follows by (18.4) and (18.12) that

$$|\det A| \geq \frac{1}{m}.$$

Let τ denote the radius of the ball inscribed in C and ρ_A the radius of the ball inscribed in AK. The ratio ω/τ is always equal to $\gamma = \sqrt{q}$, we thus have

$$\frac{2\varepsilon\omega}{\tau\rho_A}(qk)^{q-1} = \frac{2\varepsilon\gamma}{\rho_A}(qk)^{q-1} < \frac{1}{m\rho_A} \leq \frac{|\det A|}{\rho_A}$$

$$\leq \sigma_A^{q-1} < (q\|A\|)^{q-1} < (qk)^{q-1},$$

by Theorem 9.2 and inequalities (9.1). Hence $2\varepsilon\omega/\tau\rho_A = 2\varepsilon\gamma/\rho_A < 1$, and in view of Lemma 18.4 we have

$$\left(1 - \frac{2\varepsilon\gamma}{\rho_A}\right)A(C-y) \subset \psi(C-y),$$

where y is the centre of C. But the equality $\psi(x-y) = \varphi(x) - \varphi(y)$ implies $\psi(C-y) = \varphi(C) - \varphi(y)$, thus $(1-2\varepsilon\gamma/\rho_A)(AC-Ay) \subset \varphi(C) - \varphi(y)$, and hence

$$(1-2\varepsilon\gamma/\rho_A)^q \int AC \leq \int \varphi(C).$$

By the known Bernoulli inequality it follows that

$$(1-2q\varepsilon\gamma/\rho_A)\int AC \leq \int \varphi(C)$$

and by (6.1),

$$\left(1-q\frac{2\varepsilon\gamma}{\rho_A}\right)|\det A|\int C \leq \int \varphi(C).$$

Hence in view of Theorem 9.2 we get

$$|\det A|\int C - 2\varepsilon q\gamma\sigma_A^{q-1}\int C \leq \int \varphi(C).$$

Since $Ax = \alpha'(x)$ for $x \in C$, we obtain by (9.1),

$$\int_C |\det \alpha'| - 2\varepsilon q\gamma(qk)^{q-1}\int C \leq \int \varphi(C)$$

$$= \int \varphi(C \cap X) + \int \varphi(C \setminus X) \leq \int \varphi(C \cap X) + \int |\det \varphi'|,$$

in view of inequality (J1). Summing over all C_n, we get

$$\int_Y |\det \alpha'| - 2\varepsilon\gamma q(qk)^{q-1}\int Y \leq \int \varphi(Y \cap X) + \int_{Y \setminus X} |\det \varphi'|$$

$$\leq \int \varphi(Y \cap X) + \int_{Y \setminus X} q!k^q \leq \int \varphi(Y \cap X) + \varepsilon q!k^q,$$

by (8.4) and (18.1). Since $X_0 = X \cap Y \subset Y$, we hence get

$$\int_{X_0} |\det \alpha'| - 2\varepsilon\gamma q(qk)^{q-1}\left(\int X + \varepsilon\right) \leq \int \varphi(X_0) + \varepsilon q!k^q.$$

Substituting here (18.10) and letting $\varepsilon \to 0$, we obtain

$$\int_{X_0} |\det \varphi'| \leq \int \varphi(X_0).$$

But $\int (X \setminus X_0) = 0$, we thus also have

$$\int_X |\det \varphi'| \leq \int \varphi(X),$$

which together with (J1) yields equation (J2).
We now release the additional assumptions on X and φ. Let X_{km} $(k, m = 1, 2, \ldots)$ denote the subset of X on which the derivatives of φ satisfy

$k - 1 \leqslant \max_j |\varphi^{(e_j)}| < k$, $1/m \leqslant |\det \varphi'| < 1/(m-1)$, and let X_0 be the set on which $|\det \varphi'| = 0$. All the sets X_{km} are disjoint and measurable. Let $Y_1, Y_2, \ldots$ be a sequence of disjoint bounded measurable sets such that $\bigcup_n Y_n = \mathbf{R}^q$. Then the sets $X_{km} \cap Y_n$ are also disjoint, bounded and measurable and, by what we have proved so far, we have

$$\int \varphi(X_{km} \cap Y_n) = \int_{X_{km} \cup Y_n} |\det \varphi'(x)| \, dx,$$

$$\int \varphi(X_0) = \int_{X_0} |\det \varphi'(x)| \, dx;$$

the last equation follows by (J1). Summing over all $X_{km} \cap Y_n$ ($k, m, n = 1, 2, \ldots$) and X_0, we get the wished equation (J2).

19. The substitution theorem

The following theorem is a generalization of formula (J2) in the Jacobian theorem.

Theorem 19. *We suppose that a function φ whose values are in $\mathbf{R}^q$ is fully derivable on a measurable set $X \subset \mathbf{R}^q$. Let X_0 be the subset of X on which $\det \varphi' = 0$. We suppose that φ is invertible on $Y = X \backslash X_0$. Moreover, we assume that a function f whose values are in a Banach space is integrable on the image $\varphi(X)$. Then the product $|\det \varphi'(x)|.f[\varphi(x)]$ is integrable on X and we have*

$$\int_{\varphi(X)} f(x) \, dx = \int_X |\det \varphi'(x)| f[\varphi(x)] \, dx. \tag{19.1}$$

In the proof, we shall need the following simple

Lemma 19. *For each function φ defined on sets X and Y we have*

$$\varphi(X) \backslash \varphi(Y) \subset \varphi(X \backslash Y).$$

Proof. Assume that $y \in \varphi(X) \backslash \varphi(Y)$. Since $y \in \varphi(X)$, there exists a point $x \in X$ such that

$$y = \varphi(x).$$

Evidently, $x \notin Y$, because otherwise we would have $y \in \varphi(Y)$, which is not true. Thus, $x \in X \backslash Y$, and therefore $y \in \varphi(X \backslash Y)$, proving Lemma.

Proof of Theorem 19. We shall use the widespread notation $f \circ \varphi$ for the composition of functions f and φ, thus $(f \circ \varphi)(x) = f[\varphi(x)]$ (though, the symbol $\circ$ is not quite adequate, because it is symmetric and the composition is not symmetric).

By (J1) we find

$$\int \varphi(X_0) \leq \int_{X_0} 0 = 0.$$

The image $\varphi(X_0)$ is thus a null set and so is the set $\varphi(X)\backslash\varphi(Y)$, in view of Lemma 19. On the other hand, $\int_{X_0} |\det \varphi'|(f \circ \varphi) = \int_{X_0} 0 = 0$ and, consequently,

$$\int_{\varphi(X)\backslash\varphi(Y)} f = \int_{X_0} |\det \varphi'|(f \circ \varphi). \tag{19.2}$$

Suppose we have also proved that

$$\int_{\varphi(Y)} f = \int_{Y} |\det \varphi'|(f \circ \varphi). \tag{19.3}$$

Then, summing up (19.2) and (19.3) we get (19.1). It thus remains to prove (19.3).

Since the function f is integrable on $\varphi(X)$, it is also integrable on $\varphi(Y)$, because this set differs from $\varphi(X)$ by the null set $\varphi(X)\backslash\varphi(Y)$. This means that the integral on the left side of (19.3) exists. It turns out on the same to say that the function g which equals to f on the set $\varphi(Y)$ and vanishes outside it is integrable on $\mathbf{R}^q$. Thus, there exist elements λ_n in the considered Banach space and brick functions $f_1, f_2, \ldots$ such that

$$g \simeq \lambda_1 f_1 + \lambda_2 f_2 + \cdots,$$

i.e.,

$$|\lambda_1| \int f_1 + |\lambda_2| \int f_2 + \cdots < \infty \tag{19.4}$$

and

$$g(x) = \lambda_1 f_1(x) + \lambda_2 f_2(x) + \cdots \tag{19.5}$$

at all $x \in \mathbf{R}^q$ at which the series converges absolutely. It is also evident that

$$g \simeq \lambda_1 g_1 + \lambda_2 g_2 + \cdots, \tag{19.6}$$

where $g_n = f_n$ on $\varphi(Y)$ and $g_n = 0$ outside $\varphi(Y)$. Let X_n denote the set on which $g_n = 1$. Thus, g_n is the characteristic function of X_n. Moreover, let Y_n be the set on which $f_n \circ \varphi = 1$, so that $f_n \circ \varphi$ is the characteristic function of Y_n. We shall prove that

$$X_n = \varphi(Y_n \cap Y). \tag{19.7}$$

In fact, if $x \in X_n$, then $g_n(x) = 1$ and there exists a point $y \in Y$ such that $x = \varphi(y)$. Hence $f_n[\varphi(y)] = 1$, i.e., $(f_n \circ \varphi)(y) = 1$. Subsequently $y \in Y_n \cap Y$ and thus $x \in \varphi(Y_n \cap Y)$. If we assume, conversely, that the last relation holds, then there exists a point $y \in Y_n \cap Y$ such that $x = \varphi(y)$. This implies that $(f_n \circ \varphi)(y) = 1$ and $y \in Y$. Hence $f_n[\varphi(y)] = 1$ and $x \in \varphi(Y)$. Consequently, $f_n(x) = g_n(x) = 1$, i.e., $x \in X_n$. By (19.7) and (J2) we find

$$\int g_n = \int X_n = \int \varphi(Y_n \cap Y) = \int_{Y_n \cap Y} |\det \varphi'| = \int |\det \varphi'| \cdot (f_n \circ \varphi) \cdot \psi,$$

where ψ is the characteristic function of Y. Letting

$$h_n = |\det \varphi'| \cdot (f_n \circ \varphi) \cdot \psi,$$

we have $\int h_n = \int g_n \leq \int f_n$, and by (19.4),

$$|\lambda_1| \int h_1 + |\lambda_2| \int h_2 + \cdots < \infty. \tag{19.8}$$

We shall show that the equation

$$[|\det \varphi'| \cdot (f \circ \varphi) \cdot \psi](x) = \lambda_1 h_1(x) + \lambda_2 h_2(x) + \cdots \tag{19.9}$$

holds at all $x \in \mathbf{R}^q$ at which the series converges absolutely. If $x \notin Y$, then $\psi(x) = 0$, $h_n(x) = 0$, and equation (19.9) obviously holds. We thus assume that $x \in Y$. Then $\det \varphi'(x) \neq 0$ and, consequently, the series

$$\lambda_1 (f_1 \circ \varphi)(x) + \lambda_2 (f_2 \circ \varphi)(x) + \cdots \tag{19.10}$$

converges absolutely. In other words, the series $\lambda_1 f_1 + \lambda_2 f_2 + \cdots$ converges absolutely at the point $\varphi(x)$. Its limit must be $g[\varphi(x)]$, by (19.5). This proves that (19.10) converges to $(g \circ \varphi)(x)$ and, therefore, (19.9) holds, in view of definition of h_n.

Relations (19.8) and (19.9) mean, together, that

$$|\det \varphi'| \cdot (f \circ \varphi) \cdot \psi \approx \lambda_1 h_1 + \lambda_2 h_2 + \cdots.$$

The function on the left side is thus integrable and we have, by (19.6),

$$\int [|\det \varphi'|(f \circ \varphi)\psi] = \lambda_1 \int h_1 + \lambda_2 \int h_2 + \cdots$$

$$= \lambda_1 \int g_1 + \lambda_2 \int g_2 + \cdots = \int g = \int_{\varphi(Y)} f.$$

Since ψ is the characteristic function of Y, the obtained equation can be equivalently written as the wished equation (19.3).

20. Examples of application

The standard form of Substitution Theorem, given usually in text books, is:

Theorem 20. *We suppose that φ is a diffeomorphism in an open set X, i.e., φ is of class C^1, invertible and such that* det $\varphi' \neq 0$ *at all points of X. Moreover, we assume that a real valued function f is integrable on $\varphi(X)$. Then*

$$\int\limits_{\varphi(X)} f(x) = \int\limits_{X} |\det \varphi'(x)| f[\varphi(x)] \, dx.$$

It is evident that Theorem 20 is a particular case of Theorem 19, because any function of class C^1 in an open set is fully derivable in X. We are going to consider two very simple examples in which Theorem 20 is not applicable without additional argument, while Theorem 19 is.

Example 1. Let X be the one-dimensional open interval $(-1, 1)$, $\varphi(t) = t^3$ and $f(x) \equiv 1$. Since $\varphi'(t) = 3t^2$ and $\varphi(X) = (-1, 1)$, we have, by Theorem 19,

$$\int\limits_{-1}^{1} dx = \int\limits_{-1}^{1} 3t^2 \, dt.$$

However, this simple equation cannot be obtained by Theorem 20, because φ is not a diffeomorphism (we have $\varphi'(0) = 0$).

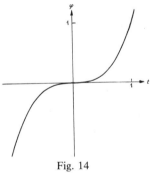

Fig. 14

Example 2. Let X be the two-dimensional set defined by the inequalities

$$0 \leqslant r < 1,$$
$$0 \leqslant \alpha < 2\pi.$$

The thick lines on the enclosed picture mean that the points of those lines belong to X.

The function φ is the map

$$x = r \cos \alpha,$$
$$y = r \sin \alpha;$$

here, the points (r, α) are arguments and the points (x, y) values of φ. When (r, α) ranges over X, then the corresponding values form the image $\varphi(X)$.

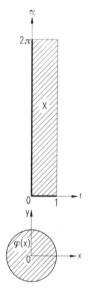

Fig. 15

The function φ is, as a matter of fact, defined for all points (r, α) of the plane $\mathbf{R}^2$ and its derivatives

$$\frac{\partial \varphi}{\partial r} = \left\{ \begin{matrix} \cos \alpha \\ \sin \alpha \end{matrix} \right\}, \qquad \frac{\partial \varphi}{\partial \alpha} = \left\{ \begin{matrix} -r \sin \alpha \\ r \cos \alpha \end{matrix} \right\}$$

are continuous in $\mathbf{R}^2$. The function φ is thus fully derivable in $\mathbf{R}^2$ (by Theorem 14.3) and, in particular, on X. Its Jacobian is

$$\det \varphi' = \begin{vmatrix} \cos \alpha & -r \sin \alpha \\ \sin \alpha & r \cos \alpha \end{vmatrix} = r$$

and vanishes on the boundary X_0 of X belonging to the α-axis. The function φ is invertible on the set $Y = X \backslash X_0$, we thus may apply Theorem 19. If $f \equiv 1$, then we get

$$\text{area of the circle } \varphi(X) = \int_{\varphi(X)} 1 = \int_X r = \int_0^{2\pi} d\alpha \int_0^1 r \, dr = 2\pi \cdot \tfrac{1}{2} = \pi.$$

In this calculation, Theorem 20 fails for 3 reasons: 1° X is not an open set, 2° the function φ is not invertible on X and 3° the Jacobian vanishes at some points of X (on the common part of X and α-axis).

These two examples show that Theorem 19 is of greater utility in comparison with the standard Theorem 20. It is true that, using additional reasoning, one can overcome the difficulties so that Theorem 20 can be applied, too. But just the necessity of such an additional work spoils the elegancy and makes applications more difficult. One can imagine that, in more complicated cases, the difficulty will increase.

In both examples, the full derivatives of φ exist in the whole considered Euclidean space and, consequently, is of class C^1 in that space. In general, it may however happen that the measurable set X and the function φ in Theorem 19 are such that the largest set on which φ is of class C^1 is the interior X^0 of X, $X^0 \neq X_0$. This follows for example, from

Lemma 20. *If ψ is of class C^1 in $\mathbf{R}^q$, and X is a measurable subset of $\mathbf{R}^q$, then there exists a function φ, fully derivable on X, which coincides with ψ on X as well as its derivatives, but the greatest set on which φ is of class C^1 is the interior of X.*

Proof. Let $\sigma(\xi)$ be a function defined and continuous on $\mathbf{R}^1$ which has all its full derivatives at points of the form $\xi = m/2^n$, where m and n are integers, and does not have full derivatives at the remaining points. Moreover, we assume that $\sigma'(0) = 0$. [Such a function can be obtained, e.g., from the function $f(x) = \sum_{n=1}^{\infty} 6^{-n} r(2^n x)$, considered in section 13, on letting $\sigma(\xi) = f(\xi + \frac{1}{3}) - \xi f'(\frac{1}{3})$.] We still introduce another auxiliary function ω such that

1°   if $x \in \bar{X}$ (closure of X), then $\omega(x) = 0$,

2°   if $x \notin \bar{X}$, then $\omega(x) = \sigma[\rho(x)]$, where $\rho(x)$ is the distance of x from the set X.

The function $\omega(x)$ has full derivatives, equal to 0, in the interior X^0. Moreover, it tends to 0 fast enough to ensure the existence of full derivatives, equal to 0, at points $x \in X$ which lie on the boundary of $\bar{X}$. However, ω is not of class C^1 outside X^0, which easily follows from the fact that σ is not fully derivable at any point. Now, the function $\varphi = \psi + \omega$ has evidently the required properties.

Remark. It is possible to replace the assertion in Lemma 20 by a stronger assertion that φ is not fully derivable at any point outside X. This result is due to CZESLAW KLIŚ [to appear in "Wiadomości Matematyczne"].

Chapter XIII

Integration and Derivation

The reader who has attentively studied the preceding pages of this book might be perhaps taken aback, when being asked to calculate numerically the Lebesgue integral of an explicitly given function, e.g., $(1-x^2)^{-1/2}$ in the interval $(0, 1)$. Extremely awkward would be trying to apply the definition given in section 3 of Chapter I and looking, for an expansion of $(1-x^2)^{-1/2}$ in a series of brick functions.

The proper way to solve this question, as well as to evaluate Lebesgue integrals for other elementary functions, is the use of *primitive functions*. Roughly speaking, F is called a primitive function of a given function f, if f is the derivative of F. Since the derivative can be defined in various ways, also the concept of primitive functions can be defined variously. In this chapter we consider primitive functions of continuous functions and of locally integrable functions. The relation between primitive functions and indefinite integrals is studied. Also the derivability almost everywhere is discussed.

All integrals considered in this chapter are meant as Bochner integrals or, if the integrand is real valued, as Lebesgue integrals. Thus, the word 'integrable' will always mean 'Bochner integrable' or 'Lebesgue integrable'.

1. Two convergence theorems

We first prove

Theorem 1.1. *If f is an integrable function on $\mathbf{R}^q$ and Z_n is a sequence of integrable sets such that $\int Z_n \to 0$, then $\int_{Z_n} f \to 0$.*

Proof. The sequence of functions fZ_n (which coincide with f on the sets Z_n and vanish outside them) converges locally in measure and therefore asymptotically to 0 (see Theorem 9.1, Chapter VI). Since $|fZ_n| \le |f|$, it follows by the generalized dominated convergence theorem (Theorem 10, Chapter IV) that $\int fZ_n \to 0$, which is our assertion.

If the integrable function f is fixed, then the integral $\phi(Z) = \int_Z f$ can be considered as a *set function*, i.e., a function whose arguments are measurable sets Z. Then the property expressed in Theorem 1.1 is called *absolute continuity* of $\phi(Z)$.

Corollary 1.1. *If f is an integrable function on an interval $I \subset \mathbf{R}^1$ (closed or open) and $x_0 \in I$, then the indefinite integral $F(x) = \int_{x_0}^{x} f$ is continuous on I.*

Proof. We extend the definition of f onto the whole real line $\mathbf{R}^1$, on letting $f = 0$ beyond I. Then f is integrable over $\mathbf{R}^1$. It suffices to show that $F(x + h_n) - F(x) \to 0$, as $h_n \to 0$. But the last difference equals, up to the sign, to $\int_{Z_n} f$, where Z_n is the interval joining the points $x + h_n$ and x. Thus, if $h_n \to 0$, the length of Z_n tends to 0 and, by Theorem 1.1, we obtain $\int_{Z_n} f \to 0$, which is our assertion.

Corollary 1.1 plays an important role in applications. It may be therefore of interest to finish the preceding proof without use of Theorem 1.1. To this end, we write $\int_{Z_n} f = \int f Z_n$ and note that the sequence $f Z_n$ is bounded by $|f|$ and converging to 0 a.e. Consequently, the ordinary dominated convergence theorem of Lebesgue can be applied, which ensures that $\int f Z_n \to 0$.
Corollary 1.1 also follows from

Theorem 1.2. *If f is an integrable function on $\mathbf{R}^q$, then*

$$\lim_{h \to 0} \int_{\mathbf{R}^q} |f(t + h) - f(t)| \, dt = 0.$$

Proof. The assertion is evidently true, if f is a brick function. If f is an arbitrary Bochner integrable function, it can be expanded into a series of brick functions

$$f \simeq \lambda_1 f_1 + \lambda_2 f_2 + \cdots.$$

Hence

$$\Delta_h = \int |f(t + h) - f(t)| \, dt \leq \sum_{n=1}^{\infty} |\lambda_n| \int |f_n(t + h) - f_n(t)| \, dt.$$

Given any number $\varepsilon > 0$, there exists an index n_0 such that

$$\sum_{n=n_0+1}^{\infty} |\lambda_n| \int f_n < \varepsilon/2.$$

This implies that

$$\Delta_h \leq \sum_{n=1}^{n_0} |\lambda_n| \int |f_n(t + h) - f_n(t)| \, dt + \varepsilon.$$

Since the sum on the right side is actually finite, we get $\lim_{h \to 0} \Delta_h \leq \varepsilon$. This proves the theorem, because the number ε can be chosen arbitrary small.

To see that Corollary 1.1 also follows from Theorem 1.2, it suffices to note that

$$\left| \int_{x_0}^{x} [f(t+h)-f(t)]\, dt \right| \le \int_{\mathbf{R}^q} |f(t+h)-f(t)|\, dt.$$

Corollary 1.2. *If f is a locally integrable function in $\mathbf{R}^q$, then for every bounded measurable set I,*

$$\lim_{h \to 0} \int_I |f(t+h)-f(t)|\, dt = 0.$$

Proof. Let J be a bounded interval such that I is inside J (i.e., the closure of I is in the interior of J). Let $g = f$ on J and $g = 0$ elsewhere. The function g is evidently integrable over $\mathbf{R}^q$. If $t + h \in J$ for $t \in I$, then

$$\int_I |f(t+h)-f(t)|\, dt = \int_{\mathbf{R}^q} |g(t+h)-g(t)|\, dt.$$

Hence, the assertion follows by Theorem 1.2.

2. Primitive functions

Now, we restrict our considerations to vector functions of a single real variable. By a vector function we mean a function whose values are in a Banach space. We say that a function F is *primitive* for a function f, if $F' = f$ holds at each point. Of course, if F is a primitive of f, then so is every function of the form $F + c$ ($c = $ constant). Conversely, if F and G are primitives for a function f, then their difference $F - G$ is constant. This follows from

Theorem 2.1. *If the derivative H' of a vector function H vanishes everywhere, then H is constant.*

This is a fundamental theorem in Calculus. For real valued functions it is usually proved by applying a mean value theorem. But this method fails, if the values of H are in an arbitrary Banach space. We therefore must look for another proof. It can be based on the Heine-Borel covering theorem, but we prefer to give a direct proof of about the same length.

Proof of Theorem 2.1.   Let $x < y$ and $\varepsilon > 0$. We define numbers $x_0, x_1, \ldots$ such that $x = x_0 < x_1 < \cdots \le y$ and x_n is the greatest of numbers $z \in [x, y]$ such that

$$\left| \frac{H(z)-H(x_{n-1})}{z-x_{n-1}} \right| \le \varepsilon,$$

if $x_{n-1} < y$. The existence of such a number x_n follows from the equation $H' = 0$ and from continuity of H. We shall show that there is an index m such that $x_{m-1} < y$ and $x_m = y$. In fact, assume that the sequence $x_0, x_1, \ldots$ is infinite. Since it is increasing and bounded by y, it converges to some limit $y_0 \leqslant y$. Let u be the least of numbers $v \in [x, y_0)$ such that

$$\left| \frac{H(y_0) - H(t)}{y_0 - t} \right| \leqslant \varepsilon \quad \text{for each } t \text{ satisfying} \quad v \leqslant t \leqslant y_0.$$

As before, the existence of such a number u follows from $H' = 0$. Since $x_n \to y_0$, there is an index m such that $u < x_{m-1} < y_0$. We thus have

$$\left| \frac{H(y_0) - H(x_{m-1})}{y_0 - x_{m-1}} \right| \leqslant \varepsilon.$$

This implies, in view of construction of the sequence $x_0, x_1, \ldots$, that $x_m \geqslant y_0$, which is impossible.
This contradiction proves that there exists a finite set of numbers $x_0, \ldots, x_m$ such that $x = x_0 < \cdots < x_m = y$ and

$$\left| \frac{H(x_n) - H(x_{n-1})}{x_n - x_{n-1}} \right| \leqslant \varepsilon \quad \text{for } n = 1, \ldots, m.$$

Hence

$$|H(y) - H(x)| \leqslant \sum_{n=1}^{m} |H(x_n) - H(x_{n-1})| \leqslant \varepsilon \sum_{n=1}^{m} (x_n - x_{n-1}) = \varepsilon(y - x).$$

But the number ε can be taken arbitrary small so that we must have $H(y) - H(x) = 0$. Since x and y are arbitrary points, the function H is constant.

Theorem 2.2. *If f is a continuous vector function in an interval $I \subset \mathbf{R}^1$, then the indefinite Bochner integral*

$$F(x) = \int_{x_0}^{x} f \qquad (x_0 \in I)$$

is, in I, a primitive function for f.

Proof. The existence of the integral follows from the continuity of f, because each continuous function is locally integrable (see section 3, Chapter XI). If x and $x + h$ belong to I, then

$$\frac{F(x+h) - F(x)}{h} = \frac{1}{h} \int_{I_h} f, \tag{2.1}$$

where I_h denotes the interval whose endpoints are x and $x + h$. But

$$\left| \frac{1}{h} \int\limits_{I_h} f - f(x) \right| = \left| \frac{1}{h} \int\limits_{I_h} [f(t) - f(x)]\, dt \right| \leqslant \frac{1}{|h|} \int\limits_{I_h} |f(t) - f(x)|\, dt. \qquad (2.2)$$

If x is kept fixed and h tends to 0, then $f(t)$ approaches $f(x)$, because of the continuity of f, and $|f(t) - f(x)|$ becomes less than an arbitrary given number ε. Thus, the last expression in (2.2) becomes less than

$$\frac{1}{|h|} \int\limits_{I_h} \varepsilon\, dt = \varepsilon.$$

This proves that the difference quotient (2.2) tends to $f(x)$, as $h \to 0$. In other words, we have $F' = f$ in I.

Theorem 2.3. *If a function f is continuous in an interval (a, b) and F is continuous on $[a, b]$ and has f for its local derivative in (a, b), then the Bochner (or Lebesgue) integral $\int\limits_a^b f$ exists and we have*

$$\int\limits_a^b f = F(b) - F(a).$$

The above theorem is of great importance for applications and is constantly used in practical calculations. It gives an immediate answer to the question raised at the beginning of this chapter how to calculate the Lebesgue integral of, the function $(1 - x^2)^{-1/2}$ in the interval $(0, 1)$. In fact, we take $F(x) = \arcsin x$ and find $\int\limits_0^1 (1 - x^2)^{-1/2}\, dx = \arcsin 1 - \arcsin 0 = \pi/2$. This technique is handier than that used in the traditional course of the Riemann integral, because the Riemann integral is defined for bounded functions only. The evaluation of the above integral would therefore require, to be exact, the concept of the so called improper Riemann integral so that an additional passage to the limit would be necessary.

Proof of Theorem 2.3.   Evidently, F is a primitive for f in (a, b), we thus have

$$\int\limits_x^y f = \int\limits_{x_0}^x f - \int\limits_{x_0}^y f = F(y) - F(x) \qquad (a < x < y < b),$$

in view of formulae (5.2) and (5.3), Chapter VI, and by the fact that all primitives differ by a constant one from another. Letting $x \to a$ and $y \to b$, we get $\int\limits_a^b f = F(b) - F(a)$, in view of Corollary 1.1 and continuity of F.

Theorem 2.2 tells us that the class of primitive functions is larger than the class of indefinite integrals. To see that it is essentially larger it suffices to note that the indefinite integral $\int_{x_0}^{x} f$ for the function $f = 0$ is always 0, whereas each constant function is primitive. On the other hand the whole class of primitives can be obtained from indefinite integrals by adding arbitrary constants.

The last statement can also be extended to primitives of arbitrary locally integrable functions, provided the concept of a primitive is properly extended.

3. Local derivatives and local primitives

By a *local-derivative* of a function f of a real variable we mean the local limit of the expression

$$\frac{1}{h}[f(x+h)-f(x)],$$

as $h \to 0$. In other words, g is a local derivative of f, if

$$\lim_{h \to 0} \int_a^b \left| \frac{1}{h}[f(x+h)-f(x)] - g(x) \right| dx = 0 \qquad (3.1)$$

holds for every bounded interval (a, b). In order to have this definition sensible, we always assume that the integrand in (3.1) is a locally integrable function of x.

Evidently, if f' is a local derivative of f, then every function equivalent to f' is also a local derivative of f. No other function has this property. In other words, a local derivative, if it exists, is determined up to equivalent functions.

Theorem 3.1. *If a measurable function f has a local derivative f', then both f and f' are locally integrable.*

Proof. If $h_n \neq 0$ and $h_n \to 0$, then $(1/h_n)[f(x+h_n)-f(x)] \to f'(x)$ locally. Consequently, there is a subsequence h_{p_n} such that $(1/h_{p_n})[f(x+h_{p_n})-f(x)] \to f'(x)$ a.e. Since the elements of the sequence are measurable functions, the limit f' is also measurable.

The function

$$K(x, h) = \frac{1}{h}[f(x+h)-f(x)] - f'(x) \qquad (h \neq 0),$$

considered as a function of two variables x and h is measurable in each rectangle

$$x_1 < x < x_2, \qquad 0 < h < h_0$$

and the integral $\int_{x_1}^{x_2} |K(x, h)| \, dx$ tends to 0, as $h \to 0$. We thus can fix h_0 so that this integral is bounded by 1 in the interval $0 < h < h_0$. Hence, by the Tonelli theorem, the function $K(x, h)$ considered as a function of h is, for almost every fixed x, an integrable function in $0 < h < h_0$. Consequently, for almost every fixed x, the function $f(x + h) = f(x) + hf'(x) + hK(x, h)$ is integrable in $0 < h < h_0$. We can also say that the function f is integrable in almost every interval of length h_0 whose initial point belongs to (x_1, x_2). This implies that f is integrable in an interval (x_0, x_2) contained in (x_1, x_2). Since the interval (x_1, x_2) can be chosen arbitrarily, the function f is locally integrable. So must be also the derivative f', for it is a limit of a locally convergent sequence $(1/h_n)[f(x + h_n) - f(x)]$ of locally integrable functions.

Theorem 3.2. *If a local derivative f' of a measurable function f vanishes a.e., then f is constant a.e.,*

Proof.   Consider the functions

$$F_n(x) = n \int_0^{1/n} f(x + t) \, dt.$$

For each fixed $x \in \mathbf{R}^1$, we have

$$\left| \frac{1}{h}[F_n(x + h) - F_n(x)] \right| \leq n \int_0^{1/n} \left| \frac{1}{h}[f(x + h + t) - f(x + t)] \right| dt$$

$$= n \int_x^{x+1/n} \left| \frac{1}{h}[f(t + h) - f(t)] \right| dt \to 0,$$

as $h \to 0$. This proves that $F_n' = 0$ everywhere and, consequently, the functions F_n are constant.
Now, we have

$$\int_a^b |F_n(x) - f(x)| \, dx = \int_a^b dx \left| n \int_0^{1/n} [f(x + t) - f(x)] \, dt \right|$$

$$\leq \int_a^b dx \, n \int_0^{1/n} |f(x + t) - f(x)| \, dt$$

$$= n \int_0^{1/n} dt \int_a^b |f(x + t) - f(x)| \, dx.$$

By Theorem 1.2, given any $\varepsilon > 0$, there exists an index n_0 such that

$$\int_a^b |f(x+t) - f(x)|\, dx < \varepsilon \quad \text{for} \quad 0 < t < \frac{1}{n_0}.$$

Hence

$$\int_a^b |F_n(x) - f(x)|\, dx \leq n \int_0^{1/n} \varepsilon\, dx = \varepsilon \quad \text{for} \quad n \geq n_0,$$

i.e., F_n converges locally to f. Since the functions F_n are constant, it follows that f is constant a.e.

A function F will be called a *local primitive* of f, if f is a local derivative of F.

Theorem 3.3. *If f is locally integrable, the indefinite Bochner integral*

$$F(x) = \int_{x_0}^x f$$

is a local primitive for f.

Proof. We have

$$\int_a^b \left| \frac{1}{h}[F(x+h) - F(x)] - f(x) \right| dx = \int_a^b dx \left| \frac{1}{h} \int_x^{x+h} [f(t) - f(x)]\, dt \right|$$

$$= \int_a^b dx \left| \frac{1}{h} \int_0^h [f(x+t) - f(x)]\, dt \right| \leq \frac{1}{h} \int_0^h dt \int_a^b |f(x+t) - f(x)|\, dx.$$

The last expression tends to 0, which follows like in the preceding proof (we only have to replace n by $1/h$). This proves that the local derivative of F is f. Consequently, F is a local primitive of f.

Theorems 3.2 and 3.3 imply that the class of all local primitives can be obtained from indefinite integrals by adding functions which are constant almost everywhere. In particular, if we add functions which are constant everywhere, we obtain the subclass of local primitives which are continuous. Each local primitive is equivalent to a continuous local primitive.

Theorem 3.4. *Continuous local primitives are derivable almost everywhere and their derivatives are equal to their local derivatives. More exactly, if F is* *a continuous local primitive of f, then*

$$\lim_{h \to 0} \frac{F(x+h)-F(x)}{h} = f(x) \tag{3.2}$$

holds for almost every x.

The proof of this theorem is rather difficult. It will be displayed in the next sections. Here, we are going to make a few remarks.

For real functions, the class of continuous local primitives coincides with the class of absolutely continuous functions (see remarks by the end of section 5). The following example shows that this is not true for vector functions.

Example. Let E be the space of real functions $a(t)$, Lebesgue integrable over the interval $(0, 1)$ and let $|a| = \int_0^1 |a(t)| \, dt$ be the norm of a. Let f be a function defined for $0 < x < 1$, whose values are in E, such that the value of f at the point x is the function $a(t) = H(t-x)$ $(0 < t < 1)$, where H is the Heaviside function:

$$H(t) = \begin{cases} 1 & \text{for} \quad t \geq 0, \\ 0 & \text{for} \quad t < 0. \end{cases}$$

Then we have, for $0 < x < y < 1$,

$$|f(y) - f(x)| = \int_0^1 |H(t-y) - H(t-x)| \, dt.$$

Evidently, the integral equals to 1 for $x < t < y$ and vanishes elsewhere, which implies

$$|f(y) - f(x)| = |y - x|.$$

Thus, the function f satisfies the Lipschitz condition with the constant 1. On the other hand, it is not derivable at any point. In fact, let a be any element of E. Then, for $h > 0$ small enough, we have

$$\left| \frac{f(x+h) - f(x)}{h} - a \right| = \int_0^1 \left| \frac{H(t-x-h) - H(t-x)}{h} - a(t) \right| dt$$

$$= \int_x^{x+h} \left| \frac{1}{h} - a(t) \right| dt \geq 1 - \int_x^{x+h} |a(t)| \, dt.$$

Since the last integral tends to 0, as $h \to 0$, the inequality proves that $(f(x+h) - f(x))/h$ does not tend to a, whatever the element $a \in E$ is. In other words, f has no derivative at any point.

The function f in the above example satisfies the Lipschitz condition, which is much more than being absolutely continuous. Thus, absolutely continuous vector functions are not derivable, in general, and their local derivatives do not exist either, which follows from Theorem 3.4. For this reason, the role of absolutely continuous functions is, in the theory of Bochner's integral, of no great importance.

Also Theorem 3.4, in spite of its undeniable beauty, has not many applications. It is true that it ensures existence of a sequence of continuous functions f_n converging to F', but such a result follows much easier from the fact that

$$n\left[F\left(x+\frac{1}{n}\right)-F(x)\right]\to F'(x) \text{ loc.}$$

Since the sequence on the left side converges locally, it contains a subsequence f_n which converges almost everywhere, by Theorem 2, Chapter XI.

Continuous local primitives can be considered as continuous solutions of the differential equation

$$F' = f,$$

where the derivative is meant as a local derivative. The whole class of such solutions depends, for a given equation, on one arbitrary parameter c. It seems that similar applications of local derivatives could extend to other differential equations, also of higher order (whereas the use of almost everywhere derivatives would be rather inadequate).

4. A local convergence theorem

In order to prove Theorem 3.4 from the preceding section we shall use a theorem on local convergence, given below. We say that a function $f(x, \alpha)$ in which the argument x belongs to $\mathbf{R}^q$ and α is considered as a parameter, *converges locally* to $f(x)$, as $\alpha \to \alpha_0$, if for each bounded interval $I \subset \mathbf{R}^q$ we have

$$\lim_{\alpha\to\alpha_0} \int_I |f(x, \alpha)-f(x)|\, dx = 0.$$

Then we also write

$$f(x, \alpha)\to f(x) \text{ loc.} \quad \text{for } \alpha\to\alpha_0.$$

This relation holds if and only if, for each sequence α_n converging to 0, the sequence $f(x, \alpha_n)$ converges locally to $f(x)$ (see section 2, Chapter XI).

Theorem 4.1. *If f is a locally Bochner integrable function in $\mathbf{R}^q$, then for almost every point $x_0\in\mathbf{R}^q$ we have*

$$f(x_0+\alpha x)\to f(x_0) \quad \text{loc.,} \quad \text{as } \alpha\to 0.$$

In spite of conciseness of the theorem, its proof will be rather long and laborious. The reader who is interested mainly in applications of the theory may quietly skip this proof and the remainder of this chapter, because no use of Theorem 4.1 or 3.4 will be made beyond.

Let C denote the q-dimensional closed cube of center at 0 and length of edges 1.

Lemma 4.1. *If f is a non-negative locally integrable function in $\mathbf{R}^q$, then*

$$K_\alpha(x) = \int_C f(x + \alpha t)\, dt \to f(x) \qquad \text{a.e.,} \qquad \text{as } \alpha \to 0.$$

Proof. Letting

$$m(x) = \liminf_{\alpha \to 0} K_\alpha(x), \qquad M(x) = \limsup_{\alpha \to 0} K_\alpha(x),$$

we plainly have

$$0 \leqslant m(x) \leqslant M(x) \leqslant \infty.$$

Assume that $M(x) = \infty$ holds on a set A which is not a null set. Then there is a subset A_0 contained in a bounded open interval J, which is not a null set either.

Let $\alpha C + x$ denote the closed cube of centre x and length of edges equal $|\alpha|$. Let $\mathfrak{F}_v$ be the family of cubes $\alpha C + x$ such that $K_\alpha(x) > v$. This family covers A_0 in the Vitali sense (see section 17, Chapter XII). We thus can select from $\mathfrak{F}$ a sequence of disjoint cubes $C_n = \alpha_n C + x_n \subset J$ which covers almost every point of A_0. By a simple linear substitution we find that

$$\int_{C_n} f = |\alpha_n|^q \int_C f(x_n + \alpha_n t)\, dt = |\alpha_n|^q K_{\alpha_n}(x_n).$$

But $|\alpha_n|^q$ is the measure $\int C_n$ of C_n, we thus may write

$$\int_{C_n} f > v \int C_n,$$

because $K_{\alpha_n}(x_n) > v$. Since the cubes C_n are disjoint and contained in J, we hence obtain, for $G = C_1 \cup C_2 \cup \cdots$,

$$\int_J f \geqslant \int_G f \geqslant v \int G.$$

Let a be the greatest lower bound of $\int Z$ for integrable sets Z which cover A_0 a.e. Then $\int G \geqslant a > 0$, for A_0 is not a null set. Hence $\int_J f \geqslant va$.

Since v can be taken arbitrary large, it follows that f is not locally integrable. This contradiction proves that the assumption $M(x) = \infty$ is false and we instead must have

$M(x) < \infty$.

Assume now that the set B of points x such that

$$m(x) < M(x) < \infty \tag{4.1}$$

is not a null set. We shall show that there exist two numbers u and v, and a non-null subset B_0 of B, contained in an open interval J, such that

$$m(x) < u < v < M(x) \tag{4.2}$$

holds for $x \in B_0$. In fact, there exists a non-null subset B_1 of B, contained in an open interval J, such that (4.2) holds for $x \in B_1$. For every point $x \in B_1$ we can find two rational numbers u and v such that (4.1) holds at that point. If we denote by $B_{u,v}$ the set of points where the inequalities (4.2) hold, then clearly B_1 is the union of all sets $B_{u,v}$ with rational u and v $(u < v)$. Since the number of such sets is countable, there must exist at least one of the sets $B_{u,v}$ which is not a null set, because otherwise B_1 would be a null set. This set $B_{u,v}$ can be selected for B_0.

Next, we shall show that inequalities (4.2) cannot hold on B_0, if B_0 is not a null set. This contradiction will prove that $m(x) = M(x)$ holds a.e. Let b be the greatest lower bound of $\int Z$ for integrable sets Z which cover B_o. Since B is supposed to be a non-null set, we have $b > 0$. There exists an open set $Q \supset B_0$ such that

$$\int Q < \sqrt{v/u}\, b,$$

since $\sqrt{v/u} > 1$ (by Theorem 6.3, Chapter XI). Let $\mathfrak{G}_u$ be the family of cubes $\alpha C + x$ such that $K_\alpha(x) < u$. This family covers B_0 in the Vitali sense, which follows from the inequality $m(x) < u$. We thus can select from $\mathfrak{G}_u$ a sequence of cubes $\Gamma_n = \gamma_n C + y_n$ which covers almost every point of B_0. We have

$$\int_{\Gamma_n} f = |\gamma_n|^q \int_C f(y_n + \gamma_n t)\, dt = |\gamma_n|^q K_{\gamma_n}(y_n).$$

Since $|\gamma_n|^q = \int \Gamma_n$, we may write

$$\int_{\Gamma_n} f < u \int \Gamma_n,$$

because $K_{\gamma_n}(y_n) < u$. Since the cubes are disjoint, we obtain for

$$\Gamma = \Gamma_1 \cup \Gamma_2 \cup \cdots,$$

$$\int_\Gamma f < u \int \Gamma \leq u \int Q \leq \sqrt{uv} \cdot b. \tag{4.3}$$

Since $\sqrt{v/u} > 1$, there is an open set $P \supset \Gamma$ such that

$$\int_P f \leq \sqrt{v/u} \int_\Gamma f. \tag{4.4}$$

Let $\mathfrak{H}_v$ be the family of cubes $\alpha C + x$ such that $v < K_\alpha(x)$. This family covers $P \cap B_0$ in the Vitali sense which follows from the inequality $v < M(x)$. Thus, we can select from $\mathfrak{H}_v$ a sequence of cubes $\Delta_n = \delta_n C + z_n \subset P$ which covers almost every point of $P \cap B_0$. Since $P \supset \Gamma$ and Γ covers almost every point of B_0, the sequence Δ_n covers almost every point of B_0'. From

$$\int_{\Delta_n} f = \int_C f(z_n + \delta_n t)\, dt = |\delta_n|^q K_{\delta_n}(z_n)$$

it follows that

$$\int_{\Delta_n} f > v \int \Delta_n.$$

If $\Delta = \Delta_1 \cup \Delta_2 \cup \cdots$, we hence obtain,

$$\int_P f \geq \int_\Delta f > v \int \Delta.$$

Since Δ covers B_0 a.e., we have $\int \Delta \geq b$ and, consequently,

$$\int_\Gamma f > \sqrt{uv} \cdot b,$$

by (4.4). This contradicts (4.3) and proves that $m(x) = M(x)$ a.e. The last equation means that $K_\alpha(x)$ converges a.e. to a finite limit, as $\alpha \to 0$.

In order to complete the proof of Lemma 4.1, we must show that this limit is equivalent to $f(x)$. In fact, we have for each bounded interval I,

$$\int_I |K_\alpha(x) - f(x)|\, dx = \int_I \left| \int_C [f(x + \alpha t) - f(x)]\, dt \right| dx$$

$$\leq \int_I dx \int_C |f(x + \alpha t) - f(x)|\, dt = \int_C dt \int_I |f(x + \alpha t) - f(x)|\, dx.$$

Given any $\varepsilon > 0$, we have by Corollary 1.2, $\int_I |f(x + \alpha t) - f(x)| \, dx \le \varepsilon$ for $|\alpha t|$ less than a properly chosen $h_0 > 0$. Since $t \in C$ implies $|t| \le \frac{1}{2}$, we get

$$\int_I |K_\alpha(x) - f(x)| \, dx \le \int_C \varepsilon \, dt = \varepsilon \quad \text{for} \quad |\alpha| < 2h_0.$$

This proves the local convergence of $K_\alpha(x)$ to $f(x)$. Our assertion now follows from Theorem 3, Chapter XI.

A function f whose values are in a Banach space E will be called *separable*, if there is a sequence $a_1, a_2, \ldots$ of elements of E such that each value of f is a limit of a subsequence $a_{p_1}, a_{p_2}, \ldots$.

Lemma 4.2. *Each locally Bochner integrable function is equivalent to a separable function.*

Proof. Each Bochner integrable function can be expanded into a series of brick functions

$$f \simeq \lambda_1 f_1 + \lambda_2 f_2 + \cdots.$$

Let $g = f$ at points at the series converges absolutely and $g = 0$ elsewhere. Then f is equivalent to g, and g is evidently separable. If f is locally integrable, then the functions

$$fJ_1, \qquad f(J_2 - J_1), \qquad f(J_3 - J_2), \ldots \tag{4.5}$$

are integrable for any sequence $J_1, J_2, \ldots$ of characteristic functions of bounded intervals. We assume that the sequence J_n tends monotonically to 1. By what we have already proved, the functions in (4.5) are respectively equivalent to functions $g_1, g_2, g_3, \ldots$ which are separable. We may assume that these functions have disjoint carriers. Since each function g_n is separable, so is their sum. This proves the lemma, since we plainly have $f \sim g$.

Proof of Theorem 4.1. We first assume that f is separable. There thus exists a sequence of elements $a_n \in E$ such that each value of f is the limit of some subsequence. For each n the function $|f(x) - a_n|$ is non-negative and locally integrable. According to Lemma 4.1 we thus have

$$\int_C |f(x + \alpha t) - a_n| \, dt \to |f(x) - a_n|, \quad \text{as} \quad \alpha \to 0, \tag{4.6}$$

for every point $x \in \mathbf{R}^q$, except for a null set Z_n; C denotes, as before, the q-dimensional closed cube of centre 0 and length of edges 1. Consequently, (4.6) for every $n = 1, 2, \ldots$ and every $x \in \mathbf{R}^q$ beyond the null set $Z = Z_1 \cup Z_2 \cup \cdots$. Since f is separable, we can choose, for every $\varepsilon > 0$ and every point x_0 an element a_n such that $|f(x_0) - a_n| < \varepsilon$. If $x_0 \notin Z$, then by (4.6) we have, for sufficiently small α,

$$\left| \int_C |f(x_0+\alpha t)-a_n|\,dt - |f(x_0)-a_n| \right| < \varepsilon$$

and hence

$$\int_C |f(x_0+\alpha t)-a_n|\,dt < 2\varepsilon.$$

Consequently, for sufficiently small α,

$$\int_C |f(x_0+\alpha t)-f(x_0)|\,dt \leq \int_C |f(x_0+\alpha t)-a_n|\,dt + \int_C |f(x_0)-a_n|\,dt < 3\varepsilon.$$

This proves that, for each fixed $x_0 \not\in Z$, we have

$$\int_C |f(x_0+\alpha t)-f(x_0)|\,dt \to 0, \quad \text{as} \quad \alpha \to 0.$$

If we replace t by nt and α by α/n, we get, after cancelling the factor n^q on the left side,

$$\int_{nC} |f(x_0+\alpha t)-f(x_0)|\,dt \to 0, \qquad \text{as} \quad \alpha \to 0,$$

where nC is the cube of centre 0 and length of edges n.

Given any bounded interval $I \subset \mathbf{R}^q$, there is an integer n such that $I \subset nC$. In consequence,

$$\int_I |f(x_0+\alpha t)-f(x_0)|\,dt \to 0, \quad \text{as} \quad \alpha \to 0,$$

This holds for all x_0 outside a null set Z and proves Theorem 4.1. We still have to release the hypothesis that f is separable. But if it were not, there would exist, by Lemma 4.2, a separable function g such that $f(x)=g(x)$ would hold for all x except for a null set Z_0. We thus would have, for $x_0 \not\in Z_0$,

$$\int_I |f(x_0+\alpha t)-f(x_0)|\,dt = \int_I |g(x_0+\alpha t)-g(x_0)|\,dt$$

and Theorem 4.1 would easily follow from the just obtained result.

5. Derivability almost everywhere

The proof of Theorem 3.4, which was not yet given, can be now easily deduced from Theorem 4.1. In fact, Theorem 4.1 implies, in the one dimensional case, that

$$\int_0^1 f(x+ht)\,dt \to f(x) \qquad \text{a.e.,} \qquad \text{as } h\to 0.$$

Substituting $x+ht=u$, we get

$$\frac{1}{h}\int_x^{x+h} f(u)\,du \to f(x) \qquad \text{a.e.,}$$

and hence,

$$\frac{F(x+h)-F(x)}{h} \to f(x) \qquad \text{a.e., as } h\to 0. \tag{5.1}$$

And this is already the assertion of Theorem 3.4.

The above result can be generalized to any number of dimensions. In fact, we have, according to Theorem 4.1,

$$\int_C |f(x+ht)-f(x)|\,dt \to 0 \qquad \text{a.e.,} \qquad \text{as } h\to 0,$$

where C is the unit cube as in section 4. Substituting $ht=u$, we get

$$\frac{1}{|h|^q}\int_{hC} |f(x+u)-f(x)|\,du \to 0 \qquad \text{a.e.,} \qquad \text{as } h\to 0.$$

If $Y_{x,h}$ denotes a set of points t, included in hC, such that its measure $\int Y_{x,h}$ is greater than $\lambda\,|h|^q$, then evidently

$$\frac{1}{\int Y_{x,h}}\int_{Y_{x,h}} |f(x+t)-f(x)|\,dt \to 0 \qquad \text{a.e.,} \qquad \text{as } h\to 0,$$

which implies

$$\frac{\displaystyle\int_{Y_{x,h}} f(x+t)\,dt}{\int Y_{x,h}} \to f(x) \qquad \text{a.e.,} \qquad \text{as } h\to 0. \tag{5.2}$$

Formula (5.2) is susceptible of various interpretations, but none of them looks as natural and nice as the formula (5.1).

If F is a real function of one real variable, the limit of

$$\frac{F(x+h)-F(x)}{h} \tag{5.3}$$

exists a.e., whenever F is absolutely continuous. Recall that a function F (whose values may belong to any Banach space) is called *absolutely continuous*, if for any $\varepsilon > 0$ there exists some $\delta > 0$ such that, for every finite set of non-overlapping intervals

$$(a_1, b_1), \ldots, (a_n, b_n)$$

such that $(b_1 - a_1) + \cdots + (b_n - a_n) < \delta$, we have

$$|F(b_1) - F(a_1)| + \cdots + |F(b_n) - F(a_n)| < \varepsilon.$$

The almost everywhere derivability of absolutely continuous functions follows from the fact (whose proof is left to the reader) that the class of those functions coincides, whenever one considers real valued functions, with the class of local primitives. The almost everywhere derivability evidently holds always, when both mentioned classes coincide. This is true, for example, if the space E the functions take their values from is a Hilbert space or any so called reflexive Banach space.

More general than the class of absolutely continuous functions is the class of functions of *bounded variation*. A function F (whose values are in an arbitrary Banach space) is called of *bounded variation*, if there is a number M such that, for any finite set of non-overlapping intervals $(a_1, b_1), \ldots, (a_n, b_n)$, we have

$$|F(b_1) - F(a_1)| + \cdots + |F(b_n) - F(a_n)| < M.$$

It turns out that the limit a.e. of (5.3) continues to exist for functions of bounded variation, whenever they are real valued. Of course this is not true, if the values of functions are in an arbitrary Banach space.

Almost everywhere derivability of real functions of bounded variation was already stated by Lebesgue, however, because of little applicability of that theorem we shall not enter into details. The extension of the concept of bounded variation is quite awkward for functions $F(x)$ with $x \in \mathbf{R}^q$. It becomes nicer for set functions, but nevertheless seems to be of minor interest in applications. In addition, the main theorems fail, if the values of functions are in an arbitrary Banach space.

6. Product of two local primitives

All functions considered in this section are functions of a single real variable; their values are in a given Banach space. We first recollect a few facts from section 3.

Although the class of absolutely continuous functions plays an important role in real analysis, it is not so in analysis of vector valued functions, where rather the class of the local primitives is of importance. Since each local primitive is equivalent to a *continuous local primitive*, we can practically restrict ourselves to the class of such functions. This class will be denoted by $\mathfrak{A}$. Each function $f \in \mathfrak{A}$ is locally derivable and its derivative f' is locally integrable. The class $\mathfrak{A}$ evidently includes the class C_1 (of continuously derivable functions). All functions in $\mathfrak{A}$ are derivable a.e.

(according to Theorem 3.4), but this fact will not be used in this or in the next section.

Theorem 6.1. *If* $f, g \in \mathfrak{A}$, *then also* $fg \in \mathfrak{A}$, *and the ordinary formula*

$$(fg)' = f'g + fg' \qquad (6.1)$$

holds a.e. Moreover, the products $f'g$ *and* fg' *are locally integrable.*

Proof. We have to prove that the integral

$$\int_a^b \left| \frac{1}{h} [f(x+h)g(x+h) - f(x)g(x)] - f'(x)g(x) - f(x)g'(x) \right| dx \qquad (6.2)$$

tends to 0, as $h \to 0$. Let M, N and ε be positive numbers such that $|f(x)| < M$ for $a \leqslant x \leqslant b$, and $|g(x)| \leqslant N$ for $a - \varepsilon \leqslant x \leqslant b + \varepsilon$. Then, for $|h| < \varepsilon$, the above integral is less than or equal to the sum

$$N \int_a^b \left| \frac{1}{h} [f(x+h) - f(x)] - f'(x) \right| dx$$

$$+ M \int_a^b \left| \frac{1}{h} [g(x+h) - g(x)] - g'(x) \right| dx,$$

which implies the wanted convergence of (6.2) to 0. This also proves that $fg \in \mathfrak{R}$. To see that the product $f'g$ is locally derivable, it suffices to note that f' is locally integrable and g locally bounded (i.e., bounded in each bounded interval). For similar reasons, the product fg' is locally integrable.

7. Integration per parts

As in the preceding section, all functions considered below are functions of a single real variable and take their values in a Banach space.

Theorem 7.1. *If* $f, g \in \mathfrak{A}$ *and* $-\infty < a < b < \infty$, *then*

$$f(b)g(b) - f(a)g(a) = \int_a^b f'g + \int_a^b fg'. \qquad (7.1)$$

Proof. We have $fg \in \mathfrak{A}$, by Theorem 6.1, the product fg is thus continuous and locally integrable. Integrating formula (6.1) from a to b, we obtain the required equation (7.1).

It is readily seen that, in Theorem 7.1, the values of f and g at points beyond (a, b) play no role. We therefore may state the theorem in a slightly sharper form:

Theorem 7.2. *If f and g are continuous functions in $[a, b]$ and have their local derivatives integrable over that interval, then (7.1) holds.*

Proof. We put $f' = g' = 0$ outside (a, b) and extend suitably the functions f and g beyond $[a, b]$ so as to get them continuous in $(-\infty, \infty)$. The extended functions belong to and the assertion follows from Theorem 7.1.

Chapter XIV

Convolution

Convolution has become one of the most important tools in Analysis. An extensive study of this concept was given in [1], but only for real valued functions (or distributions). In this book the theory is presented for vector valued functions (which needs a few modifications). For convenience of the reader, we present it from the very beginning so that the chapter is selfcontained.

The most difficult theorem on convolution is the Titchmarsh theorem. Since its proof requires special methods, it will be discussed in the next, separate chapter.

I am indebted to A. KAMIŃSKI for his efficient assistance in preparing the present Chapter XIV.

1. Convolution of two functions

By the convolution of two functions f and g we mean the integral

$$\int_{\mathbf{R}^q} f(x-t)g(t)\, dt. \tag{1.1}$$

The convolution exists at a point x, whenever the product $f(x-t)g(t)$ is Bochner integrable with respect to t. We assume that the values of f and g are in Banach spaces A and B, respectively, and that the values of the product $f(x-t)g(t)$ are in a Banach space C. Therefore, if the convolution exists at some point x, its value is in C.

In order to have the convolution defined at as many points as possible, we adopt the following convention: if one of the factors $f(x-t)$ or $g(t)$ is 0 for some x and t, then the product $f(x-t)g(t)$ is taken to be 0, even if the second factor is not defined.

Theorem 1.1. *The equation*

$$\int_{\mathbf{R}^q} f(x-t)g(t)\, dt = \int_{\mathbf{R}^q} f(t)g(x-t)\, dt$$

holds at a point x, whenever at least one of the integrals is sensible (then also the other integral is sensible).

Proof. The assertion follows by a simple substitution in the integral.

We shall denote the convolution (1.1) by $f * g$.

Corollary. *If $A = B$, and the product is commutative i.e., if $ab = ba$ holds for all $a, b \in A$, then the equation*

$$f * g = g * f \tag{1.2}$$

holds (at a given point x), whenever at least one of the convolutions exists (at x).

By simple calculations we also obtain the following theorems.

Theorem 1.2. *If the convolution $f * g$ exists at a point x, then, given any real number λ, the convolutions $f * (\lambda g)$ and $(\lambda f) * g$ exist and the equations*

$$(\lambda f) * g = f * (\lambda g) = \lambda(f * g)$$

hold at that point.

Theorem 1.3. *If the convolution $f * g$ and $f * h$ exist at a point x, then also the convolution $f * (g + h)$ exists and the equality*

$$f * (g + h) = f * g + f * h$$

holds at that point.

Because of the axiom **M** (Chapter IV, section 1) the existence of the convolution $f * g$ at x implies the existence, at x, of the integral

$$\int_{\mathbf{R}^q} |f(x - t) g(t)| \, dt.$$

This integral will be denoted, for convenience, by $f \stackrel{*}{*} g$. Since $|ab| \leqslant |a| \, |b|$, we generally have

$$|f * g| \leqslant f \stackrel{*}{*} g \leqslant |f| * |g|. \tag{1.3}$$

In particular, if

$$|ab| = |a| \, |b| \quad \text{for} \quad a \in A, \ b \in B \tag{1.4}$$

(for example, this condition is satisfied, when one of the Banach spaces A or B is the set of real numbers), then we have

$$f \stackrel{*}{*} g = |f| * |g| \tag{1.5}$$

and the existence of one of the convolutions is equivalent to the existence of the other one.

However, this is not true in general. In fact, let $A = B = \mathbf{R}^2$ and let the product ab be the ordinary scalar product. In particular, if we take for a and b two orthogonal vectors of length 1, then we have $|ab| = 0$ and $|a| \, |b| = 1$. If we now put $f = a\varphi$ and $g = b\varphi$, where φ is a positive function such that $\varphi * \varphi$ does not exist, then evidently $f \stackrel{*}{*} g = 0$ but the convolution $|f| * |g| = \varphi * \varphi$ does not exist.

Theorem 1.4. (a) If $f * g$ exists at a point x, then $f \bar{*} g$ exists at x. If, moreover, condition (1.4) holds, then also $|f| * |g|$ exists at x. (b) If f and g are Bochner measurable and $|f| * |g|$ or $f \bar{*} g$ exists at x, then also $f * g$ exists at x.

Proof. The first part of the theorem is followed by axiom **M** (see the preceding remarks). In order to prove the second part, it suffices to show, by (1.3), that the function $h(x, t) = f(x - t)g(t)$ is Bochner measurable (see Theorem 3.1, Chapter VI). But, in view of Theorem 6.3, Chapter X, this will be done, if we prove that the functions $\bar{f}(x, t) = f(x - t)$ and $\bar{g}(x, t) = g(t)$ are measurable.

The measurability of $\bar{g}$ is a consequence of the Fubini theorem. The measurability of $\bar{f}$ follows from

Lemma 1.1. If $f(x)$ is Bochner measurable in $\mathbf{R}^q$, then the function $\bar{f}(x, t) = f(x - t)$ is Bochner measurable in $\mathbf{R}^{2q}$.

Proof. If $f(x)$ is locally integrable in $\mathbf{R}^q$, then $\bar{f}(x, t)$ is locally integrable in $\mathbf{R}^{2q}$, which is an easy consequence of the Fubini theorem. Using the transformation $x = x' - t'$, $t = t'$, we see that the function $\bar{f}(x', t') = f(x' - t')$ is locally integrable in $\mathbf{R}^{2q}$. Instead of x', t' we may of course use the letters x and t.

If $f(x)$ is a measurable function in $\mathbf{R}^q$, then there are locally integrable functions $f_n(x)$ such that $f_n(x) \rightarrow f(x)$. By the just obtained result the functions $\bar{f}_n(x, t) = f_n(x - t)$ are locally integrable in $\mathbf{R}^{2q}$. Moreover, $\bar{f}_n(x, t) \rightarrow \bar{f}(x, t)$ which proves that $\bar{f}(x, t)$ is measurable in $\mathbf{R}^{2q}$.

Theorem 1.5. If f and g are measurable and the convolution (1.1) exists almost everywhere, then the convolution $f * g$ is a measurable function.

Proof. The function $h(x, t) = f(x - t)g(t)$ is measurable in $\mathbf{R}^{2q}$ (see Lemma 1.1). Let $p_n(x, t)$ be a sequence of brick functions in $\mathbf{R}^{2q}$, convergent everywhere to the limit 1. Then the functions $h_n(x, t) = h(x, t) \cap np_n(x, t)$ are integrable in $\mathbf{R}^{2q}$, by Theorem 3.1, Chapter VI. Since $f(x - t)$ is, for every fixed x, a measurable function of t, the function $h_n(x, t)$ is also measurable with respect to t. Moreover, it is bounded by $np_n(x, t)$, thus integrable with respect to t. Hence the function $K_n(x) = \int h_n(x, t) \, dt$ is integrable (in $\mathbf{R}^q$), by the Fubini theorem.

Let Z be the set of all points x for which the integral $\int f(x - t)g(t) \, dt$ exists. Then also the integral $\int |f(x - t)g(t)| \, dt$ exists for $x \in Z$. Since $h_n(x, t) \rightarrow h(x, t)$ and $|h_n(x, t)| \leqslant |h(x, t)|$, it follows by the Dominated Convergence Theorem that

$$k_n(x) = \int h_n(x, t) \, dt \rightarrow \int h(x, t) \, dt \quad \text{for} \quad x \in Z,$$

i.e., almost everywhere. Thus $\int h(x, t)\, dt = (f * g)(x)$ is a measurable function of x.

In general, convolution is not associative, i.e., it may happen that

$$(f * g) * h = f * (g * h) \tag{1.6}$$

does not hold, even if all convolutions involved in (1.6) exist everywhere. In fact, let $f(x) = 1$, $g(x) = -xe^{-x^2}$ $(x \in \mathbf{R}^1)$ and let $h(x) = \int_{-\infty}^{x} e^{-t^2}\, dt$. It is easy to see that $f * g = 0$. This implies that $(f * g) * h = 0$ as well. On the other hand, a straightforward calculation gives

$$g * h = \frac{1}{2}\sqrt{\frac{\pi}{2}}\, e^{-x^2/2}$$

and hence $f * (g * h) = \frac{1}{2}\pi$, i.e., (1.6) does not hold. In the next section we state some sufficient conditions for associativity.

2. Convolutions of three functions

In this and next sections we suppose that the equality $(ab)c = a(bc)$ holds for any elements a, b and c from the considered Banach spaces A, B and C, i.e., that the product is associative. In this case, we may neglect the parentheses and simply write abc. Let f, g and h be measurable functions whose values belong to A, B and C, respectively.

By the convolution $f * g * h$ of three functions we mean the double integral

$$\iint_{\mathbf{R}^{2q}} f(x-t)g(t-u)h(u)\, dt\, du. \tag{2.1}$$

The convolution exists at a point $x \in \mathbf{R}^q$, whenever the product $k(x, t, u) = f(x-t)g(t-u)h(u)$ is Bochner integrable over $\mathbf{R}^{2q}$ at x. As before, we understand that, if one of the factors $f(x-t)$, $g(t-u)$ or $h(u)$ is 0 for some x, t and u, then the product is always taken to be 0, even if the remaining factors are not defined.

The existence of $f * g * h$ implies the existence of $f \bar{*} g \bar{*} h$, the last expression being defined by

$$(f \bar{*} g \bar{*} h)(x) = \iint_{\mathbf{R}^{2q}} |f(x-t)g(t-u)h(u)|\, dt\, du.$$

The converse implication also holds, provided we assume that the product $f(x-t)g(t-u)h(u)$ is measurable.

Theorem 2.1. *(a) If $f * g * h$ exists at a point x, then $f \bar{*} g \bar{*} h$ exists at x. If, moreover, condition $|abc| = |a| |b| |c|$ holds for every $a \in A$, $b \in B$, $c \in C$, then also $|f| * |g| * |h|$ exists. (b) If f, g and h are Bochner measurable and $|f| * |g| * |h|$ or $f \bar{*} g \bar{*} h$ exists at x, then also $f * g * h$ exists at x.*

Proof. Like in Theorem 1.4, it suffices to prove that the function $k(x, t, u) = f(x - t)g(t - u)h(u)$ is measurable. From Lemma 1.1 follows that the functions $f(x - t)$ and $g(t - u)$ are measurable in $\mathbf{R}^{2q}$. Hence, by Theorem 5.4, Chapter X, we conclude the measurability of the functions $f(x - t)$, $g(t - u)$ and $h(u)$ in $\mathbf{R}^{3q}$. Then it remains to apply twice Theorem 6.3, Chapter X.

Theorem 2.2. *If the convolution $f * g * h$ exists, then*

$$f * g * h = f * (g * h) = (f * g) * h. \tag{2.2}$$

More precisely: if $f * g * h$ exists at some point x, then the convolutions $h_1 = f * g$ and $f_1 = g * h$ are defined on sets such that the convolutions $f * f_1$ and $h_1 * h$ exist at x.
Moreover, the equality

$$f * g * h = f * f_1 = h_1 * h \quad \text{holds at x.}$$

Proof. Suppose that $f * g * h$ exists at some fixed point x. Then, by the Fubini theorem, the functions

$$k_1(t) = \int_{\mathbf{R}^q} f(x - t)g(t - u)h(u) \, du \tag{2.3}$$

and

$$k_2(u) = \int_{\mathbf{R}^q} f(x - t)g(t - u)h(u) \, dt \tag{2.4}$$

are defined for almost every t and for almost every u, respectively. Moreover we have

$$\int_{\mathbf{R}^q} k_1(t) \, dt = f * g * h = \int_{\mathbf{R}^q} k_2(u) \, du. \tag{2.5}$$

Let Z be the set of points t for which the function $k_1(t)$ is defined. Furthermore, let Z_1 and Z_2 denote the sets of such points t of Z that $f(x - t) \neq 0$ and $f(x - t) = 0$, respectively.
If $t \in Z_1$, we can write

$$k_1(t) = f(x - t) \int_{\mathbf{R}^q} g(t - u)h(u) \, du \tag{2.6}$$

and the integral in (2.6) exists for every $t \in Z_1$.

If $t \in Z_2$, then the product on the right side of (2.6) exists and equals to 0, according to our convention, no matter whether the integral in (2.6) exists or not (it is worth noting that the set of points for which this integral does not exist can be non-null). But for $t \in Z_2$ also $k_1(t) = 0$, by (2.3). Thus the equality (2.6) holds for every $t \in Z$.

From (2.5) and (2.6) follows that

$$f * g * h = \int_{\mathbf{R}^q} f(x - t)\, dt \int_{\mathbf{R}^q} g(t - u)h(u)\, du = f * (g * h).$$

Similarly, starting from (2.4) we can show that

$$f * g * h = (f * g) * h.$$

which completes the proof.

Corollary 2.1. *If the convolution $|f| * |g| * |h|$ exists, then*

$$|f| * |g| * |h| = |f| * (|g| * |h|) = (|f| * |g|) * |h|$$

holds in the same sense as in Theorem 2.2.

Proof. These equations follow from Theorem 2.2., if we replace f, g, h by $|f|$, $|g|$, $|h|$, respectively.

Theorem 2.3. *If f, g and h are Bochner measurable and the convolution (2.1) exists almost everywhere, then this convolution is a measurable function.*

Proof. Since the convolutions $f * g$ and $g * h$ may happen to be un-defined on null sets, the last theorem does not reduce to Theorem 1.5. However, we can repeat word for word the proof of that theorem, making only natural modifications.

It is easy to see that if $A = B = C$ and the product is commutative (its associativity being still postulated), i.e., if A is a commutative Banach algebra, then

$$f * g * h = f * h * g = g * f * h = g * h * f = h * f * g = h * g * f.$$

This result can be obtained by proper substitutions.

3. Associativity of convolution

As we saw at the end of section 1, the associativity law

$$(f * g) * h = f * (g * h)$$

$$(3.1)$$

does not hold in general. On the other hand, Theorem 2.2 tells us that (3.1) does hold whenever $f * g * h$ exists. For applications it is important to have sufficient conditions for (3.1) in which the existence of the convolution of three functions is not postulated.

Theorem 3.1. *If the convolution* $|f| * (|g| * |h|)$ *exists at a point x and the functions f, g, h are measurable, then (3.1) holds at x. More precisely, if the convolution* $|g| * |h|$ *is defined on a set such that the convolution* $|f| * (|g| * |h|)$ *exists at x, and f, g, h are measurable, then the convolutions* $h_1 = f * g$ *and* $f_1 = g * h$ *are defined on sets such that the convolutions* $f * f_1$ *and* $h_1 * h$ *exist and are equal at x.*

Proof. We can write,

$$|f(x)| * (|g(x)| * |h(x)|) = \int_{\mathbf{R}^q} |f(x-t)|\, dt \int_{\mathbf{R}^q} |g(t-u)|\, |h(u)|\, du.$$

This implies, by the Tonelli theorem, the existence of $f * g * h$ (as well as $|f| * |g| * |h|$), and our assertion follows by Theorem 2.2.

Corollary 3.1. *If the convolution* $|f| * (|g| * |h|)$ *exists at a point x and the functions f, g, h are measurable, then the equality*

$$(|f| * |g|) * |h| = |f| * (|g| * |h|) \tag{3.2}$$

holds at x in the sense like in Theorem 3.1.

Proof. This follows from Theorem 3.1, if we replace f, g, h by $|f|$, $|g|$, $|h|$, respectively.

Theorem 3.2. *If* $|f| * (|g| * |h|)$ *exists almost everywhere and the functions f, g, h are measurable, then (3.1) and (3.2) hold almost everywhere. Moreover, if the integral* $\int |f|$, $\int |g|$ *or* $\int |h|$ *(respectively) does not vanish, then the convolution* $|g| * |h|$, $|f| * |h|$ *or* $|f| * |g|$ *(respectively) exists almost everywhere.*

Proof. The first part of the assertion follows immediately from Theorem 3.1 and Corollary 3.1. We can state, furthermore, as in the proof of Theorem 3.1, that the convolution $|f| * |g| * |h|$ exists almost everywhere. From Corollary 2.1 it also follows that $|f| * (|g| * |h|)$ exists almost everywhere.

Now, we show that the convolution $|g| * |h|$ exists a.e., if $\int |f| > 0$. We assume that the convolution $|g| * |h|$ is not defined almost everywhere, so that if Z denotes the set of points at which $|g| * |h|$ does not exists, then Z is not a null set.

Let f_1 and f_2 be two real functions such that $f_1 - f_2 = 1$ on Z and $f_1 = f_2 = |g| * |h|$ on $\mathbf{R}^q \backslash Z$. Then

$$\int_{\mathbf{R}^q} (f_1 - f_2) > 0. \tag{3.3}$$

Now let x be a point at which the convolution $|f| * (|g| * |h|)$ exists. Then we must have $f(x - t) = 0$ for almost every $t \in Z$. Consequently,

$$\int_{\mathbf{R}^q} |f(x - t)|(|g| * |h|)(t) \, dt = \int_{\mathbf{R}^q} |f(x - t)| f_1(t) \, dt$$

$$= \int_{\mathbf{R}^q} |f(x - t)| f_2(t) \, dt.$$

Since $|f| * (|g| * |h|)$ exists almost everywhere, this means that

$$|f| * f_1 = |f| * f_2 \qquad \text{a.e.}$$

Hence we have

$$\int_{\mathbf{R}^q} [|f| * (f_1 - f_2)] = 0. \tag{3.4}$$

On other hand, by the Tonelli theorem,

$$\int_{\mathbf{R}^q} [|f| * (f_1 - f_2)] = \int_{\mathbf{R}^q} |f| \int_{\mathbf{R}^q} (f_1 - f_2) > 0.$$

This contradiction proves the assertion for $\int |f| > 0$. In the cases $\int |g| > 0$ or $\int |h| > 0$, the assertion can be deduced from the preceding result, using commutativity and associativity of the convolution of $|f|, |g|, |h|$.

4. Convolutive dual sets of functions

According to Theorem 1.4, if f and g are Bochner–measurable functions and the convolution $|f| * |g|$ exists, then also the convolution $f * g$ exists. This allows us to reduce the study of $f * g$ to the case of real functions. We therefore restrict our consideration in this section to real functions. All functions considered in this section are assumed real valued and measurable.

Let U be any set of such functions defined in $\mathbf{R}^q$. We denote by U^* the set of all measurable functions g such that the convolution $f * g$ exists a.e. for each $f \in U$. The set U^* will be called the *convolutive dual set* of U. If the convolution $f * g$ exists, then also the convolution $|f| * |g|$ exists, by

Theorem 1.4. More generally, if $|g| \leq |g_1|$, the existence of $f * g_1$ implies the existence of both the convolutions $f * g$ and $|f| * |g|$ so that $g \in U^*$. A set V of functions g such that the conditions $|g| \leq |g_1|$, $g_1 \in V$ imply $g \in V$ will be called *standard*. Thus:

Theorem 4.1. *A convolutive dual set is standard.*

Example 1. Let U consist of a single function $f = 1$ in $\mathbf{R}^q$. Then the convolution $f * g$ reduces to the integral $\int g$ so that U^* is the set of all integrable functions in $\mathbf{R}^q$.

Example 2. Let U be the set of all bounded measurable functions in $\mathbf{R}^q$. We shall show that then U^* is, as before, the set of all integrable functions in $\mathbf{R}^q$. In fact, if $f \in U$ and g is integrable, then the integral $\int f(x - t)g(t)dt$ exists for every x so that $g \in U^*$. If we assume conversely, that $g \in U^*$, then the convolution $f * g$ must exist for each $f \in U$ and thus for $f \equiv 1$, in particular. Hence g must be integrable, like in Example 1. It is worth remarking that in both cases we have obtained the same dual set, although the generating set U in Example 2 is much larger than in Example 1.

Theorem 4.2. *If relations $f \in U$, $g \in U^*$ imply $|f| * |g| \in U$, then relations $g \in U^*$, $h \in U^*$ imply $g * h \in U^*$. (Thus, U^* is a convolutative semi-group under convolution.)*

Proof. Assume that $f \in U$ and $g, h \in U^*$. Since $|f| * |g| \in U$, it follows that also $(|f| * |g|) * h \in U^*$. By Theorem 3.1 it follows that the convolution $f * (g * h)$ exists. Since f is arbitrary within U, we have $g * h \in U^*$, according to the definitions of U^*.

Corollary 4.1. *The convolution of two integrable functions exists* a.e. *and is another integrable function.*

Proof. We take for U the set of bounded measurable functions. Then U^* is the set of integrable functions (see Example 2). If $f \in U$, $|f| \leq M$ and $g \in U^*$, then

$$|f| * |g| \leq M * |g| = M \int g = M_1 < \infty \quad \text{for each} \quad x \in \mathbf{R}^q.$$

Hence $|f| * |g| \in U$ and the first implication in Theorem 4.2 holds. Consequently, the second implication holds, proving Corollary.

The preceding method can be generalized, on multiplying the factors f and g of the convolution by properly chosen functions u and v. Let U_0 be a class of real valued functions, defined in $\mathbf{R}^q$, such that for any $u \in U_0$ there is a positive function $v \in U_0$ satisfying

$$|u(x + y)| \leq v(x)v(y) \quad \text{for each} \quad x, y \in \mathbf{R}^q. \tag{4.1}$$

The class U_0 may consist of a single function, e.g., e^x. Another class U_0 with this property is the set of all polynomials.

In the following theorem, we denote by $\bar{v}$ the function such that $\bar{v}(x) = v(-x)$ for each $x \in \mathbf{R}^q$.

Theorem 4.3. *Let U be a standard set and let V be the set of functions such that*

$$f \in V, \quad iff \quad \frac{f}{u} \in U \text{ for some positive } u \in U_0.$$

Then the set V is standard and its dual V^* consists of functions g such that

$$g \in V^*, \quad iff \quad \bar{v}g \in U^* \text{ for each positive } v \in U_0.$$

Moreover, if U has the property that $f \in U$, $g \in U^*$ imply $f * g \in U$, then V has a similar property, i.e., $f \in V$, $g \in V^*$ imply $f * g \in V$.

Proof. Assume that g is a function satisfying $\bar{v}g \in U^*$ for each positive $v \in U_0$. If $f \in V$, then $f/u \in U$ for some positive $u \in U_0$. There is a positive $v \in U_0$ satisfying (4.1). Hence

$$|f * g| \leq \int_{\mathbf{R}^q} |f(x-t)g(t)| \, dt = \int_{\mathbf{R}^q} \left| \frac{f(x-t)}{u(x-t)} \right| |u(x-t)g(t)| \, dt$$

$$\leq v(x) \int_{\mathbf{R}^q} \left| \frac{f(x-t)}{u(x-t)} \right| |v(-t)g(t)| \, dt.$$

Since $f/u \in U$ and $\bar{v}g \in U^*$, the last integral exists almost everywhere. This implies the existence of the convolution and, consequently, $g \in V^*$.

Assume now, conversely, that $g \in V^*$ is given. Then the convolution $f * g$ exists almost everywhere for each $f \in V$. We shall show that, if $u \in U_0$, then $\bar{u}g \in U^*$, i.e., the convolution $f * \bar{u}g$ exists almost everywhere for any $f \in U$. In fact, there is a function $v \in U_0$ satisfying (4.1) and therefore,

$$|(f * \bar{u}g)(x)| \leq \int_{\mathbf{R}^q} |u(t-x)g(x-t)f(t)| \, dt$$

$$\leq v(-x) \int_{\mathbf{R}^q} |g(x-t)v(t)f(t)| \, dt = v(-x)(|g| * |vf|)(x).$$

Since $vf/v \in U$, we have $vf \in V$ and, consequently, the convolution $vf * g$ exists almost everywhere. This implies that also the convolution $f * \bar{u}g$ exists almost everywhere. Thus $\bar{u}g \in U^*$, proving the first part of the theorem.

To prove its second part, assume that $f \in V$ and $g \in V^*$. There exist functions $u, v \in U_0$, $v > 0$ such that (4.1) holds, $f/u \in U$ and

$$\frac{|f * g|}{v} \leq \frac{1}{v(x)} \int_{\mathbf{R}^q} \left| \frac{f(x-t)}{u(x-t)} \right| |u(x-t)g(t)| \, dt$$

$$\leq \int_{\mathbf{R}^q} \left| \frac{f(x-t)}{u(x-t)} \right| |\bar{v}(t)g(t)| \, dt = \left| \frac{f}{u} \right| * |\bar{v}g|.$$

By the first part of Theorem 4.3, we have $\bar{v}g \in U^*$. Since $\dfrac{f}{u} \in U$, $\bar{v}g \in U^*$ and the sets U, U^* are standard, we have $\dfrac{f}{v} \in U$ and $|\bar{v}g| \in U^*$. This implies that $\dfrac{f}{u} * |\bar{v}g| \in U$, by hypothesis. Since

$$\left| \frac{f * g}{v} \right| \leq \left| \frac{f}{u} \right| * |\bar{v}g| \in U$$

and U is standard, we get $\dfrac{f * g}{v} \in U$. This means that $f * g \in V$, proving the second part of the theorem.

We shall still show some applications of Theorem 4.3. A function f is called *slowly increasing*, iff there is a polynomial p such that $|f| \leq p$. A function g is called *rapidly decreasing*, iff the product gp is bounded for every polynomial p.

Corollary 4.2. *If f is slowly increasing and g is rapidly decreasing, then the convolution $f * g$ exists a.e. and is slowly increasing.*

Proof. We take for U_0 the set of all polynomials and for U the set of all bounded measurable functions. Then V is the set of all slowly increasing functions and V^* is the set of all rapidly decreasing functions, and the assertion follows from the first part of Theorem 4.3.

Corollary 4.3. *If f and g are rapidly decreasing functions, then their convolution $f * g$ exists and is a rapidly decreasing function.*

Proof. We use the notation from the preceding proof and apply the second part of Theorem 4.3.

5. Application to vector valued functions

The functions considered in this section are assumed to be Bochner integrable in $\mathbf{R}^q$. All integrals are stretched over $\mathbf{R}^q$.

Theorem 5.1. *If f and g are Bochner integrable functions, then the convolution $f * g$ exists and is Bochner integrable. Moreover,*

$$\int (f * g) = \int f \cdot \int g \quad \text{and} \quad \int |f * g| \leqslant \int |f| \cdot \int |g|.$$

Proof. By Corollary 4.1, the convolution $|f| * |g|$ exists a.e. and is integrable. By (1.3) and Theorem 1.4, the convolution $f * g$ also exists a.e. and is Bochner integrable. By the Tonelli theorem we have

$$\int (f * g) = \int dx \int f(x - t)g(t)\, dt = \int\int f(x - t)g(t)\, dx\, dt = \int f \cdot \int g.$$

The last equality follows by a simple linear substitution. The inequality for the moduli follows similarly, on using inequality $|f * g| \leqslant |f| * |g|$.

The definitions of a *slowly increasing* function and of a *rapidly decreasing* function given in the preceding section apply also when values of the function are in a Banach space. However the polynomials involved are to be taken always with real coefficients.

Theorem 5.2. *If f and g are Bochner measurable functions and one of them is slowly increasing and the other one is rapidly decreasing, then their convolution exist a.e. and is a slowly increasing.*

Proof. The functions $|f|$ and $|g|$ have similar properties, but are real valued. This allows us to apply Corollary 4.2 and implies that the convolution $|f| * |g|$ exists a.e. and is slowly increasing. By inequality $|f * g| \leqslant |f| * |g|$, the convolution $f * g$ also exists and is a slowly increasing function.

From Corollary 4.3 we similarly obtain

Theorem 5.3. *If f and g are Bochner measurable and rapidly decreasing functions, then their convolution $f * g$ is also rapidly decreasing.*

All these theorems have been derived from the basic Theorem 4.3. They give, in fact, existence criteria for convolution. Those criteria are based on the rate of growth of involved functions. In the next sections, we are going to give another type of existence criteria in which the rate of growth is completely irrelevant. Instead, the shape of the carriers plays a striking role. We shall introduce the concept of compatibility of carriers and show that the convolution of two locally integrable functions always exists, whenever their carriers are compatible. The definition of compatibility makes also sense for sets which are not considered as carriers of functions.

6. Compatible sets

Let X and Y be arbitrary subsets of $\mathbf{R}^q$. We denote by $X(t)$ and $Y(t)$ their characteristic functions. If $x \in \mathbf{R}^q$, we denote by S^x the set consisting of the points t such that $X(x - t)Y(t) = 1$, The set S^x is completely determined by the point x and the sets X, Y. We say that the sets X and Y are *compatible*, iff for every bounded interval $I \subset \mathbf{R}^q$ there is another bounded interval $J \subset \mathbf{R}^q$ such that $x \in I$ implies $S^x \subset J$.

Example 1. Assume that the set X is arbitrary and the set Y is bounded. Then X and Y are compatible.

Example 2. Assume that the points of X and Y have positive coordinates. Then X and Y are compatible.

In Example 1, one of the sets is bounded. In Example 2, both the sets are bounded from the left-hand side. There are compatible sets which are both unbounded from each side, but their construction is somewhat sophisticated.

Theorem 6.1. *The following condition is necessary and sufficient for sets X and Y to be compatible:*

$$(*) \qquad \text{If} \quad x_n \in X, \; y_n \in Y \quad \text{and} \quad |x_n| + |y_n| \to \infty, \quad \text{then} \quad |x_n + y_n| \to \infty.$$

Proof. If condition (*) is not satisfied, then there exist sequences x_n and y_n such that $x_n \in X$, $y_n \in Y$, $|x_n| + |y_n| \to \infty$ and $|x_n + y_n| < M < \infty$. Let $z_n = x_n + y_n$. Then $X(z_n - y_n)Y(y_n) = 1$ and $|z_n| < M$. The points $x = z_n$ are in a bounded interval I, but the set of points $t = y_n$ is not bounded. This proves that the sets X and Y are not compatible and, consequently, that condition (*) is necessary.

On the other hand, if the sets X and Y are not compatible, then there exists a bounded interval I and sequences z_n, t_n such that $z_n - t_n \in X$, $t_n \in Y$, $z_n \in I$ and $t_n \to \infty$. Letting $x_n = z_n - t_n$ and $y_n = t_n$, we have $x_n \in X$, $y_n \in Y$, $|x_n| + |y_n| \to \infty$ and $|x_n + y_n| = |z_n| < M < \infty$. This shows that condition (*) is not satisfied, and completes the proof.

Theorem 6.1 shows that the relation of compatibility is symmetric. Moreover, condition (*) has a simple geometrical interpretation. In fact, since $x + y = 2(x + y)/2$, condition (*) tells us that *if a point x ranges over X and y ranges over Y so that at least one of them tends to infinity, then their arithmetic mean* $\dfrac{x + y}{2}$ *also tends to infinity.*

Theorem 6.2. *If X, Y are compatible sets and $V \subset X$, $W \subset Y$, then V, W are compatible. In other words, subsets of compatible sets are compatible.*

The proof follows immediately from Theorem 6.1.

Condition (*) can easily be reformulated for three (or more) sets X, Y, Z:

(**)   If $x_n \in X$, $y_n \in Y$, $z_n \in Z$ and $|x_n| + |y_n| + |z_n| \to \infty$, then

$$|x_n + y_n + z_n| \to \infty.$$

This condition allows us to extend the concept of compatibility onto three sets. We namely say that the sets X, Y, Z are *compatible*, if they satisfy condition (**).

Theorem 6.3. *The sets X. Y. Z are compatible, iff X, Y are compatible and $X + Y$, Z are compatible.*

Proof.   If the sets $X + Y$ and Z are compatible, then

$$x_n \in X, \ y_n \in Y, \ z_n \in Z \text{ and } |x_n| + |y_n| + |z_n| \to \infty \text{ imply } |x_n + y_n + z_n| \to \infty,$$

$$(6.1)$$

by condition (*). Let p_n an increasing sequence consisting of all positive integers such that $|x_{p_n}| + |y_{p_n}| \geqslant |z_{p_n}|$, and let q_n be the sequence of the remaining positive integers. Then $|x_{q_n}| + |y_{q_n}| < |z_{q_n}|$, If both the sequences p_n, q_n are infinite and $|x_n| + |y_n| + |z_n| \to \infty$, we have

$$|x_{p_n}| + |y_{p_n}| \to \infty \quad \text{and} \quad |z_{q_n}| \to \infty.$$

7. Functions with compatible carriers

The concept of a *carrier* or *support* was introduced, for distributions, by Laurent Schwartz in his famous book 'Théorie des distributions' ([26], p. 17 and 27). This concept turns out to be useful also in the study of ordinary functions. For a continuous function f the support can be simply defined as the closure of the set of points x at which $f(x) \neq 0$. We can equivalently say that the support of f is the smallest closed set outside which f vanishes. If f is not continuous, then its value at a separate point plays minor role and it thus is more natural to say that *the support of f is the smallest closed set outside which f vanishes* a.e. (almost everywhere). This is the definition we adopt in this book. It differs from the original Schwartz definition, but agrees with it, if the distribution is a function. E.g., if f is the characteristic function of a closed interval, then that interval is the support of f.

However, a similar statement would be false for arbitrary closed sets. In fact, let f be the function which takes the value 1 at the origin and 0 elsewhere. Then f is the characteristic function of the set consisting of a single point, the origin, but the support of f is the empty set. This might seem strange to a reader acquainted with Theory of Distributions, because the delta distribution also vanishes everywhere except for the origin and, nevertheless, the non-empty set, consisting of the origin, is considered as its support. The explanation of this apparent paradox is that our definition, given above, applies only to functions. For arbitrary distributions, another definition must be given so that the structure of distributions is taken in account. Since Theory of Distributions does not belong to the subject of this book, we refer the interested reader to special literature (e.g., [1]) for more details.

Theorem 7.1. *If two Bochner locally integrable (in* $\mathbf{R}^q$*) functions f and g have compatible carriers X and Y, then the convolution f * g exists almost a.e. and represents a locally integrable function whose carrier is contained in X + Y, i.e., in the set of points* $x + y$ *such that* $x \in X$ *and* $y \in Y$.

Proof. Let a bounded interval $I \subset \mathbf{R}^q$ be given. Since X and Y are compatible, there exists another bounded interval $J \subset \mathbf{R}^q$ such that $x \in I$ implies $S^x \subset I$. There exists a third bounded interval K such that $J \subset K$ and $I - J \subset K$ where $I - J$ is the set of all points $x - t$ such that $x \in I$ and $t \in J$. Let $f_1(x) = f(x)K(x)$ and $g_1(x) = g(x)K(x)$, where $K(x)$ is the characteristic function of the set K. Since the set K is bounded, the functions f_1 and g_1 are integrable in $\mathbf{R}^q$. Hence the convolution $f_1 * g_1$ exists a.e. in $\mathbf{R}^q$ and represents an integrable function in $\mathbf{R}^q$, according to Corollary 4.1. If $x \in I$, then $f(x - t)g(t) = 0$ for $t \notin J$ and $K(x - t)K(t) = 1$ for $t \notin J$. Hence

$$\int_{\mathbf{R}^q} f(x - t)g(t)\, dt = \int_{\mathbf{R}^q} f(x - t)K(x - t)g(t)K(t)\, dt = \int_{\mathbf{R}^q} f_1(x - t)g(t)\, dt.$$

$$(7.1)$$

This implies that the integral on the left side exists a.e. in I and represents an integrable function there. This holds for arbitrary bounded interval I, and therefore means that the convolution $f * g$ exists a.e. in $\mathbf{R}^q$ and represents a locally integrable function. To complete the proof, note that given any x not belonging to $X + Y$, we have either $x - t \notin X$ or $t \notin Y$ so that integral (7.1) vanishes for that x.

Corollary 7.1. *If f and g are Bochner locally integrable functions in* $\mathbf{R}^q$ *and one of them is of bounded carrier, then the convolution f * g exists a.e. and is a locally integrable function.*

Proof. It suffices to remark that the carrier which is bounded is compatible with every other set.

8. Associativity of the convolution of functions with compatible carriers

In this section we shall assume, as before, that the functions f, g, h have their values in the Banach spaces A, B, C and equality

$$(ab)c = a(bc)$$

holds for every $a \in A$, $b \in B$, $c \in C$.

The concept of compatibility of three sets allows us to formulate the following associativity theorem.

Theorem 8.1. *Let f, g and h be locally Bochner integrable functions in* $\mathbf{R}^q$, *whose carriers are X, Y and Z, respectively. If X, Y, Z are compatible, then all the convolutions involved in the equality*

$$(f * g) * h = f * (g * h) \tag{8.1}$$

exist a.e. and the equality holds.

Proof. The moduli $|f|$, $|g|$, and $|h|$ are also Bochner locally integrable (axiom **M**) and have the same carriers X, Y, and Z. The convolution $|f| * |g|$ therefore exists and represents a locally integrable function, by Theorem 5.1. Since the carrier of $|f| * |g|$ lies in $X + Y$, the convolution $(|f| * |g|) * |h|$ also exists, by Theorems 6.7 and 3.1. The assertion now follows, by Theorem 3.2.

Remark. The hypothesis concerning the sets $X + Y$ and Z cannot be replaced, in Theorem 8.1 by the hypothesis that the carrier of $f * g$ be compatible with Z. In fact, if f, g, h are real valued functions such that

$$\int f = 0, \quad \int |f| > 0, \quad g = 1, \quad h = 1,$$

then $(f * g) * h = (f * 1) * 1 = 0 * 1 = 0$.

On the other hand $f * (g * h)$ does not make sense because $g * h = \infty$. From (*) and from Theorem 8.1 we obtain

Corollary 8.1. *If f, g, h are locally integrable functions and f, g have bounded carriers, then all the convolutions involved in (8.1) exist a.e. and the equality holds a.e.*

However, the following much stronger corollary follows directly from Theorem 3.2.

Corollary 8.2. *If f, g, h are locally integrable functions, f has bounded carrier and the convolution* $|g| * |h|$ *exists a.e. and is a locally integrable function, then all the convolutions involved in (8.1) exist a.e. and the equality holds a.e.*

Proof. If the assumptions of the Corollary are satisfied, then the convolution $|f| * (|g| * |h|)$ exists a.e., by Theorem 5.1. This implies, by Theorem 3.2 that the outer convolutions in equality (8.2) exist a.e. and the equality holds. Furthermore the inner convolutions in (7.1) exist a.e.; in fact, $g * h$ exists by hypothesis, and $f * g$ exists by Theorem 5.1, because f is of bounded carrier.

Remark. Note that the pair of functions f, g can be replaced in the second assumption of Corollary 8.1 by g, h or by f, h.

One can also modify the second assumption in this way: 'h has a bounded carrier and $|f| * |g|$ exists a.e.'. The third version of the assumption: 'g has a bounded carrier and $|f| * |h|$ exists a.e.' cannot be adopted in general. This is however possible, if $A = B = C$ is a commutative Banach algebra. These facts follows from Remark in section 3.

9. A particular case

We consider two real numbers α and β satisfying

$$0 < \alpha < 1 \quad \text{and} \quad -\alpha < \beta \leq \alpha. \tag{9.1}$$

Let w be a point of $\mathbf{R}^q$ such that $|w| = 1$. By X we denote the set of points $x \in \mathbf{R}^q$ such that $wx \geq \alpha|x|$ and by Y the set of points $y \in \mathbf{R}^q$ such that $wy \geq \beta|y|$, where wx and wy are scalar products. We shall show that X and Y satisfy condition (*). In fact, let $x_n \in X$, $y_n \in Y$, and

$$m_n = \min (|x_n|, |y_n|) = \frac{|x_n| + |y_n| - \||x_n| - |y_n|\|}{2}.$$

If $|x_n| + |y_n| \to \infty$ and the sequence m_n is bounded, then the relation $|x_n + y_n| \to \infty$ follows from the inequality

$$|x_n + y_n| \geq \||x_n| - |y_n|\| = |x_n| + |y_n| - 2m_n.$$

If the sequence m_n is not bounded, we can split it into two subsequences m_{p_n} and m_{q_n} such that m_{p_n} is bounded and $m_{q_n} \to \infty$, as $n \to \infty$. Then

$$|x_{p_n} + y_{p_n}| \to \infty, \tag{9.2}$$

like in the preceding case. For members with indices q_n we use the general inequality

$$|x_{q_n} + y_{q_n}| \geq m_{q_n}|u_{q_n}|, \quad \text{where} \quad u_{q_n} = \frac{x_{q_n}}{|x_{q_n}|} + \frac{y_{q_n}}{|y_{q_n}|}.$$

(If $x = 0$, we assign $x/|x|$ the value 0.) Since $|wu_{q_n}| \geq \alpha + \beta > 0$, we conclude that u_{q_n} is greater than a fixed positive number. Since $|u_{q_n}| \to \infty$, it follows that also

$$|x_{q_n} + y_{q_n}| \to \infty. \tag{9.3}$$

From (9.2) and (9.3) we obtain $|x_n + y_n| \to \infty$, which proves that X and Y satisfy (*) and, therefore, are compatible.

One can easily give a geometrical interpretation of the sets X and Y. We namely have $wx = |x| \cos (w, x)$, and so X is the set of all points x such that the angle θ between the vectors w and x satisfies the inequality $\cos \theta \geq \beta$. The set X is thus a cone whose apex coincides with the origin and whose axis is the line joining the origin to the point w. The cone is convex, if $\alpha \geq 0$, and concave, if $\alpha < 0$. Similarly, Y is another cone, but it is always convex and contained in X.

If Z is the set of all points $x + y$ such that $x \in X$ and $y \in Y$, then $Z = X$. In fact,

$$w(x + y) \geq \beta |x| + \alpha |y|. \tag{9.4}$$

But, by (9.1)

$$|x + y| \leq |x| + |y| \leq |x| + \frac{\alpha}{\beta} |y| \quad \text{for} \quad \beta > 0$$

and

$$|x + y| \geq |x| - |y| > |x| + \frac{\alpha}{\beta} |y| \quad \text{for} \quad \beta < 0.$$

In both cases, and also for $\beta = 0$, we have

$$\beta |x + y| \leq \beta |x| + \alpha |y|,$$

which, together with (9.4), leads to the inequality

$$w(x + y) \geq \beta |x + y|$$

and so $Z \subset X$.

Conversely, given any point $x \in X$, we can write $x = x + y \in Z$, where $y = 0 \in Y$. Thus $X \subset Z$ and, consequently, $Z = X$.

Assume now that U_X is the set of all locally integrable functions f whose values are in a Banach space A, and the carriers are contained in the cone X. Similarly, U_Y will denote the set of all locally integrable functions g whose values are in a Banach space B, and the carriers are contained in the cone Y. If $f \in U_X$ and $g \in U_Y$, then by Theorem 6.1 the carriers of f and g are compatible. Thus, by Theorem 7.1 the convolution $f * g$ exists and represents a locally integrable function. Moreover, the carrier of $f * g$ is contained in the cone X, which implies $f * g \in U_X$.

Chapter XV
The Titchmarsh Theorem

About 50 years ago, E. C. Titchmarsh discovered, by the occasion of investigating zeros of some analytical functions, an interesting theorem on convolution. That theorem plays an important role in modern Analysis and is actually called *the Titchmarsh Convolution Theorem*. The original proof of Titchmarsh is difficult and involves deep theorems on analytical functions. Simpler proofs consisting in examining the rate of growth of analytical or harmonic functions were given by M. CRUM [6] in 1941 and J. DUFRESNOY [8] in 1947. At present there exist a large number of proofs, based on various methods.

We shall give, in section 2 of this chapter, two equivalent formulations of the Titchmarsh theorem. The proof we give in section 4 was found in 1959 [19]. It is simpler than other known proofs and does not make use of analytical functions. In comparison with the original version we modify it, in section 4, so as to obtain the theorems for functions whose values are in certain Banach algebras. In this way we obtain results which are somewhat stronger rather than in the traditional formulation.

An extension of the Titchmarsh theorem to several variables was given by J. L. LIONS [17] and, independently, by J. MIKUSIŃSKI and C. RYLL-NARDZEWSKI [21]. This matter will be discussed in section 5 of this chapter. The main subject of this chapter is preceded by some theorems on moments which are needed in the sequel.

1. Theorems on moments

Lemma 1. *If g is a Bochner integrable function over the one dimensional interval $(0, T)$, then*

$$\lim_{x \to \infty} \sum_{k=1}^{\infty} \frac{(-1)^{k-1}}{k!} \int_0^T e^{kx(t-\tau)} g(\tau) \, d\tau = \int_0^t g(\tau) \, d\tau \tag{1.1}$$

for all $t \in (0, T)$.

Proof. By the dominated convergence theorem the left side of formula (1.1) can be written in the form

$$\int_0^T g(\tau) \lim_{x \to \infty} \sum_{k=1}^{\infty} \frac{(-1)^{k-1}}{k!} e^{kx(t-\tau)} \, d\tau,$$

i.e.,

$$\int_0^T g(\tau) \lim_{x\to\infty} [1 - \exp(-e^{x(t-\tau)})]\, d\tau. \tag{1.2}$$

Since

$$\lim_{x\to\infty} \exp(-e^{x(t-\tau)}) = \begin{cases} 0 & \text{for } \tau < t, \\ 1 & \text{for } t < \tau. \end{cases}$$

Hence, applying the dominated convergence theorem to (1.2), we get $\int_0^t g(\tau)\, d\tau$, proving Lemma 1.

Theorem 1.1. *If f is a Bochner integrable function over $(0, T)$ and there exists a number N such that*

$$\left| \int_0^T e^{nt} f(t)\, dt \right| \leq N \quad \text{for} \quad n = 1, 2, \ldots, \tag{1.3}$$

then $f = 0$ a.e. in $(0, T)$.

Proof. Formula (1.1) can be written in the form

$$\lim_{x\to\infty} \sum_{k=1}^{\infty} \frac{(-1)^{k-1}}{k!} e^{-kx(T-t)} \int_0^T e^{kx(T-\tau)} g(\tau)\, d\tau = \int_0^t g(\tau)\, d\tau \tag{1.4}$$

for each $t \in (0, T)$.

If k and x are positive integers and $g(\tau) = f(T - \tau)$, then by (1.3) we have

$$\left| \int_0^T e^{kx(T-\tau)} g(\tau)\, d\tau \right| = \left| \int_0^T e^{kx(T-\tau)} f(T-\tau)\, d\tau \right| = \left| \int_0^T e^{kxt} f(t)\, dt \right| \leq N.$$

Consequently the expansion preceded by the sign 'lim' in (1.4) is not greater than

$$N \sum_{k=1}^{\infty} \frac{1}{k!} e^{-kx(T-t)} = N[1 - \exp(e^{-x(T-t)})]$$

and therefore tends to 0, as $x \to \infty$. This proves that $\int_0^t g(\tau)\, d\tau = 0$ in $(0, T)$ and, consequently, $g = 0$ a.e. in $(0, T)$, by Theorem 3.4, Chapter XIII.

Theorem 1.2. *If g is a Bochner integrable function over the one dimensional interval $(1, X)$ and there exists a number N such that*

$$\int_1^X x^n g(x)\, dx \leq N \quad \text{for} \quad n = 1, 2, \ldots, \tag{1.5}$$

then $g = 0$ a.e. in $(1, X)$.

Proof. By the substitution $x = e^t$, $X = e^T$ and $xg(x) = f(t)$, inequalities (1.5) change into (1.3). It follows hence that $f(t) = 0$ a.e. in $(0, T)$, i.e., that $xg(x) = 0$ a.e. in $(1, X)$ which proves our theorem.

Theorem 1.3. *If a function f is Bochner integrable and*

$$\int_0^T t^n f(t)\, dt = 0 \tag{1.6}$$

holds for $n = 1, 2, \ldots,$ *then* $f = 0$ *a.e. in* $(0, T)$.

Proof. Let Θ be an arbitrary number from $(0, T)$. By the substitution

$$t = \Theta x, \qquad T = \Theta X \quad \text{and} \quad f(t) = g(x),$$

equation (1.6) yields

$$\Theta^{n+1} \int_0^X x^n g(x)\, dx = 0 \quad \text{for} \quad n = 1, 2, \ldots,$$

and hence

$$\left| \int_1^X x^n g(x)\, dx \right| = \left| \int_0^1 x^n g(x)\, dx \right| \leq \int_0^1 |g(x)|\, dx = N \quad \text{for} \quad 1, 2, \ldots$$

Thus, by Theorem 1.2, we have $g = 0$ a.e. in $(1, X)$, i.e. $f = 0$ a.e. in (Θ, T). It follows hence that $f = 0$ a.e., in $(0, T)$, because Θ can be taken arbitrary small.

2. Formulation of the Titchmarsh theorem

The simplest form of the Titchmarsh theorem on convolution is

Theorem 2.1. *If the convolution of two functions f and g, is integrable over an interval* $(0, T)$, *vanishes a.e. in* $(0, T)$, *then at least one of them vanishes a.e. in* $(0, \frac{1}{2}T)$.

However, it is usually stated in the equivalent form of the following

Theorem 2.2. *If f and g satisfy the hypothesis of the preceding theorem with* $T < \infty$, *then there are two numbers* $t_1 \geq 0$ *and* $t_2 \geq 0$ *such that* $t_1 + t_2 \geq T$ *and f, g vanish almost everywhere in* $(0, t_1)$ *and* $(0, t_2)$, *respectively. (If* $t_1 = 0$, *then we mean that the interval* $(0, t_1)$ *is an empty set. A similar remark applies also to* t_2.)

Traditionally, the involved functions f and g are assumed real or complex valued. However the above theorems continue to be true, if the values of

f and g belong to any Banach algebra A such that

$$|a^2| = |a|^2 \tag{2.1}$$

for each $a \in A$. By a *Banach algebra* A we mean a Banach space in which, additionally, a product ab is defined for each pair a, b of elements of A so that the following conditions hold:

$$ab = ba,$$

$$(ab)c = a(bc),$$

$$a(b+c) = ab + ac,$$

$$|ab| \leqslant |a|\,|b|.$$

In section 6, Chapter X a definition of a product ab with $a \in A$, $b \in B$, $ab \in C$ was given. If $A = B = C$, then A is a Banach algebra. To prove the equivalence of Theorems 2.1 and 2.2, assume first that $T < \infty$ and that Theorem 2.2 holds. Then it is evident that also Theorem 2.1 is true. Since it is true for each $T < \infty$, it plainly continues being true for $T = \infty$.

Assume now that Theorem 2.1 holds and that $T < \infty$. Denote by $(0, t_1)$ and $(0, t_2)$ the largest intervals in which f and g vanish a.e. Then

$$h(t) = \int_0^t f(t - \tau)g(\tau)\, d\tau = \int_{t_2}^{t - t_1} f(t - \tau)g(\tau)\, d\tau$$

$$= \int_0^u f(t_1 + u - \tau)g(t_2 + \tau)\, d\tau$$

for $t = t_1 + t_2 + u$. Since Theorem 2.1 holds, h cannot vanish a.e. in any right-hand neighbourhood of $t_1 + t_2$. Thus $t_1 + t_2 \geqslant T$. This completes the proof of equivalence.

3. A lemma

To prove Theorems 2.1 and 2.2 we shall need the following

Lemma 3.1. *If $f * f = 0$ a.e. in $(0, T)$, then $f = 0$ a.e. in $(0, \frac{1}{2}T)$.*

Proof. According to the hypothesis we have

$$\int_0^t f(t - \tau)f(\tau)\, d\tau = 0 \quad \text{a.e.} \quad \text{in} \quad (0, T) \tag{3.1}$$

and hence

$$I_n = \int_0^T e^{n(T-t)} \, dt \int_0^t f(t-\tau)f(\tau) \, d\tau = 0. \tag{3.2}$$

By the Tonelli theorem, the iterated integral (3.2) can be represented as a double integral

$$I_n = \iint_A e^{n(T-t)}f(t-\tau)f(\tau) \, d\tau \, dt$$

over the triangle A defined by the inequalities

$$0 \leqslant \tau \leqslant t \leqslant T.$$

After the substitution

$$t = T - u - v, \qquad \tau = \frac{1}{2}T - v$$

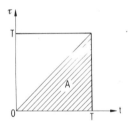

Fig. 16

this integral becomes

$$I_n = \iint_B e^{n(u+v)}f(\tfrac{1}{2}T - u)f(\tfrac{1}{2}T - v) \, du \, dv,$$

where B is the triangle defined by the inequalities

$$0 \leqslant u + v, \qquad 2u \leqslant T, \qquad 2v \leqslant T.$$

We can write

$$\iint_{B \cup C} = \iint_B + \iint_C$$

where C is the triangle defined by the inequalities

$$-T \leqslant 2u, \qquad -T \leqslant 2v \qquad u + v \leqslant 0,$$

and the union $B \cup C$ is the square

$$-T \leqslant 2u \leqslant T, \qquad -T \leqslant 2v \leqslant T.$$

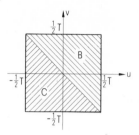

Fig. 17

Since $\iint\limits_{B} = I_n = 0$, we have

$$\iint\limits_{B \cup C} e^{n(u+v)} f(\tfrac{1}{2}T - u) f(\tfrac{1}{2}T - v) \, du \, dv$$

$$= \iint\limits_{C} e^{n(u+v)} f(\tfrac{1}{2}T - u) f(\tfrac{1}{2}T - v) \, du \, dv.$$

If $n > 0$, then the factor $e^{n(u+v)}$ in the integral on the right-hand side is less than 1. We thus have

$$\left| \int\limits_{-\frac{1}{2}T}^{\frac{1}{2}T} e^{nu} f(\tfrac{1}{2}T - u) \, du \int\limits_{-\frac{1}{2}T}^{\frac{1}{2}T} e^{nv} f(\tfrac{1}{2}T - v) \, dv \right| \leqslant M^2,$$

where

$$M^2 = \iint\limits_{C} |f(\tfrac{1}{2}T - u) f(\tfrac{1}{2}T - v)| \, du \, dv.$$

Now, using property (2.1) of the considered Banach algebra, we obtain

$$\left| \int\limits_{-\frac{1}{2}T}^{\frac{1}{2}T} e^{nu} f(\tfrac{1}{2}T - u) \, du \right| \leqslant M.$$

Hence

$$\left| \int\limits_{0}^{\frac{1}{2}T} e^{nu} f(\tfrac{1}{2}T - u) \, du \right| \leqslant N,$$

where

$$N = M + \int\limits_{-\frac{1}{2}T}^{0} |f(\tfrac{1}{2}T - u)| \, du.$$

This inequality being valid for any $n > 0$, we have, by Theorem 1.1, $f(\tfrac{1}{2}T - u) = 0$ a.e. in $(0, \tfrac{1}{2}T)$, which is equivalent to $f = 0$ a.e. in $(0, \tfrac{1}{2}T)$.

4. Proof of the Titchmarsh theorem

In the proof, we shall denote the convolution $\int_0^t f(t-\tau)g(\tau)\,dr$ by fg. The ordinary product of f by the variable t will be denoted by f'. Under this notation, it is easy to check that $(fg)' = f'g + fg'$, which recalls the ordinary formula for differentation of the product. The product of f by t^n will be consequently denoted by $f^{(n)}$.

Lemma 4.1. *If f and g are continuous and $fg^{(n)} = 0$ in $[0, T]$, $n = 1, 2, \ldots$, then at least one of the functions f or g vanishes in $[0, \frac{1}{2}T]$.*

Proof. The explicit form of $fg^{(n)} = 0$ is

$$\int_0^t \tau^n f(t-\tau)g(\tau)\,d\tau = 0 \qquad (0 \leq t \leq T).$$

By Theorem 1.3 it follows that $f(t-\tau)g(\tau) = 0$ a.e. in $0 < \tau < t$. Since f and g are continuous it follows that $f(t-\tau)g(\tau) = 0$ for all t and satisfying $0 \leq \tau \leq t \leq T$.

Assume that the assertion is not true, i.e., there are in the interval $[0, \frac{1}{2}T]$ points τ_0 and τ such that $f(\tau_0) \neq 0$ and $g(\tau) \neq 0$. Letting $t = \tau_0 + \tau$ we then have $f(t-\tau)g(\tau) \neq 0$ with $0 \leq \tau \leq t \leq T$. This contradiction proves the assertion of Lemma 4.1.

Lemma 4.2. *If f and g are continuous and $fg = 0$ in $[0, T]$, then also $fg' = 0$ in $[0, T]$.*

Proof. Let α be the greatest number, satisfying $0 \leq \alpha \leq 1$, such that, for any f and g, the equation

$$fg = 0 \quad \text{in} \quad [0, T] \tag{4.1}$$

implies

$$fg' = 0 \quad \text{in} \quad [0, \alpha T]. \tag{4.2}$$

The particular value $\alpha = 0$ is allowed and the interval $[0, 0]$ consists then of a single point $t = 0$. At this point the convolution fg' always vanishes because both the functions f and g are continuous.

It is important to note that the number α does not depend on T. Assume that $T_1 \neq T_2$ and that α_1, α_2 are values of α corresponding to T_1 and T_2. Let $f_1(t) = f_2(\varkappa t)$, where $\varkappa = \dfrac{T_2}{T_1}$. Then, substituting $\varkappa t = u$ and $\varkappa\tau = \sigma$, we get

$$\int_0^t f_1(t-\tau)g_1(\tau)\,d\tau = \frac{1}{\varkappa}\int_0^u f_2(u-\sigma)g_2(\sigma)\,d\sigma. \tag{4.3}$$

Similarly

$$\int_0^t f_1(t-\tau)\tau g_1(\tau)\, d\tau = \int_0^u f_2(u-\sigma)\sigma g_2(\sigma)\, d\sigma. \tag{4.4}$$

Assume that $f_2 g_2 = 0$ in $[0, T_2]$. Then we have $f_1 g_1 = 0$ in $[0, T_1]$, by (4.3). Hence, $f_1 g_1' = 0$ in $[0, \alpha_1 T_1]$ and, consequently, $f_2 g_2' = 0$ in $[0, \alpha_1 \varkappa T_1]$, by (4.2), i.e., in $[0, \alpha_1 T_2]$. By the definition of α_2, it follows that $\alpha_2 \leqslant \alpha_1$. For symmetry reasons, we similarly obtain $\alpha_1 \leqslant \alpha_2$, which proves that $\alpha_1 = \alpha_2$. In other words, α does not depend on T.
Since (4.1) implies (4.2), in turn (4.2) implies

$$f' g' = 0 \quad \text{in} \quad [0, \alpha^2 T], \tag{4.5}$$

because of commutativity of convolution. We shall also need the equation

$$f' g + f g' = 0 \quad \text{in} \quad [0, T], \tag{4.6}$$

which follows from (4.1).
We now extend the functions f and g continuously beyond the interval $[0, T]$. Then equation (4.5) and (4.6) imply

$$f g' (f' g + f g') = 0 \quad \text{in} \quad [0, T + \alpha T],$$

i.e.,

$$f g \cdot f' g' + (f g')^2 = 0 \quad \text{in} \quad [0, T + \alpha T]. \tag{4.7}$$

But it follows from (4.1) and (4.5) that the first term in (4.7) vanishes in $[0, T + \alpha^2 T]$, which implies that $(f g')^2 = 0$ in $[0, T + \alpha^2 T]$. Hence we infer that $f g' = 0$ in $[0, \frac{1}{2}(1 + \alpha^2) T]$, by Lemma 3.1 and continuity of $f g'$. According to the definition of α we have $\frac{1}{2}(1 + \alpha^2) \leqslant \alpha$, which implies $(1 - \alpha)^2 \leqslant 0$ and $\alpha = 1$. This proves Lemma 4.2.

From Lemmas 4.1 and 4.2, Theorem 2.1 follows, but under additional assumption that the functions f and g are continuous. If f and g are integrable, and $f g = 0$, in $(0, T)$, then the functions

$$f_0(t) = \int_0^t f(\tau)\, d\tau, \qquad g_0(t) = \int_0^t g(\tau)\, d\tau$$

are continuous and $f_0 g_0 = 0$ holds everywhere in $[0, T]$. Thus our proof applies to the functions f_0 and g_0 so that at least one of them vanishes in $[0, \frac{1}{2} T]$. This implies that at least one of functions f or g vanishes a.e. in $(0, \frac{1}{2} T)$.

5. Convex support of a convolution

By the *convex support* or *convex carrier* of a function f we mean the smallest closed convex set outside which the function vanishes a.e. This set will be denoted by

conv supp f.

By the *arithmetic sum* of two subsets X and Y of $\mathbf{R}^q$ we mean the set of all vectors $x + y$ such that $x \in X$ and $y \in Y$.

Theorem 5.1. *If f and g are locally integrable and of bounded carriers in $\mathbf{R}^q$ then*

conv supp$(f * g) = $ conv supp $f + $ conv supp g.

This theorem is due to J. L. LIONS [17] and was proved (for real valued functions) in 1951. We shall show that in one-dimensional case, i.e., for $q = 1$, Theorem 5.1 is equivalent to Theorem 2.1 so that it can be considered as a generalization of the Titchmarsh theorem. In fact, assume that f and g are integrable functions in $(0, T)$ such that $\int_0^t f(t - \tau)g(\tau)\, d\tau = 0$ a.e. in $(0, T)$. We extend the functions f and g onto the whole line $(-\infty, +\infty)$, by letting $f = g = 0$ beyond $(0, T)$. Then the convolution $f * g$ is also a function in $(-\infty, +\infty)$, vanishing in $(0, T)$ a.e. Consequently, the initial point x_0 of conv supp $(f * g)$ satisfies $x_0 \geq T$. If x_1 and x_2 are the initial points of conv supp f and conv supp g, respectively, then of course $x_1 \geq 0$ and $x_2 \geq 0$. Moreover, we have $x_1 + x_2 = x_0$, according to Theorem 5.1. Since $x_0 \geq T$, it follows that at least one of numbers x_1 or x_2 is $\geq \frac{1}{2} T$, proving the Titchmarsh theorem.

In order to prove, conversely, that the Titchmarsh theorem implies Theorem 5.1 (in case $q = 1$) assume that

$X = $ conv supp f and $Y = $ conv supp g.

Let x_1 be the initial point of X, and y_1 the initial point of Y. Without loss of generality, we may assume that $-\infty < x_1 < +\infty$ and $-\infty < y_1 < +\infty$. We put $f_1(t) = f(t - x_1)$ and $g_1(t) = g(t - y_1)$ and assume that there exists a number $T > 0$ such that

$$\int_0^T f_1(t - \tau)g_1(\tau)\, d\tau = 0 \quad \text{a.e.} \quad \text{in} \quad (0, T). \tag{5.1}$$

Then, by the Titchmarsh theorem, at least one of the functions f_1 or g_1 vanishes a.e. in the interval $(0, \frac{1}{2} T)$ and, consequently, either f vanishes a.e. in $(x_1, x_1 + \frac{1}{2} T)$ or g vanishes a.e. in $(y_1, y_1 + \frac{1}{2} T)$. This contradicts that $x_1 \in X$ and $y_1 \in Y$ and proves that there exists no point $T > 0$ such that (5.1) holds. In other words, the initial point of conv supp $(f_1 * g_1)$ is 0. Coming back to functions f and g, we infer that the initial point of conv supp $(f * g)$ is $x_1 + y_1$. Similarly, the end point of conv supp $(f * g)$ is the sum $x_2 + y_2$ of the endpoints x_2 and y_2 of conv supp f and conv supp g. To prove this fact, it suffices to introduce the functions $f_2(t) = f(x_2 - t)$, $g_2(t) = g(y_2 - t)$ and apply the preceding argument.

It is easy to show that if we replaced, in Theorem 5.1 convex supports by ordinary supports, the theorem would become false. In other words, the equation supp $(f * g) = $ supp $f + $ supp g does not hold in general.

In 1951, J. MIKUSIŃSKI and C. RYLL-NARDZEWSKI [21] proved the following

Theorem 5.2. *If $f(t_1, \ldots, t_n)$ and $g(t_1, \ldots, t_n)$ are two functions, integrable in the simplex*

$$S_c : 0 < t_i \ (i = 1, \ldots, n), \qquad t_1 + \cdots + t_n < c$$

such that the convolution

$$\int_0^{t_1} d\tau_1 \cdots \int_0^{t_n} d\tau_n f(t_1 - \tau_1, \ldots, t_n - \tau_n) g(\tau_1, \ldots, \tau_n)$$

vanishes a.e. on S_a. then there are two positive numbers a, b such that $a + b \geq c$, and f, g vanish on S_a and S_b, respectively.

It turns out that the above theorem is equivalent to Theorem 5.1. A proof of equivalence can be found in MIKUSIŃSKI's paper [20]. In that paper also are given other equivalent formulations of the Lions theorem and its slight generalization. For proofs we refer the reader to original papers.

Appendix I

Integrating Step Functions

In Chapter I, section 1, we were considering step functions of the form

$$f = \lambda_1 f_1 + \cdots + \lambda_n f_n, \tag{1}$$

where $f_1, \ldots, f_n$ were brick functions and $\lambda_1, \ldots, \lambda_n$ were real coefficients. The integral of f was defined by the formula

$$\int f = \lambda_1 \int f_1 + \cdots + \lambda_n \int f_n. \tag{2}$$

In case of a single real variable, it is almost obvious that the value $\int f$ does not depend on the representation (2). In Chapter I, we admitted formula (2) for several variables, relying on analogy only. There are various methods to prove that formula precisely. In this Appendix we are going to give a proof which uses the concept of Heaviside functions. Since the geometrical intuition, above all in multidimensional case, might be deceptive, all the given arguments will be purely algebraic.

1. Heaviside functions

The Heaviside function $H(x)$ on the real line $\mathbf{R}^1$ admits the value 1 for $x \geq 0$ and vanishes elsewhere; it thus can be defined on writing

$$H(x) = \begin{cases} 1 & \text{for} \quad x \geq 0, \\ 0 & \text{for} \quad x < 0. \end{cases}$$

By a Heaviside function $H(x)$ in the plane $\mathbf{R}^2$, where x actually denotes points $x = (\xi_1, \xi_2)$ of $\mathbf{R}^2$, we understand the function which admits the value 1 for $x \geq 0$, i.e., for $\xi_1 \geq 0, \xi_2 \geq 0$, and vanishes elsewhere. In symbols,

$$H(x) = \begin{cases} 1 & \text{for} \quad x \geq 0, \\ 0 & \text{for} \quad x \not\geq 0. \end{cases} \tag{1.1}$$

Note that we cannot use here the notation $x < 0$ (which would mean $\xi_1 < 0, \xi_2 < 0$) instead of $x \not\geq 0$, because then $H(x)$ would not be defined in the whole plane $\mathbf{R}^2$.

Similarly, in Euclidean q-dimensional space $\mathbf{R}^q$, the Heaviside function $H(x)$, where $x = (\xi_1, \ldots, \xi_q) \in \mathbf{R}^q$, is defined on assuming their values equal to 1 for $x \geq 0$, i.e., for $\xi_1 \geq 0, \ldots, \xi_q \geq 0$, and to 0 elsewhere. The notation (1.1) can be used also in this general case.

The Heaviside functions belong to the simplest non-constant real valued functions; they admit the values 1 or 0 only. Note that

$$H(x) = H(\xi_1) \cdots H(\xi_q);$$

this equality can be considered as another, but equivalent, definition of the q-dimensional Heaviside function, provided we already know what a one dimensional Heaviside function is.

If $x = (\xi_1, \ldots, \xi_q)$ and $a = (\alpha_1, \ldots, \alpha_q)$ are points of $\mathbf{R}^q$, then the difference

$$x - a = (\xi_1 - \alpha_1, \ldots, \xi_q - \alpha_q)$$

is another point of $\mathbf{R}^q$. Evidently, the value of H at $x - a$ equals to the product

$$H(x - a) = H(\xi_1 - \alpha_1) \cdots H(\xi_q - \alpha_q). \tag{1.2}$$

This implies that

$$H(x - a) = \begin{cases} 1 & \text{for} \quad x \geqslant a, \\ 0 & \text{for} \quad x \not\geqslant a. \end{cases}$$

2. Bricks and brick functions

Let $a = (\alpha_1, \ldots, \alpha_q)$ and $b = (\beta_1, \ldots, \beta_q)$ be points of $\mathbf{R}^q$ such that $a < b$, i.e., $\alpha_i < \beta_i$ for $i = 1, \ldots, q$. By a *brick* $[a, b)$ we understand the half closed interval $a \leqslant x < b$, i.e., the set of all points $x = (\xi_1, \ldots, \xi_q)$ of $\mathbf{R}^q$ satisfying $\alpha_j \leqslant \xi_j < \beta_j$ for $j = 1, \ldots, q$.

A point $c = (\gamma_1, \ldots, \gamma_q)$ such that, for each $j = 1, \ldots, q$, we have $\gamma_j = \alpha_j$ or $\gamma_j = \beta_j$ is called a *vertex* of the brick $[a, b)$. A brick has exactly 2^q vertices. A vertex is even, if the number of the β_j's appearing among the coordinates $\gamma_1, \ldots, \gamma_q$ is even. It is odd, if that number is odd. The point a is always an even vertex of $[a, b)$. The point b is an even vertex, if the number q is even, and an odd vertex, if the number q is odd. A brick has exactly 2^{q-1} even vertices and 2^{q-1} odd vertices.

Let I_{ab} denote a function, related to the brick $[a, b)$, such that

$$I_{ab}(x) = \begin{cases} 1, & \text{if } x \text{ is an even vertex,} \\ -1, & \text{if } x \text{ is an odd vertex,} \\ 0, & \text{if } x \text{ is no vertex.} \end{cases}$$

It is easy to see that, if q is even and x is an even or odd vertex of $[a, b)$, then $-x$ is an even or odd vertex of $[-b, -a)$, respectively. If q is odd and x is an even or odd vertex of $[a, b)$, then $-x$ is, conversely, an odd or even vertex of $[-b, -a)$. This implies that

$$I_{-b,-a}(-x) = (-1)^q I_{ab}(x). \tag{2.1}$$

Let K_{ab} denote the characteristic function of the brick $[a, b)$, i.e., a function such that

$$K_{ab}(x) = \begin{cases} 1 & \text{for} \quad a \leqslant x < b, \\ 0 & \text{elsewhere.} \end{cases}$$

Characteristic functions of bricks are called *brick functions*. Evidently, every q-dimensional brick function can be expressed as a product of one-dimensional brick functions

$$K_{ab}(x) = K_{\alpha_1\beta_1}(\xi_1) \cdots K_{\alpha_q\beta_q}(\xi_q).$$

On the other hand, each of the one dimensional brick functions equals to a difference of shifted Heaviside functions

$$K_{\alpha_j\beta_j}(\xi_j) = H(\xi_j - \alpha_j) - H(\xi_j - \beta_j).$$

Hence

$$K_{ab}(x) = \prod_{j=1}^{q} [H(\xi_j - \alpha_j) - H(\xi_j - \beta_j)].$$

On expanding this product, we can write

$$K_{ab}(x) = \sum_c I_{ab}(c)H(x - c), \tag{2.2}$$

where the sum is extended over all $c \in \mathbf{R}^q$. Since the number of c such that $I_{ab}(c) \neq 0$ is finite (equal to 2^q), the sum consists, in fact, of a finite number of summands.

It is interesting that, beside (2.2), also the formula

$$K_{ab}(x) = (-1)^q \sum_c I_{ab}(c)H(c - x) \tag{2.3}$$

holds. In fact,

$$K_{ab}(-x) = K_{-b,-a}(x) = \sum_c I_{-b,-a}(c)H(x - c)$$

and, by (2.1),

$$K_{ab}(-x) = (-1)^q \sum_c I_{ab}(-c)H(x - c) = (-1)^q \sum_c I_{ab}(c)H(x + c).$$

Substituting $-x$ instead of x, we obtain hence formula (2.3).

3. Step functions

By *step functions* we shall understand linear combinations

$$\lambda_1 H(x - a_1) + \cdots + \lambda_n H(x - a_n), \tag{3.1}$$

where the coefficients λ_i are real numbers, and x, a_i are points of $\mathbf{R}^q$. The sum (3.1) can also be written in the form

$$\sum_{i=1}^{n} \lambda_i H(x - a_i). \tag{3.2}$$

It is almost obvious that a linear combination of step functions is another step function. However, it is awkward to write down an exact proof of this fact in symbols like (3.1) or (3.2). A more convenient notation is

$$\sum_c \lambda_c H(x - c),$$

where the summation runs over all points $c \in \mathbf{R}^q$. But we assume that there is only a finite number of points c for which $\lambda_c \neq 0$. This assumption will be kept throughout the whole Appendix I.

In particular, from (2.2) follows that each brick function K_{ab} is a step function.

Now, if

$$f(x) = \sum_b \mu_b f_b(x)$$

is a linear combination of step functions

$$f_b(x) = \sum_c \lambda_{bc} H(x - c),$$

we can write

$$f(x) = \sum_b \mu_b \sum_c \lambda_{bc} H(x - c) = \sum_c \sum_b \mu_b \lambda_{bc} H(x - c),$$

because the number of non-vanishing summands is finite in each sum, and the order of summation can therefore be interchanged. Letting $\varkappa_c = \sum_b \mu_b \lambda_{bc}$, we get

$$f(x) = \sum_c \varkappa_c H(x - c).$$

This proves that a linear combination of step functions is a step function.

Theorem 3. *For each step function f there is only one representation in the form $f(x) = \sum_c \lambda_c H(x - c)$.*

Proof. Assume there is another representation $f(x) = \sum_c \mu_c H(x - c)$. Letting $\rho_c = \lambda_c - \mu_c$, we get $\sum_c \rho_c H(x - c) = 0$ for each $x \in \mathbf{R}^q$. If $[a, b)$ is a brick and I_{ab} its vertex function defined as in section 2 we can write

$$\sum_x I_{ab}(x) \sum_c \rho_c H(x - c) = 0$$

or, interchanging the order of summation,

$$\sum_c \rho_c \sum_x I_{ab}(x) H(x - c) = 0.$$

If we apply now formula (2.3), with interchanged roles of x and c, we get after cancelling the factor $(-1)^q$

$$\sum_c \rho_c K_{ab}(c) = 0, \tag{3.3}$$

where K_{ab} is the characteristic function of the brick $[a, b)$.

Let d be an arbitrary fixed point of $\mathbf{R}^q$. Since there is only a finite number of points c such that $\rho_c \neq 0$, we can choose the brick $[a, b)$ such that d is the only point in $[a, b)$ with $\rho_d = 0$. Then $K_{ab}(c) = 0$ for each point $c \neq d$ such that $\rho_c \neq 0$ and, subsequently, the sum in (3.3) reduces to the only summand $\rho_d K_{ab}(d) = \rho_d$. Hence $\rho_d = 0$. Since d is arbitrary, we have $\rho_d = 0$ and, in turn, $\lambda_d = \mu_d$ for all $d \in \mathbf{R}^q$.

4. Step functions of bounded carrier

A function is said to be of bounded carrier, iff it vanishes outside a bounded set. Since a brick is a bounded set and, moreover, each bounded set is included in a brick, we can also say that a function is of bounded carrier, iff it vanishes outside a brick. Evidently, each brick function is of bounded carrier. A linear combination of functions of bounded carriers is a function of bounded carrier.

Theorem 4. *A step function is of bounded carrier, iff it can be represented in the form*

$$f = \sum_a \lambda_a K_{aa^*}, \tag{4.1}$$

where the K_{aa^*} denote characteristic functions of pairwise disjoint bricks $[a, a^*)$.

Proof. Since brick functions K_{aa^*} are step functions, so is their linear combination (4.1). Moreover, since the number of the K_{aa^*} in (4.1) is finite, and each of the K_{aa^*} vanishes outside a bounded interval, there is a common bounded interval which all the K_{aa^*} vanish outside. Subsequently, also the function f vanishes outisde that interval. In other words, f is of bounded carrier.

It remains to prove that, conversely, if a step function

$$f(x) = \sum_c \mu_c H(x - c)$$

is of bounded carrier, then it can be represented in the form (4.1). Denote by A the set of all points a such that, for each $j = 1, \ldots, q$, the jth coordinate of a equals to the jth coordinate of some point c such that $\mu_c \neq 0$. The set A is finite and has a minimal point a' and a maximal point a'', i.e., we have $a', a'' \in A$ and $a' \leq a \leq a''$ for all $a \in A$.

We have $f(x) = 0$ outside $[a', a'')$. In fact, if $x = (\xi_1, \ldots, \xi_q) \notin [a', a'')$, then there is an index k such that $\xi_k < \alpha_k'$ or $\xi_k \geq \alpha_k''$, where α_k' and α_k'' denote the kth coordinates of a' and a'', respectively. Let $x + \omega e_k$ be the point which has the same coordinates as x, except for the kth coordinate which is $\xi_k + \omega$. If $\xi_k \geq \alpha_k''$, then the values of $f(x + \omega e_k)$ are constant for all $\omega \geq 0$ (x being fixed). Since f is of bounded carrier, i.e., vanishes outside a brick, the values of f are 0 for large ω, thus we must also have $f(x) = 0$. If $\xi_k < \alpha_k'$, the argument is similar, but we take $\omega \leq 0$.

Now, the points of A divide the brick $[a', a'')$ into a finite number of smaller bricks $[a, a^*)$ such that all vertices of $[a, a^*)$ belong to A, but a is the only point of A, belonging to $[a, a^*)$. The point a^* is determined uniquely by a. The function f is constant on each brick $[a, a^*)$ and admits the value $f(a)$ on it. All the bricks $[a, a^*)$ are pairwise disjoint and their union is $[a', a'')$. Subsequently we have

$$f(x) = \sum_a f(a) K_{aa^*}(x),$$

where the sum is extended on all $a \in A$ such that $a^* \in A$. Letting $\lambda_a = f(a)$, whenever $a, a^* \in A$, and $\lambda_a = 0$ for all remaining $a \in \mathbf{R}^q$, we get the required formula (4.1).

Corollary 4. *The absolute value of a step function of bounded carrier is a step function of bounded carrier.*

Proof. From the representation (4.1) it follows that

$$|f| = \sum_a |\lambda_a| K_{aa^*},$$

for the functions K_{aa^*} are non-negative. This proves the assertion.

5. The integral of a step function of bounded carrier

If $[a, b)$ is a one-dimensional interval, then by the integral of its characteristic function K_{ab} we understand the length of that interval; in symbols, $\int K_{ab} = b - a$. A two-dimensional interval is, in fact, a rectangle $\alpha_1 \leq \xi_1 < \beta_1$, $\alpha_2 \leq \xi_2 < \beta_2$. By the integral of its characteristic function K_{ab} we understand the area of the rectangle. Thus $\int K_{ab} = (\beta_1 - \alpha_1)(\beta_2 - \alpha_2)$. A three-dimensional interval $[a, b)$ is a parallelopipede $\alpha_1 \leq \xi_1 < \beta_1$, $\alpha_2 \leq \xi_2 < \beta_2$, $\alpha_3 \leq \xi_3 < \beta_3$. Then the integral $\int K_{ab} = (\beta_1 - \alpha_1)(\beta_2 - \alpha_2)(\beta_3 - \alpha_3)$ is the volume of the parallelopipede. Generally, if $[a, b)$ is an interval in Euclidean q-dimensional space $\mathbf{R}^q$, then we put by definition

$$\int K_{ab} = \prod_{j=1}^{q} (\beta_j - \alpha_j). \tag{5.1}$$

On expanding the product on the right side, we obtain 2^q products of coordinates of vertices of $[a, b)$, equipped with the sign $+$, if the vertex is even, and with the sign $-$, if the vertex is odd. Denote, generally, by $\dot{c}$ the product of the coordinates of $c = (\gamma_1, \ldots, \gamma_q)$; thus we have $\dot{c} = \gamma_1 \cdots \gamma_q$. Then we get

$$\int K_{ab} = \sum_c I_{ab}(c) \cdot \dot{c}, \tag{5.2}$$

where I_{ab} is the vertex function of $[a, b)$, defined as in section 11.

We are going to generalize the integral from brick functions K_{ab} to the whole class $\mathfrak{B}$ of step functions having bounded carriers. We wish to have this generalization such that the integral of linear combinations of functions from $\mathfrak{B}$ should be equal to the corresponding linear combination of integrals. Otherwise speaking, we wish to have

$$\int \left(\sum_a \lambda_a f_a \right) = \sum_a \lambda_a \int f_a \tag{5.3}$$

for $f_a \in \mathfrak{B}$. Property (5.3) is called the *linearity* of the integral; it is also common to say that the integral (satisfying (5.3)) is a *linear functional on* $\mathfrak{B}$.

Now, Theorem 4 says that each function $f \in \mathfrak{B}$ can be represented in the form

$$f = \sum_a \lambda_a K_{aa*}, \tag{5.4}$$

where K_{aa*} are brick functions. Thus, if (5.3) holds, we get

$$\int f = \sum_a \lambda_a \int K_{aa*}. \tag{5.5}$$

This equality can be taken for the definition of the integral of $f \in \mathfrak{B}$, because the values of $\int K_{aa*}$ are given by (5.2). The meaning of this definition is the following: in order to find the integral of f, we decompose f into brick functions K_{aa*} and the take the corresponding linear combination of integrals $\int K_{aa*}$, whose values are given by any of formulae (5.1) or (5.2). However, the point is that the decomposition (5.4) can be performed in various ways and we therefore do not know at first whether the value (5.5) is determined uniquely for all decompositions of f.

Theorem 5. *If we represent a function $f \in \mathfrak{B}$ as a linear combination* (5.4), *then the value of the integral, defined by* (5.5), *does not depend on the representation* (5.4). *Thus, the value of the integral is defined uniquely for each function $f \in \mathfrak{B}$. Moreover, the integral is a linear functional on $\mathfrak{B}$, i.e.,* (5.3) *holds for any $f_a \in \mathfrak{B}$.*

Proof. The idea of the proof is the following. We define an integral $\hat{\int}$ for a larger class than $\mathfrak{B}$, in which the consistency of the definition follows easily. Then we show that the integral $\hat{\int}$, when restricted to the class $\mathfrak{B}$, coincides with the integral $\int$, defined by (5.5).

For all step functions (not necessarily of bounded carrier)

$$f = \sum_c \lambda_c H(x - c),$$

we put

$$\hat{\int} f = \sum_c \lambda_c \dot{c}.$$

This definition determines the value $\hat{\int} f$ uniquely for each step function f, by Theorem 3. Moreover, property (5.3) holds for $\hat{\int}$, i.e., we have

$$\hat{\int} \left(\sum_a \lambda_a f_a \right) = \sum_a \lambda_a \hat{\int} f_a. \tag{5.6}$$

In fact, since the f_a are assumed step functions, we can write

$$f_a(x) = \sum_c \mu_{ac} H(x - c).$$

Thus

$$\sum_a \lambda_a f_a = \sum_a \lambda_a \sum_c \mu_{ac} H(x - c) = \sum_c \left(\sum_a \lambda_a \mu_{ac} \right) H(x - c).$$

Hence

$$\hat{\int} \left(\sum_a \lambda_a f_a \right) = \sum_c \left(\sum_a \lambda_a \mu_{ac} \right) \dot{c} = \sum_a \lambda_a \sum_c \mu_{ac} \dot{c} = \sum_a \lambda_a \hat{\int} f_a.$$

Thus (5.6) holds.

In view of (5.6), equality (5.4) implies

$$\hat{\int} f = \sum_a \lambda_a \hat{\int} K_{aa*}.$$

Observe that from (2.2) it follows that $\hat{\int} K_{aa*} = \sum_c I_{aa*}(c) \dot{c}$, which, in view of (5.2) implies $\hat{\int} K_{aa*} = \int K_{aa*}$. Subsequently,

$$\hat{\int} f = \sum_a \lambda_a \int K_{aa*}.$$

But the value of $\int f$ has been defined uniquely for each step function f. Hence it follows that formula (5.5) defines the integral $\int f$ uniquely for each $f \in \mathfrak{B}$ and we have $\int f = \hat{\int} f$ for $f \in \mathfrak{B}$. Subsequently, if $f_a \in \mathfrak{B}$, we can replace $\hat{\int}$ by $\int$ in formula (5.6) which gives the required property (5.3).

6. Fundamental properties of the integral

If $\lambda_0 = \lambda$, $f_0 = f$ and $\lambda_a = 0$ for $a \neq 0$, then formula (5.3) becomes

$$\mathbf{H} \quad \int (\lambda f) = \lambda \int f.$$

This property is called *homogeneity* of the integral.

If $\lambda_{a_1} = \lambda_{a_2} = 1$, $f_{a_1} = f$, $f_{a_2} = g$, and $\lambda_a = 0$ for $a \neq a_1, a_2$, then formula (5.3) becomes

$$\mathbf{A} \quad \int (f+g) = \int f + \int g.$$

This property is called *additivity* of the integral.

Both the properties **H** and **A** follow from (5.3). We shall show that, conversely, property (5.3) follows from **H** and **A**. In fact, formula (5.3) can be written as

$$\mathbf{L} \quad \int (\lambda_1 f_1 + \cdots + \lambda_n f_n) = \lambda_1 \int f_1 + \cdots + \lambda_n \int f_n.$$

If $n = 1$, then **L** reduces to **H**, thus is true. For $n = 2, 3, \ldots$, **L** follows by an easy induction.

Note that in particular we have

$$\int (f-g) = \int f - \int g.$$

We shall prove that

$$\mathbf{M_0} \quad f \leqslant g \quad \text{implies} \quad \int f \leqslant \int g.$$

In fact, we have $g - f \geqslant 0$. By Theorem 4 we can write

$$g - f = \sum_a \lambda_a K_{aa^*} \geqslant 0,$$

where the brick functions K_{aa^*} have disjoint carriers. This implies that $\lambda_a \geqslant 0$ for all a. Subsequently,

$$\int (g-f) = \sum_a \lambda_a \int K_{aa^*} \geqslant 0,$$

since we always have $\int K_{aa^*} \geqslant 0$, by (5.1). This in turn implies $\int g - \int f \geqslant 0$, which proves $\mathbf{M_0}$. Property $\mathbf{M_0}$ is called the *monotony* of the integral. Let us also note the property

$$\mathbf{M} \quad \left| \int f \right| \leqslant \int |f|,$$

which easily follows from $\mathbf{M_0}$. In fact, we have

$$-f \leqslant |f| \quad \text{and} \quad f \leqslant |f|.$$

Hence, by $\mathbf{M_0}$,

$$-\int f \leqslant \int |f| \quad \text{and} \quad \int f \leqslant \int |f|,$$

which proves **M**. Property **M** can be called the *modulus property*.

It is interesting to remark that, conversely, **M** implies $\mathbf{M}_0$. In fact, by **M** we have $|\int (g-f)| \leq \int |g-f|$. Hence $\int |g-f| \geq 0$. If $f \leq g$, then $|g-f| = g-f$, thus $\int (g-f) \geq 0$ and, subsequently, $\int g - \int f \geq 0$. This proves $\mathbf{M}_0$. We shall still prove

Theorem 6. *Given any step function of bounded carrier f and any number $\varepsilon > 0$, there is another step function of bounded carrier g and a number $\eta > 0$ such that*

$$g(x) - f(y) \geq 0, \quad whenever \quad |x-y| < \eta,$$

$$\int g \leq \int f + \varepsilon.$$

Proof. For any $x = (\xi_1, \ldots, \xi_q) \in \mathbf{R}^q$ and $\eta \in \mathbf{R}^1$, we generally admit the notation: $x - \eta = (\xi_1 - \eta, \ldots, \xi_q - \eta)$, $x + \eta = (\xi_1 + \eta, \ldots, \xi_q + \eta)$.
Assume that $|x - y| \leq \eta$. If $y \in [a, b)$, then evidently $x \in [a - \eta, b + \eta)$ and consequently $K_{a-\eta, b+\eta}(x) = 1$. Hence

$$K_{a-\eta, b+\eta}(x) - K_{a,b}(y) \geq 0.$$

But the same inequality also holds, if $y \in [a, b)$, because then $K_{a,b}(y) = 0$. Thus it holds for all $x, y \in \mathbf{R}^q$ satisfying $|x - y| \leq \eta$. By (5.1) we have

$$\int K_{a-\eta, b+\eta} - \int K_{a,b} = \prod_{j=1}^{q} (\beta_j - \alpha_j + 2\eta) - \prod_{j=1}^{q} (\beta_j - \alpha_j)$$

and hence we see that

$$\int K_{a-\eta, b+\eta} - \int K_{a,b} \leq \varepsilon,$$

provided η is small enough. Thus the theorem is true for $f = K_{a,b}$. Similarly we can prove that it is true for $f = -K_{a,b}$. In fact, assume that $|x - y| \leq \eta < \frac{1}{2}(b - a)$. If $x \in [a + \eta, b - \eta)$, then $y \in [a, b)$ and hence $K_{a,b}(y) = 1$. Thus

$$-K_{a+\eta, b-\eta}(x) + K_{a,b}(y) \geq 0.$$

If $x \notin [a + \eta, b - \eta)$, then the above inequality also holds, because then $K_{a+\eta, b-\eta}(x) = 0$. It thus holds for all $x, y \in \mathbf{R}^q$ satisfying $|x - y| < \eta$. Again by (5.1) we have

$$-\int K_{a+\eta, b-\eta} + \int K_{a,b} = -\prod_{j=1}^{q} (\beta_j - \alpha_j - 2\eta) - \prod_{j=1}^{q} (\beta_j - \alpha_j),$$

and we see that

$$-\int K_{a+\eta, b-\eta} + \int K_{a,b} \leq \varepsilon,$$

provided η is small enough.

Now, by **H** it follows easily that the theorem is true for any function $f = \lambda K_{a,b}$, no matter whether λ is positive or negative. Using property **A** we see that the theorem is true for functions of the form $f = \lambda_1 K_{a_1,b_1} + \lambda_2 K_{a_2,b_2}$, and by induction, for arbitrary linear combinations $f = \lambda_1 K_{a_1,b_1} + \cdots + \lambda_q K_{a_q,b_q}$, i.e., for arbitrary step functions of bounded carrier.

Appendix II

Equivalence of the New Definitions of Integrals with the Old Ones

1. Equivalence of the original Lebesgue definition of the integral with the definition given in Chapter I

Instead of formulating in detail the Lebesgue definition, which would lead us to Measure Theory as its background, we shall base our reasoning on a few facts which are established in every traditional course of the Lebesgue integral.

It is plain that, if f is a characteristic function of a brick I, then the Lebesgue integral of f is defined as the product of the lengths of edges of I so that the meaning of $\int f$ is the same, no matter whether the integral is meant in the Lebesgue sense or in ours.

A subset X of $\mathbf{R}^q$ is said *of Lebesgue measure* 0, iff for any $\varepsilon > 0$ it can be covered by a sequence $I_1, I_2, \ldots$ of bounded q-dimensional intervals the sum of volumes of which is less than ε. It is obvious that it does not matter if the intervals I_n are open, closed or half-closed (bricks). We thus can say that a set X is of Lebesgue measure 0, iff for any $\varepsilon > 0$ there is a sequence of brick functions f_n such that $\int f_1 + \int f_2 + \cdots < \varepsilon$ and $f_1 + f_2 + \cdots \geq f$, where f denotes the characteristic function of X. Hence the meaning of sets of measure 0, or *null sets*, is the same in the Lebesgue theory and ours.

Moreover, *convergence almost everywhere*, i.e., convergence beyond a null set, means the same in both theories. More generally, we say that a property holds almost everywhere or a.e., if it holds everywhere except for a null set.

Let L denote the set of Lebesgue integrable functions. As said, we shall not go into the question what the Lebesgue integrable functions are, we only shall use the following of their properties (where $\int$ denotes the integral in Lebesgue's sense):

(i)   If f is a brick function, then $f \in L$.
(ii)   If $f_j \in L$ and $\lambda_j \in \mathbf{R}^q$ $(j = 1, \ldots n)$, then $\lambda_1 f_1 + \cdots + \lambda_n f_n \in L$ and $\int (\lambda_1 f_1 + \cdots + \lambda_n f_n) = \lambda_1 \int f_1 + \cdots + \lambda_n \int f_n$.
(iii)   (Monotone Convergence Theorem.) If $s_1, s_2, \ldots$ is a monotone sequence of real valued functions such that $s_n \in L$ and $|\int s_n| \leq M$, then there exists a function $s \in L$ such that $s_n \to s$ a.e. and $\int s_n \to \int s$.
(iv)   (Dominated Convergence Theorem.) If $t_n \in L$, $t_n \to f$ a.e. and $|t_n| \leq s \in L$ a.e., then $f \in L$ and $\int t_n \to \int f$.

Assume that f is a function, integrable in the sense of Chapter I, i.e., there are real numbers $\lambda_1, \lambda_2, \ldots$ and brick functions $f_1, f_2, \ldots$ such that

1° $|\lambda_1| \int f_1 + |\lambda_2| \int f_2 + \cdots < \infty,$

2° $f(x) = \lambda_1 f_1(x) + \lambda_2 f_2(x) + \cdots$ at points x at which the series converges
absolutely.

Then $s_n = |\lambda_1| f_1 + \cdots + |\lambda_n| f_n \in L$, by (i) and (ii), and

$$\int s_n = |\lambda_1| \int f_1 + \cdots + |\lambda_n| \int f_n.$$

The hypothesis 1° implies that the sequence s_n converges monotonically
almost everywhere, by (iii), to a function $s \in L$. Consequently, the series
$\lambda_1 f_1 + \lambda_2 f_2 + \cdots$ converges absolutely and almost everywhere to f, by (ii).
But the partial sums $t_n = \lambda_1 f_1 + \cdots + \lambda_n f_n$ are commonly bounded a.e. by
$s \in L$. In view of (iv) we thus have $f \in L$ and $\int t_n \to \int f$, i.e., $\int f = \lambda_1 \int f_1 + \lambda_2 \int f_2 + \cdots$.
This proves that, if f is integrable in the sense of Chapter I, then it is
integrable in the sense of Lebesgue and both integrals coincide.

In order to prove that, conversely, if $f \in L$, then $f \in U$ (i.e., f is integrable
in the sense of Chapter I), we shall use the property

(v)   If $f \in L$, then f can be represented as a difference $f = g - h$ of two
functions $g \in L$ and $h \in L$ such that each of them is the limit almost
everywhere of a non-decreasing sequence of step functions.

This property was used by Riesz and Nagy as a definition of the Lebesgue
integral in their monography 'Leçons d'analyse fonctionnelle' [24].
Since each step function is a linear combination of brick functions, it
easily follows that g and h expand into almost everywhere convergent
series

$$g = \mu_1 g_1 + \mu_2 g_2 + \cdots, \qquad h = \nu_1 h_1 + \nu_2 h_2 + \cdots, \tag{1.1}$$

where μ_n and ν_n are positive numbers and g_n, h_n are brick functions. It
thus exists a null set E such that equations (1.1) hold outside E.
Moreover, by (ii) and (iii) we have

$$\int g = \mu_1 \int g_1 + \mu_2 \int g_2 + \cdots < \infty, \qquad \int h = \nu_1 \int h_1 + \nu_2 \int h_2 + \cdots < \infty.$$

Let $\varepsilon_1, \varepsilon_2, \ldots$ be positive numbers such that $\varepsilon_1 + \varepsilon_2 + \cdots < \infty$. There are
bricks I_{in} such that, for each $i = 1, 2, \ldots$ we have $E \subset \bigcup_n I_{in}$ and $\sum_n k_{in} < \varepsilon$,

where the k_{in} are brick functions, characteristic for I_{in}, respectively. The
double sequence $\{k_{in}\}$ can be ordered into a simple sequence $k_1, k_2, \ldots$
Then the series

$$\mu_1 g_1 + k_1 - \nu_1 h_1 - k_1 + \mu_2 g_2 + k_2 - \nu_2 h_2 - k_2 + \cdots \tag{1.2}$$

diverges at each point $x \in E$, because $k_1(x) + k_2(x) + \cdots = \infty$ for $x \in E$. If, for some x, series (1.2) converges absolutely, then the series $k_1(x) + k_2(x) + \cdots$ has a finite number of non-null elements and, consequently, (1.2) converges absolutely to $g - h$, i.e., to f. Moreover,

$$\mu_1 \int g_1 + \int k_1 + \nu_1 \int h_1 + \int k_1 + \mu_2 \int g_2 + \int k_2 + \nu_2 \int h_2 + \int k_2 + \cdots$$
$$< \int g + \int h + 2(\varepsilon_1 + \varepsilon_2 + \cdots) < \infty.$$

This proves that $f \in L$ implies $f \in U$. The equivalence of classes U and L is thus established. It is also seen that the value of $\int f$ is the same, no matter whether the integral is meant in the sense of Chapter I or in the sense of the original definition of Lebesgue.

2. Equivalence of the original Bochner definition of the integral with the definition given in Chapter III

In Bochner's approach to integration, the concept of L-*measurability*, i.e., measurability in the Lebesgue sense, is of importance. We shall show that L-measurability coincides with measurability defined in Chapter VI, which will be referred to, in this section, as to M-*measurability*.

Assume that a set $X \subset \mathbf{R}^q$ is L-measurable. Let I_n be an increasing sequence of bounded intervals that cover $\mathbf{R}^q$, and let f_n be the characteristic functions of the intersections $X \cap I_n$. As shown in section 1, the functions f_n are integrable. In the Lebesgue theory, *each L-measurable function, bounded by an integrable function, is itself integrable*. Hence the functions f_n are integrable. According to section 1, the f_n are also integrable in the sense of Chapter I. Hence, they are M-measurable, by Axiom **P** (Chapter VI, section 2). Consequently, the limit $f = \lim_{n \to \infty} f_n$ is M-measurable, by Theorem 3.2, Chapter VI. But this limit is the characteristic function of the set X which is, in consequence, M-measurable (by the definition given at the beginning of section 4, Chapter VI).

Assume now, conversely, that X is M-measurable. Then the functions f_n, defined as above, are integrable (Theorem 3.1, Chapter VI). But in the Lebesgue theory, *each integrable function is L-measurable*, and *the limit of a sequence of L-measurable functions is still L-measurable*. Thus, f is L-measurable. It is also known that, *for each L-measurable function, the set of points at which the value is different from 0 is L-measurable*. Hence X is L-measurable.

This completes the proof that L-measurable sets are M-measurable, and conversely. Therefore, there will be no confusion, if, for sets, the same word *measurable* will be used, without specifying the letter L or M.

In Bochner's theory, a function g from $\mathbf{R}^q$ to a Banach space E is called *finite-valued* or *simple*, if there is a finite number of disjoint measurable sets $X_1, \ldots, X_p$ such that $X_1 \cup \cdots \cup X_p = \mathbf{R}^q$, and f is constant on each of these sets. A function f will be said B-*measurable* (Bochner measurable), if there exist simple functions f_n such that $f_n \to f$ a.e.

We shall show that, if a function f is B-measurable, then it is also M-measurable (i.e., measurable in the sense of section 2, Chapter VI), and conversely.

In fact, assume that f admits only two values: 0 or $c \in E$ (E Banach space). We assume, moreover, that the set X on which f takes the value c is measurable. Then we can write $f = c \cdot X$, where c can be interpreted as a constant function, and X as the characteristic function of the considered set. Since c and X are M-measurable, so is the function f, by Theorem 8.1, Chapter VI. Now, each B-measurable function is, by definition, a limit a.e. of a sequence of simple functions, and is therefore M-measurable, by Theorem 3.2, Chapter VI. Assume now, conversely, that f is M-measurable. Then, by Theorem 9.3, Chapter VI, there are integrable functions f_n such that $f_n \to f$ a.e. But each integrable function is a limit a.e. of a series of brick functions. The partial sums of such a series are simple functions so that f is B-measurable.

In this way we have proved that B-measurability (of functions) coincides with M-measurability and, in both cases, we thus may use the same word *measurability*.

Note that measurability of functions is always concerned with the given Banach space E, in contrast to measurability of sets.

Finally, we shall show that B-integrability and M-integrability (where the meaning of letters B and M is obvious) coincide with each other. In fact, assume that f is B-integrable. Then it is measurable, and the real valued function $|f|$ is integrable. Hence, f is M-integrable, by Theorem 3.1, Chapter VI. Assuming, conversely, that f is M-integrable, we conclude that f is measurable, by **P**, section 2, Chapter VI. Moreover, $|f|$ is integrable, by Axiom **M** (section 1, Chapter IV), which proves that f is B-integrable. Thus, the B-integrable and the M-integrable functions constitute the same class, and we may call them simply *integrable*, without running into misunderstanding.

If f is integrable, then there are brick functions f_n and elements λ_n from E such that

1° $\quad |\lambda_1| \int f_1 + |\lambda_2| \int f_2 + \cdots < \infty$, and

2° $\quad f = \lambda_1 f_1 + \lambda_2 f_2 + \cdots$ a.e.

It is plain that, for brick functions f_n, the B-integral and the M-integral coincide so that the integrals in 1° can be meant in any sense. Also, for simple functions

$$s_n = \lambda_1 f_1 + \cdots + \lambda_n f_n$$

the integral

$$\int s_n = \lambda_1 \int f_1 + \cdots + \lambda_n \int f_n$$

can be meant as B-integral or M-integral as well.

Since $|s_n| \leq s = |\lambda_1||f_1| + |\lambda_2||f_2| + \cdots$ and the real valued function s is integrable, we have

$$\int f = \lim_{n \to \infty} \int s_n,$$

no matter whether the integrals are meant as B-integrals or M-integrals (because in both cases the dominated convergence theorem holds). This proves the equivalence of B-integrals and M-integrals.

Remark.   In the paper mentioned above, Bochner considers functions whose values are in a Banach space over the field **C** of complex numbers. This makes at first an impression that his approach is more general. After a while of reflexion, one could believe, conversely, that his approach is less general, because each Banach space over **C** is also a Banach space over the field **R** or real numbers, so that our definitions of Chapter III may be applied. In fact, both approaches are equivalent, because Bochner does not use in his approach, multiplication by complex numbers.

EXERCISES

to Chapter I:

1. Prove that, if f is the characteristic function of any of bounded intervals (a, b), $[a, b]$ or $(a, b]$, then it is integrable.

2. Prove that, if f is integrable, then also the function g such that $g(x) = f(-x)$ is integrable.

to Chapter II:

1. Check that the following sets are linear spaces:
    a) the set of the real numbers,
    b) the set of the complex numbers,
    c) the set of all continuous functions on the interval $[0, 1]$,
    d) the set of all sequences of real numbers, tending to 0.

2. Check that, if by "addition" we mean the ordinary multiplication, by "multiplication by λ" the ordinary λth power, then the set of all positive numbers is a linear space.

3. Show that the space of all polynomials with real coefficients is a linear normed space, if we take for the norm of the polynomial p the expression $|p| = \max_{[0, 1]} |p(x)|$. Show that this space is not a Banach space. (Hint: show that it is not complete.)

4. Check that the set of all continuous functions on $[0, 1]$ is a Banach space, if we take the norm $|f| = \max_{[0, 1]} |f(x)|$.

5. Prove that, if a and b are elements of a Banach space, then either $|a + b| \geqslant |a|$ or $|a - b| \geqslant |a|$.

to Chapter III:

1. The space of the complex numbers can be considered as a particular Banach space. Show that a complex valued function is Bochner integrable, if and only if its real part and its imaginary part are Lebesgue integrable.

2. Let L denote the space of the Lebesgue integrable functions. In particular, each brick function belongs to L. Let χ_x denote the brick function which is the characteristic function of the interval $[x, x + 1)$.

Show that the function

$$f(x) = \begin{cases} \chi_x, & \text{if } x \in [0, 1), \\ 0, & \text{if } x \notin [0, 1) \end{cases}$$

(whose values are in the Banach space L) is Bochner integrable. What is its integral?

to Chapter IV:

1. Prove that norm convergence satisfies Urysohn's condition L^*.

to Chapter V:

1. Prove the following formulae, on reducing them to equivalent formulae but with ordinary algebraic operations:

$A \cup A = A,$

$(A \backslash B) \cap B = 0,$

$(A \cap B) \cup (A \backslash B) = A.$

2. Prove that

a) If $f_n \to f$ i.m., then $\lambda f_n \to \lambda f$ i.m., for each real λ;

b) If $f_n \to f$ i.m., and $g_n \to g$ i.m., then $f_n + g_n \to f + g$ i.m.;

c) If $f_n \to f$ i.m., then $|f_n| \to |f|$ i.m.

to Chapter VI:

1. Prove that $f \cap (-f) = f.$

2. Prove that if a sequence of measurable functions f_n converges to f almost everywhere, then it converges to f locally in measure.

3. Prove that if $f \geqslant 0$, then $\displaystyle\int_{Z_1 \cap Z_2} f \leqslant \int_{Z_1 \cup Z_2} f \leqslant \int_{Z_1} f + \int_{Z_2} f.$

4. Give an example of two functions f and g, f being continuous and g measurable, such that the superposition $h(x) = g(f(x))$ is not measurable.

5. Show that a real valued function f is measurable, if and only if, for any real number α, the set of points where $f < \alpha$ is measurable.

6. Prove that if f is measurable and $f \neq 0$ everywhere, then $\dfrac{1}{|f|}$ is measurable.

to Chapter VII:

1. Show that a vector valued function $f(x)$ is continuous at x, if and only if $x_n \to x$ implies $f(x_n) \to f(x)$. In the proof, axiom of choice is needed. Where?

2. Show that if a set X of real numbers is measurable, then the set of points x such that $x^3 \in X$ is also measurable.

3. Show that if the outer cover of a set X is equivalent to its inner cover, then X is measurable.

to Chapter VIII:

1. Let $f(x) = \dfrac{1}{q}$ if $x = \dfrac{p}{q}$, where p and q are relatively prime positive integers, and let $f(x) = 0$ if x is irrational. Prove that f is Riemann integrable over the interval $(0, 1)$.

2. Prove that conditions C and C' in section 6 are equivalent.

to Chapter X:

1. Prove that if f is integrable over X and g is integrable over Y, then the product $f(x)g(y)$ is integrable over $X \times Y$.

2. Prove that if the function $f(t, u)$ of two variables t and u is integrable over the triangle $\Delta: 0 \le t \le u \le T$, then

$$\int_0^T dt \int_0^t f(t, u) \, du = \int_0^T du \int_u^T f(t, u) \, dt$$

(this formula is sometimes called the Dirichlet formula).

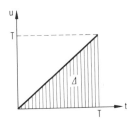

Fig. 18

to Chapter XI:

1. Prove that, if $f(x, y)$ is a function of two real variables x and y, continuous on a closed and bounded rectangle $I: (a \le x \le b, c \le y \le d)$, then

$$\int_a^b dx \int_c^d f(x, y) \, dy = \int_c^d dy \int_a^b f(x, y) \, dx.$$

(Hint: use the Fubini theorem).

2. Prove that if f is Bochner integrable over $\mathbf{R}^1$, then the functions

$$F(x) = \int_{-\infty}^{\infty} \sin xt \cdot f(t) \, dt \quad \text{and} \quad G(x) = \int_{-\infty}^{\infty} \cos xt \, f(t) \, dt$$

are continuous.

to Chapter XII:

1. Prove that if f and g are functions of a real variable, integrable in $(0, T)$, then the convolution

$$h(t) = \int_0^t f(t-u)g(u)\, du$$

is also integrable in $(0, T)$. (Hint: consider the integral $\int_0^T h(t)\, dt$ and apply the Tonelli theorem).

2. Prove that, if $x \in \mathbf{R}^q$ and A_n denotes the set of the x such that $2^{-n-1} \leq |x| < 2^{-n}$, then

$$\int_{A_n} |x|^p = 2^{-(q+p)n} \int_{A_0} |x|^p.$$

Deduce hence that the function $|x|^p$ is locally integrable in $\mathbf{R}^q$, iff $p > -q$.

3. Show that an antiaureole of a square is another square and an aureole of a square never is a square.

4. Show that the function $F(x) = x^2 \sin \dfrac{1}{x^2}$ with $F(0) = 0$ has its ordinary derivative 0 at $x = 0$, but the full derivative does not exist at $x = 0$.

5. Show that the function $F(x, y) = (x^2 + y^2) \sin \dfrac{1}{x^2 + y^2}$ has a Stolz's differential at the origin, but is not fully derivable there.

6. Interpret inequality $(J1)$ in the following one-dimensional case: $X = [-1, 1]$, $\varphi(x) = x^3 - x$. Show that the left side of the inequality is then $\dfrac{2}{\sqrt{3}}$ and its right side is $\dfrac{8}{3\sqrt{3}}$.

to Chapter XIII:

1. Prove that the function $|x|$ has, in $\mathbf{R}^1$, its local derivative equal to sgn x.

2. Prove that the Heaviside function $H(x) = \begin{cases} 1 & \text{for } x \geq 0, \\ 0 & \text{for } x < 0, \end{cases}$ has no local derivative in any interval containing the point $x = 0$.

3. Let $a_1, a_2, \ldots$ be a sequence containing all rational numbers from the interval $(0, 1)$. Let $f(x) = \sum_{n=1}^{\infty} 2^{-n} H(x - a_n)$. Prove that f is non-decreasing in the interval $(0, 1)$ and has no local derivative in any subinterval of $(0, 1)$.

to Chapter XIV:

1. Prove that if $f(x) = e^{-(x^2/\alpha^2)}$, $g(x) = e^{-(x^2/\beta^2)}$, then

   $$f * g = \sqrt{\alpha^2 + \beta^2}\ e^{-x^2/(\alpha^2 + \beta^2)}.$$

2. If H is the Heaviside function, then

   $$\underbrace{(H * \ldots * H)}_{n}(x) = \frac{x^{n-1}}{(n-1)!} H(x).$$

BIBLIOGRAPHY

[1] P. Antosik–J. Mikusiński–R. Sikorski, Theory of distributions. The sequential approach, Amsterdam-Warszawa 1973.

[2] S. Banach, Théorie des opérations linéaires, Warszawa 1932.

[3] ——, Sur un théorème de M. Vitali, Fund. Math. 5, 130–136 (1924).

[4] S. Banach–A. Tarski, Sur la décomposition des ensembles de points en parties respectivement congruentes, Fund. Math. 6, 244–277 (1924).

[5] S. Bochner, Integration von Funktionen, deren Werte die Elemente eines Vektorraumes sind, Fund. Math. 20, 262–276 (1933).

[6] M. M. Crum, On the resultant of two functions, The Quaterly Journal of Mathematics, Oxford Series 12, 108–111 (1941).

[7] P. J. Daniell, A general form of integral, Ann. of Math. 19, 279–294 (1917–1918).

[8] J. Dufresnoy, Sur le produit de composition de deux fonctions, Comptes Rendus Ac. Sci. 225, 857–859 (1947).

[9] ——, Autour du théorème de Phragmén -Lindelöf, Bull. Sci. Math. 72, 17–22 (1948).

[10] P. Fatou, Séries trigonométriques et séries de Taylor, Acta Math. 30, 335–400 (1906).

[11] G. Fubini, Sugli integrali multipli, Atti Ac. Naz. Lincei, Rend. 16, 608–614 (1907).

[12] K. Gödel, The consistency of the axiom of choice and of the generalized continuum hypothesis, Proc. Natl. Ac. Sci. 24, 556–557 (1938).

[13] C. Kliś–C. Ryll–Nardzewski, On a problem of J. Mikusiński on HEM-integral, Bul. Pol. Ac. Sci. 25, 301–304 (1977).

[14] H. Lebesgue, Leçons sur l'intégration et la recherche des fonctions primitives, Paris 1904.

[15] ——, Sur l'intégration des fonctions discontinues, Ann. Ecole Norm. 27, 361–450 (1910).

[16] B. Levi, Ricerche sulle funzioni derivate, Atti Ac. Naz. Lincei, Rend. 15_1, 433–438 (1906).

[17] J. L. Lions, Supports de produits de composition I, Comptes Rendus 232, 1530–1532 (1951); II, Comptes Rendus 232, 1622–1624 (1951).

[18] J. Mikusiński, Operational Calculus, Pergamon Press, PWN, Second edition (1967).

[19] ——, Une simple démonstration du théorème de Tichmarsh sur la convolution, Bul. Ac. Sci. 7 (1959), 715-717.

[20] ——, Convolution of functions of several variables, Studia Math. 20 (1961), 301–312.

[21] J. Mikusiński–C. Ryll–Nardzewski, Sur le produit de composition, Studia Math. 12 (1951), 52–57.

[22] T. Rado–P. V. Reichelderfer, Continuous transformations in analysis, Springer (1955).

[23] F. Riesz, Sur l'intégrale de Lebesgue, Acta Math. 42, 191-205 (1920).

[24] F. Riesz–B. Sz.-Nagy, Leçons d'analyse fonctionnelle, Budapest 1965.

[25] S. Saks, Theory of the integral, Warszawa-Lwów 1937.

[26] L. Schwartz, Théorie des distributions, I, Paris 1950, II, Paris 1951.

[27] M. H. Stone, Notes on integration, Proc. Nat. Ac. Sci. U.S.A. 34 (1948): Note I, 336–342, Note II, 447–455, Note III, 483–490; 35 (1949): Note IV, 50–58.

[28] E. C. Titchmarsh, The zeros of certain integral functions, Proc. Lond. Math. Soc. 25, 283–302 (1926).

[29] ——, Introduction to the theory of Fourier Integrals, Oxford (1948).

[30] L. Tonelli, Sull'integrazione per parti, Atti Ac. Naz. Lincei 18_2, 246–253 (1909).

[31] E. Zermelo, Beweis dass jede Menge wohlgeordnet werden kann, Math. Ann. 59, 514–516 (1904).

Bibliography added in proof

P. Antosik, Some conditions for mean convergence, Bul. Ac. Pol. Sci. XVI (1968), 641–644.

J. Mikusiński, A theorem on moments, Studia Math. XII (1951), 191–193.

——, A new proof of Titchmarsh's theorem on convolution, Studia Math. XIII (1953), 56–58.

J. Mikusiński–C. Ryll-Nardzewski, A theorem on bounded moments, Studia Math. XIII (1953), 51–55.

W. Sierpiński, Sur un problème concernant les ensembles mesurables superficiellement, Fundamenta Math. 1, 112–115 (1920).

K. Skórnik, Postać funkcji lokalnie całkowalnej, której m-ta pochodna lokalna znika prawie wszędzie (The form of a locally integrable function whose m-th derivative vanishes almost everywhere), Zeszyty Naukowe WSP 5, Katowice, 1966, 127–152.